WHEN MISSOURI TOOK THE TROLLEY

by

Andrew D. Young

First published 2007

ARCHWAY PUBLISHING

PO Box 410903 St. Louis MO. 63141-0903
E-mail Archway@brick.net
Design and Layout by Cenveo, St. Louis
© 2007 Andrew D. Young

ISBN 9780964727953

Library of Congress Control Number: 2006931753

TABLE OF CONTENTS

Front Cover: When Missouri took the trolley. A view of Washington Avenue in St. Louis, looking west from Sixth Street circa 1906. People spill out from the busy sidewalks onto the roadway as a Page car carefully threads its way along the street. This stunningly beautiful hand-colored postcard, issued by the V.O. Hammon Publishing Company of Chicago, is nevertheless incorrect for at that time St. Louis streetcars were painted cadmium orange, not the green shown here.

Title Page: An already-jammed southbound two-car train, headed by car 1074, is besieged by would-be-riders exiting St. Louis Sportsman's Park (Grand and Dodier). So are other cars further back along the line on this bright 6th of October, 1944. Why? It's the end of a game in baseball's 1944 all-Missouri World Series, the St. Louis Cardinals against the St. Louis Browns. STLMOT

Front endpaper: St. Louis, 1942. G.M. Sebree, Motor Coach Age.

Opposite: A late snowstorm of March 3rd 1952 has caused this mess at the merger of Delaware and Main in Kansas City. In the center background a jam of nine trolleys is blocked by autos turning into their path because their own traffic lane is blocked by illegally-parked vehicles.

Rear endpaper: Kansas City, 1949.

PREFACE

This is a book about Missouri's trolley, street railways and interurbans, a fond look back for those "of a certain age," a newly-told tale for younger folk interested in Missouri of old. The historical record, however, is patchy. Large trolley systems were organized as joint-stock corporations. They had a perpetual thirst for cash and were constantly scrutinized by newspapers and trade journals. But lines in smaller towns, such as Chillicothe, Keytesville and Warrensberg began and often remained partnerships or family businesses evolving from a general carrier or a livery stable. These often slipped under the reporter's radar. For example, concrete information on Lebanon's short-lived line surfaced only in July 2006 while this book was already in pre-press. Moreover, other than for Kansas City and St. Louis, few corporate records have survived and so it's possible one or two Missouri street railways may have been missed.

Census figures are quoted from 1880 to 2000, but caution is advised. City boundaries were fluid and entries can be flat-out wrong. For example, St. Joseph's 1890 population was 52,324, not enough for its civic boosters, some of whom got the 1900 census-takers drunk before whisking them repeatedly through the same neighborhoods to "score" a St. Joseph population of 102,979. A more plausible 77,403 was recorded in 1910, an embarrassing "loss" over the decade.

Rosters of individual trolley systems have been omitted in favor of brief notes as Joplin/Webb City, Illinois Traction, Kansas City and St. Louis rosters have been published elsewhere (see the bibliography), records of smaller towns are few, of dubious accuracy or unavailable, and animal railway records are long gone.

Andrew D. Young, St. Louis, March 2007.

Reams of paper, thousands of words and gallons of ink have been used to describe the state of Missouri's 19th century streets and roads, but it's all summed up in one good photograph. This is Kansas City MET's grip 119 and open trailer 112 outside Laclede Car Company, St. Louis in 1887, prior to delivery. Rails have been placed on top of the mud solely for this photograph and were taken up again when the shoot was over. This St. Louis city street (believed to be North Second) remains unpaved well into the horsecar age, an ocean of mud and slurry. Missouri's rural roads were as bad, if not worse.

ACKNOWLEDGEMENTS

My thanks to Jim Worton, Molly Butterworth, Nick Ohlman and Ron Goldfeder (St. Louis Museum of Transportation), Rosy Thacker (John H. Price Memorial Library, Crich Tramway Village U.K.), to Roy G. Benedict (River Grove IL) for Alton, Jacksonville and Peoria material, Edward A. Conrad (Blue Springs MO) for maps of Tri-State interurbans, Carroll Cruise (City Utilities Transit, Springfield), State Historical Society of Missouri (Columbia), Special Collections and Archives of Southeast Missouri State University (Cape Girardeau), Zelli Fischelli (University of Missouri St. Louis), for Cassidy papers in Western History Manuscripts collection, Chillicothe Public Library, Ron Leake (Ralls County Historical Society, Perry), Mayor Sharon E. Metz and Cathy McGuinness (Carrollton), Jeffrey Moreau (Orangevale CA) for notes from the late Allison Chandler, Ron Mosbaugh (Carthage MO), Lowell H. Rott (Madison MO) for notes on Missouri and Kansas interurbans, former Mayor George Schwartz (Hannibal), G. Mac Sebree (Vancouver WA), Tom Shrout (Citizens for Modern Transit, St. Louis), Ann Sundermeyer (Hannibal Free Public Library), St. Joseph Public Library, The Library Center of Springfield, the History Museum for Springfield-Greene County and Joanne Trainor of Kansas City for photos taken by her late father Earl McMechan.

Thanks also to Steve Binning, Tom Boland, Russell E. Carter, Boris Cefer, Dr. Harold Cox, Bob Eastin, Kevin T. Farrell, Ray Gehl, Mark Godwin, Mark Goldfeder, the late Willis Goldschmidt, Charles Hamann, Bill Heger, Bob Hepp, Tom Konieczny, Don Maag, David J. Neubauer, Jim Ozment, Stephen M. Scalzo, Lew Schneider, Cliff Scholes, Don Scott, Ira Schreiber, Andy Sisk and Bill Volkmer for practical help and encouragement. Pictures are from the author's collection unless credited. "Streetcar" or "street railway" refers to all traction modes, "trolley" to electric cars and "interurban" to electric lines and cars linking rural areas and towns. Population figures are based on U. S. census data.

The Western frontier; Springfield Public Square looking southwest circa 1881. Horsecar tracks (left) sprout a passing siding, allowing north and southbound cars to pass each other in the Square without hindrance.

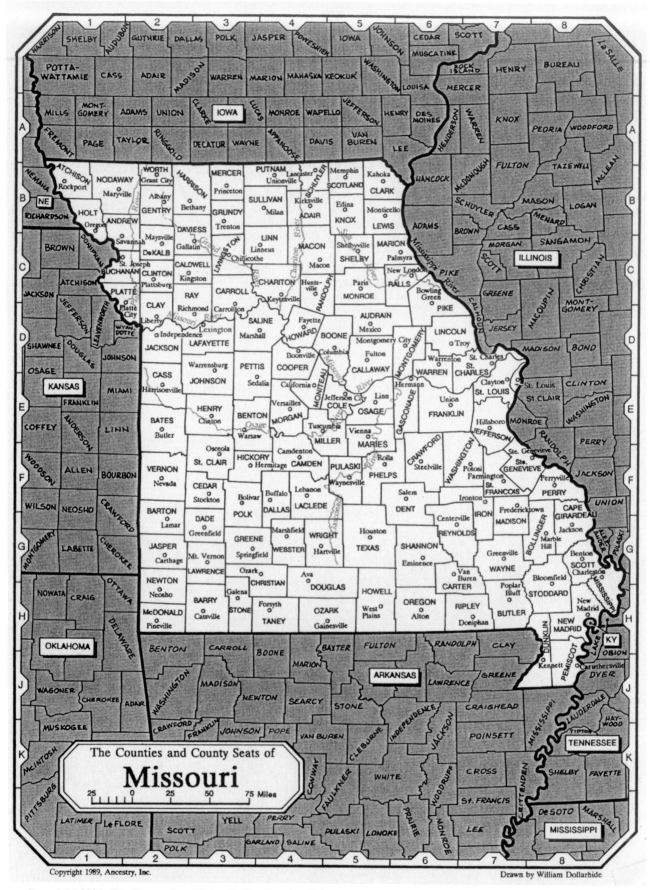

The Counties and County Seats of
Missouri

25   0   25   50   75 Miles

THIS IS MISSOURI

An almost-forgotten chapter of transportation history, the street railway era in Missouri ran from 1859 to 1966. It peaked between 1895 and 1920 when electric trolleys dominated town transit. But the date range is misleading. Omit Kansas City, St. Joseph and St. Louis, and the state's street railways gave just a half-century of service, say 1880 to 1930. Smaller systems like Chillicothe, Clinton, Lebanon, Lexington, Mexico, Trenton and Warrensburg were more ephemeral. Some didn't electrify and a few didn't even make it to the 20th century.

In fact, Missouri had relatively few street railways. Neighboring states had more. Indiana from 1890s until the 1940s had a large network radiating from Indianapolis and Fort Wayne, linking cities, county seats and small towns, some with their own local systems. Yet Indiana had less population than Missouri before 1920.

"Commenting recently on the growth of 38% for Indianapolis and on 19% for St. Louis in the last census decade, the St. Louis Republic said 'A number of railroad systems are managed from St. Louis. Not one road of any size is managed from Indianapolis. St. Louis lies just across the Mississippi from the greatest deposit of good steam coal adjacent to any American city. Indianapolis gets its coal from considerable distances. St. Louis has a river channel connecting it with the sea, Indianapolis has no navigable water. St. Louis is located on rolling hills...Indianapolis is as flat as the top of a dinner table. St. Louis is far from any other large city, Indianapolis has achieved its remarkable growth within 183 miles of Chicago. St. Louis has two important universities; Indianapolis has none...St. Louis is the world's center in a number of...manufacture(s), Indianapolis has many small, prosperous shops but few large ones. (Yet) fast interurban trolley lines have made it easy for people of a circle of 250 miles in diameter to visit Indianapolis.In the streets...the man from Fort Wayne rubs elbows with the man from Terre Haute, the shopper from Columbus meets her old school friend from Logansport. A trolley map of Indiana looks like the spokes of a wheel whose hub is Indianapolis. A city without great wealth, without large industries, without a university, without navigable water, without coal, without natural beauty of site, has grown because it made it easy for its neighbors for 100 miles around to drop in before dinner, per trolley car, and leave after an early supper to get home by bedtime.' "(ERJ August 28th,1915 p. 380.)

West meets east; a well-known but still worthwhile glimpse of Kansas City and Westport cars on the Walnut Street passing siding at City Market in 1871. Not a single building here is more than a decade old in this, the largest of America's cowboy and frontier towns, but despite its western "cow town" look, the landscape is unmistakably urban. The appalling state of the road speaks for itself, yet private transport is already there in the form of buckboards and other parked wagons.

The industry's principal historians point out that,*"in the Deep South, the Northern Plains states and the arid west there (was) little mileage. Low rural population densities, an absence of large cities, and, in the South, low rural incomes made these areas unattractive to...promoters."* (The Electric Interurban Railway in America by George W. Hilton and John F. Due p. 42). That was a fact of life realized very early in Missouri.

"Missouri, while in the front rank of states in the greater number of improvements, has been sadly behind in...electric railways. There is probably no other state...in the Middle West with as few...Outside the suburban electric railways of St. Louis County, one in Southeast Missouri and the road connecting Carthage and Joplin, Missouri has no trolley lines except in the cities. None...was equipped or built with expectation of...through and rapid service... (but) with the sole view of supplying a local need." (P-D August 11th, 1906 p. 1.)

A city or town's need for street railways was self-evident, but rural areas needed them for different reasons; primarily to satisfy a craving for a link to the outside world. From 1910 reliable autos and trucks supplied that need, years before roads were paved. Yet it is remarkable just how many Missouri dreamers and schemers not only planned rural trolleys and interurbans but spent good money trying to make them happen. Many succeeded but many more did not, though securities may have been issued, rights of way graded, bridges built, tracks, ties, wires, poles and even cars delivered. Their backers either weren't aware of or chose to ignore the warnings.

So in Missouri the question isn't why so few rural lines were built but why were so many attempted? Much of the answer lies in the state's physical geography. The Missouri and Mississippi, North America's longest rivers, define and bisect the state, a meeting of the waters that from the outset put the focus firmly on St. Louis, just south of the confluence. Established in 1764, the Mississippi gave the city, almost a thousand miles from an ocean, a link to the outside world centuries before airfreight, highways and railroads. From the north, the river brought furs and timber. To the south lay New Orleans and the world. To the east, the Ohio led to Ohio, Kentucky and Tennessee. To the west, the Missouri flowed in from the Great Plains and the western frontier. Missouri was French until 1763, Spanish until 1800 and French again until 1803's Louisiana Purchase. Most was terra incognita before 1804's Lewis and Clark expedition.

Missouri's towns, often called "cities" but in truth little more than hamlets, were mostly built on or within reach of navigable rivers such as the Black, Chariton, Gasconade, Grand, Meramec, Osage, St. Francis and White that fed the big two. Boat landings made these

settlements markets for produce, feed, seed, and livestock. Often plants were set up to process raw materials before shipping, and some towns became local distribution and manufacturing centers. But beyond town lines was a terrible wilderness in which settlements with more than 500 souls were rare. Hard-scrabble subsistence farmers, struggling to survive, could not easily create new communities out there, nor the economic infrastructure to support them. Since the trader and trapper era of the 18th century, that fact of life has colored rural Missouri's outlook. It is conservative, skeptical and dour. Not for nothing does Missouri call itself the "Show-me" state.

It was an outlook at odds with those who poured in from New England and the South, from England, Scotland, Ireland, Italy, Poland, Hungary and Germany, all seeking a fresh start in a benign climate on their own land. It was an outlook at odds with those with the vision and funds to specialize in viticulture, fruit, livestock, poultry,

East going west meets south. The Mississippi and Missouri rivers dominate the state's geography, history, settlement, economy and growth. Hannibal, St. Louis and Cape Girardeau in Missouri, Alton, Granite City and East St. Louis in Illinois, were all on the Mississippi. Kansas City, Jefferson City, Lexington, St. Charles and St. Joseph in Missouri and Kansas City and Leavenworth in Kansas were all on the Missouri. On the Mississippi, looking south towards St. Louis's Eads Bridge, we see the steamboat Queen Saint Paul. Trolleys on the Eads Bridge top deck are from East St. Louis. Within five years of this 1930 scene, they were gone. By 1940 the buildings on the levee had gone as well, clearing space for the Gateway Arch memorializing the pioneers bound for the Western frontier. After years of disuse and eventual demolition, the road deck on the Eads Bridge was built anew and re-opened in 2005. The rail deck (below) was disused between 1974 and 1992 when MetroLink light rail cars began service. In the rear is the double-decked Municipal Bridge whose road deck (top) has been disused for years.

Population of Missouri and other Midwest states

STATE	1880	1890	1900	1910	1920	1930	1940	1950	1960	1970	1980	1990	2000
ARKANSAS	802,525	1,128,211	1,311,564	1,574,449	1,752,204	1,854,482	1,949,387	1,909,511	1,786,272	1,923,322	2,286,357	2,350,725	2,673,400
ILLINOIS	3,077,871	3,826,352	4,821,550	5,638,591	6,485,280	7,630,654	7,897,241	8,712,176	10,081,158	11,110,285	11,427,409	11,430,602	12,419,293
INDIANA	1,978,301	2,192,404	2,516,462	2,700,876	2,930,390	3,238,503	3,427,796	3,934,224	4,662,498	5,195,392	5,490,214	5,544,159	6,080,485
IOWA	1,624,615	1,912,297	2,231,853	2,224,771	2,404,021	2,470,939	2,538,268	2,621,073	2,757,537	2,825,368	2,913,808	2,776,755	2,926,324
KANSAS	996,096	1,428,108	1,470,495	1,690,949	1,769,257	1,880,999	1,801,028	1,905,299	2,178,611	2,249,071	2,364,236	2,477,574	2,668,418
MICHIGAN	1,636,937	2,093,890	2,420,982	2,810,173	3,668,412	4,842,325	5,256,106	6,371,766	7,823,194	8,881,826	9,262,044	9,295,297	9,938,444
MISSOURI	2,168,380	2,679,185	3,106,665	3,293,335	3,404,055	3,629,367	3,784,664	3,954,653	4,319,813	4,677,623	4,916,766	5,117,073	5,595,211
NEBRASKA	452,402	1,062,656	1,066,300	1,192,214	1,296,372	1,377,983	1,315,834	1,325,510	1,411,330	1,485,333	1,569,825	1,578,365	1,711,263
OHIO	3,196,062	3,672,329	4,157,545	4,767,121	5,759,394	6,646,697	6,907,612	7,946,627	9,706,397	10,657,423	10,797,603	10,847,115	11,353,140
OKLAHOMA	—	258,657	790,391	1,657,155	2,028,283	2,396,040	2,336,434	2,233,351	2,328,284	2,559,463	3,025,487	3,145,585	3,450,654
WISCONSIN	1,315,497	1,693,330	2,069,042	2,333,860	2,632,067	2,939,006	3,137,587	3,434,575	3,951,777	4,417,821	4,705,642	4,891,769	5,363,675
US POP'L'N	50,189,209	62,979,766	76,212,168	92,228,496	106,021,537	123,202,624	132,164,569	151,325,798	179,323,175	203,302,031	226,542,203	248,709,873	281,421,906

(Bureau of the Census, United States Department of Commerce)

mules, tobacco and hogs. Most of all, it was an outlook at odds with the unending stream of pioneers flowing through the state to find and settle land further west. It was a fault line that split society. It left Missouri hopelessly divided during the Civil War.

Though one of the few slave states to stay with the Union, many legislators and state officials from the governor on down seceded, setting up a feisty Confederate Government-in-exile in the south and much of central and west Missouri. Scores of crucial battles were fought, while guerillas from both sides mounted bloody skirmishes for years before and after the war. Entire communities were split, towns and villages were annihilated and decades passed before the scars healed.

But the fact that Missouri's Civil War is still regarded as an anarchic side-show rather than an integral part of the national conflict is a tangible reminder of the state's irrelevance, its remoteness from the minds of America's eastern political, intellectual and financial elite, then and now. And not just the elite. Folks all over the long-settled east, if they gave any thought to it at all, saw Missouri beyond St. Louis as just a remote backwater where fields of waving corn blended into cowboy and cattle country, a land bridge to the west and the Great American Desert.

So, like barnacles on a ship's bottom, an unholy accretion of myth, fantasy, and pernicious nonsense has latched on to national perception of Missouri. It was partly fueled by Mark Twain. The "civilized" east, with its cultural cringe to Europe (expressed in the flowery "literary" prose of high Victoriana), was initially appalled by Twain's "vulgarity" and "tall tale" language of the west. It came from an America beyond the eastern experience, a brash, self-sufficient place, owing nothing to no one. But Twain's rough, sardonic voice was authentic, refreshing and seductive. Soon the east began to laugh and Twain became the first western celebrity since President Andrew Jackson. His fame has lasted.

For our purposes, however, Twain is a liability. His best-known works teem with the rude and the crude, with unwashed hicks, boozers, know-nothing rednecks, mule skinners, riverboat pilots, flatboatmen, fire-and-brimstone preachers and unrepentant slave owners as stubborn as the mules they raise, bristling with spurious notions of "honor" that could goad bewhiskered thugs, masquerading as southern gentlemen, into murderous one-sided "duels."

Shoot-outs at high noon on a western town's dusty streets, ancient and unending Ozark family feuds, bushwhackers and lynch mobs are pervasive Missouri stereotypes. So are images of gilded sternwheelers chugging along the big river, infested with fancy-waistcoated, cigar-chomping, whisky-guzzling card-sharps and con-men, trailing posses of high-spirited, parasol-twirling women, fluttering their eyelashes or snapping their fans at anything promising in trousers and mutton-chop whiskers. A short step then to imagine these same southern belles later on in darkened cabins, prostrated by an attack of the vapors or luxuriating after a vigorous tussle in defense of their honor (victorious or otherwise) with one of the aforementioned "gentlemen." Or from having ingested too many mint juleps. Or both.

This farrago of nonsense about Missourians and Missouri life persisted. In the 1930s an Easterner's quick take was a similar bunch of unreflective platitudes, updated by Depression images of the blues, abandoned homesteads and dilapidated bible-belt towns, a U. S. 66 drive-through state where tourists in smart and fancy new autos jostled for road space with dust-bowl refugees in overloaded, overheating jalopies, all California-bound. For that, you can thank Woody Guthrie, John Steinbeck and Thomas Hart Benton's classic 1930s murals "The Social History of the State of Missouri" that adorn the interior of the state capitol and which so outraged Missourians for years after completion.

Yet *"hicks from the sticks"* generalizations about Missouri predate Twain. They're in the American writings of Charles Dickens (1842), of mother and son Frances (1830) and Anthony (1861/2) Trollope and the paintings of George Caleb Bingham (1840s and beyond). By satirizing these cliches Twain merely reinforced them.. So long as people are introduced to Missouri by <u>Tom Sawyer</u>, <u>Huckleberry Finn</u> or <u>Life on the Mississippi</u>, by endless re-runs of the Beverly Hillbillies or the Jerome Kern/Oscar Hammerstein movie musical <u>Showboat</u> on cable TV, they'll never end. But better that than seeing Missouri and its neighbors as empty "fly-over" states, as so many easterners do today.

For a more exact if less colorful picture, let's examine the regions, each distinct in economy, outlook and orientation.

1. <u>Northern Plains.</u> This runs from the Iowa line in the north to the Missouri. The Mississippi is a natural and unambiguous eastern boundary. When in 1837 the U. S. Government completed the Platte purchase, its western boundary became the state's; the Missouri River south from Iowa to St. Joseph. Physically and climatically an extension of Iowa and Illinois, it's a typical Midwest "granger" area of intensively cultivated farmland. It was and is corn country, but there were/are hogs, dairy cattle, orchards, wheat, soybeans later,

vineyards and some tobacco. There are no sizeable towns away from the major rivers.

2. <u>Western Plains</u> Drier and colder, this region is climatically closer to the Great Plains states, though a continuation of "granger" Missouri. Osage City, close to where the Osage river meets the Missouri, is about as far east as this region extends. The point where the Missouri Ozarks become an obstacle to farming rather than a scenic backdrop marks its southern boundary and its western boundary runs from St. Joseph south to Joplin, Neosho and Arkansas, a triangular wedge of territory. When Abilene KS became trail's end for Texas cattle drives, animals were shipped by rail from there to Kansas City to be killed, processed and packed for onward distribution. As trails followed the railheads or minerals were found, townships sprang up overnight. Cattle, cowboys, mines and miners drove their economies. The demand for whiskey and whores was prodigious. Kansas City and St. Joseph were just the largest of Missouri's many "wide-open" western towns. But this wasn't the whole picture.

The frontier and urbanization eras (as represented by permanent settlers of both sexes) overlapped. The Pony Express of 1860 came and went a scant few years before St. Joseph's first streetcar line began in 1866. It was already a western boom town, a mini-Kansas City sustained by cattle, meat-packing and flour milling, crammed with cattlemen, day laborers, grifters and drifters. But its entrepreneurs, bankers, lawyers, clergy, teachers, doctors and merchants, aspired to be (or already were) middle class, socially and spiritually "superior" in their own estimation than those they'd left behind on their way up. Determined to put down roots with their wives and kids, thousands had moved to the suburbs of St. Joseph by the 1880s, to live the same orderly, civilized life as middle-class folks back east in St. Louis, proud of their gassed, watered and sewered new homes and enjoying convenient links with downtown supplied by streetcars. Some already had phones, while homes and car lines were soon to be hooked up to electrical services. The outlaw Jesse James, living under an alias, was killed in April 1882 not in the streets of a one-horse town or on some hot and dusty trail, but straightening a picture in his suburban St. Joseph home.

3. <u>Southeast Missouri.</u> This includes the bootheel area south of Sikeston. Warmer, wetter and less populous than the rest of the state, it is physically and psychologically part of the ante-bellum south. Its eastern boundary is the Mississippi and it lies south of a line running west through Sikeston and Poplar Bluff. Its economy ran on corn, hogs, cotton, tobacco and rice, generally raised on family farms.

4. <u>Southwest Missouri.</u> West from Poplar Bluff to Springfield and on to the Kansas line, it's mostly forest and hills. From Springfield south to Arkansas, the Missouri Ozarks blossom in all their topographically challenging splendor and this was Missouri's most isolated area until Branson took off around 1970. With few railroads, (some counties had none) and with mountain trails masquerading as roads, only the poorest subsistence farmers stuck it out here, gaining a national reputation (rightly or wrongly) as Ozark hillbillies. But grapes and apples were commercially grown and when iron ore was found, local forges and furnaces began. From the early 1900s, the promise of cheap hydro-electric power from local rivers led to visions of electric interurbans out of Springfield opening up the area. It didn't happen, though that city's trolleys were hydro-powered in part. So were those of Hannibal and St. Louis from 1913, albeit by the Mississippi, dammed at Keokuk IA over 200 miles to the north. The same Keokuk hydro-electric plant served St. Louis's MetroLink light rail at peak times during the 1990s.

These boundaries and economies are not rigid. At best they blend seamlessly. At worst there is overlap and duplication. All had small towns and hard-scrabble farms settled by folks from the Old South. More common in southern Missouri, their habitats were often regarded as "Little Dixies," farms generally being worked with just a handful of slaves. Larger farms and plantations of the kind found in slave states further east and south existed in Missouri, but were uncommon. All regions had areas of intense commercial farming, while the archetypal one-street Wild West frontier town of the movies was defined by 1870s Springfield, Carthage, Clinton and Sedalia. Farms, smelters and mines around Joplin and Flat River co-existed for decades; many miners worked their own farms when not underground.

Coal made Bates and Macon counties. Iron ore was a staple of Iron County. Local boom-and-bust industry (oil and gas wells, logging and steam-powered sawmills) spawned mushroom-like growth in towns that shrivelled when the ore ran out or the forests were gone. Quarrying and brick-making were local activities, though Carthage began commercial harvesting of limestone in the 1880s. But except for Kansas City and St. Louis, the state's urban bookends, Missouri had no industrial towns and few railroad junctions or sizeable settlements in the 19th and early 20th centuries. Its four regions conform with Hilton and Due's definition of areas where interurban and rural trolleys could not flourish. "Build it and they will come" could never apply here. Rural and frontier Missouri was simply an inappropriate place to try.

Of all Missouri's cities, St. Louis was the key national player, an integral part of the U. S. economy even before Missouri statehood. Without St. Louis, the U.S. might have lost the Mississippi to a hostile power before 1814 or to the Confederacy in 1861, with the direst of consequences. From industrialization in 1870 until at least 1950, St. Louis was one of America's ten largest cities (fourth in the 1900-1910 period), flanked by an adjoining county with further 100,000-plus souls and rising.

Not that the city's national significance, then or now, registers with the locals, who harbor an enduring schizoid take on their city's place in the scheme of things. For more than a century, they've argued endlessly whether St. Louis is America's most western eastern city or its most northern southern city (and vice-versa). Because they've yet to find an answer, St. Louis still spends more psychic energy than is good for it trying to face all directions at once.

But St. Louis registers on national and international radar. It is in but not of Missouri, just as New York City is in but not of New York State. Nowhere else in Missouri can make that claim, not even Kansas City. A late bloomer compared to St. Louis, it's a western town with a frontier history and outlook. It began in the 1850s but not until the 1860s, with St. Louis already a century old, did it take off. Bridging of the Missouri in 1869 allowed it to outpace St. Joseph. Flour milling and grain was big, but meatpacking was bigger, the speedy conversion of animals on the hoof into food products, shipped in colossal amounts world-wide. So it was for over fifty years. Everything was up-to-date in Kansas City if you and your kin were rural folk, slack-jawed with wonder at its urban marvels. But to the rest of America (including St. Louis) Kansas City until 1930 was just a frontier cow town on steroids, a brash, raw, rowdy, uncivilized place.

St. Louis, not Kansas City, was and remains the state's biggest deal. Not just an animal chow, baseball, beer and shoe town, it was one of America's top five industrial centers from 1870 to 1930. In street railways, it was number one, Kansas City a distant second, with 740 trolleys at its 1920s peak to St. Louis's 1667. In trackage, KC had 326 miles, St. Louis 485. Omit St. Louis and over half of Missouri's trolleys vanish. Take out Kansas City, St. Joseph and their linking interurban, delete the Carthage, Webb City and Joplin system and all that's left are a few small-town lines and isolated farm-to-market lines. Had autos come a decade sooner or the trolley a decade later, they would not have been built.

Big city and small town transit needs differed and Missouri in the street railway era was nothing if not a state of small towns. In 1880, 197 of its "towns and cities" had 400 to 4,000 inhabitants, 238 in 1890 and 340 by 1920. In 1880 fourteen of its towns had over 4,000 but only four had more than 10,000. In 1890, 29 exceeded 4,000 and six had over 10,000. By 1920, 34 had 4000-plus population and thirteen over 10,000 but four of these were municipally-independent Kansas City or St. Louis suburbs (Missouri Manual, 1891/2 p.p. 332-334, Missouri Manual 1921/22 p.p. 248-258).

The main impetus behind rural and small town trolley projects was getting (name your community here) out of the mud with a reliable all-weather rail link to a county seat, city, river landing or railroad, using private investors to finance and build it. Given the dismal history of rural trolley lines one has to wonder if building private toll roads, as was done in the 1840s and 1850s in similar circumstances, might not have been a better use of their money? But investors of the time didn't see it that way. Their fixation for rail, not road, links was part of the era's rural branch line craze and the fact that railroads, not highways, were where it was at in land transport. Missouri's disastrous experience with privately-built local roads forty-plus years before, remained etched in collective memory.

There were two types of rural trolley. One was a farm-to-market line linking hamlets with towns or a county seat and hauling freight in areas poorly served by railroads, which in Missouri had interstate or transcontinental ambitions and minimal interest in local traffic. The other linked a railroad station with a downtown or a spa, a type satirized in Fontaine Fox's "Toonerville Trolley" cartoon strip. Planning Disneyland in the 1950s, Walt Disney drew on memories of his Missouri childhood in Marceline for the park's idealized 1910-1920 Main Street setting, where horse cars meet all the trains. Strangely, his memory must have failed him. Marceline never had any.

When good roads, automobiles, buses and trucks converged from 1910 onwards. Missouri rejoiced and never looked back. Rural trolleys were finished. But good roads were hardly a new idea, any more than mechanised road vehicles. Steam could and did power 19th-century road vehicles as well as riverboats, ships and locomotives. Indeed, the first application of steam power other than to a pump was to a three-wheel road wagon built by Frenchman Nicholas Cugnot in 1769, though its reliable forward progress was impeded by design flaws that fouled the steering. More successful were a trio of steamers built in 1800 by Englishman Richard Trevithick. They worked fine; poor roads were their undoing. Trevithick, however, is better known as the builder of the world's first steam railroad locomotive in 1804.

By 1810, there were several all-weather roads in the eastern states, to which was added the federally-funded National Road going west from Cumberland MD to Wheeling (West) Virginia from 1810/11. Soon after, a privately-funded eastern extension (the Baltimore Pike) was added. The initial project was complete by 1818. This was no rough scar, hacked out of existing forest, Indian or buffalo trails, but a solidly-engineered highway. Western extensions followed and

Vandalia IL was reached in the 1850s. But the final 65 miles to St. Louis wasn't built, nor the branch to Alton IL, nor any other Federally-funded highways. The subsidy had been withdrawn.

That was incredibly shortsighted. The National Road was America's best pre-20th century highway by far, heavily used from dawn until well past dusk. Stagecoaches made up to 70 miles a day and even six-horse Conestoga wagons hauling four tons of heavy freight managed a daily 15 miles. Long before railroads, the National Road opened up the "western" states by providing a rock-solid and reliable eastern link. Had it reached the Mississippi as originally intended, eastern Missouri would have grown larger and faster than it did. But with the ending of the subsidy, the road got into bad repair. Tolls imposed to finance maintenance were never enough. When the Pennsylvania Railroad reached Pittsburgh and the Baltimore and Ohio Railroad passed Wheeling, the National Road declined, not to revive until the 1920s as U.S. 40.

In Missouri, a pack-horse road of the mid-1740s tied lead mines to St. Genevieve. St. Louis County's St. Charles Road was hacked from the forest in the 1770s by the Spanish who by the 1790s had also "built" El Camino Real from New Madrid to St. Louis via Sikeston, Cape Girardeau and St. Genevieve. Today's U. S. 61, this route originated with De Soto who in 1541 traveled it from New Madrid to Cape Girardeau, sending scouts even further north. In 1805, it was designated the first official U. S. highway west of the Mississippi. A series of "trails" then developed, Boone's Lick being the first, starting in St. Charles and heading west. Western trails were crucial to U. S. interests and the Federal Government appointed three commissioners to oversee the southwest extension of Boone's Lick as the Santa Fe Trail.

An embryonic system of Post Roads began circa 1818 and some inter-city stage-coaches navigated them as best they could. St. Charles Road became a post and stage road in 1819. In 1822, Missouri made each county responsible for road maintenance, all free men age 16-45 giving several days to this duty annually. Illinois had similar laws. Unhappily, results varied from appalling to "what road, where?" Each county, concerned only with its own needs, was indifferent to intercounty and intrastate links. Roads were unsigned and unbridged, teeming with ruts, roots, mud and chuckholes. A cleared road might be 50' wide but stumps up to 10" high could remain, making travel hazardous. Missourians soon reckoned a passable road was one where mud didn't reach your boot-tops when in the saddle.

In the 1840s, livery stables, taverns, road houses and bridges were built, making journeys marginally less irksome. A movement to build private toll roads, turnpikes or plank roads had limited success. St. Charles Road became a turnpike in 1837. But toll collectors were seen as fair game by those who couldn't, or wouldn't, pay and investors lost their shirts as the new roads bled money. Yet without money, there was no maintenance. Plank roads were useless within months.

Most of Missouri's 19th-century "roads" were farm-to-market routes unsuited to mechanical (steam) traction. Had they been of the National Road's quality, had more advanced and compact steam propulsion units been available for larger road vehicles, there would have been little need for rural, local or even intra-state railroads. But as it was, steam railroads delivered speed and comfort far beyond anything a stagecoach on a trail masquerading as a highway could provide. They could outhaul a road vehicle by at least a factor of four.

Once iron (later steel) rails and steam-powered trains were seen as transport's way ahead, speculation, promotion and construction gripped Missouri.

Macadamising of St. Charles Road in 1865 was an exception proving the rule (it was then it acquired its "Rock Road" name). Otherwise roads languished as rail flourished. Reliable farm-to-market or farm-to-railhead roads were sorely needed, but failing that, then a "local-interest" light railway or interurban would have served, taking people and freight to a nearby town or railhead a few times a day. They could have been built cheaply with partial state or federal subsidy.

Belgium had a national system of such secondary rural lines, the government giving private operators franchises to build and run segments of a planned national network, mainly between 1885 and 1914. These steam lines opened up Belgium's rural areas and many were electrified from 1894. After 1918, when franchises were vacated as unprofitable, the government ran the lines itself. The first closures were in the 1920s, but more were built or electrified into the 1950s. Survivors were fused into new Light Rail projects from the 1970s and remain part of privatized Belgian mass transit.

With state/federal subsidy, rural Missouri too might have had a coherent rural network of light rail or interurbans, to its lasting benefit. But without subsidy, little would have been gained even had the many "hot-air" lines contemplated been built, for as commercial investments they were all no-hopers.

Early in 1913, a Highway Commission was created. Each Missouri county appointed a three-man highway board which could apply to the State Highway Commissioner to set up an inter-county road system of connecting highways between county seats on any route agreed by that county's highway board and the State Highway engineer. The former would let contracts for the roads to be dragged, the latter would make an annual $15.00 a mile appropriation for them. The phrase "road dragging" implied these new roads would be unpaved, still far short of the all-weather roads needed.

The July 1916 Federal-Aid Road Act gave subsidies to states that built rural post roads and roads "for other purposes," widely interpreted as authorizing the building of a connecting interstate road system. Experiments then began to determine the best hard surface and St. Charles Rock Road was the first in Missouri to be concreted. The next five years saw huge growth in auto traffic and a pressing need for all-weather interstate roads. The 1921 Federal-Aid Road Act identified 7% of existing rural mileage as eligible for aid, enough to establish the present U. S. highway system.

Following passage of a $60 million bond issue in 1920, Missouri's 1921 Centennial Road Law supplemented the Federal Act, setting up today's Missouri Highway Commission and designating 7,600 miles of state highways. A new Highway Department selected 1500 miles of road to receive better paving than the typical clay-bound gravel of the time, paid for out of revenue (gas taxes and the like) and state bond issues. Each county was to be linked with its neighbor by at least one north-south and one east-west paved road. Road construction, realignment and paving plus the funding that sustains it all, has been unceasing ever since.

Motor vehicle registrations of Missouri and other Midwest states

STATE	1900	1910	1920	1930	1940	1950	1960	1970	1980	1990	2000
ARKANSAS	20	1,150	59,082	221,441	261,396	477,265	707,551	1,043,336	1,573,718	1,447,660	1,813,919
ILLINOIS	800	35,580	568,924	1,646,127	1,939,358	2,650,968	3,776,079	5,237,878	7,478,832	7,873,189	8,889,635
INDIANA	170	10,110	333,087	879.800	1,008,923	1,434,885	2,048,302	2,817,991	3,825,852	4,365,780	5,487,920
IOWA	40	10,410	437,378	782,510	802,804	1,072,290	1,325,392	1,790,061	2,329,465	2,631,973	3,058,058
KANSAS	220	10,480	294,159	597,581	588,984	853,462	1,163,414	1,547,643	2,006,868	2,012,353	2,266,868
MICHIGAN	360	20,670	412,717	1,338,018	1,571,272	2,432,684	3,308,325	4,589,319	6,488,070	7,208,217	8,296,331
MISSOURI	180	12,270	297,008	765,575	929,529	1,261,420	1,720,029	2,407,887	3,271,288	3,904,879	4,546,282
NEBRASKA	80	11,340	219,000	427,771	416,689	569,497	733,538	974,158	1,254,095	1,383,848	1,582,203
OHIO	480	32,940	83,300	1,772,733	1,941,699	2,795,073	4,086,772	5,973,901	7,771,238	8,410,468	10,323,179
OKLAHOMA	10	880	212,880	554,546	584,297	831,368	1,183,550	1,712,552	2,582,999	2,649,051	2,941,824
WISCONSIN	160	14,200	293,298	788,134	912,740	1,201,188	1,600,163	2,181,510	2,940,911	3,814,311	4,300,759
U.S.TOTAL	8,000	468,500	9,239,181	26,749,853	32,453,233	49,161,691	73,857,788	108,418,197	155,798,219	188,797,914	217,566,789

(U. S. Department of Transportation, Federal Highway Administration. Totals are autos, trucks & buses combined but excludes motor cycles. Early year totals are approximations as records are incomplete and contradictory)

HERE COMES THE TROLLEY:
THE WIRES GO UP,
THE RAILS GO DOWN

When brand new, horsecars were among the most colorful and showy vehicles to be seen. Even after service on the less-than-pristine streets of St. Louis, cars still stood out. This is Fourth and Morgan looking south circa 1886. People's Railway closed car 8 is about to head south. One of the city's principal streets it is macadamized but not yet paved. The Fourth Street and Arsenal "bobtail" (believed to be car 10) has people on board but as yet no horse or mule to pull it. One-man operated "bobtail" cars lacked a rear platform. Instead passengers climbed the iron step and entered through the center rear. The nickel fare was rolled down to the driver at the front using a chute.

Railroads could not go everywhere. Good local roads remained vital, not just as rural farm-to-market links but as a way to clear clogged urban arteries, a pressing need since the 1820s when American cities, grown beyond "walking" size, still lacked paved streets and easy passage for wagons and carriages. In St. Louis, cabs arrived in 1838, horse buses in 1843. Both ran on mostly unpaved, undrained streets. But even on paved surfaces, the big wheels of a cab or horse bus rode over cobblestones with all the resilience of the average brick. Something better was needed.

That something was a vehicle on metal rails, aka the streetcar. Missouri's first graced St. Louis's Olive Street from 4th to 12th Streets on July 4th, 1859, and was extended two weeks later to 17th and to Leffingwell. Three thousand people showed up for the opening, though many others were absent on steamboat excursions or Independence Day trips. A Market Street line began in August. St. Joseph followed in 1866, Kansas City in 1869 and Hannibal in July 1878. Legend has it that one Hannibal driver celebrated opening day by getting smashed in a local saloon. He was fired.

The streetcar was an advance on the animal bus. Two beasts pulling a car could haul double the number of passengers and the metal rails gave a smoother ride. When Charles Dickens returned to America in the early 1860s after a twenty-year absence, he praised the streetcars that eased his travels round Manhattan and roundly denounced the London authorities who had got rid of their "American Railway" within a few months of its 1861 opening. Had he made a return trip to St. Louis, he would have been just as impressed with its cars.

Still, animal traction was expensive. Not every neighborhood could be served nor could rush-hour demands for extra cars be met. Adding a car meant two more men to staff it and four to six horses to pull it, for animals could manage only three or four hours daily. A tripper car supplementing service at busy times had to be on the streets for at least nine. A regular car and crew could be out for 18 hours a day and with the Civil War continuing, men and livestock were in short supply. So experiments with mechanical traction began in 1864, with a steam dummy (a small locomotive disguised so as not to frighten horses) pulling horse cars at ten mph on St. Louis's Grand Avenue (Easton to the Fairgrounds), and west on Easton to the Abbey race track near Sarah.

The experiments showed the dummy to be technically feasible but not cost-effective. For example, it was hoped fuel would cost less than animal feed. It didn't. Worse, heavier rail was needed, silent and smoke-free running (required by city ordinance) wasn't possible and 18-hour days with just a few brief stops for coke and water, proved unworkable.

In later years, some of these limitations were overcome, but St. Louis and Kansas City relied on animal cars until 1884, developing dense and sophisticated systems run by numerous competing companies.

The generation that saw animal cars and buses arrive in the 1850s and 1860s saw them as a luxury. Their sons and daughters saw them as vital adjuncts to urban living, whatever their inconveniences.

"They call it the tramway in England and it is so much more compact and expressive a name than the one we use that it ...ought to be adopted universally...in progressive America. The street railway...has within a few years...reached a high degree of perfection and is an important factor in the lives of (city) dwellers...Without the streetcars the great city of St. Louis would in a very short time retrograde to its condition of forty or fifty years ago, when the sububs began at Ninth Street and the region of Eighteenth Street and beyond was 'way out in the country'...(But) any part of the city can (now) be reached quickly and cheaply. Property that would otherwise be a dull sale by the acre now brings a smart price by the foot and miles...of handsome residences are eagerly rented by small tradesmen and men on moderate salaries who would be doomed to a life in a greasy boarding house were it not for the bounding streetcar.

"Some lines run in an exclusively aristocratic and pretentious neighborhood...Others are divided in their course between high and low where the wealthy merchant sits beside the grimy workman and the silks of the lady of fashion come in contact with the soiled dress of the boarding-house drudge. Streetcars are essentially democratic. There are no reserved seats and ladies must depend for courtesy upon the breeding of patrons of the line. In streetcar travel the bobtail car holds a prominent place...The manifold duties of a bobtail driver are so...various as to call for wonder that one man could be found competent to attend to it all. He must see that each fare is paid...attend to his mule or mules with his hand ever on the brake, hand out packages of change to all who ask...keep a lookout for passengers on each corner and up and down each intersecting street, remember to let the fat lady off at criss-cross street, and the thin lady with glasses at the center of

the crossing at twenty-fourth and in his unoccupied moments give the family history and geneaology of the occupants of each prominent residence the car passes to the passenger of an enquiring mind who is disposed to be friendly... (<u>G-D</u> June 20th, 1880 p. 8)

After years of heavy service, once-shiny horsecars were shabby and neglected, especially now mechanical replacements were on hand. Cars such as this weary St. Louis Union Railroad bobtail car, used on the Lee Avenue line until circa 1893 were anything up to fifteen years old, and were subject to much ridicule in the local papers from the late 1870s onwards. The idea of cramming fifty or more people onto a vehicle intended to seat no more than sixteen appears ludicrous today, but in the 1880s it was a much-resented fact of daily life. STLMOT

"A car rattles down to the (Olive) terminus, the team is changed, the car is then driven over the switch and onto the right-hand track... Before the driver has his team changed and the eastbound passengers are out, the car is invaded by stragglers from the multitude. By the time the gates are hitched to the driver's platform, the car is half-filled and when it is moved to the side-track, every seat is taken and one or two people are standing...When it is driven away it has become crowded and...at every crossing from Fourth to Ninth Street, numerous additions will be received.

"(At) the corner of Fourth and Pine, the observer will see a crowd on both sides of Pine Street waiting for cars. The minute a car reaches the turntable and is swung around there is a grand rush for entry and before the driver can note down the time in his book, the car is packed...The same scene (is) enacted at the terminus of each of the roads that take on passengers at Fourth Street. This is all supposed to occur on any ordinary fine evening. What is the case when the streets are rendered unfit for walking by rain? Simply this. Almost double the usual number of people...wait for cars and...crowd into unwholesome, malodorous conveyances, submitting...to pushing, dragging and stamping and be carried away to reach their destination at about the same time...had they walked." (P-D November 15th, 1883 p.2.)

Early in 1884 a reporter rode from St. Louis's West End *"and not only enjoyed the society of thirty-seven horny-handed sons of toil, but was given thirty-seven opportunities to study how much worse-smelling one kind of tobacco could be than another. An analytical chemist, who was a fellow-sufferer, declared he could recognize in the atmosphere of the car nine distinct noxious gases, continued exposure to any one of which would produce serious illness if not a torturesome death. The women, as usual, insisted upon crowding into the smoking car, although the point is made to run another car within one minute of the smoker. After haughtily accepting the seat of the man with the tin pail who is going to a hard day's labor, she, as a rule, occupied the remainder of the trip by casting indignant glances at the puffers of cigars and pipes. As usual, no cars seemed to be filled in the minds of the conductors. There was always room for more...* (P-D January 18th, 1884)

While riding the cars could be a pain, a job on the cars was highly prized, long hours, poor to terrible conditions and low pay notwithstanding. For country boys, used to working all hours and seasons in the great outdoors, this was a chance to make it in the big city with wages of almost $2.00 a day if they were lucky and the pride of working with the latest technology once a system cabled or electrified. Moreover, country boys were docile, not inclined to make trouble however marginal their working conditions and were generally polite to the passengers. Management loved that. When St. Louis and Kansas City hired, country boys were given preference, a practice common until at least World War One.

City men also worked the cars but they were a different breed of cat. For every crew who in winter froze their fingers to the brake handles at their post on an open platform or choked in the sweat and fug of an overcrowded car in pre-deodorant days, there was another happy to share the profits from illegally skimming or "knocking down" fares to supplement their wages. Many quit after a few years with enough money to start a saloon or small business. City men also had the reputation of being curt and offhand with passengers. Not that the latter were paragons of virtue. Scams abounded; girls of fifteen or more passing themselves off as fourteen or less so they could ride for half-fare, mothers who scattered children all over a car hoping to get away with paying only for some, folks passing bad coins,

Kansas City Cable Railway open grip car 9. This engraving was made soon after opening in 1886, and shows the grip under the car (bottom center) engaging the cable.

"When John Woollam came to St. Louis in 1882, he had a friend working on the Broadway line and got a job driving a pair of mules...from Gano Avenue 5200 north to Jefferson and Keokuk. There were no paved streets and (when) the road was...not muddy, it was dusty. The company had barrels of water and brushes at each end of the line and it was the driver's duty to wash the outside of the car while the conductor scrubbed the inside. The men worked two 'short' days of 15 hours and one long day of 18 hours alternately. Compensation was $1.65 for the 'short' day, $1.98 for the long. There were no stoves...or windshields and in winter floors were covered with straw...Derailments were frequent and it was up to the passengers to get out and help put the car back on track. At one time, conditions were so bad the cars were run over granite blocks covered with tar and sand in place of rails. There were no plows and in winter the company depended upon salt to keep lines open..." (UR *magazine July 15th, 1921)*

and jumpers who by alighting when asked for a fare and getting on the next car, avoided paying completely. Mashers, sleepers, drunks and the malodorous were occupational hazards to those riding or working the cars and in a state where pistol-packing was still a way of life, there was always a chance of armed robbery especially after midnight. Many crews packed their own heat. Every rider knew it and many took their own precautions.

In electric days, men still worked cars with open platforms in all weathers and were frozen, soaked or steamed, often all three on the same shift. John McCombs and Harry Lofflin began as animal car drivers in the 1890s and transferred to electrics until retiring along with St. Joseph's streetcars in January 1938. Each had a permanently stiff finger from years of wrestling a car's handbrake. Enclosing and heating a car and its platforms didn't bring an end to physical affliction. McCombs had a similarly stiff finger on his other hand, caused by years of gripping a Birney "Safety" car's "deadman" handle after this new type of vehicle arrived in 1918 (St. Joseph News-Press, January 30th, 1938 p.4).

Life on small town trolleys was more laid-back. Animal-car crews did not trouble themselves with fare-paying riders if they didn't want to carry them. Lost revenue seemed immaterial. When Cape Girardeau ridership was especially poor, street railway officials would ask passengers to ride around a bit more for the same fare to make business look better. On rainy days, when mules slipped in the mud and cars derailed, passengers would be triaged into those who got off and pushed, those who got off to walk and those who wouldn't get off but told the others what to do.

In Sedalia, animal cars *"used to jog along, sometimes on the tracks, sometimes off the tracks...Some of the young men of the city who lived east of Third and Engineer, would ride to the end of the line, relieve the driver of the reins and drive on to their homes (beyond the tracks).*

They outnumbered the driver and he was helpless in their hands. There was nothing...to do but to acquiesce and when they had climbed out, to return to the tracks. One gentleman of Sedalia, who as a boy was one of the numerous ones who would 'hop the cars,' got on one day carrying two dozen eggs. The driver jogged the car purposely the man now believes, and he fell backwards landing on the eggs." (The Sedalia Democrat, October 4th, 1931 p. 2).

Most small towns had no street lighting. Would-be passengers could neither see nor hear an approaching animal car at night, though all cars were supposed to carry oil lamps to denote their presence. In 1879, Hannibal ordered the company to put bells on the mules, advising riders to strike a match to let the crew of an oncoming car know they wanted to be picked up. Similar arrangements were made elsewhere; indeed on 1950s St. Louis and Kansas City suburban trolley lines the same thing had to be done if the electric light that marked a car stop was missing or out.

Cable cars were the first practical mechanized transit, but were capital-intensive, best suited to first-tier city systems such as St. Louis and Kansas City. Both built cable lines from 1884. At their peak, each was among the nation's top ten in size and ridership. But electricity was the coming thing. Kansas City, St. Joseph and St. Louis began experimenting with electric cars and by 1890 cable traction was obsolete. Though the last new cable wasn't opened until 1891, cable cars left St. Louis in March 1901 and Kansas City by 1906, except the 12th Street cable which soldiered on until 1913.

Missouri's first electric cars ran in Kansas City in 1884 when Grand Avenue Railway President Walton Holmes took on a project of one John C. Henry, a Canadian who after losing a farm and a couple of stores to grasshoppers in Wakeeney KS, had come to KC in 1880 as a dispatcher for the Kansas City, Fort Scott and Memphis Railroad. Henry did not claim to be a pioneer. His electric cars, for example, used Van Depoele motors, already in limited production. Instead he claimed that after four years of experiments he'd solved the problem of getting

Kansas City Cable Railway's 9th Street viaduct circa 1886. A train comprising an open grip and trailer crosses the railroad tracks before climbing the 18.5% grade up the bluffs to downtown Kansas City.

power from the motor to the wheels, using a constant-speed motor and "manual transmission" with gears operating in an oil bath.

After setting up the Henry Electric Railway Company, Holmes offered Henry an old open car, a half-mile of track and a used steam-thresher to run a generator. Wires (one positive, one negative) were strung between 39th Street and West Linwood Boulevard (Hunter Avenue). A two-wheel collector in a frame ran along the wires, linked to the car by a power cord. All worked fine, but the light track derailed the car on its first run (December 15th, 1884).

Later experiments were done on the Kansas City, Fort Scott and Memphis Railroad's Union Depot-Westport Fairgrounds switch (near Linwood and Broadway) with a new Brownell open car named "Pacinnoti." The overhead was now a single wire with current return through the rails. Again, the car derailed at 12 mph on the first run, dumping itself and its passengers into a hedge. But later, it hauled a railroad boxcar up a 3% grade, a first for electric power, achieved on January 29th, 1886.

Kansas City Electric Railway Company (Henry car) circa 1887.

The Twelfth Street Cable April 9th, 1888-October 12th, 1913.
By Walter P. Neff
(Kansas City Daily Drovers Telegram, October 1913, reprinted in The Railwayan, January 1923 p. 10).

In nineteen hundred and fifty-seven, a white-haired man, near the gates of heaven,
Will say: "Come closer and you shall hear, a tale of the city you hold so dear
A tale that will sound like a fairy's fable, of a street car line called the Twelfth Street cable."

And around his chair they will kneel to listen, and their childish eyes with wonder glisten,
As his feeble voice depicts the scenes the old man witnessed in his teens,
And describes as well as he is able, the wondrous thing called the Twelfth Street Cable.

And the children still unborn today, will hear their doddering granddad say:
"A rope of steel, secure and strong, ran in a conduit ten miles long
T'was an endless rope, from the carbarn stable, it made a loop did the Twelfth Street cable.

"It held the cars with a mighty grip that took them along at a merry clip,
They ran much faster than you can walk and made so much noise that we didn't talk.
They were larger too than this dinner table, yet were pulled along by the powerful cable.

"The streetcar company fixed it so, that the cars would rock, rock to and fro,
And the girls who worked indoors would prize, a trip on the line for the exercise,
And Madge and Mary and Ruth and Mabel, would healthy be through the Twelfth Street cable.

"I remember a hill that the line traversed and the feeling I had when I rode it first.
My health had been bad and I longed to die and go to the mansions in the sky.
So I boarded a train of the Twelfth Street label, but it went straight down and was held by the cable.

There was sweet romance on the jostling line, the manager worked the thing out fine,
Young men stood up and held onto the straps, that let them fall into the maidens' laps,
And girlish hopes that ere this were stable, grew bright from a trip on the Twelfth Street cable.

Much more could I tell of the line so queer, on which I rode for twenty-six year,
But I'm growing tired and fain would press, my aching head in sleeps' caress.
Good night my dears, God grant I'm able, to sleep and dream of the Twelfth Street cable."

And thus in 1957, the gray-haired man so near to heaven
Related a tale ere he came to die, that shows how memory takes a lie
And dresses it up in the form of a fable, as the old man did of the Twelfth Street cable.

In July 1887, Henry electrified the East Fifth Street horse line (Kansas City Electric Railway Company) between Grand and Lydia, using 250V D.C. and four open cars, the first electric cars in regular Missouri service. But the backers (including Willard E. Winner) were focused on the real estate for which it had been sponsored, open cars were wickedly cold in winter and the Henry transmission was unreliable. They were replaced by animal cars at year's end though Poor's 1889 still listed the KCERC with "four cars and four electric motors," on two miles of standard-gauge track. With some foresight, Henry sold his patents to the Westinghouse Company who soon hired him as an electrical engineer, but not before he'd moved to Coronado CA and opened a more successful electric line there.

At this time, Kansas City traction affairs were settling down after a major shake-up. Until 1886, they'd been dominated by the Corrigan brothers and their Corrigan Consolidated Transit Company, an early attempt to coerce independent operations into one unified company. However, they were bought out in 1886 by a combination of interests including the Armour and Adams families, major investors in the stockyards and anxious to cable or electrify existing lines to serve them. The Metropolitan of Kansas City, which took over the Corrigan system, inherited some awful old cars.

"Through your kind permission of a little space in your valuable paper, we may be enabled to enlighten some wanderer who has thousands of dollars to invest…not knowing where or how to do so. The old maxim is, you know, that all appreciate good work, good dealing and cannot help but respect the same…Many people… appreciate the uniform good work of a good real estate firm. No class of people on the face of the globe can do more for a town, for a city or for a community than a good, substantial real estate firm. It points out places that are dark and throws light upon the same.. They build a town in fact in a few years with fine buildings and residences. They run their street cars, they run their cable lines… they improve streets and cause a general satisfaction and pride to come gradually on…

"The firm of Hobson and Co, consisting of W. J. Hobson and C. W. Hobson is one of the most reliable and prominent in the State of Missouri. No one has done more for the building up of St. Joseph in the short space of a few months than Hobson and Co. Think of making sales in one day amounting to $100,000 and over…A few days ago…(we closed) one of the largest deals ever made in St. Joseph, that of selling the Francke, Brittain and Hall tracts, covering…180 acres. This purchase…will improve its locality and in a short space of time add…thousands of people to St. Joseph. Think of it! In a few months, St. Joseph will have her people riding in cable cars. Have patience citizens. Stick to your old shoes. Don't speak of your long walk. Don't bother your brain as to how you shall reach your wife at dinner or tea on a wet day. In a few months, all will be well. No more tired limbs, no more sore feet…we shall ride with satisfaction from one end of St. Joseph to the other on our cable line." (<u>St. Joseph Daily Gazette</u>*, editorial page, September 6th, 1887).*

"Many still have vivid recollections of…Corrigan horse cars, 10' bobtails with mules inured to all kinds of service. The tracks, (what there was of them), were single with turnouts. These…were… superfluous, as when the cars met one simply turned towards the gutter and traveled along until it struck the track again.This…did not trouble the public any as it was difficult to tell whether the cars were on the track or not. The first step (MET)…took was to have these cars washed…It is said the price of soap in Kansas City advanced…in consequence." (<u>The Railwayan</u>, January 1923 p. 9.)

By 1889, manufacturers could offer complete electric installations, from generation and distribution to tracks, overhead wires, cars, staff training and public education. (*"No sir, your expensive watch won't be magnetized by the electric motor. Yes ma'am, it's safe. You cannot be shocked if you have one foot on the track, unless at the same time your other foot is on the overhead wire.)"* The MET, gradually merging all cable and animal lines in the city under its banner, knew electricity was the coming thing and made its plans accordingly.

In April 1887, the Lindell Railway of St. Louis and the Union Railway of St. Joseph had begun electric experiments by ordering motors from the Sprague company plus Julien batteries and motors. The Union examined naptha-powered motors as well, soon rejecting batteries and naptha as impractical. Instead, they erected poles and wires in July and in late August fitted a car with a Sprague motor. Its first test run was between Highland and New Ulm Park on September 6th. The rival Wyatt Park Railway had already bought materials to build St. Joseph's

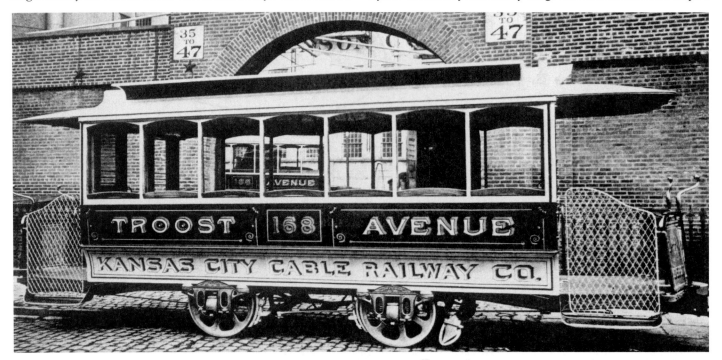

Trailer for Kansas City Cable Railway's Troost Avenue extension outside the John Stephenson plant, New York, 1887.

Cable car winding gear was a high point of Victorian mechanical and metallurgical engineering proficiency. This is the St. Louis Cable and Western installation. (SRJ January 1890 p. 45).

first cable line. It was keenly anticipated. The Union's success prompted them to electrify instead.

The Lindell persevered with the Julien battery and motor, each set costing $1,600 and weighing two tons. Testing began in April 1887 on Washington Avenue between 3rd and 23rd Streets, but the 80-mile range was less than claimed by the Julien folks, insufficient for a day's work. The batteries smelled bad, often splashing sulphuric acid onto passengers' legs, a public relations problem despite the laconic observation of one Julien director that *"the acid employed is a 90% dilution and...one may bathe his face and hands in it with impunity."* (SRG October 1888 p.144).

Recharging soon exceeded an acceptable five hours, battery life was only six to eight months and replacements were neither as well made nor as powerful. The Julien motor was ineffective and the gears were of poor-quality metal. Two Sprague motors were expected but the Lindell couldn't get a shipping date. When their electrical engineer talked with Frank Sprague at the 1887 American Street Railway Association's Philadelphia convention, he was brushed off. Recovering from typhoid fever and intensely focused on the problems of the Richmond VA electric trolley system due to start tests by the end of October, Sprague was too busy to focus on a few motors for a backwoods western state. Once Richmond was up and running, Sprague's St. Joseph back-orders were filled, but the Lindell cancelled.

Instead, a car with Brush motors and gears and powered by Julien batteries went into service from February 5th 1888. While it did fine (a second car was added), the Lindell's quest for better, cheaper batteries proved fruitless and their first overhead wire line opened on Finney Avenue early in 1889. A mile of the St. Louis Railway between Wyoming (Wild Hunter's) and Keokuk on Broadway had been experimentally wired for 90 days on November 1st, 1888. The cars were a

success but the north-south Broadway line was busy and with a blanket ban on downtown overhead wires (the Lindell's Finney line was in suburbs west of Grand), and electric cars believed too fragile for heavy city service, the St. Louis Railway decided to cable the busy central portion. The ban was lifted on April 4th, 1890, thanks to bribery of compliant city fathers by the trolley companies' agent. The other companies soon extended their wires downtown but the Broadway line stayed with cable, electric cars running extension shuttles at north and south ends.

The St. Louis and Suburban took things a step further. Its narrow-gauge steam railroad division ran from Enright (near Grand) to Wellston and Florissant, its cable division ran downtown from Enright. In late 1891, it electrified both divisions, a total of twenty miles from Washington and Third out to Florissant. One of America's first electric interurbans, it boasted passenger, freight, express and mail service.

Animal cars were better than no cars at all and for rural towns the opening of their first line, whatever the motive power, was a milestone in local life, no matter how short its existence. Trenton opened in 1890. It was gone by 1896.

"To Captain N. A. Winters must be given the honor of putting down the first streetcar line in Trenton...The steel rails are new, heavy and first-class and...laid on solid oak cross ties...Captain Winters had announced that he would start his first car at 8 o'clock Thursday morning (December 4th), but at a late hour Wednesday evening it was discovered that the gauge of the track was not the same as the car...The Captain bought the car with the understanding that it was standard gauge and he laid the track at standard gauge, which was on measurement found to be an inch and a half too wide. Nothing daunted, the Captain put on a force of 20 men who worked all Wednesday night setting in one of the rails in and at 10 o'clock Thursday forenoon, the first

One of St. Joseph's pristine new electric trolley cars. Car 23 of the Peoples' Railway, as a Frederick Avenue Mail car in the still-rural suburbs during the early 1890s.

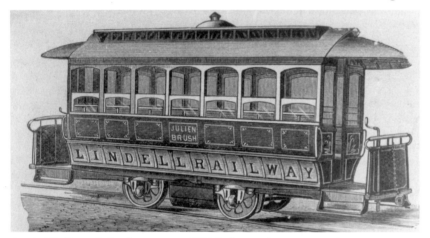

Lindell Railway Julien battery car 1887. Julien equipment was tried all over the-world between 1887 and 1890, including the U.K., Belgium and Australia. At best only modest successes were recorded.

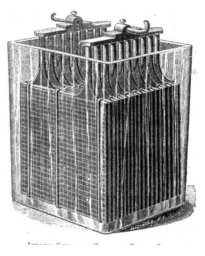

Julien storage battery cell.

trip was made…Members of the press had the honor of the first ride, after which the car was run free frseveral hours." Trenton Daily Republican *(December 4th, 1890 p. 2.)*

While getting a streetcar line was a consumation devoutly to be wished, an unending litany of contradictory moans began once cars ran. Fares were too high, fares were too low, cars came late, cars came early, they were too hot, they were too cold, they were unbearably noisy, they were dangerously quiet. Law-abiding citizens innocently strolling in the street could be maimed or disemboweled by electric cars with weak handbrakes, but when ordinances dictated power (air) brakes be fitted, riders would be hurled against the interior bulkhead in promiscuous heaps of bruised ribs and broken bones as cars came to an over-enthusiastic halt. At bottom, the scorn heaped on the operating companies was emotional; the caustic aftermath of a brief, torrid and failed love-affair. Nothing was ever right so far as the public

was concerned and the transit soap opera, an enduring feature of city life, is with us yet. Kansas City and St. Louis especially were national and not just state bellwethers and the trade press ran stories on their travails for decades.

Initial financing of Missouri's big city systems came from locals with national prominence and deep pockets. These included such groups as the Krugs and Steinackers in St. Joseph, the Adams, Armour, Heim and Winner interests in Kansas City, and in St. Louis the "Big Cinch" group (pillars of the social register, dominant in banking, utilities and railroads) including David Francis, Julius Walsh and Edwards Whitaker, plus Big Cinch wannabees like George Kobusch, H. F. Vogel, George Baumhoff and James Houseman. All were used to getting their way and not squeamish about the methods used to do it. But it wasn't long before bigger groups were attracted from other parts of the country.

St. Joseph was among the earliest, when New York's R. B. Newcombe and Company, representing a venture capitalist group, injected itself into the city's system. By 1905, St. Louis's United Railways was part of the North American Company, Federal Light and Traction Company of New York owned Springfield Traction by 1912, while Sedalia and St. Joseph were in Henry Doherty's Cities Service Company by 1912 and 1913 respectively. McKinley's Illinois Traction, originally backed by Canadian and British investors, was in North American by 1926 and the locally-promoted Kansas City, Clay County and St. Joseph used Chicago and New York money from the outset.

In Joplin and Webb City, local and outside finance built the Southwest Missouri, an interurban system that eventually served towns in three states. But for decades it was under the daily supervision of A. H. Rogers, an Iowa-born Harvard alumnus who at various times owned a wholesale grocery, was President of Springfield Bank and had local newspaper interests. His fundraising skills were legendary, Charles L. Henry of Indiana and the E. Z. Wallower investment syndicate of Harrisburg PA (among others) being persuaded to put money into Southwest. The Wallower group kept it there for over forty years and also had money in local zinc mines. Wallower himself owned and built Joplin's Keystone Hotel at Fourth and Main in 1892, which may have

been how he first met Rogers. But from 1890 until he died in 1920, this was Mr. Rogers' neighborhood and Southwest's cars were his trolleys. For the smaller investor, however, street railway "securities" were anything but. Regular folk got into trolley stocks around 1890, some hoping to get out again in a few years having made a comfortable profit, others such as widows, orphans and bachelor uncles hoping to live for years off the sure-fire dividends. All hopes were disappointed. Pillaging carpet-baggers would sweep in, make big bucks from selling franchises or overpriced stock, then sweep out again leaving small investors with portfolios of worthless paper that paid no dividends and only pennies on the dollar.

Kansas City had home-grown pillagers in the shape of Thomas and Bernard Corrigan, but it exported others. Robert Snyder was one. Well-known in KC as the colossus of town gas, Snyder easily shook down St. Louis. In 1898, he bought himself a blanket St. Louis traction franchise by paying $250,000 for the votes of the obligingly venal Board of Alderman, outbidding the Board's usual paymaster, the local "Big Cinch" crowd's agent "Boss" Ed Butler. Then in 1899 he turned round and sold the franchise for $1.25 million to "Big Cinch" interests. Some of this money built his "Ha-Ha-Tonka" castle near Camdenton but Snyder didn't live to see it finished, being killed in a 1906 auto wreck.

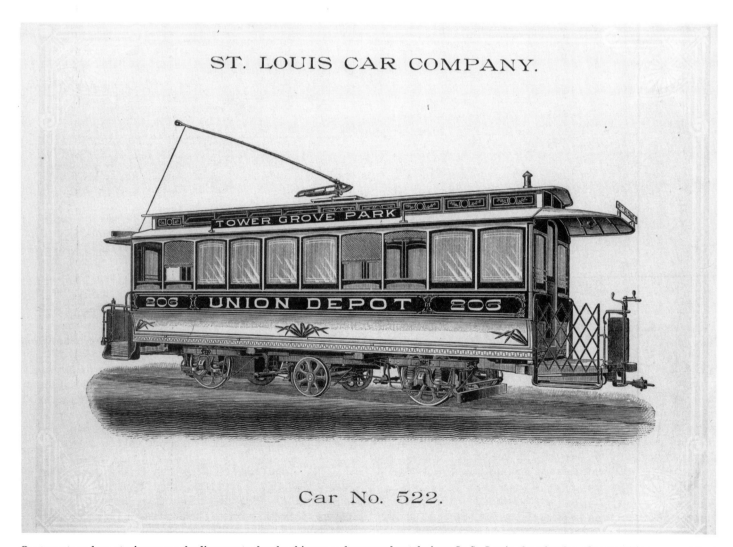

One way to reduce strains on car bodies was to develop bigger and more robust designs. In St. Louis, the stimulus of competition ensured that such cars appeared early in the 1890s, many years before similar cars arrived in Kansas City or even New York or Chicago. Union Depot 206 of 1892 is mounted on a Robinson "radial" six-wheel truck and with its many sisters was big enough to make a dent in the rush-hour crowds.

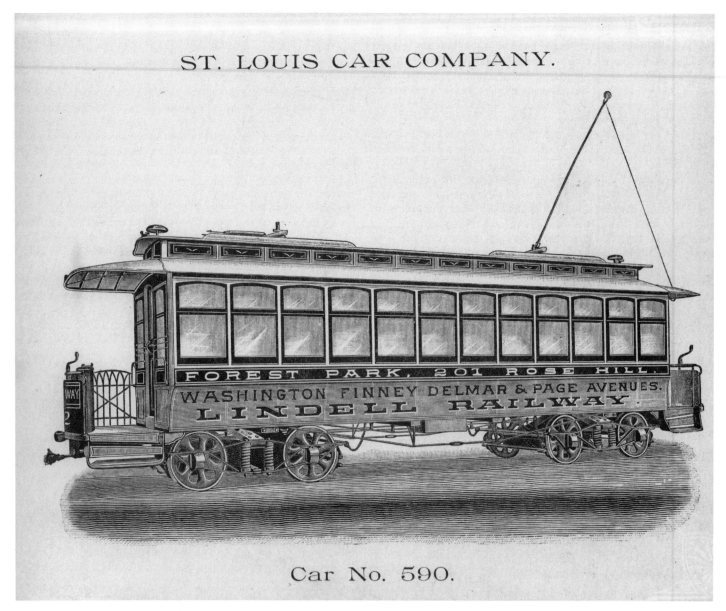

Lindell Railway (St. Louis) 201 circa 1892 was one of America's first double-truck electric cars.

His family used the place for years, but after a fire the ruins and land were donated to Missouri for the present state park.

Still, St. Louis's "Big Cinchers" weren't pikers. The embarrassment of paying a carpetbagger $1.25 million for a franchise on their own turf was nothing in the face of their planned multi-million dollar trolley consolidation. Transit conspiracy theories of recent years don't hold water, but the conspiracy behind the creation of St. Louis's United Railways in 1899 was genuine and criminal, a audacious betrayal of the public interest. Within five years the "Big Cinch's" consolidation had issued over $101 million of paper for a city-wide system valued at just $38 million in 1913.

And where did the rest go? Into their pockets and those of the management company and lawyers working on their behalf. The bribes paid to city Aldermen for a "yes" vote on the consolidation were tiny by comparison, though no less reprehensible—an Alderman's ice cream parlor remodeled here, another sent on an expensive vacation there, their leader given $50,000 to distribute as he saw fit to keep his voting bloc in line. So where were the state regulators that could hold companies and individuals accountable? There were none. Only crusading city attorneys like Joseph Falk (later St. Louis's Mayor and Missouri's Governor) could hold feet to the fire through indictments for bribery and fraud. Even then, getting convictions wasn't plain sailing. Several principals hurriedly decamped for Mexico or Europe, others refused to talk while Judge Henry Priest, an otherwise honorable "Big Cinch" lawyer and UR's defense attorney in the fraud trials, gained national notoriety by declaring that "after all, bribery is only a conventional offense."

Criminality was not confined to big city streetcar systems. When the largest stakeholder in the Alton, Jacksonville and Peoria (IL) interurban died in 1909, his daughter's husband and brother-in-law became president and treasurer. Already driving their St. Louis Fire Insurance Company into the ground, they began milking the AJ&P of $500,000 while raising loans from the owner of the McGuire-Cummings Car Company to fix cash-flow problems in building the Godfrey-Jerseyville extension. When the line went into receivership in July 1911, they skipped town to avoid an embezzlement indictment, surfacing three months later in Los Angeles only after an investigative reporter tracked them down. Confronted with the charges, they feigned surprise. Ultimately, it turned out that the AJ&P's total worth was less than one-seventh of the money raised in its name, but it took until 1914 to convict them. The road itself died in 1918.

America's entire traction industry was a case study in the ugly side of capitalism. Anarchic, idiosyncratic and corrupt, it was an unsupervised Darwinian free-for-all. Nominally, there was local regulation but only later did it become comprehensive and effective. In Missouri, trolleys were initially under the overlapping jurisdictions of the Board of Railroad and Warehouse Commissioners and the State Board of Equalization. By 1898, the latter only required street railroads be assessed for taxation at full market value. Cities imposed their own fees and franchises, though street paving and similar obligations were common. So were property taxes, to be paid on tracks, poles, overhead and other street furniture. A city could claim supervisory and tax authority over any aspect of operation. For example, in 1903, St. Louis imposed a tax of one mill for every passenger carried on city street railways. Collect-

ing it was another matter. It was 1917, after years of litigation that twice took the parties to the U. S. Supreme Court, before it saw a single penny.

From 1907, a few cities established regulatory boards to control route changes, fares, brakes, fenders et al. In 1913, Missouri's Public Service Commission was set up to supervise (among other things) railroads, street railroads, express companies, steamboats and other common carriers statewide. Route or fare changes or substitution of car lines by buses, hitherto done at the stroke of a pen by a company with a cursory genuflection to those who issued their franchise, now sparked lengthy and time-consuming hearings. This regulatory system saw out the street railway era.

Happily, there was an economic upside to this free-for-all. From 1885 until at least 1930, St. Louis was number one in the street railway industry, the dot. com phenomenon of its age. It was a world class player in car building and design development and a center for support services, brokers and dealers. Thousands of St. Louis families were the direct beneficiaries over several generations. Its roots lay in the unending supply of wood coming down-river from the north. Since state-

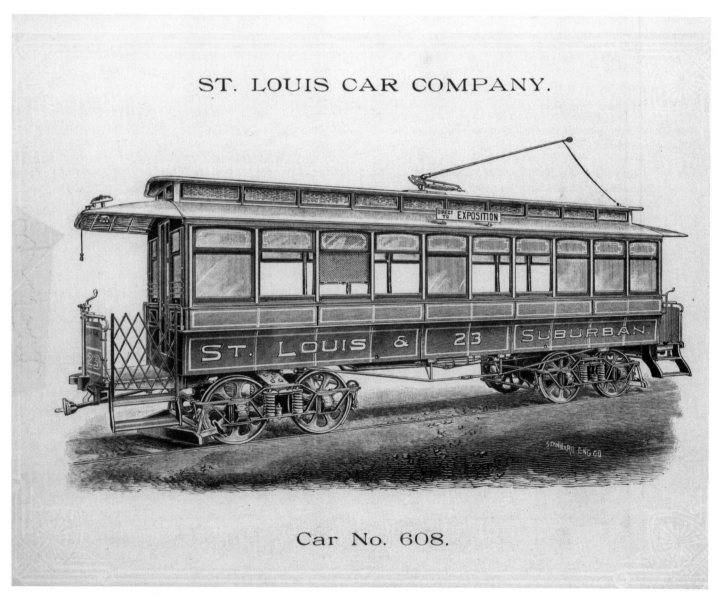

St. Louis and Suburban 23 circa 1891/2 was one of America's first electric interurban cars.

hood, scores of St. Louis workshops had thrived on building buggies, wagons and "prairie schooners," for pioneers fitting out in the city before their long trek west. After the pioneers came a demand for rail vehicles, cabs, horse buses and streetcars. All were made of wood. By 1892, St. Louis had six streetcar builders and scores of ancillary suppliers. The obstinacy of one bull-headed man made it possible.

In 1868, sixteen-year old Frederick B. Brownell was apprenticed to Andrew Wight, a St. Louis wagon and bus builder, becoming de facto manager by 1872. Wight died of tuberculosis in January 1876 and Brownell bought Wight's interests from his widow on time payments. The keen young man soon crusted over. By 1880 he was a stubborn, wrong-headed know-it-all, a 19th-century Basil Fawlty believing as an article of faith that his business ran best when he didn't have to waste his time listening to customers and their jackass obsessions with trivia like specifications, size and finish. Better they should write out their checks in full, on time and without question for the cars he felt they needed. He was the expert, their interests were his. He could be trusted. Couldn't he?

True, Brownell cars were quality products. But his strident personality and idiosyncratic catalogs grated. He was no people person. Curt to customers and high-handed with suppliers, he was autocratic and bullying with employees. A contender for bragging rights as Missouri's worst boss, his lieutenants couldn't stand him. Every so often there was an explosion and they would abruptly leave, many to set up their own plants. Skilled and experienced workpeople would follow. The Laclede, American and St. Louis Car companies began this way. By late 1897, at the peak of demand for cars, Brownell's refusal to update designs or soften his demeanor had power-driven his company into the ground. By 1900, the Brownell Car Company was bankrupt and he was out of business before the age of 50.

Some 19th-century St. Louis builders, like Missouri Car and St. Charles Car, specialized in railroad vehicles. Others made buggies, surreys, cab and carriages. The Dorris and Moon companies later eased into automobiles. St. Louis Car between 1904 and 1945 made caskets,

Victrola cabinets, three different kinds of automobile and airplanes. After 1910, when the industry had shaken down, St. Louis and American remained, plus American Car and Foundry (ACF Industries) into which the Missouri and St. Charles companies were merged. To these should be added the United Railways shops at 39th and Park, which from 1904 to 1929 built hundreds of its own cars from scratch rather than buy locally, and remodeled thousands more to the same standards, either for their own use or for resale elsewhere

From 1874 to 1974, when the last subway car for New York City (and jetway for JFK airport) left St. Louis Car's Baden plant, scores of thousands of finished streetcars and rail vehicles were shipped to customers across the globe. Only Philadelphia's J. G. Brill came close to matching the St. Louis output. Indeed, in 1902 Brill took over American Car (and the shell of Brownell), and ran it until 1931. St. Louis Car took over Laclede in 1904 but closed it soon after.

Second-tier cities such as Hannibal, Nevada and Sedalia, operating far below the national radar, had as much attitude and ambition as first-tier cities. Trolleys brought a touch of urban glamor to civic life, tangible evidence to local boosters they were on the way to better things. A trolley on a postcard of your main street was a symbol of progress even if it had yet to boast a line. And if you were blessed with that rara avis, a presidential visit, why then electric trolleys were the only way to move his retinue, no matter how many automobiles might try to assist, as in Cape Girardeau on October 26th, 1909 when all 300lbs of President Taft stepped off a riverboat to give a speech in town.

Still, some of Missouri's animal lines never electrified. Lexington and Trenton didn't even survive the 19th century while Chillicothe and Clinton barely made it to 1901 and 1903 respectively before quitting. An account of the Clinton "closure" in 1903 is in W. Lamkin's History of Henry County Volume 1 (p. 209) and while as a historian Mr. Lamkin clearly seems to be a man who'd never let facts get in the way of a good story, his tale remains worth telling.

"Citizens gave themselves metropolitan airs over the…cars… but once

Summer streetcar equipment. Missouri Railroad cable grip 20, trailer 172 at unknown St. Louis location circa 1894.

AMERICAN CAR COMPANY.

No. 164. Trailer.

Length over corner posts, 20 feet.   Seating capacity, 28 persons.

No. 172. Grip Car.

Length over corner posts, 11 feet 9 inches.   Seating capacity, 16 persons.

Winter streetcar equipment. Missouri Railroad trailer 309 and cable grip 16, from American Car Company 1895 catalog.

the popularity of the artesian well went into decline, all attempts at holding down a schedule were abandoned and trips were made rarely, sometimes...30 days apart...The question of paving the streets came up...It was proposed to put brick paving down...The...track was an obstacle...(but) no one ever knew what became of it. The only thing we can be certain of...is that one evening as the sun set, track was ready to carry the cars...and at daylight the next morning there was none... Some resident ...might have seen the rail and ties being carried away during the night by unknown parties but...nothing was ever said"

Sedalia's animal cars began in September 1881, electrics in March 1890. Hannibal's animal lines began in 1878, electrics in June 1890. Springfield's animal lines began in 1881, electrics in early 1891. Whenever they made their debut, they were joyously greeted. This report, headlined *"The Lightning Flash"* describes Springfield's first test run.

"There has been...speculation...whether the Electric Street Car... would in its initiatory (sic) trips prove as successful as its friends hoped but doubt upon that point has been happily put to sleep for ever...During the afternoon Mr. J. Loney, in charge of the electrical construction, put car 26 in condition for the route...The result demonstrates that he is the right man in the right place...(while) Superintendent Frank Smith was everywhere and bossing things in the most gentlemanly and courteous manner possible. Shortly before 5 o'clock, the establishment on Booneville Street was cleared of outsiders and the car brought out...Mr. Parker, electrical engineer of the Metropolitan...was in charge and in a distinguished, and successful manner presided at the throttle valve, lever—whatever you want to call it. After a few preliminary strokes of the gong, Mr. Parker sent his car, with its cargo of prominent citizens, northward on Boonville, thence along Commercial Street to Benton Avenue, along that highway to Center Street, down Jefferson and into the Square. The enthusiasm along the route was splendid. Men women and children shouted, waved handkerchiefs and indulged in every plauditory (sic) demonstration.

"The car was decorated with...banners and it was throughout a gala affair amounting to a triumphal procession. The car was followed by a number of gentlemen in buggies...While a low rate of speed was adopted, this being only a trial trip, the followers were left ignominiously in the rear, and a number on horseback found it difficult to maintain the pace set, especially on the long straight stretch on Benton Avenue. When the car...arrived in the Square, there was a great shout of welcome and a thousand people around to see the new motor in all its glory...Arriving at the stable, a conductor appeared with his cap of office on his head, and Chief of Police Dryden was the first man to relinquish his nickel...Thereafter the car was run on the paying principle...The whole business worked like a charm...Electrical illumination about the wheels...due to sand on the track and the fragments of rock...will disappear as the track gets into better condition, though it was rather an attractive part of the program as the evening shades began to gather...to the thousands who witnessed the novel phenomenon for the first time." (Springfield Leader December 5th, 1890 back page).

Carthage's 1883 animal line went electric in 1895 and was extended to Carterville as an interurban. Cape Girardeau's first animal line began January 1893 but it was December 1905 before electric trolleys began. Mexico had an animal line for a few months in 1889, but electrics didn't arrive until 1911, a year late.

Some towns had no animal lines. Carollton's downtown was a mile north of the station, but the ground was swampy and road vehicles had a hard time making it. Several businesses sprang up around the station, including a stock yard and grain elevator. A small hotel followed, the owner having two daughters. One caught the eye of local businessman Frank V. Crouch, who lived uptown. Legend has it that Crouch promoted a rail line to the station so he could more easily visit her. Maybe, maybe not, but 1893's Carrollton steam dummy was a fact. By 1897 it had been electrified.

"Hurrah! The electric line goes. The cars walk up the hill. Will run regular (sic) tomorrow. The fondest hopes...of our citizens has been realized. For...years people have talked about an electric line and now we have it. About 6 o'clock Monday evening (August 30) Car No. 1 climbed the hill but stuck at the corner. The top of the hill was soon lined with people and the crowds grew larger and larger...Mr. Crouch reversed the motor and slowly backed down the hill to remedy the defect. The crowd lingered...until 8:30 when they began to scatter to their homes. But a few moments later the electric car shot across the square to the Florence Hotel corner...greeted with loud cries and cheers... Everybody is proud of the line and...the energy and push of Mr. Crouch who for the past two years has worked almost incessantly for the road. Nothing...will do more for the town...Already people are beginning to throw back their heads and put on city airs and these people were made to feel better by a passenger on a westbound Santa Fe train who thought he'd reached Kansas City and wanted to get off. (<u>Carrollton Democrat</u>, September 3rd, 1897 p. 5)

Jefferson City too had no animal cars. Its electrics came only in 1910. Their absence was a scandal for years. Acres of newsprint were dedicated to editorial harrumphing on the subject, in the vain hope something might get done.

"We unhesitatingly declare that one of the most...imperative needs...is a streetcar line...In addition to the necessity for such an enterprise, it would constitute one of the greatest advertisements we could have. The only expression of astonishment by strangers coming here is that the State Capital of Missouri has no streetcar...No city in this day and age begins its development or indicates its growth without the useful street car and the omission of it marks...a city... behind the times. Our council has had

Interior of Missouri Railroad trailer 309-note upholstery, gas lights in the ceiling and general high standard of finish, including rattan (cane) upholstered transverse (cross) seats, unusual in all but the biggest city operations.

Keytesville's 1889 animal line ran until 1919 when its octogenarian owner decided he wante labor-saving autos. By then it was a curiosity, an ancient relic, good for a newspaper's Sunday supplement human-interest feature.

"H. J. Moore, senior member of the company operating the Keytesville horsecar line...is still...serving the people of his county with the most satisfactory transportation circumstances permit. Realizing the motor is the modern way, he has plans for an autobus and freight system all worked out so soon as the roads are made permanent... It's a good-natured, social crowd—those who travel on the Keytesville Limited—and they don't kick on being shoved over by ice cream and milk, because such things make life better. No matter what hour of the day or night a Wabash passenger train stops at the depot, the horse car is there. The writer recollects getting off at the lonely station once between midnight and dawn. Desolation reigned on every side, a regular rural wilderness. He was wondering how he would ever find his way to town when he noticed a man standing at the corner of the depot. 'Going to town, sir?' inquired the man politely.

"'Yes, but where is it?' The man smiled and led the way. There, hidden by the end of the depot, was a little oil-lighted car with its patient horses quietly dozing. There was only one passenger. The driver...went out on the platform, signaled to his team and hung up the lines. Then, as it was a cold night, he came in the car and sat down with his guest. 'The horses know the way...They know every tap of the bell, just what it means. If they see anybody standing by the roadside, they know just where to stop and when the passenger gets aboard, they start at the sound of the bell. They're educated, these horses are. First time you ever went over our road? There ain't a line in the State that has finer scenery.

"'We start you out of a live American city—if your hotel bill's paid—with stores and moving picture shows and courthouse and jail and every convenience. Next you're whirling through the suburbs, Queen Ann cottages and King Henry hen houses and barns. Then we pass into the corn country. Some raise 80 to 100 bushels an acre; ship it out over our line. Then you're in the heart of the big Chariton valley...Next we go through hickory, walnut and cottonwood; second growth. Used it all up first time to burn them in old Mother Hubbard engines and for ties and things...and then comes the tobacco. That's where we win out. When a man has ten acres of Chariton County tobacco, his fortune's made. By and by, we swing around the curve and the Union depot is in sight—junction of the Keytesville horse-car and the Wabash steam-cars which will take you to any place on earth!' (<u>St. Louis Republic</u>, March 18th, 1919 p. 5)

a number of offers...and has driven such hard bargains as to frighten them off. But the next opportunity should be...the occasion for meeting investors more than half way...St. Louis capitalists... would ... be glad to make an investment...The exercise of a little public spirit on the part of our...business men who have close relations with capitalists in the large cities would in a few months result in the building of a car line... Let them try it and see how much more business would come to this town—one of the most beautiful and healthful in all Missouri." (Jefferson City Daily Tribune, March 22nd, 1893 editorial).

Locally-funded small-town systems were often adjuncts to real-estate projects, with judges and retired colonels the big investors, promoters or figureheads, town boosters to a man. Often they'd be on the line themselves, doing hands-on work or helping run cars once service began.

Directors would generally be entitled to gold passes, allowing them to ride free of charge. This could be taken to extremes, and not always in the largest cities. G. M. Sebree, a Springfield attorney, included among his clients the Cassville and Exeter Railroad and Springfield Traction, for whom he acted as general counsel. According to family legend, not only did he have a gold pass for Springfield's cars, so did his dog.

But most Missouri towns never had streetcars at all, even if they had a few horse-buses. The most obvious candidates for streetcars and thus remarkable in that they didn't get them, were second-tier cities such as Columbia, Fulton, Kirksville, Louisiana, Macon, Moberly, Poplar Bluff, Rolla and Sikeston. Some were well-served by railroads and didn't see the need. Others not as well-served were disappointed by abortive projects. Still, those towns that did get cars soon found the experience to be more than they bargained for. Profits were rarely made, debts were crippling and investors over-exposed. Maintenance was deferred then abandoned as the money ran out, and what was the pride of the town in (say) 1905 was an embarassment by 1920. Only if it was swept into a utility chain, part of a larger power and light group like Cities Services or Stone and Webster, could a wilting traction property be adequately funded.

In Cape Girardeau for example, a car barn fire on January 3rd, 1913 destroyed six of eight cars, the sheds and a boiler room. The phones didn't work, the Fire Company was late, losses were estimated at $30,000 and unhappy local investors wanted out. An arrangement made with Light and Development Company of St. Louis (the Cape's electric utility) to power the line for surviving cars led to a sale offer and an agreement was signed on January 13th. Given the glacial pace with which the Cape's trolley affairs usually moved, this was fast. In trying to persuade the MOPSC, at a December 1913 hearing, that unloading the trolleys was a good thing all round, the witnesses told a rueful tale of their unwise speculation. President W. H. Harrison declared that once the novelty wore off, the line had tanked and little could be done to change the habits of this conservative town.

At first, it had been *"something new and everybody had to ride it two or three times...Now they will come and look up and down the street, and especially if he is a German... will walk downtown ...(That nickel fare) gets a glass of beer... (so) he walks...Ladies and other people ...(who) cannot see a car...they (too) will walk."* When asked the value of company stock, he replied *"You couldn't give it away,"* grumbling that if he'd known he was to be grilled, he'd have come better prepared to show its worthlessness. All officers were small businessmen, carrying $350,000 of obligations with no offsetting income and that was a recipe for disaster. He'd tried to sell the company for years, but Light and Development was *"the only sucker I have found."* So *"for the good of the town,"* MOPSC approved the sale.

In 1912 Sedalia's trolleys joined the Cities Services group, which attacked ridership decline and competition with vigor. A series of newspaper ads was placed, entitled *"Is a Traction system a necessity in Sedalia."* The ad *"Shoe Leather vs. Traction Service"* claimed that a pedestrian count at intersections in rush-hours revealed 3,200 people walking. *"Did you know that is more than ride our cars, all of them, from 5:30 a.m. to 11:30 p.m.? If 10% of those people rode the cars, we would have shown progress last year (1915) instead of a loss in passengers carried of 109,938."* An influx of new lightweight cars in 1916 helped reverse that trend.

St. Louis County Street Railway car 2 in the muddy wastes of St. Charles Rock Road/Lucas and Hunt Road circa 1899. This was the last St. Louis area animal line, although in both Kansas City and St. Louis animal cars continued to provide cable car owl service so that cables acould be stopped for routine maintenance during the night. This practice continued until cable lines were electrified. STLMOT

Without the large utility companies, only federal or state subsidy might have kept rural lines going. Yet not only was the legislative and administrative machinery absent, the entire concept had been off the political map since the policy of state subsidies for regional railroad and highway building had imploded in the 1860s. To Missouri's elected officials and electorate, rural trolleys, like railroads, were a matter for private enterprise. You had a proposition? Go to the local commercial or business mens' club in towns on your route, apply for franchises from every local council and ask the locals for "bonuses" or subsidies, giving them a chance to get in on the ground floor of a sure-fire thing.

In this climate, successful promoters had to be (indeed were) part salesmen, part hellfire evangelist and part con-men, pouring on the emotional and oratorical platitudes as they exhorted listeners to join other right-minded citizens in lifting their small towns out of the mud and setting them on the road to prosperity. Often, local papers echoed the pitch.

"An effort has been made by citizens of Nevada, Jerico Springs and Montevallo to build an electric line...It means development of the entire district. The line could be built...at reasonable cost, a few bridges would have to be constructed, possibly not over three or four. The grade could be made with very little trouble and people are...in the position where they are almost compelled to have the line...The shopping point that it will make Nevada and many other advantages derived from the line are ample reasons for our citizens to...work for the line. All the minerals and produce shipped over this line will come to Nevada. The farmer nearby will be able to send his produce to Nevada every day...when the roads are in condition that make it impossible to drive to town. He can pick up his basket of eggs and butter, take the car, come to Nevada, do his buying and return home in a very short time.

"This is the opportunity that now awaits Nevada. Not only that; build the line and others will be built. Nevada will be the center of all the

The Railroad comes to Ava.

The Ava and Mansfield, long rumored to have either had or at least considered electric operation, spent its life as a steam-operated branch railroad. But opening speeches expressed the same kind of hope as those at similar rural interurban and trolley ceremonies, evidence that the mode of traction was unimportant in the face of a small town's final liberation from oppressive isolation.

"When the train arrived, Mayor Burdett spoke from 'This beautiful and magnificent passenger coach...with the words Kansas City, Ozarks and Southern Railroad inscribed along its length with shining golden letters ...Today, I see Ava, a little village...budding into a great city whose influence is destined to be felt in all the commercial interests of this, the great state of Missouri...The seeds were sown when a $20,000 bonus was subscribed for construction of a railroad from Mansfield to Ava. I want to congratulate every person who subscribed to this bonus...I want also to congratulate those of you who did not subscribe to the bonus for having the privilege of living among a class of people who saw into the future and keenly realized the fact that $20,000 was...a small sum ...compared to the advantages of a railroad to a people living in a rich and undeveloped section like ours." (Douglas County Herald *March 3rd, 1910 p. 1).*

Northern Central 117, open trailer 60, probably at the Fairgrounds terminal, St. Louis, circa 1890. Electric cars of this period were either converted horsecars or (in this case) beefed-up horsecar types on a single truck. The open trailer is almost certainly a converted horse car. The structure on the roof with small windows, on top of which is the trolley pole and its base (to pick-up power) is known as a deck or clerestory roof. These structures gave better ventilation and circulation of air—provided each little window panes was pushed to the open position. STLMOT.

Many of the Lindell Railway's earliest electrics were spliced from two horse car bodies to make one large high-capacity, center-entrance car. This was done with both winter (closed) and summer (open) equipment. Car 313 and another are seen here at the end of the Delmar line (De Baliviere) circa 1891, some time before the fields were built over, the road paved and the line extended into Forest Park, St. Louis.

lines and she will double her population in a very short time… Mr. Hightower, secretary of the Jerico Springs Commercial Club said (to the Nevada Commercial Club yesterday)… 'We are here to get this line. We know it takes money…(but) our little town is full of energetic people that are ready to give their support to an electric line. We have coal beds that start at our city and run south for eight miles. The coal vein is from 24 to 42 inches in thickness. The quality is superb and can be found from 16 to 20 feet below the surface. We have the best fruit section in the state and thousands of bushels of apples can be shipped from Jerico springs…' (The Daily Mail [Nevada] June 16th, 1900, p. 1.) This particular line never materialized.

The fad for mineral springs and spas seemed a good bet for a rural trolley or interurban. The Kansas City, Clay County and St. Joseph's Excelsior Springs branch was a notable Missouri example. The Pertle Springs line in Warrensburg had a steam dummy that ran for over thir-ty years between the railroad station and the springs. From 1890, Lebanon's one single-truck electric car met all the trains, taking passengers to the Magnetic Springs and the Gasconade Hotel. However. tourists and locals eyed each other with mutual incomprehension and the advertising hype based on the water's magnetic properties proved to be a hoax perpetrated by one of the workman who'd drilled the original well. Visitors fell off, trains were relatively few and the bored motorman often passed the time getting sozzled in the local saloons. One day he drove the car into the barn, smashed through the rear wall and ran out the other side. The hotel was in receivership by November 1893 and gone by 1896, along with the trolley.

Other spa lines didn't even open. The St. Louis and Montesano in its various incarnations, built just a few miles out from St. Louis before running out of cash. It never got near Montesano Springs. The stately cars it ordered languished unsold at St. Louis Car for years. The Moberly, Huntsville and Randolph Springs Railroad Company, franchised in 1909, didn't build until 1913. It stopped when the Randolph Springs Hotel's future was put in doubt after a fire and the promoter took off for foreign parts with the remaining money. In March 1915, the hotel/spa complex and the incomplete line were bought "as is" by Charles H. Dameron. Loans were raised and building resumed. But cash again ran out when two "tunnels" had to be built to avoid grade crossings on entering and exiting Huntsville. The

On interurban lines, car body design soon became substantial and railroad-like. Equipment was slower to catch up. This is Southwest 14, a former Carthage "White Line" (Jasper County Electric Railway) car of 1895, which has derailed circa 1898 on the Center Creek trestle near Lakeside Park. The Center Creek trestle was replaced by a concrete bridge in 1913. Earl E. McMechan.

"It took Mark Pilcher and John Abbay, well-known local merchants, about five minutes Friday afternoon to realize that Mexico is the southern terminal at present, of a live, hustling little railroad. They made the trip to Molino... on the electric car and noted with surprise the large number of passengers...Especially noticeable...were the packages ...loaded on at Mexico and taken off by the passengers at the stops...The beauties of the country seemed never more apparent as the little single-truck car glided past fields on level stretches and bounced along through the woods and pastures. 'It's great, Mark,' said John Abbay, lighting a fresh cigar. 'It certainly is great, John,' replied Mr Pilcher, removing cigar ashes from his eyes. When the car stopped at Molino it was ascertained that many... passengers had come from Santa Fe and had hitched their horses in a feed barn at Molino while they shopped in Mexico...

"Mexico merchants and the reporter inspected the tracks Bill Mundy is building toward his house...Mr. Munday hitherto has shone as an expert in buying and selling swine but he had a ?-mile of track built in about two days...The steel is laid on good, solid ties...and a bunch... were ...shoveling dirt and leveling up the track. Straight oak poles for the trolley wire...are set and the wire is being strung. The track is now up to the Molino street and...will proceed a ?-mile further north...A trailer...(will) handle the big crowds...a flat car with a...wood railing...and seats on the sides.

"Everybody connected with the traction company works. The secretary, C. W. Gaither, forgot his office Friday and with hammer and saw built the railing and seats on the flat car. He formerly was a contracting carpenter.S. D. Robison exchanged his title as General Manager for a hatband and a metal plate bearing the words 'Conductor No. 1' and took up the change. Coming back, the car stopped to pick up a large party of Mexico folks who had gone out for a picnic in the woods. A stray fisherman or two got on at Skull Lick and several women and children rode...returning home or going to spend the evening with friends. 'We've sure got an electric railroad, John,' said Mark Pilcher when they alighted in Mexico. 'That's the truth, Mark,' replied Mr. Abbay" (Mexico Intelligencer, May 13th, 1911 p. 2).

hotel remained closed. A "windstorm" took off its roof in July 1918. Dameron defaulted and the hotel and spa were foreclosed in April 1920, ownership passing to an Afro-American investment syndicate.The interurban was never finished, but many concrete abutments survive. The hotel ruins were demolished in the summer of 1930.

A "nearly" interurban without a spa en-route, was the Hannibal and Northern Missouri Railroad, an ambitious 1909 project to build 110 miles from Hannibal northwest via Palmyra to Kirksville (plus branches) with a powerhouse on the Salt River. Incorporated for $2 million, little capital was paid up. While surveys were completed and twelve miles of bridges and grades built, grading got no further west than Bethel in Shelby county before the company went bust. Its promoter bought the line at foreclosure in March 1912 for $12,500 but did no more.

Ample finances could elude even the most successful promoters. At a

A May 1896 tornado caused terrible damage in St. Louis and took the roof off the People's Railway Company cable powerhouse. The damaged cable winding gear can be seen on the left as Union Depot Company double-truck car 372 stands marooned amid the debris of Geyer Avenue. The photo looks west from Missouri Avenue to Jefferson Avenue. Every building in the background and on the right has been damaged or destroyed. STLMOT

(Left) This copy of a contemporary newspaper photograph shows more of the damage. The falling roof has mangled the flimsy horse and electric car bodies. STLMOT

(Below) Electric trolley lines stimulated new real estate ventures, if they weren't already sponsored by one. St. Louis Post-Dispatch, May 18th 1893.

June 14th, 1914 after-dinner speech to the Jefferson City Commercial Club at the Central Hotel, William B. Mckinley of Illinois Traction, a straight arrow if ever there was one, talked gloomily of prospects for building interurbans from Jefferson City to the north and to Columbia.

"I know you appreciate that money is…hard to get hold of at present. My business is developing public utilities of all kinds, my particular preference being for interurbans…My eyes are always directed toward available localities for building and operating them. We came to Jefferson City two years ago and bought the street railway and the bridge. I felt then and I feel now, there is a splendid field for development around here…not because it would be a profitable investment in itself, but…with this as a nucleus we could develop an interurban system centered on the State capital…(But) building…requires cash…(Sufficient Missouri) money cannot be obtained…for large enterprises.

"'It must…(come) from older states where larger wealth is accumulated…To get it…public utilities owners must be encouraged to invest in it through liberal laws and good rates of interest…If a group of men have $1 million…to invest in an interurban… they select a location where the laws are the safest to preserve their principal and where the rulings will be fairest to give them a good return on their money…I have been in the mortgage loan business all my life and I know I can buy for my clients good first mortgages in Missouri at 7% and 8% where there is no risk or loss of principal. This being the case, I cannot expect my clients to invest their money in interurbans…in Missouri, where there is a chance for a loss, at as low a rate as they could buy first mortgages on real estate." (MDI June 15th 1915 p.4)

Missouri's street railways peaked around 1915. But most barely made operating profits and none gave worthwhile rates of return on capital. In the 1920s, with automotive transport clearly here to stay, power, water and light conglomerates began cutting loose from the transit millstone long before 1935's Public Utilities Holding Act targeted interlocking, shell and holding companies. Most systems survived the exit of big money as bus rather than trolley operators, often financed by easy payments from General Motors Acceptance Corporation, a more user-friendly process than floating bonds or relying on credit that could be called in at any time. None of their remaining riders seemed to mind.

PASSENGERS AND FREIGHT

The St. Louis and Suburban's lengthy St. Louis county routes were ideal for sightseeing by private parties in specially-fitted cars. An early and little-known example was the St. Louis and Suburban's "Ramona." Elaborate window treatments, wicker chairs and high-grade parlor furnishings add to the charm.

The coming of the streetcar wasn't just a question of a smooth ride compared to a horse bus. It was knowing that at frequent intervals a car would take you most places you needed to go for a small fee. Once the electric trolley arrived, "always a car in sight" was the ideal, meaning that if you missed one, you could see the next on its way. That wasn't always practical, even in Kansas City or St. Louis, but 5-minute service was common on their trolley lines and in smaller towns as well. The latter, however, were as likely to see a car every ten to fifteen minutes; on lighter lines every twenty to thirty minutes. But the customers were no less delighted, at least at first. Punctuality and predictability were the key, whether a car came every 90 seconds or every 30 minutes.

The "Ramona" was replaced after a few years by newer and even more sumptuous vehicles. St. Louis and Suburban's Kinloch" (the second so-named), was built in 1903 by St. Louis Car as a private car for the line's president, but available for charter at other times. This picture and that of the "Ramona" were made for inventory purposes circa 1908.

City streets were arteries; it was crucial trolleys flowed freely through them, especially in small towns where there was an alternative—walking or cycling. Jefferson City, Nevada, Sedalia and Cape Girardeau trolleys were especially vulnerable once their novelty wore off. In larger towns, where streets were often choked with traffic (horse-drawn before 1910, increasingly automotive afterwards) that obstructed and delayed the cars, the perception that trolley companies were uninterested in good service soon became universal,

often accompanied by agitation to reduce the 5-cent fare, or resist increases once inflation took hold. These tensions were largely focused on journeys to and from work, as they had been since the 1880s. Perversely, riders continued to demand immediate service and a seat at these times. But maintaining enough cars to do that meant 70% would be idle outside the rush-hour.

System owners were reluctant to tie up money this way and the result was insuffereable overcrowding. Yet it was clear no red-blooded American would tolerate being barred from a car just because all the seats were taken and eventually the trolley companies bowed to the inevitable and built up a rush-hour fleet from older, depreciated cars that had been replaced in base service by newer models. These were assigned to the tripper runs seen earlier on the animal railways, to bring the time between cars down from (say) five to 2.5 minutes. Or they could run an overlapping short-turn service for those not riding to the outer terminal. But were riders pleased to have a seat on the old-timers trundled out at peak hours? Alas for human nature. They were not.

When car lines ran smoothly (and for much of the time they did) all

"*All who work for a living have to reach their place of business at a certain time. They arise at a fixed hour... allowing so much time for breakfasting and so much for the trip...The breakfast time is improved upon and... minutes ...gained. A serene consciousness of being on time causes one to overlook...a few minute's delay waiting on a corner for a car...The car rumbles slowly along with human being bulging from all openings in it...A stop is made at every corner...until the lower tier of streets is reached, when (it) stops to allow (those)...packed in close to the driver to struggle their way through the crowd and drop into the street...The car has been delayed by frequent stoppages and the prospect of a superior storming over one for being late...is contemplated until a hysterical wish to throttle the measly directors who allow cars to be over-crowded in such a beastly manner ranges up and down one's soul...*

"*Now where the streetcar companies are lamentably deficient in gratitude as well as in common decency...where they show a greediness that is disgusting, is in taking advantage of their patrons... compelling them to make their trips in cars crowded to suffocation and from 10 to 15 minutes late ...No one who has seen the grand outpouring of men and women from the business houses and factories in the heart of the city when the 6 o'clock evening hour has been reached, has failed to be struck by the sight. Human beings pour out of the hives of industry as thick as swarming bees and surge through the...streets in heavy black waves...At the corner of Fourth and Olive...Chouteau Avenue, cars rumble past, crowded on both platforms and packed in the center...Grouped in front of Polack's old store are probably a half-dozen girls who make frantic gashes in the air with their parasols or umbrellas...The driver sees them, stops his car and some two or three...wedge themselves into the crowd of young and old men who are puffing cigars on the platform*"
(P-D November 15th, 1883 p.2.)

THE ELECTRIC · RAILWAY
—OF—
THE UNION LINE

Affords our citizens, as well as the visitor and the stranger, one of the most interesting, unique and pleasant short excursions that can be made out of the city. The cars run past Union Depot and Market Square through the lovely New Ulm Valley to

✦ KRUG PARK ✦

A picturesque piece of ground improved by the Union Railway for gratuitous public use, and crowned on its summit with a high tower, from which an enchanting view of the city and surrounding country is obtained.

Easy and cheap access to city parks made it possible for thousands of city dwellers to enjoy fresh air and leisure time and the street railway companies were quick to encourage this kind of riding. This St. Joseph example graced 1890's City Directory.

City parks could never have justified their existence without easy access and in the 19th century at least, parks and streetcars were fellow travelers. This is St. Louis's Grand Avenue on June 4th, 1908. In the distance a southbound car approaches the entrance to Tower Grove Park, a Victorian gem to this day. STLMOT

was right with the world. But when they didn't, all hell broke loose. The St. Louis Post-Dispatch, (*"the people's organ in everything"* as Pulitzer's editors repeatedly reminded its readers) began its first anti-streetcar campaign on November 16th, 1883 when *"a score or more of the heroic souls who do journalistic work for this paper whitened the frosty atmosphere with their breaths during the early morning hours today when otherwise they would have been engaged in reading the morning papers by a crackling fire."* Headlined *"Packed like Sardines,"* or *"Cattle cars, Grave cars and Hoodlum cars,"* these pieces ridiculed the companies and their *"vile monopolies"* for weeks but achieved little, other than for boosting circulation.

Trolley lines often paralleled passenger-carrying railroads. This could be advantageous or ruinous for both parties. Tower Grove station in St. Louis was for years a transfer point between the MoPac and the ckity's trolley companies. Riders coming in from Valley Park and Kirkwood transferred from train to trolley to better access where they needed to be in St.Louis rather than be taken to a single downtown railroad terminal. On the journey back to the suburbs, the train won hands-down for speed and convenience until St. Louis and Suburban's "Meramec Valley" division, which paralleled the MoPac most of the way to Kirkwood, opened in 1897. Serving more places en route, with cheaper fares and better service, it abstracted most of the railroad's business and generated more that was exclusively its own.

The Quincy Omaha and Kansas City Railroad Company (the OK) ran passenger service from points north into Kansas City Southern's Grand Central Station at the north end of Kansas City, just south of the Missouri (not the original Union Station in the West Bottoms near the confluence of the Kaw and Missouri Rivers). To reach it, the OK crossed the Missouri on the Hannibal bridge. When the Clay County interurban opened in 1913, OK passengers found they could reach downtown KC more cheaply if they left the train

at Avondale station and changed to Clay County cars. KCS abandoned Grand Central for the new Union Station at 20th and Main when it opened in October 1914. Losing business to the interurban and now having no KC terminal of its own, the OK decided to terminate at Avondale.

Moody's Railroad Manual 1916 noted that in December 1914 the Clay County *"began a terminal service to the Kansas City Union Station for the Quincy Omaha and Kansas City RR Co."* Indeed, from its opening in 1913, the Kansas City Clay County and St. Joseph was the preferred rail route between the two cities, being shorter, quicker, cleaner, cheaper and more frequent. The steam roads, down in the Missouri Valley, could not match the directness of the Clay County's high-country route and its better access to Kansas City and St. Joseph.

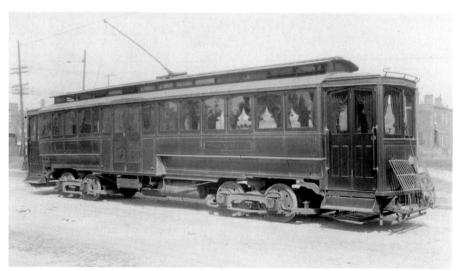

The splendid funeral car "Dolores" was home-built in 1897 by St. Louis's Lindell Railway, using two former horse-car bodies spliced together. Suitable internal decor was provided, black crepe drapes, tassels and other funerary accessories being visible through the windows. Mourners entered front and rear, the offset center doors admitted the casket. The car was freshened and remodeled in 1912 (as seen here) for further service, but automotive hearses soon ate into the business and after languishing unemployed from 1918, it was converted circa 1924 for the use of United Railway's Medical Department.

This view near Maltby KS and the Kansas City Western Railway's right-of-way comes from publicity material circa 1908 featuring the sightseeing possibilities of their scenic line to Leavenworth.

By the end of 1896, the Southwest Missouri ran a Carthage-Galena KS main line via Webb City and Joplin, parallelling the Frisco railroad. It normally ran as two separate divisions. Joplin-Galena was the west division, a forty-five minute run for a dime every half-hour from 6:00 a.m. to 11:00 p.m. Carthage-Joplin was the east division, a ninety-minute run for 20 cents, every half-hour from 6:00 a.m. to 11:00 p.m. Both gave a better, cleaner, cheaper, more convenient and comprehensive service than the railroad. That didn't prevent a war with the Frisco, beginning July 11th 1897. The Frisco put on hourly trains and Southwest cut fares by 2/3rds. Fares later went up again, but the Frisco kept the hourly trains. So from March 1st, 1899 "Empire County Express" limited service was added to Southwest's east division, every 90 minutes from 8:00 a.m. to 11:00 p.m., with four stops and four grade-crossing stops taking just one hour. Frisco's Carthage-Joplin trains only needed fifty minutes, but needed "free hacks" from the stations to downtown.

The St. Louis, St. Charles and Western used these primitive open trailers (converted freight cars) for heavy weekend tourist and picnic traffic to the German Protestant Orphan's Home on St. Charles Rock Road in Pattonville. This is trailer 1 near the home circa 1902. STLMOT.

AN EASTON AVENUE CAR, SHOWING CONGESTION COMMON ON TROLLEY LINES

The journey to and from work was, is and always will be a trying experience, as any commuter from 1859 to the present day could testify. St. Louis Post-Dispatch, January 2nd 1907.

Illinois Traction lines out of St. Louis competed with the railroads for traffic to Springfield, Peoria, Bloomington, Decatur and Danville. Its services rivalled the best of them. There were sleeping cars right up to 1940, there were diners and when the railroads began air-conditioning cars in the early 1930s, so did the IT. This was rare on North American interurbans at this or any other time. Their new air-conditioned streamlined trains were superior to all but the "dome" passenger cars going into post-war railroad service. But ridership decline saw the demise of IT passenger services in 1956, years before railroad passenger services were merged into Amtrak.

Streetcars were often targets for adolescent mischief and petty lawbreaking. In the 1870s, kids hitching a "free" ride on the back of a bobtail car were a common pest, undeterred by an irate driver with a whip. The trick was not to get caught. Staid, conservative upper-middle class St. Louisans, now respectable and distinguished seniors and

pillars of their communities, talk of their childhood sixty and more years ago when they'd pull the Clayton "dinky's" trolley pole off the wire just to hear to hear the motorman ("Red" Carroll likely as not) cuss, or save a dime the hard way by riding the rear fender. Putting pennies on the track to be squashed by the car's wheels was kid's stuff. Far more interesting was seeing how big a rock needed to be before a car would fail to squash it to powder and instead spit out the fragments faster than a speeding bullet in every direction—so long as the rock wasn't big enough to derail the car, an occurrence which even the stupidest knew crossed the line from mischief to criminal vandalism.

Soaping or greasing the rails to watch a car fail to make a grade was harmless on St. Louis's quiet suburban Clayton line but potentially fatal in urban St. Joseph. Motorman John McCombs *"still shudders when he thinks of a wild ride he took because of a...prank. Coming in on the Jules line, he started to apply the hand brake as the car*

In addition to its city services in Joplin and Webb City, the Southwest Missouri's interurban cars were used for journeys to and from work by miners. This is Southwest 49, stopped at the Davey #3 (Big Shaft) Mine of the American Lead and Zinc Company in Prosperity MO, full of miners returning from lunch on June 20th, 1914. Motorman Bert Matt (right) and Conductor J. H. McMechan (father of Earl E. McMechan), pose for the camera. Earl E. McMechan.

St. Louisans often took long leisure-time trolley trips on the interurbans that fanned out into Illinois. Here are observation car 7 and interurban 3 of the Alton, Granite and St. Louis in Alton prior to World War 1. This line, however, was in heavy daily use as well and ran until 1953. The drumhead sign on the observation car's railing reads "Alton-St. Louis Limited. Electric Way."

Don't mind if the cars are all crowded;
Don't rush, for that's indiscreet.
When you wear good style,
With a radiant smile,
You are sure, my dear, of a seat.

Some folks, when handed a lemon, can always find a way to make lemonade. (<u>UR Bulletin</u>, April 15, 1916.)

started gaining speed down the hill at Eighteenth...The brakes did not retard...Someone had soaped the rails. The car plunged down the hill at breakneck speed and over the grade at Fifteenth and startedregaining speed on that hill. Mr McCombs...was scared. He could not halt the car until it got to Ninth and Frederick." (<u>St. Joseph News-Press</u>, January 30th, 1938 p. 4)

Outside the harrowing rush hours, trolley riding for leisure and pleasure was popular for years. Evening travel to theaters and other attractions was routine, as was travel to railroad stations, amusement parks (often owned by the trolley company), beauty spots, sports venues, picnics and cemeteries. There also was leisure riding in smaller towns like Mexico, Farmington and Nevada. Cars to Hannibal's Mount Olivet cemetery would stop for riders to visit a flower shop, buy their blooms, then go on to the cemetery. Lakeside Park's many attractions from 1908 included a local baseball league and between 6,000 and 8,000 rode the Southwest from Carthage, Webb City, Joplin, Galena KS and even Picher OK to take in a game. On Sundays Carrollton folks would ride the car from the Square to the station just to watch the trains roll by. The first segment of the Alton Jacksonville and Peoria opened on August 20th 1907, earlier than planned, so folks could attend the Bethany Horse Thief Detectives' Association picnic. The St. Joseph and Savannah for years carried picnic parties to Glendale Park until paved roads and autos provided an alternative.

The Kansas City-Western Railway charged $25.00 an hour to charter a 44-seat car in the 1906-1916 period, $30.00 for a 52-seat car. For this sum, a group boarded in Kansas City and rode over the Intercity viaduct into Kansas (for which the MET charged an extra nickel) for a scenic ride on the Missouri's west bank to Lansing. An hour's stopover was taken to inspect the State Pentientiary where, as the brochure advertising the service quaintly put it, *"every courtesy is shown by the Warden and his deputies."* From Lansing the party continued to the Leavenworth Soldiers' Home and picnic grounds, where on summer afternoons the company hired a military band for concerts. The trip ended at Fort Leavenworth (the Federal Penitentiary was passed over-one prison per trip was more than enough) and after sightseeing the party returned to KC, the MET again extracting a nickel for crossing the Intercity viaduct.

Winnwood Lake, beach, zoo and dance hall, Excelsior Springs, the cemeteries, Swope Park and the new Union Station were other favorite Kansas City area trolley excursions. The Country Club line originally was an enjoyable summer trip into the country with a cool-of-the-evening return, but the later development of Country Club Plaza and the Pratt and Whitney aircraft motor plant changed its ridership profile to that of an embryonic Light Rail line.

St. Louis's long county lines were ideal for summer Sunday excursions, especially night trips on open cars when cooling breezes blew. During Prohibition, a ride west on St. Louis's Clayton "dinky" to Price Road was an incredibly popular diversion, for up the hill from the line, at Price and Ladue, was Busch's Grove. Were the veranda lights on of an evening? Was there a light in the cupola? Yes? Then bootleg hooch was on tap and G-men were elsewhere. Cars to the cemeteries and St. Charles were favorites into the 1930s and folks still rode to Creve Coeur Lake in summer 1950.

The more ambitious took day trips from St. Louis to Lincolnland (Springfield) on Illinois Traction interurbans. Runs from Eads Bridge on the East St. Louis and Suburban were a staple of the "trolley for pleasure" era, fanning out to Horseshoe Lake, Alton, Belleville and Lebanon. Cars on its "Scenic Loop Route of the Great East Side Electric Lines," rolled over the Illinois prairies to Mitchell and Edwardsville. Charles Dickens rode on horseback from St. Louis to Belleville around 1842 specifically to see these prairies. One of his sons re-enacted the trip decades later as a company guest in either "The Mounds" or "The Bluffs," in part to showcase transportation developments since his father's time. These charter cars, with their buffets and elegant dull-green silk hangings were the pride of the line.

Of all the tourist attractions and beauty spots accessible by St. Louis area trolleys, however, none surpassed Forest Park. Until the 1904 World's Fair, several lines ran right into the park, ending at trim little stations that harmonized with their pleasant surroundings. The Louisiana Purchase exposition of 1904 put an end to that, but the Lindell Railway's station is there yet, heavily rebuilt and expanded from its first days (around 1895) as a trolley terminal. During 1904,

---

In the 1890s, private cars were fashionable among the smart set. Kansas City and St. Louis had several. "'*Mrs John Smith requests the pleasure of your company, Friday September first. Private car Kinloch (sic). Rendezvous 9 o'clock. Sarah and Suburban.' This dainty note of invitation on the most approved of gray-blue paper was received on a Thursday morning by the friends of Mrs. Smith…There has been no fashionable form of entertainment more popular these pleasant summer evenings than the trolley party. It is all very well to say you don't care if you didn't get an invitation, that there are other trolley cars and you can ride 17 miles for a nickel, but…the public trolley is not the pleasantest place in the world this hot weather with so many people riding who have neglected the preliminaries of toilet so essential to the comfort of the individual who take his tub regularly before he takes his dinner.*

"*There is no way of taking little journeys in the world quite so delightful as the trolley…The automobile may in time prove the rival…but at present there is nothing here to divide honors and when it comes to spending a whole evening spinning over the rails with one's best friends beside one, there is little wonder that the trolle party has become a popular entertainment…Mrs Smith herself likes to give trolley parties 'for it is a great nuisance in hot weather' she says 'to have your house opened for company… It is too hot in St. Louis to be comfortable indoors and then it is hard on the servants working in such sultry weather.' So Mrs Smith, who dearly loves to entertain, asks her friends to her trolley party, feeling that she has saved herself and her servants lots of fuss and worry…*

"*The details of the affair are very easily arranged, a few minutes' talk over the telephone being all that is necessary…A private car may be engaged for the small sum of $20 or $25…this charge including fees for the motorman, conductor and porter. The car has regular chairs for eighteen and, besides, camp*

stools are furnished…These chairs are very comfortable, of the split bamboo kind and…may be turned in any direction. The light panelings, mirrors and various crystal effects make the car as pleasant and cool looking as one's own apartments. The rows of electric lights on the outside give a festive appearance to the outing, which is very exhilerating. The evening lasts until 1 o'clock…there are many miles of electric railway that may be traversed and whatever choice is made, one is sure to be satisfied….

"*Above all things, when you choose a trolley crowd, be sure that you have congenial people. It is not necessary that tin horns be blown all the time…but fun of the more or less rollicking kind is…sure to be expected by the freedom and joyousness of the occasion, and if you are not likely to be in sympathy with it, probably it were just as well not to accept the invitation. Music is…a necessary part of the program and varies from the expensive band to the amateur violinist and solo and chorus singing are as naturally indulged in as laughter …Topical songs, comic recitations, fortune telling and parlor games are all indulged in as the taste and inclination of the guests may determine…*

"*The hamper, which always goes along, is a mattter of no small concern. There are generally sandwiches made with minced meats, chicken, ham or tongue, relishes of some sort, iced drinks and ice cream or sherberts. The commonest sort of trolley party, however, is the one on the picnic plan at which expenses of the car are divided among the young men…The young ladies 'furnish the delicacies of the occasion.' Now that the summer travelers have returned, the trolley party… will be usually only preliminary to the supper…served at the home club of the host. As the nights are cooler and dancing is in order, a princely entertainment will consist of a trolley ride to the Country Club with dancing for a couple of hours, then supper and another ride, the longest way home. (G-D September 17th,1899, part 3 p.7).*

UNITED RAILWAYS BULLETIN

PUBLISHED MONTHLY FOR DISTRIBUTION AMONG THE EMPLOYES OF THE UNITED RAILWAYS CO. OF ST. LOUIS.

VOLUME TWO   *ST. LOUIS, AUGUST 15, 1916*   *NUMBER EIGHT*

Many trolley and interurban companies built their own amusement parks as a way to stimulate leisure riding. Creve Coeur Park in St. Louis, Krug Park in St. Joseph and Winnwood Lake on the Clay County interurban north of Kansas City were among the best known in Missouri. The trolleys in this 1916 drawing are the legendary Creve Coeur "Moonlight" summer cars, which ran until 1929.

Several of the Southwest's more flimsy bridges and trestles were replaced, grade crossings bridged and the lines to Lakeside Park doubled over the years. This is the 1913 Missouri Pacific overpass at King's Crossing, just east of Lakeside Park circa 1922, with car 67 speeding another load of leisure-time riders to the park. Earl E. McMechan.

trolleys could even whisk you round Forest Park on the exposition's Intramural Railroad.

In the auto-scarce 1940s, trolley touring enjoyed a mild revival and tourist cars ran in many Canadian and U. S. cities. St. Louis missed out on this, but touring Kansas City on the "The Scout" was a major treat. It ran 26 miles twice daily, touching the best of KC including Union Station, the Gallery of Art and Swope Park. There was even a night run, complete with record-player, sound system and an "announcer" DJ who took requests.

Contrary to expectations, trolley freight was never a big earner. But with creative "drumming" by a line's agents, it could play a large part in sustaining revenues. Except for package express, freight was largely absent from city trolleys after the 1890s, unless an existing freight operation was taken over. The St. Louis and Suburban to Wellston and Florissant which electrified in 1891, continued freight, express and mail services from its earlier incarnation as a steam railway. But as the suburbs gradually encroached, freight services ceased. U.S. Mail cars ran regular routes on the Suburban and United Railways until the contract was withdrawn in 1913.

Though its franchise forbade freight traffic as such, package express and other revenue-generating services were staples of UR's St. Louis operation before 1920. Spurs into quarries and building sites were used to haul excavated dirt or construction refuse. There were funeral cars, express cars and refrigerator cars and in the 1890s an ambulance car. Kansas City enjoyed similar facilities including a unique service of cement trains, where work cars hauled one to three cement trailers converted from old passenger cars, to Kansas and Missouri customers. The cement originated at the Bonner Springs Portland Cement Company in Kansas and was brought to KC by the Kansas City and Kaw Valley.

On October 12th, 1904, Missouri Governor David Francis spoke to the American Street Railway Association's 23rd annual convention about the Intramural and its development.

"We (originally) suggested to the street railways…that they operate a line…within the limits of the exposition that would be the joint property of the two companies and on…which line they could run the cars from their systems throughout the city. When I went to Europe in the interests of this Fair early in 1903, it was my understanding that we had about perfected an arrangement whereby an intramural road could be constructed and be the joint property of the city street railway systems, the St. Louis Transit Company and the Suburban…Upon my return—and I was not gone over six weeks—I found the entire project had been abandoned. I found the Suburban…had become discouraged because of a fire which destroyed about…sixty of its car and that the Transit Company had…(made) such extraordinary preparations for the Fair…it had incurred a larger debt than planned and…was compelled to take a temporary loan of some millions…(that) seriously affected the value of the stocks I was holding in that company.

"I found, furthermore, that the exposition management had about decided that the crowds within these walls could be handled by automobiles. I threw up my hands in despair and said that…handling the crowds…by automobiles without fixed routes was in my judgment…erroneous… It was necessary to have an Intramural road…They said 'you will have to build it yourselves.' That meant the Exposition authorities. I have no personal interest in anything on these grounds, unless it is the entire grounds. I am staking more on this exposition than I have staked on any enterprise in my life and I do not know why…(But) I immediately set about…to arrange for an Intramural road …under control of the Exposition authorities. In order to utilize the tracks already laid, it was necessary…the gauge be…4' 8½" instead of 4' 10" as on the street railways of this city…Without going into further details, we ask you to look at the road.

"It is operated daily except Sunday. The Government does not permit us to open the Fair on Sundays. I do not know your ideas about Sunday observances but…that prohibition…has cost this Exposition $1 million. If we had been permitted to operate…it would not only never have injured the morals of the people who patronized it, but it would have attracted them to pursuits less injurious than those in which many of them now indulge…On every other day, the Intramural…carries an average of 55,000…55% of the paid admission to these grounds…(It) is one of the best sources of revenue that the Exposition management has. Now imagine gentlemen, how we could have transported the crowds, if you can imagine—I cannot—without an intramural road. Think of having 150,000 people a day on these grounds on roller chairs, automobiles and jinrickshaws. Think of the…distances between these buildings. These grounds are two miles east and west and one mile north and south…about twice that of the Chicago Fair. What would you think of it if we did not have the Intramural…in operation inside?" (<u>SRJ</u> October 22nd 1904 pp 740-2).

Southwest's Lakeside Park, between Webb City and Carterville was a major attraction for leisure-time riders. Car 30, seen at the park entrance circa 1911, is well-filled with folks headed home. Many will likely make the full journey west to Galena KS. Earl E. McMechan.

A sunny February day in 1939 and eastbound car 1086 accelerates away from the Crow's Nest loop on its way back to University City, St. Louis. Until the 1940s, the far reaches of the Creve Coeur line were as isolated as any of Missouri's rural lines and about as likely to generate any meaningful traffic, other than on summer weekends.

The Southwest Missouri originally carried no freight at all except express packages on front platforms. Motormen and conductors were given 20% of all express charges. Fearing losses, the Southwest had no agents and no dedicated freight vehicles so this was the only expense for an activity which in 1910 grossed $10,000. But extra income was needed and from 1915 the company began serving mines and railroad interchanges in Kansas and Oklahoma, soon shifting multiple carloads of coal, chat and ore daily. An extension to Picher OK opened in 1918, with Miami OK the ultimate goal. Yet E. Z. Wallower and A. H. Rogers were fretting over adverse industry trends well before it was built. Wallower, on behalf of his Harrisburg investors, was even considering cashing out.

On September 18th, 1917 he wrote Rogers *"This will be a hard time to finance our complete line to Miami, and we may have to wait after building to Baxter or Picher*

Catalan loop was the southern terminus of St. Louis's Broadway line. A suburban extension carried trolleys a further two and a half miles into Jefferson Barracks and the military cemetery until 1932 and at the time of this May 1940 photograph of "Witt" car 765, shuttle buses continued to do so. The loop itself spawned its own leisure-time attractions over the years, including Sauter's park, which now is beginning to look run-down and seedy.

Oakland Avenue on St. Louis's Forest Park line was a prime leisure destination. Attractions included the Forest Park Highlands amusement park, St. Louis Zoo and the park itself. In the 1940s, ridership was exceptionally high trnd this scene at Oakland and Hampton was typical of summer weekends or holidays at that time. It's a Labor Day crowd (September 3rd, 1945) that surrounds PCC car 1578, "Witt" car 1329 and a surviving "World's Fair" class car, now more than forty years old and still in heavy-duty service. STLMOT

By the late 1940s, it was clear that while ridership remained high, the return of the automobile was imminent. An impressive array of 1940s sedans and station wagons waits for the traffic cops outside the St. Louis Arena on Oakland Avenue, who are allowing more pedestrians to join the throng leaving the May 4th 1947 Police Circus for their car ride home. STLMOT

This school picnic group has arrived at Forest Park Highlands on June 6th, 1945 after riding car 1013 and one of the last trailer cars to remain in service. STLMOT

...Will be glad to go over the proposed route to Picher with you. I hope it is through the center of development and not too far north ...There is not much prospect of a sale these times. I believe, however, that the proposed extension will help...with any prospective purchaser, and one may come along sooner than we expect. We will need that extension ...to make up in the falling-off in the towns north and east of Joplin."

On October 27th Rogers wrote Wallower saying *"In running from Joplin to Baxter and Picher we shall have entered a territory the like of which the S.W... has not heretofore known...Before offering to go to Miami we had better first try the Baxter and Picher business to determine to what extent...facilities may be inadequate and what...additional money is needed to make them right...My estimate of cash cost of...building...15 miles of RR from the junction near the State line to our Picher depot is $550,000 against which we can get authority to issue 80% in bonds, say $440,000. Believe we can (get) our State Commissions to let us sell these bonds at not less than 70% par. $440,000 par value of bonds sold at 70 would yield $308,000. Stockholders would...each take his pro rata of bonds on the above basis. Our floating debt would...be extinguished and the dividend-paying problem only would remain for solution."*

"RUBBERNECK" SERVICE IN WARTIME

THE "SCOUT" — OUR OPEN-AIR STREET CAR — NOW CONSTITUTES KANSAS CITY'S ONLY REGULARLY OPERATED SIGHT-SEEING SERVICE

Four regular tours will operate daily at 10:30 A. M., 2:30 P. M., 7:30 P. M. and 9:30 P. M. All trips will leave from 9th & Main.

Day-time Trips—40c plus tax.
Night-time, Sunday & Holiday
Trips—50c plus tax.

ODT regulations having eliminated motor bus sight-seeing service and Gray Line tours, the "Scout," which started operation June 14th, is expected to handle big loads during the summer months. Weather permitting, this service will continue through Sunday, Sept. 27th.

Let's all get familiar with this service and help acquaint visitors and our many new residents with the "Scout's" delightfully cool sight-seeing trips.

Passengers on each trip will be limited to the seating capacity of car— 47 passengers. To be sure of seat secure ticket in advance. On sale at 728 Delaware and at the 48th & Harrison Division office.

Stops will be made to pick up passengers at all regular car stops in the downtown district and at the Union Station. On return trip passengers may alight at any point upon signal to operator. Free transfers *from* the "Scout" will be issued upon request and in accordance with transfer regulations.

FARES: Day trips—10:30 a. m. and 2:30 p. m. (except Sundays and Holidays), all seats 40c each, plus Federal transportation tax. Children under five, held in lap of fare-paying passenger, may ride free. Trip time 1½ hours.

Night trips—7:30 p. m. and 9:30 p. m. (also all 4 trips Sundays and Holidays), seats 50c each, plus Federal transportation tax. Children under five, held in lap of fare-paying passenger, may ride free. Trip time 2 hours.

The "Scout" may be chartered by private parties for old-fashioned trolley trips at any time other than scheduled trips. The rate for such special trips is $17.50 for two hours and $8.75 for each additional hour thereafter.

For reservations, call GR 0050—Sta. 292.

Night-time, Sunday & Holiday Route:

From 9th & Main, loop via 9th, Wyandotte & 10th Sts. to Main and south via B'way, Westport and Ward P'kway to 60th.

Returning to 39th and B'way, east to Main, south over Rockhill and Swope Park route to Swope Park.

Returning north over Swope P'kway to 47th and Troost, thence north on Troost to 8th St., loop via 8th, Wyandotte, & 10th Sts. to Main.

Day-time Route:

From 9th & Main, south to 43rd St. over Rockhill Road and Swope P'kway route to Swope Park.

Returning north over Swope P'kway to 47th and Troost, thence north over regular night-time route.

In Kansas City, "The Scout" was a well-remembered treat of the 1940s. The metal arches that sport light bulbs provide support for a canvas roof in rainy weather.

A carload of teens rides "The Scout" on a special hayride excursion in the late 1940s.

On May 14th, 1919 Wallower wrote Rogers saying Southwest was losing $100 daily on freight. Rogers agreed, replying on May 23rd that operating expenses were 24 cents a mile *"and about the only profitable traffic we have is that between Carthage and Picher."* The main line was making it but branches and local services were not. Jitneys were to blame. *"Mr. W, excuse me if I do not enthuse over the idea of campaigning against the jitney by putting on extra cars, extra advertising and enlisting assistance of the Civic Clubs…(They) should, however, aside from all reference to the… (Southwest), urge the city…that a valid indemnity bond of say $2,500 be required of each jitney."* (Letters in Southwest Missouri RR records, Western Historical Manuscripts collection, Columbia MO).

The St. Francois initially hauled coal, agricultural tools, grain, dry goods and building materials. It had private sidings for larger shippers and handled carload lots on its own account (billed through to places such as St. Louis). Trucks robbed it of business and by the 1940s, the line's sole revenue came from hauling coal to the State Hospital, just outside Farmington. It was dieselized in 1947 and closed in 1957.

In Carrolton, mail was hauled from the station to the Post Office and back. The line also picked up railroad cars with its electric switcher

Like Kansas City, St. Louis initially believed the core of the surviving trolley system was worth keeping and also ordered new cars and repaired tracks. PCC car 1730 carefully negotiates a stretch of track under repair as it heads west on Olive, between Grand and Boyle in October 1946. STLMOT

Steel rails were heavy, weighing from 16 to 30lbs per yard on the earliest horse lines, to upwards of 90 lbs per yard on heavy-duty street railways of the 1930s. Switches and crossing pieces were even heavier, often made of specialized hardened or manganese steels. This is crane 400 in St. Louis's materials yards at 39th and Park in September 1944, carefully picking up a six-ton turnout switch (the track piece that allowed one route to diverge from another) from flat car 72. Motor flat 139 and tool car 260 are in the background. STLMOT.

As late as 1951, the St. Louis materials yard was well stocked with new girder rail for track repairs. A three-man crew checks rail lengths while a White truck stands by. To its left, replacement overhead line poles are being stored, while on the right stands crane 400.

The last railroad/trolley grade crossing in St. Louis was on South Broadway, where one of the track gang is welding in new crossing pieces in the late 1940s. STLMOT

In the 1890s, a suburban, rural or interurban trolley was a lifeline to civilization, providing reliable swift passenger transport where none existed before, plus merchandise, express and general freight service. This St. Louis and Suburban mail car, seen out towards Kinloch in the late 1890s, may be the original of 1891, the first such service in the country.

and took them to its 18-car trolley freight yard on South Main for onward delivery. A spur to the powerhouse (which also supplied town current) was used for coal delivery. Traveling theatricals playing Carrolton's Opera House could take a car right to their hotel, along with their bags. Scenery was unloaded outside the theater dock from a railroad baggage car, hauled up South Folger by the switcher. The car would then be parked in the South Main yard before being reloaded when the theatricals left town. Building materials for courthouse construction came onto the grounds on railroad flat cars hauled by the switcher during 1902/3, a spur being laid for the purpose.

Keytesville's line also hauled freight, indeed after about 1905 it was the only animal-powered streetcar line to do so.

"When the new travelling salesman makes his first trip to Keytesville he steps down to the little station platform and begins to peer round through the trees for the town. The only thing he sees, however, is the little horse car and the peaceful looking team of bay horses hitched to it. "Where's the town?" he asks of the station agent. "Get on the car there and you'll soon find out," grins the agent. "How'm I going to get my trunks?" the drummer persists. The driver... rolls an ice cream freezer to the steps of the car and says "Get into the car, mister. Your trunks will get hauled to town all right." There seems to be no other way out of it and the new man squeezes past the trunk

and cases of "pop" on the platform and takes his seat. When all passengers are inside, the driver walls them in with mail sacks, empty milk cans, more cases of "pop" and ice cream freezers, placed on the platform of the car.

"Then the journey to Keytesville begins. The mile and a half of track...is clipped off in about 15 to 20 minutes and when the car at last turns into the main street, the new drummer heartily agrees with the farmer lad, grins at him and says: "This sure is some larrapin' town, ain't it?" When the car stops, the drummer picks up his hand luggage and makes for the front door, but he is balked again. The freight and baggage must be unloaded before he can get out. The ice cream freezers are put off in front of the drug store, the bottles of "pop" go to a thirst emporium and the other freight and baggage is delivered where it belongs on Bridge Street... The drummer, noticing the actions of an older man in his profession, takes his seat again and waits patiently until the mail has been put off at the Post Office and the car stops in front of the Brown Hotel. The horse car has delivered him and his trunks. (KCS August 14th, 1910 p. 7)

Having for years moved heaven and earth to get rail traffic off their streets, bigger cities were more fussy about trolley freight. St. Louis was particularly strict about Illinois Traction, which until 1925 could haul no more than two cars at a time within city limits at night and one during the day. Kansas City and St. Joseph were less strict, but

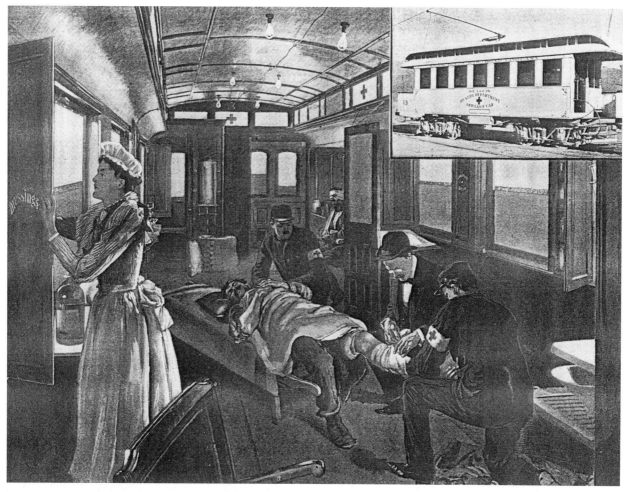

Ambulance cars seemed like a good idea but proved impractical, given that the car in front could not move to one side to let the ambulance pass. This car was fitted up in 1894 by or for the Union Depot Railroad of St. Louis.

operational limitations caused by terrain and location of railroad interchanges kept much interurban freight off Kansas City streets. Both cities had large interurban freight houses. That in St. Louis, property of the McKinley system, handled nothing but Illinois Traction freight. The KC freight house served all lines that made it across the Missouri, plus the Clay County. A smaller St. Joseph freight house interchanged between the Clay County and the St. Joseph-Savannah.

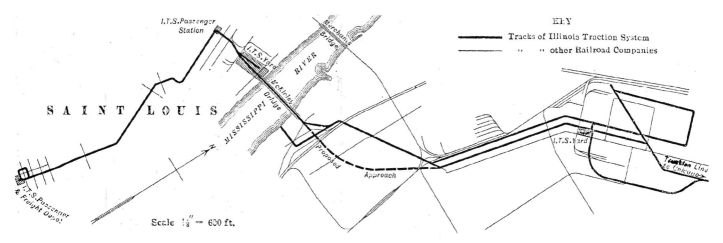

Map of St. Louis Electric Terminal Railway's Granite City-St. Louis line circa 1912, the shortest, but the most important segment of the entire Illinois Traction system. The "proposed approach" was built later-a flimsy-looking wooden trestle known as the "high line" that nevertheless survived disused but intact until parts of it fell down recently through dereliction and neglect. It has now been completely removed. (SRJ February 15th, 1913 p. 282).

The McKinley Bridge was and remains one of the greatest monuments to the trolley era in North America, having been built so that one interurban company could get unobstructed and independent rail access to the huge St. Louis market. PCC 452 heads off the bridge onto the St. Louis Diversion in 1958. The original tracks to 9th Street to the old 12th Street terminal lie disused and disconnected on the left. Ray Gehl/Mark Goldfeder collection.

The Kaw Valley ran passenger cars to KC from 1914, but initially kept freight cars out of Missouri, servicing on-line farms in Kansas and accepting carload freight on foreign equipment only for delivery to on-line industries. Business was growing, however, and by 1917 the KCKV&W had two electric locomotives, eight box cars, four flat cars and two refrigerator cars. The locomotives ran 24/7 hauling sand, crushed rock, cement, cattle, wheat, potatoes and produce.

The company badly wanted to get its freight trains to Missouri railroad interchanges. Two routes were available through KC for interchange with the Kaw Valley. Both were grossly overloaded. It could take five days to get a freight train through KC. The former Kansas City, Mexico and Orient Railroad would have provided a third water-level route, but ran out of money before it finished building. The Kaw Valley took over the project and it was functional by 1924. It was big-league stuff and the freight hauled into Missouri was heavy-duty.

The KC interurban freight house did not serve the former Kansas

City and Westport Belt Railway Company. That line's Westport terminal was at 40th and Summit. The MET's parent bought the KC&WBRC in 1905 and the MET electrified it, running cars from downtown south on Main and Wornall, joining the railroad at 43rd Street. Trolleys and railroad freights shared tracks south of 43rd Street. The railroad from 40th to 43rd Street remained a freight-only spur. In 1907, cars were extended south to 51st Street and the J. C. Nichols "Country Club" development. The MET owned the line outright from July 7th 1914, soon extending it to Dodson and 75th Street. A World War II branch left Dodson for the Pratt and Whitney plant. Cars ceased on June 22nd, 1957 (KC's last trolley line), but electric freight continued, as did the 40th and Summit materials yard. The line was dieselized at the end of July 1957 and ran to 1968. Much right-of-way survives, the core of several Kansas City Light Rail proposals.

The all-freight St. Louis and Belleville owned over 500 coal cars. Under wire until 1951, it continued as the Peabody Short Line (dieselised) and then as part of the Illinois Central to the late 1960s. But no interurban hauled freight (other than package express) into St. Louis except IT. This was partly because the Illinois riverfront had railroad yards and interchanges; the Missouri riverfront had none. It was also a matter of St. Louis being unwilling to see interurban freights on its streets. There was also the gauge; 4' 10" in St. Louis, standard on the East Side lines—after 1905.

"The gauge of the East St. Louis and Suburban... is to be changed without...a complete shut-down of the system for one day as was first contemplated...The change is to be made on the different divisions on different days. Over 100 miles of track on 12 divisions will be narrowed...in about a week...At times there will be 700 men engaged... The change will cost $75,000...Engineer of Construction Bennett has divided the entire system into sections of six miles. Fifty men in charge of a foreman are assigned to each section. Each gang is expected to change six miles in a day. On the day before the change is to be made on a branch, a gang will be sent to each six-mile section to draw the inner spike on two out of every three ties. Another gang will follow and drive spikes on each tie one and one half inches inside the rail. On the day the change is made, one gang will draw the remaining inside spikes and loosen the rail, another gang will push the rail one and one half inches against the new spike, one spiker will follow who will drive a spike on the outside of the rail to hold it and anoth-

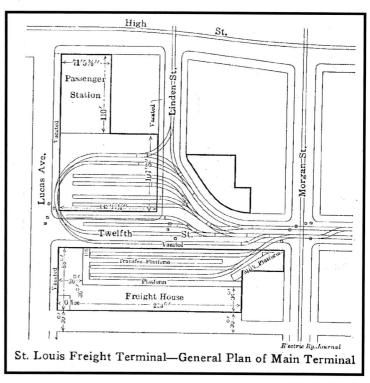

St. Louis Freight Terminal—General Plan of Main Terminal

**Map of Illinois Traction's St. Louis Terminal 1910-1931.
(SRJ February 15th, 1913 p. 283).**

Illinois Traction's Eleventh and Lucas Freight House circa 1912 with express motor 1057, express trailer 1193 and a further unidentified express trailer. Bill Volkmer collection.

New ST. LOUIS TERMINAL

The Illinois Terminal's $15,000,000 project in St. Louis now nears completion. In the main, it consists of an entirely new high speed route (elevated and subway) from the McKinley Bridge to Twelfth Boulevard and Washington Avenue — right to the heart of St. Louis where wholesale and retail shopping districts meet and adjoining St. Louis' civic center development. This new route is to be completely electrified, and will terminate in a group of gigantic buildings furnishing shipping, storage, and warehouse facilities, and offering national distributors unexcelled service by rail or truck in all directions from St. Louis and within the St. Louis area.

Passenger trains will arrive at and depart from the subway level, while the commodious concourse and waiting rooms will be located at street level—entrance will be from both Washington Avenue and Twelfth Boulevard.

Freight terminals will be underground—eleven freight tracks will enter the main building and provide space

The new terminal in the heart of the St. Louis business district as it will look when completed.

for in excess of 100 cars. Design and equipment embody the latest ideas to facilitate the rapid loading and unloading of freight.

The group of terminal buildings will cover the territory between Washington Avenue and Morgan Street, while the main building—illustrated above—will cover an entire city block with 75,000 square feet of storage space on each floor.—The entire project is scheduled for completion by January 1, 1932.

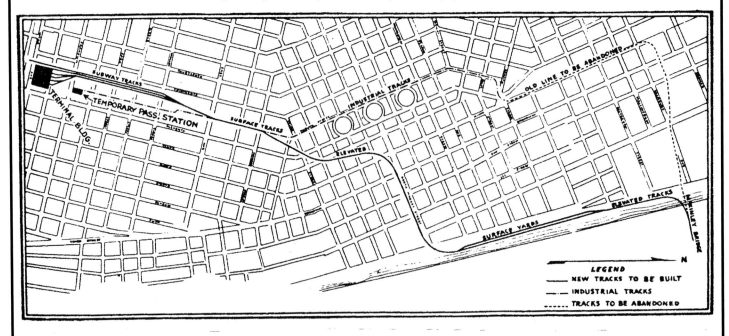

Of all the belt and diversionary lines built by the interurbans, that of the Illinois Terminal in St. Louis was among the most ambitious and longest lived, the last movement on it being made February 20th, 2006. When funds become available, it is slated for conversion to an urban bike/hike trail, perhaps the only one with an elevated stretch in all of North America.

Most Kansas City interurbans hauled railroad freight cars, though not on city streets. This is a mid-50s picture of the Country Club line's freight operation, which continued to 1968.

Often, interurbans and street railroads used their own freight vehicles, which could better cope with sharp curves or be custom-built for general utility use in around the system. This is Springfield Traction 9, a home-made box car here seen hauling heavy sacks, plus freight car 6, on a rural stretch of Broadway near Talmage on August 19th, 1912. SLMOT

er gang will follow him, drive the outside spikes and tighten those inside. The cars are now being prepared so that the wheels can be pushed over the axles the required distance. Cars along the line at the time of the changes will be raised on jacks and their axles changed and then they will go ahead.' "(P-D June 17th, 1905 p.5.)

The Terminal Railroad Association of St. Louis's Mississippi rail bridge monopoly raised the price of Illinois coal to what was seen as extortionate levels once a train arrived in Missouri, a monopoly unbroken by McKinley's 1910 bridge because of the city's restrictions on street-running freight trains. Even had the ambitious Southern Traction/Municipal Bridge/downtown St. Louis standard-gauge interurban loop and the associated all-line interurban passenger/freight depot projects of 1910-1919 worked out, it would have been the same. ST's 1911 franchise allowed no box cars into St. Louis, only an express motor with two trailers between midnight and 5:00 a.m. Coal trains would never have been allowed; a big drawback as it was already clear ST had pretensions to be a major coal-hauler.

From the 1920s, cities began insisting trolley companies pave streets and build belt lines as conditions for renewing franchises. The Jolin and Pittsburg and the Southwest were asked to build freight belts around Joplin, as IT later did around Champaign, Decatur and Springfield IL. The Southwest instead interchanged railroad freight outside town, as it did in Galena KS. The J&P still ran freight (mainly coal and mine chat) long after passenger service ceased on May 31st, 1929 but on that day, it also cut its Joplin line back to Chitwood, a quarter-mile inside Joplin city limits, to avoid paving obligations. It later retreated to Waco on the Missouri-Kansas state line. Further north, the Clay County, unable to contemplate the building of belt lines, bought motor trucks to haul its freight.

IT freights left St. Louis streets in 1931 when 2½ miles of diversionary trackage was opened from the end of the McKinley Bridge to a "subway" station in the basement of the St. Louis Globe-Democrat building. This diversion survived the merger of the IT into the

The Southwest Missouri graduated from less-than-carload to carload freight rather late, not taking up the latter until around 1915. It then built up a considerable business, investing in several electric locomotives to haul the trains. Locomotives four and five, home-built in 1927, always ran together. In February 1927, they were pictured just after delivery from the Webb City shops, together with the men who built them. Earl E. McMechan

Norfolk Southern Railroad in 1981. Once or twice a week, a small diesel locomotive delivered rolls of newsprint to the former basement station of the newspaper building, now owned by the St. Louis Post-Dispatch. This ceased in mid-2004; the line is gradually being dismantled.

Freight traffic was no guarantee of survival. Package and express business on rural and interurban lines was killed by jitneys and motor trucks. A few, including the Southwest and the Clay County, continued to use their own trucks for package, express and LCL. The Clay County closed its lines in 1933, but passenger and freight services were maintained by its buses and trucks for the few more years the company lasted. Southwest's rail freight services east of Joplin were withdrawn circa 1935 and replaced by company motor trucks before the business was sold. Rail freight service west of Galena KS was sold to the Northeastern Oklahoma Railroad, which ran diesel freights until the 1960s. But in Missouri, these two systems were exceptional. Most had no freight service, rail or otherwise, to fall back on. The towns they served were lucky if the company (or its successors) could even afford to run replacement motor buses. Still, Hannibal, St. Joseph, Springfield, Sedalia and Jefferson City can still boast regular local bus service. Other small (and not so small) Missouri towns cannot-at one point Joplin, for example, had no buses at all.

A typical sight on rural interurban lines before motor trucks took over; an electric freight express or baggage car switching a railroad box car to an on-line customer. Here St. Francois car 50 has just coupled up to a boxcar in Farmington almost at the end of electric operation on November 16th, 1947.

OLD CARS, NEW CARS

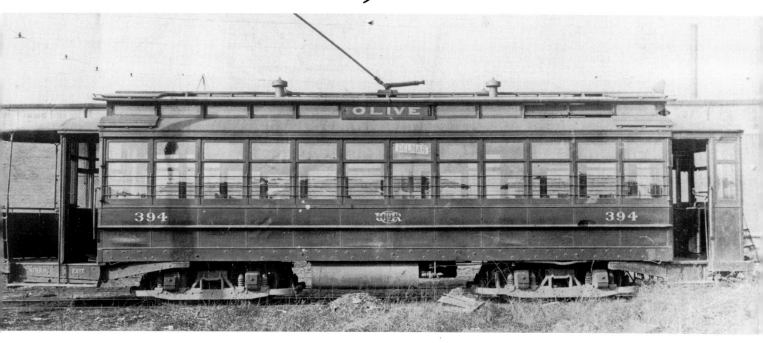

The traditional city trolley, St. Louis United Railways 394 (Laclede car, 1902). There were a hundred cars of this type. Hundreds more were similar. Seen here circa 1908 in shabby condition, some concessions to heavy service are visible, including Pay-As-You-Enter facilities and the doorless double-entrance extended "Detroit" platform at the rear (left), divided into a separate entrance and exit. The entrance is wide enough for a double stream of passengers who pay the seated conductor as they enter the car. They exit the same way they came in, or at the front through the narrow door by the motorman. The rear platform was closed off with doors after St. Louis passed an ordinance to compel such a conversion circa 1914. The cars themselves mostly lasted until the mid-1920's, although a sizeable group survived until the mid-1930s.

By the late 1890s, even with all the extra hang-ons dictated by electric propulsion, trolley design still owed much to the 1860s horse car with their wood bodies and underframes. Unfortunately, the weighty hang-ons quickly shook bodies to pieces. Platforms drooped, bodies sagged, roofs leaked or collapsed and structural members worked loose. Electric cars for heavy-duty city or interurban service sson sported larger bodies, wider doorways, reinforced wood underframes, eight rather than four wheels, all-steel underframes, then steel underframes and car-body bottoms (the "semi-steel" car). Increased weight and power consumption was the result. For a passenger, this was not all bad; heavy cars rode better and gave greater protection in a wreck—if one could avoid being stabbed by flying splinters or glass shards.

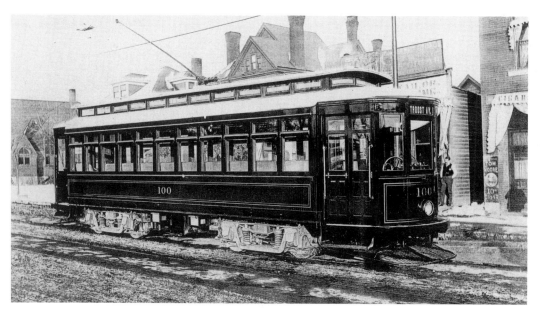

The traditional city trolley, Kansas City MET 100 of 1902 is a sturdy city car designed to handle the same type of heavy urban traffic as the St. Louis vehicle, and with a similar thirty to forty year service life. Here the double-doorway extended platform is at the front, with an extra exit door at the rear. Car 100 (seen on Troost soon after delivery from St. Louis Car on December 17th, 1902), was the first of 120 and unlike its St. Louis counterparts, was always totally enclosed.

The traditional wooden interurban, Illinois Traction 225 of 1905. Cars for this type of service were elegant and stylish, redolent of modernity, speed and cleanliness but with a weight of up to 80,000lbs, steep steps and narrow entrances were unsuited to Missouri's typical rural farm-to-market lines. Instead, these were intercity flyers. The vehicle is seen at American Car, St. Louis on August 10th, 1905 just prior to delivery

The latter exited either the way they came in or out the front door. Previously, the conductor had to roam the car after passengers sat down, with all the attendant delays and missed fares. On lighter lines, the motorman took the fares, eliminating second-man costs.

From 1905 there was a fad for further smoothing the ride by adding a thin layer of concrete to the floor, a technique used for years in subway and railroad passenger cars. A superb-riding vehicle resulted, but hauling that dead weight around cost big bucks. Existing tracks broke up under the pounding of these 70,000lbs (and more) monsters while their prodigious appetite (some interurbans had four 100 HP motors) strained generation and distribution facilities.

An early car's strength was in its underframe, making it essentially a heavy flat car with a wooden body "floating" on top having no structural or load-bearing function. Early all-steel car designs were similar, but their "fire-proof" qualities and strength made their passengers less vulnerable to injury. But substituting steel body parts for wood on a one-for-one basis was unnecessary and more innovative designs took advantage of steel's ability to increase body strength and decrease weight, using

Missed fare were a serious problem, addressed by the 1905 Pay-as-you-enter car. A large rear platform and circulating area allowed passengers to board quickly through doors separating entering and exiting streams. The former made their way past the seated conductor, to whom they paid their fare before moving on.

Illinois Traction 300 (St. Louis Car, 1907) survived only to 1936, many of those years spent more than 220 miles away from St. Louis on the lightly-traveled 16-mile Danville-Ridge Farm branch, which closed in 1933. Bill Janssen.

On a warm day around 1913, a closed car of the 101-102 group tows open trailer 111 through downtown Springfield. To modern eyes, the closed and open trolleys look as traditional as any other from that era, but the autos look ancient. To 1913 eyes, the autos would have looked modern and it would have been the trolleys that looked ancient, obstructing the progress of more efficient vehicles through public streets.

Center-entrance door city cars were fashionable for a brief period between 1910 and 1914 but otherwise this 1912 car for San Diego is a very late wood-bodied car with (uncommon by then) a wooden underframe; a classic example of specialized carpentry. Body posts are heavy and a sturdy car for city service will be the result.

standardized shapes that could be rolled or pressed in a steel mill rather than custom-made for the job in hand.

Steel side-girder body construction, where the body from underframe to roof was a single load-carrying structure, came after 1910. Such cars were cheaper to build, operate and maintain. The steel body side was one piece and continuous "T" shape steel side posts and carlines formed the roof framing. This made for a strong, lightweight body and roof as compared to the glued-and-screwed wooden structural members and panels of horse and early electric car days. Out of this came the lightweight one-man single-truck car for light lines. Petite motors (but not in horse-power), smaller wheels, and a lower floor made such cars easier to enter and exit and cheaper to run than the concrete-floor behemoths of a decade earlier.

Many one-man lightweight types incorporated some or all of these innovations. Some were ultralight (often 14,000lbs or less), others just city car "lite" in appearance and operation.

From 1912, Sedalia's trolleys were part of of Henry Doherty's <u>Cities Service Company</u>, a utilities chain which used the latest management and operating techniques and could afford to buy the new equipment needed to take advantage of them. Sedalia experimented with universal one-man operation of existing cars from November 1915 and early in 1916 ordered eight new lightweight one-man single-truck cars. Delivered in the summer, they were assigned to base service, being supplemented by the best older cars. They did the job and unlike other Missouri towns, Sedalia was in good enough shape to weather the next few turbulent years. These cars just preceded the merger of one-man operation, safety

If They Could Talk.

I AM A STREET CAR, steel jacketed,
ELECTRIC LIGHTED, sanitary,
SWIFT, SAFE. I am the
COMMON CARRIER that
MASTER BUILDERS have made to
DEFY THE ELEMENTS, to carry
TEEMING THOUSANDS to
WORK AND PLAY, to build
CITIES by bridging the miles
BETWEEN METROPOLIS and suburb for
LESS THAN A NICKEL. Traveling
HIGHWAYS OF STEEL, I laugh at
THE BLIZZARD, pierce the
DRIVING RAIN, on the job
EARLY AS THE MILKMAN, late as
THE NIGHT EDITOR homeward bound.
I AM PART of
THE CITY ITSELF,
PAYING my full share of the
PUBLIC TAX and
THEN SOME. I have only
ONE PRICE—good for
TWO MILES OR TWELVE, and good
RAIN OR SHINE, day or night,
ALWAYS.

I AM A JITNEY bus, yep,
A SASSY four-passenger
JIT that jits along the
ASPHALT JITWAY and nowhere else.
WHEN IT SNOWS I hibernate
AND WHEN it rains and
WHEN IT HAILS, and when
THE NORTH WIND blows,
I HIKE IT
BACK TO THE GARAGE, for—
DENT THIS on your
BIOGRAPH FILM—I believe in
WORKING only when
BUSINESS IS GOOD. When it's
BAD I let the street car work.
OH, I'M A CANNY lad
I CALL myself
THE POOR MAN'S TAXI and the
BOOBS BELIEVE. I don't
PAY A SOU to keep up the
STREETS, and I charge a nickel
FOR TWO MILES and more
IF I CAN, and I never
LEAVE THE ASPHALT, never—
I SHOULD WORRY!

In the 1914, the "jitney" automobile became a fact of life, lightly skewered by this unattributed piece in the Kansas City Railwayan (May 1916 p. 3). It clearly struck a nerve because it was reprinted, again without attribution by St. Louis's United Railways Bulletin on June 15th, 1916.

STREET CARS
and
AUTOMOBILES

The new street cars are going into service as fast as we can make the necessary adjustments and break in our men to the new equipment. These new SAFETY CARS are the very latest in every manner, shape and form. They embody all the approved appliances for operation and for safety. The brakes and the doors operate with compressed air and the EMERGENCY AIR VALVE on the controller stops the car automatically if for any reason the operator removes his hand from the control lever.

THE TRACK IS SANDED—THE BRAKES ARE SET—THE CURRENT IS SHUT OFF.

The new high-speed motors allow a quick get-away and a rapid accelleration for these cars, much faster than the old cars and we will be able to make better time and more regular service. You can help in this by BUYING TOKENS and having your fare ready when you get on the car.

THE AUTOMOBILISTS ARE REQUESTED

to take the above into consideration and to remember that the street cars can not get out of their way and that it is to the mutual advantage of all concerned that they endeavor to

GIVE THE STREET CARS THE RIGHT OF WAY

The new equipment is a credit to Cape Girardeau and with the proper co-operation from everyone the street cars can be maintained and operated regularly and continuously.

Cape Girardeau-Jackson
Interurban Ry. Co.

E. A. HART, Manager.

Cape Girardeau was especially anxious its new Birney "Safety" cars would work as intended and placed this ad in the local <u>Southeast Missourian</u> (p. 2) on December 29th, 1921.

features, body design and styling into a new Stone and Webster car design.

Today this company is today light-years away from its activities of ninety years ago, when in addition to engineering hydro-electric and other power projects, it was involved in over two dozen street railways as owner, manager or operator. By 1916, they had perfected a small and relatively standardized car. Designed by and named for their master mechanic Charles O. Birney, it was intended to cut costs to the bone in a vehicle using the very latest of equipment. The Birney package included a body of shaped steel pressings based on T-iron side posts, body-side girders, carlines and arch roof, plus a lower floor, smaller wheels, light-weight motors and a front entrance/exit under the motorman's control. Weight was cut by 50%. The two-motor single-truck reduced power costs.

From 1912 developments in metal body design took manufacturers into new territory, where strength, lightness and economy were paramount. This is a St. Louis Car demonstrator, sectioned for exhibition at a trade convention and later sold to a Dayton OH company for light city use. It was built at the same time as the San Diego car pictured above. It is the length of a full-size city car, but has a two-motor single truck rather than a two or four-motor double truck. The lightweight body is of the new steel T-post design, one of the developmental foundations of 1916's lightweight Birney "Safety" car. The interior fittings too have been lightened, as witness the hard polished-wood seats.

The Birney "Safety" car, designed for light small-town and rural service, could also cope with light city service. St. Louis 508 is at the Chippewa and Grand junction, already well filled with riders, on April 26th, 1931. The White Rose gas station on the right is selling regular for 25 cents. The poster on the car dash (left) exhorts riders to "Stop fretting about wet streets (and) go by Street Car." The poster on the car dash (right) advertises an imminent talk on radio station KWK entitled "Up from the Horse car." (R. V. Mehlenbeck/Mark Goldfeder collection.)

Birney car interiors were basic but reasonably airy. This is one of the first, a 1916 order for Monroe LA. In the south, but not in Missouri, Jim Crow laws applied to trolleys, even vehicles as small as these. The top rail of each seat has two metal fittings to which can be clipped the segregation signs, visible left and right on the third seats back from the motorman's position.

The "Safety" features were based on a newly-developed combined brake control valve and lightweight controller, with a spring-loaded "deadman" handle the motorman pushed down to run the car. If he fell unconscious or dropped dead, it sprang up from the operating position to shut off power, dump sand on the rail, apply the air brake for an emergency stop, release doors and lower the steps automatically. In normal service, the controller was interlocked with the safety mechanism so the car couldn't move until the door was closed and the steps raised. This virtually eliminated accidents to riders getting on or off. In an age which had just coined the slogan "Safety First," that was a very big deal.

The safety features were associated with the name of J. M. Bosenbury, superintendent of motive power and equipment for Illinois Traction. In conjunction with the Westinghouse Company, he had perfected them in 1913 for lightweight, one-man cars serving isolated IT properties such as Quincy IL, Topeka and Wichita KS where ridership was in tailspin.

"The lightweight safety car ...has been developed not so much as the result of genius foresight as from plain necessity. One of the more startling necessities for the new type car is brought out in the statement of Mr. Bosenbury that it has been estimated... 50% of the available passengers in medium-sized town are now riding in automobiles." (ERJ September 22nd 1917 p. 523).

The IT, Stone and Webster and Doherty's Cities Services all served small

Complete metal skeleton of a 1919 St. Louis Car Birney car for Milwaukee, representative of the 6,000 or so built between 1916 and 1926.

A portion of the steel erecting shop at American Car in St. Louis on September 17th, 1920, showing fabrication of formed steel shapes and pressings, visible in the foreground, into complete Birney car bodies, some of which are seen in the background.

Weaving rattan for car seats at American Car, September 17th, 1920.

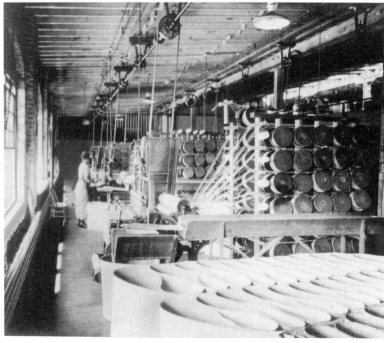

towns suffering the same decline, including Jefferson City, St. Joseph and Springfield. These were places where the Birney "Safety" car was expected to work best. Many more cars were built or remodeled with some (not all) of these features: St. Louis, Kansas City and St. Joseph recycled scores of older, heavier wood-bodied vehicles as one-man "safety" cars with all the proper gear but that didn't make them Birneys. Equally, Sedalia's 1916 lightweights had the body (slightly longer) but not the safety devices so they too were not Birneys. But any car with one or more of these features was using technology well advanced over that of a decade earlier, bringing reductions in operating costs that fully justified their purchase.

IT pioneered, Stone and Webster led, and the rest followed. The lightweight one-man "Safety" car, or Birney, became a transit craze and over 6,000 were produced up to 1925. Other Missouri trolley systems were as anxious as Sedalia to stave off catastrophe and for a while the Birney had great appeal. They were small but initially it was believed a fleet of these agile new cars running on faster schedules would make increased service possible. Cost reduction from one-man operation would pay for the extra runs. There was even an attempt by the industry press to dub them "Quick Service" cars, the theory being that with (hopefully) always a car in sight, people would be tempted away from jitneys and autos. The increased revenue would return profitability to the owning company, the safety features would reduce accidents and insurance claims and the light weight standard components would make the car cheap to buy, run and fix.

Well, that was the theory. Practice was something else. Often,

even Birneys were unprofitable in this inflationary era when transit lived and died by the farebox. Nevertheless, transit consultants and pundits continued to muddy the waters by promising savings and service levels the car could not possibly deliver, especially on heavy urban routes for which it was never intended. Still, initial reports of Birney performance on such routes were upbeat. When Birneys took over St. Joseph's Messanie Street line in November 1918, costs declined and gross receipts increased, as they did in

A Westinghouse advertisement of 1919 featuring Kansas City Birney 1514, coping with passengers at a downtown car stop.

My Auto 'Tis of Thee

My auto 'tis of thee,
Short cut to poverty,
　Of thee I chant.
I blew a pile of dough,
On you two years ago;
And now you refuse to go,
　Or won't, or can't.

　　Through town and countryside,
　　You were my joy and pride,
　　　A happy day.
　　I loved thy gaudy hue,
　　The nice white tires so new,
　　But now you're down and through,
　　　In every way.

　　To thee, old rattlebox,
　　Came many bumps and knocks,
　　　For thee I grieve.
　　Badly thy top is torn,
　　Frayed are thy seats and worn,
　　A Whooping cough affects thy horn,
　　　I do believe.

Thy perfume swells the breeze,
While good folk choke and sneeze,
　As we pass by.
I paid for thee a price,
Would buy a mansion twice,
Now all are yelling "ice,"
　I wonder why.

　　Thy motor has the grip,
　　Thy spark-plug has the pip,
　　　And woe is thine.
　　I, too, have suffered chills,
　　Ague and kindred ills,
　　Endeavoring to pay my bills,
　　　Since thou wert mine.

　　Gone is my bank roll now,
　　No more would choke a cow,
　　　As once before,
　　Yet if I had the mon'
　　So help me John, amen,
　　I'd buy a car again,
　　　And speed some more.
　　　　　　　—Walter Ashton.

After 1912 when automobiles became more affordable, people bought them in ever-increasing numbers. Most lasted a lot longer and gave less trouble than that of the poor sap of this parody, reprinted in the <u>UR Bulletin</u> July 15th, 1916 (p. 2).

The interior of cars so converted was not as fresh as the Birney and the spindle-backed hard wooden seats were not user-friendly. This is St. Joseph 163 adorned with a bunch of notices ranging from "Safety is Wisdom," in the front window, to "Do not expectorate on the floor of this car." Among the car cards advertising Lux soap, Crisco shortening, Heinz cooked macaroni, Uneeda biscuit's social tea biscuits and Jersey Ice Cream (rich in the flavor of big, ripe berries), is one for a "Star" tourer automobile, priced at $348 with easy monthly payments.

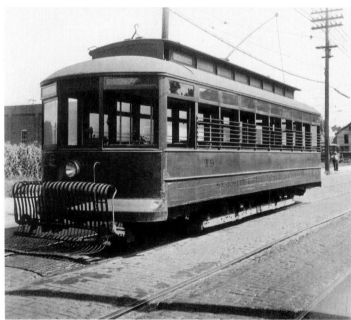

Kansas City when Birneys took over the Sunset Hill line in April 1919. But KC passengers cannot have been happy when management discovered *"the cars will carry with a fair degree of comfort a load of 60, 35 seated and 25 standing,"* (ERJ June 14th, 1919, 1171). Nor would they have been happy about the wooden seats; they were upholstered in older cars, as they were in KC's next Birneys. Performance and profitablity soon declined.

Cape Girardeau had made noises about new cars for some time, ERJ July 10th, 1920 (p. 105) noting it as in the market for four or five. But buying new cars went against all trends as they applied

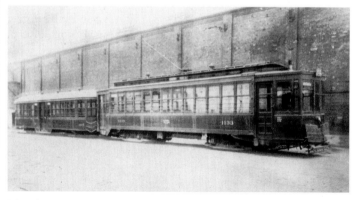

The "safety" equipped one-man car concept was attractive, even to those unprepared to spend money on new cars. The entire package other than for the lightweight car body, could be retrofitted to depreciated but otherwise serviceable old cars; the extra power cost over the Birney was offset by the money saved in not having to buy a complete new car. Missouri cities large and small upgraded older vehicles in this way to get several more years productive service from them. This is St. Joseph 19, circa 1918.

Big city responses to heavy traffic before and immediately after World War One, included the running of trains, generally a beefed-up motored car hauling a lightweight trailer. This was done in Kansas City and in St. Louis, where UR car 1133 of 1911 poses for an official picture with trailer 195 of 1914.

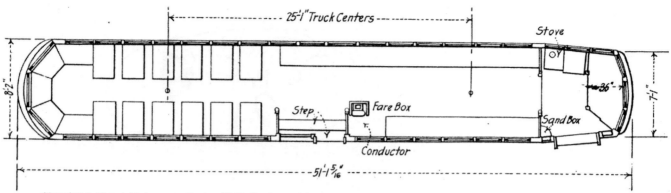

Cleveland Front-Entrance, Center-Exit Design with Prepayment Space Extending Over Forward Half of Body

A later response was to combine lightweight construction, and the Birney's safety equipment with a large body and improved interior layout, allowing a stream of passengers to flow naturally down the car from the front entrance and a second stream to exit at the center. Fares were collected by the seated conductor as each passenger passed. This was the basis of the "Peter Witt" design, first seen in Cleveland during 1914/15, of which this is a plan. Dimensions and details varied, but all "Witt" cars were of this basic front-entrance center-exit layout. Over 5400 were built for North American service alone; Toronto, Cleveland, Detroit, and St. Louis each running many hundreds. The "pre-payment" circulating space with longitudinal bench seats takes over almost all the front half in the classic version but less than half in later versions. When "Witts" were converted to one-man operation, the space generally was left unaltered, though later "Witt" designs, such as the PCC (easily adaptable to 1 or 2-person operation), often substituted one and two-person cross seats for the benches.

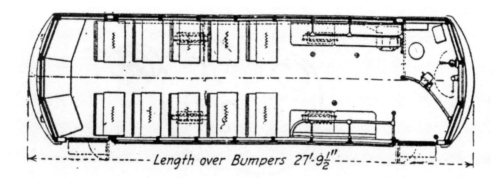

Compare this with the floor plan of a 1919 Kansas City Birney "Safety" car, modified from the original Birney standard by substitution of Witt-style longitudinal bench seats in the front, a larger entrance/exit door and the possibility of adding another at the rear. Kansas City was able to make use of these cars in a variety of light city services because of these modifications and several operated well after World War Two.

St. Louis developed its home-grown "Witt" design in 1921. Car 757, seen here southbound at Broadway and Chouteau in the late 1930s, is a typical "Witt" car, with wide entrance and exit doors, a roomy circulating area in the front half and either two-man or one-man operation.

However, unrestricted downtown parking, narrow streets and other street traffic could make nonsense out of any theories about efficient loading and punctual service. St. Louis "Witt" 703 has just crossed 7th Street as it moves west on Pine on December 31st, 1933.

to such small traction systems. Indeed, the company's attorney, at an October 18th, 1921 Chamber of Commerce meeting had said stockholders were ready to abandon ship unless the city or influential city groups could persuade them to change their minds. He'd suggested the Chamber of Commerce circulate petitions for a fare raise so the cars could continue. Unlike the long drawn-out efforts to increase fares and effect ordinance changes elsewhere, the Chamber within two days did exactly that, presenting a 1,544-signature petition to the city. On the 21st an ordinance allowing a 7-cent fare or a 4-ride token for a quarter was passed so fast that more than eighty years afterwards a strong smell of greased rails (or palms) still clings to it.

Three new Birney cars arrived less than two months later. When the first ran on December 25th, the Southeast Missourian (December 27th 1921 p.1.) reported *"more people rode this one car than have gone on the others in a month."* It wasn't just one-man operation which held out promise of rejuvenation, it was the Birney's pep and low costs that promised profitability. *"For a good many years, Cape Girardeau has boasted a streetcar system but constantly decreased earnings caused the property to get in such bad shape that finally a showdown came. It was a case of 'put up or shut up.' Believing Cape Girardeau would show the proper attitude to... the service if modernized, the money was put up and now it's up to Cape Girardians to buy tokens-and buying them they are."* (<u>Southeast Missourian</u> December 31st, 1921 p. 10).

The "Witt" approach was seen in St. Louis as better than the older car-plus-trailer train and thought was given to putting motors in existing trailers and converting them to "Witt" design, trailer 436 being done in 1928 and seen here at 39th and Park circa 1938. However it was a costly exercise and the Depression, ridership decline and subsequent bankruptcy of the St. Louis Public Service Company meant that even had the money been available, there was little need for further conversions.

This was also true of the otherwise successful 1928 quartet of front entrance-rear exit lightweight cars, as represented here by car 522 at 39th and Park circa 1938. St. Louis instead converted older cars to this standard rather than buy new, unlike Kansas City which bought scores of new cars to this design from 1914 to the Depression.

Hart had worked hard to get the needed $50,000 yet his earnings target was modest. He reckoned if the cars earned $60.00 a day, expenses would be covered. For a while, they did. Moreover, Light and Development not only paid for new cars, but renewed the entire infrastructure to give them the best possible conditions to strut their stuff. What they couldn't do was to supply riders and this was Hart's main worry. "*Unless the people ride on the cars and boost for them, I will soon be up against it because I made it strong to the owners that the people of Cape Girardeau wanted the cars...and would not be stingy in patronizing them.*" (Southeast Missourian December 17th, 1921 p. 1).

Cape Girardeau was the smallest Missouri town to buy new cars rather than let them fade away. It was not then realized how quickly even these promising rejuvenations would lapse into fiscal basket cases and for a few years it seemed new lightweight cars could stabilize small-town passenger operation. Hart was moved to recount his experience at a Missouri Association of Public Utilities convention in May 1923. He spoke of his troubles maintaining service until refinancing, the 7-cent fare,

Many Kansas City Pay-As-You-Enter cars were remodeled and updated in the late 1920s, like car 1133 of 1916. Their external appearance was smoothed out for a sleeker appearance, while a new paint job and modernized interior made them infinitely more inviting.

Kansas City 1118 of the same batch was featured in this 1928 General Electric advertisement, together with some of the new safety equipment (including a "dead-man" controller handle) with which they were fitted. This large car with its wider doors is coping better than the Birney featured in the earlier 1919 Westinghouse advertisement.

new cars, track and overhead had brightened his horizons. He believed car service was vital for continued economic development of small towns but that unprofitable service could not be provided indefinitely without becoming a detriment to the entire community (ERJ June 6th, 1923 p. 1015).

He was right. Some Missouri systems were now so unprofitable they couldn't afford or even justify new cars, never mind new track or overhead wires. Jefferson City was one. Instead, existing track and overhead were patched up and three used Birneys arrived. That appeased Mayor Thomas, pushing for new bus routes in lieu of trolley extensions that weren't going to be made, until he discovered the cars were hand-me-downs from Galesburg IL.

"Mayor Thomas today inspected the alleged 'new' street-cars...(He) was frankly and visibly disgusted... 'What do you think this is, a second-hand town?...Will the company never send us anything new? Must we always take what some other city has cast off?'...Mayor Thomas is out of patience with...Missouri Power and Light...Officials gave out... glowing accounts about the new cars and the progress of the city and all that sort of thing, and the arrival of cars no larger and only slightly modern, was a disappointment ...They...are now...being repainted so that they will at least look new. Employees ...told a reporter...this afternoon that the cars, while probably (sic) not new, were the very latest model...They have the air control and all safety appliances (and) were fortified with springs, which will guarantee easier riding...Comment on the street...was for the most part sarcastic, while others said that probably the 'new' cars, always with the emphasis on the 'new,' might help some." (Jefferson City Tribune May 20th, 1925 p 1.)

Springfield was another town that patched up its street railway and bought Birneys. They ran from 1918 to 1937; a decent span. Indeed, a few more pre-owned examples were added in 1930. But Carrollton and Nevada gave up on trolleys in the early 1920s. Hannibal got its new Birneys very late in the day, on a 1925 lease-to-own deal. They could not save the system and were repossessed by St. Louis Car the day after closure in October 1930.

(Left) Another response to all but the heaviest of city traffic was to look at motor buses, which could help bring service to new areas without the expense of laying track and stringing overhead wire. From the early 1920s buses were tried in cities of all sizes, pioneering new routes and replacing unprofitable trolley lines in poor repair. This is Springfield 11, a Ford model "T" seen in Public Square during 1921. STLMOT

(Below) Larger cities needed larger buses. This Safeway bus is for Kansas City and is seen at St. Louis Car in 1925 just before delivery.

(Left) But neither car nor bus could stem the tidal wave of automobiles. An unidentified Springfield Birney runs a gauntlet of parked autos as it heads east on Jefferson towards the camera on July 10th, 1924. History Museum for Springfield-Greene County.

(Below) Several thousand double-truck Birney "Safety" cars were built between 1922 and 1930, similar in body layout to front-entrance rear-exit city cars. Almost all were constructed by St. Louis's two surviving car builders, but only a handful were sold to Missouri operators. They used them for interurban service. Missouri and Kansas car 115 is seen circa 1937 in Overland Park KS.

Bigger systems such as Joplin, St. Joseph and St. Louis, bought Birneys for one or two basket-case lines. They were agile with a few passengers aboard, but in crowded, "always-a-car-in-sight" conditions they were underpowered and slow, throwing entire schedules out of kilter. Horror stories leaked out from Boston and Brooklyn who bought large Birney fleets but found within days of their entering service that they couldn't cope. A change from private to municipal ownership in Detroit saw 250 new Birneys enter service in 1922. By 1924, 200 had been sold.

Ironically, the most effective big city car layout, still used with little modification on most city buses to this day, had already been developed when the first Birneys were designed. The "Peter Witt" car, conceived in Cleveland OH during 1914 at the behest of the local street railway commissioner for whom it was named, was a high-capacity, single-end, front-entrance, center exit, pay-as-you-pass, two-man car. Longitudinal seats in front gave a roomy circu-

(Above left) Southwest Missouri built six lightweight interurbans in 1927 that were noticeably sturdier than double-truck Birneys and in the modern idiom already seen in St. Louis, East St. Louis and elsewhere. They were regarded by the Southwest as city cars though they ran the full length of the line. Car 92 is seen just east of the Picher OK station early in 1938, when only two passenger cars still ran. Earl E. McMechan.

(Above right) As with all modern cars of the time, the light and airy interior of Southwest's 1927 lightweights had great eye-appeal, and the comfortable leather-upholstered seats were particularly inviting. Earl E. McMechan.

In the mid-1920s, new city cars came better styled and packaged, an understated campaign to provide cars Joe and Josephine Public would be eager to ride. 351 is one of five East St. Louis front-entrance rear-exit lightweight "Rail Sedans," (St. Louis Car, 1927) seen soon after delivery. It wears its striking paint job well, whereas the older but similarly-garbed car 300 (behind) looks merely garish.

lation area as riders sat down or passed through to cross-seats further back. They paid as they left, stepping on a floor-mounted treadle switch that opened the center doors once the car stopped.

The "Witt" car could lift huge crowds off the street quickly, its layout allowed good internal flow without the car being delayed and delivered a ride far superior to the bouncy, single-truck Birney. Large cities quickly ceased their dalliance with the tiny car and gave their hearts almost unreservedly to the big "Witt." Yet though at first sight its antithesis in weight and operating costs, "Witts" owed much to the Birney in shedding pounds (often tens of thousands of pounds), often using similar lightweight motors, small wheels, safety equipment and body construction. But "Witts" could move big-city crowds quickly, efficiently and economically. The Birney, created to solve small-town problems, couldn't.

In 1922, a larger, double-truck Birney was introduced by American and St. Louis Car and several medium-sized cities (then) such as Phoenix AZ, Miami, St. Petersburg and Tampa FL either re-equipped with it or supplemented existing single-truck Birneys, gaining all the advantages of the older car plus a smoother ride and extra capacity. It sold well and had a long life. Many systems with the larger Birney survived to the late 1940s and beyond. But of all the thousands built in St. Louis, none were used in Missouri city service. Only a couple ran in North Kansas City. The Southwest, Kansas City, Leavenworth and Western and Missouri and Kansas each bought a few of the interurban version between 1925 and 1927. IT later put some on its St. Louis suburban lines.

With "Witts" and Birneys, St. Louis and Kansas City experience

The "Rail Sedan" interior was very much in the modern idiom and several steps up from the Birney in comfort and appearance. This is a 1927 St. Louis Car publicity photo of East St. Louis 350's interior. Hand-crafted advertising cards extol the virtues of the new "Rail Sedan" type.

differed. KC had no "Witts" but many Birneys. UR had few Birneys and (eventually) mostly "Witts" or their streamlined successor. Receiver Rolla Wells, originally a horse-car driver in the 1860s on his father Erastus's Market Street Railway, felt Birneys were of limited use, but he'd test a few. UR Master Mechanic Michael O'Brien felt they would work only on lines with more

From 1927 development of new car designs stagnated. So did sales. The point was made at the American Electric Railway Association' 1928 convention, where a replica battered "Toonerville" trolley (plus the "Skipper") was exhibited to contrast worn-out old cars and the latest modern vehicles. The label reads "This is the original Toonerville Trolley car used by the Betzwood Film Company of Betzwood PA when making moving pictures founded upon the famous Fontaine Fox cartoons." STLMOT.

passenger car with beefed-up motors, gears and towing equipment pulled a lightweight trailer, and 188 trailers went into service between 1913 and 1921. They lasted until the Depression's ridership decline and all but 15 were gone by the late 1930s. Four trailers were motored in the 1920s, two being converted to "Peter Witt" layout, bringing the number of St. Louis "Witt" cars to 254. After 1929, "Witts" were gradually one-manned until only rush-hour or extra-heavy lines had two-man cars. Wages were increased for this extra responsibility. One-man "Witt" cars had a foot-operated air-brake to ease the motorman's labor. Older cars were one-manned later, often retrofitted with the same foot-operated air-brake.

Between 1940 and 1946, 300 one-man streamlined President's Conference Committee (a 1929/30 industry body that commissioned a research study of the ideal city car, then set about building it) cars came to St. Louis to run with the "Witts." The lightweight car sported every "Witt" and Birney safety feature in updated form including the "Witt" internal passenger-flow, though PCC acceleration was boosted to match a 1934 Ford V-8. From the late 1930s most buses for heavy-duty city service came with the same "Witt" body layout and one-man operation.

Kansas City had a large fleet of old cars, some going back to the mid-1890s. Modern cars were

than 3 1/2 minute intervals between cars. UR Manager A. T. Perkins thought they might do on light routes and county lines but heavy lines needed two-man "Witt" cars *as light as the weight of travel will permit."* (UR Bulletin, November 1919 p. 4).

UR's shops were as versatile as those of American or St. Louis Car in dreaming up and building new designs and their first home-built "Witt" was ready in 1920. At the same time, 10 Birneys were ordered from American Car (the first UR order to an outside builder since 1903), They were put on light suburban shuttles from December 1920. One motorman assigned a Birney was Paul Vasquez, who began as a 13-year old horsecar driver in the Civil War. His last one-man car had been a bob-tail in the 1870s. After successful trials, UR's shops built 100 "Witts" from early 1921, but bought no more Birneys, instead adding safety equipment to remodeled, lightened, depreciated double-truck cars with the reserve seating capacity and good ride qualities needed for long suburban lines, without using capital to buy new cars. UR built four lightweight, double-truck one-man front-entrance, rear-exit cars in 1928 to replace four old cars wrecked by a May 1927 tornado. They were ideal (as double-truck Birneys would have been) and served the long county lines with older rebuilt cars for years. But with the Depression, no more were built and routes assigned to Birneys had gone by 1933.

On the heaviest lines, two-car three-man trains were used long before "Witts" came to St. Louis. A regular

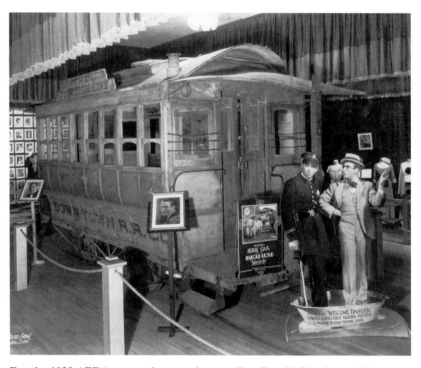

For the 1929 AERA convention, movie comedian Harold Lloyd sent this worn-out horse car (origin unknown) to again make the point. Hundreds of rural and small-town lines, out of money and resources, ended their days with cars (often horse-cars used as trailers for equally battered electric cars) in this condition, long before 1929. This car was featured in Lloyd's last silent movie "Speedy" of 1928, produced by Harold Lloyd Corporation which occasionally shows up on television classic movie channels. The car's subsequent fate is not known.

A fleet of modern new buses often got as rousing an inauguration as did electric trolleys thirty years before. Here is a group of Twin Coach TC 40s lined up outside St. Louis City Hall for inspection in December 1931, before going into service on the new 105 Gravois bus line, which supplemented the 20 Cherokee car line between downtown and Grand before heading off into new territory in southwest city. A banner on bus 515 declares them to be the last word in comfortable transportation, with safety glass, power brakes, leather seats and steel bodies.

badly needed and 148 high-capacity lightweight one-man city cars came between 1914 and 1917. Their rear-entrance front-exit door layout was similar to double-truck Birneys or St. Louis's four 1928 cars, and the fact this was fine for heavy service without going for larger "Witt" types, reflects KC's lower population density compared to St. Louis. They were supplemented in 1919-20 by 95 Birneys, most with design changes to better tailor the car for light city service. Equipment was tweaked to improve performance, an internal well step gave a less-steep entry, structural members, bolster and under frame were strengthened, grab rails and roof headlining added, two passenger streams were created by increasing front door width and changing cross-seats near the motorman for longitudinal seats, and rear doors were fitted. The austere interior was softened, rattan replaced polished-wood seats and they were given some insulation for winter use.

KC's Birneys were long-lived, unlike those in other big cities, most of which had already gone by the early 1930s. Initially, they were used on several unsuitable lines, including Country Club. In December 1920 there was a horrendous accident when a northbound Birney's brakes failed at 30th and Main and the car ran away, jumping the tracks at 27th Street and hitting a southbound car. Eight were killed and the Birneys were immediately reassigned to short, lightly-loaded lines without long grades, which they served for decades. Some were not replaced until 1949.

A further 20 one-man city cars came in 1922, multiple-unit double-truck cars which ran as two-car trains in

rush-hour on the heaviest lines. The second unit was a tripper and once the rush was over, it would go to the barns while the first car continued alone in base service. Many earlier cars were fitted with multiple-unit equipment, but like St. Louis, train operation in KC lasted only until the Depression. Still, KC had hundreds of pre-1914 cars lacking features that by the mid-1920s were seen as essential. With the advent of Kansas City Public Service Company in 1926, a huge remodeling program systematically updated at least half the fleet, including many pre-1914 cars, by adding "Safety" car equipment, improving front and rear doors by powering them from the air circuits, modernizing interiors, seats and lighting and rear-door exit treadle. Once the company went multimodal in the late 1930s, its new trolley buses and 186 PCC cars, bought between 1941 and 1946, were of the modified one-man "Witt" design, with a front entrance and center exit.

Big city buses were adopting the "Witt" streetcar layout of front entrance and center exit with either one or two man operation, like these Yellow Coach Type 40s and their smart, jackbooted drivers, seen on September 9th, 1932 just before replacing cars on St. Louis's Natural Bridge line. STLMOT.

At the 1929 AERA convention, delegates took the point made by Harold Lloyd's battered old horsecar and a committee of over two dozen street railway and manufacturer presidents (Presidents' Conference Committee) was set up to fund a research program that would stimulate development of the ideal streetcar. Their million-dollar baby was born after six years of research, a dazzlingly glamorous streamlined trolley, decades ahead of it older brethren in appearance, performance and technological advances. This PCC model was built by St. Louis Public Service Company and exhibited in a downtown Famous-Barr department store window in May 1940, a month prior to PCC cars coming into St. Louis service.

Car 1500, the first of 300 PCCs for St. Louis, at the head of a June 16th, 1940 inaugural parade of the new cars on 12th at Washington.

THE END OF THE AFFAIR: THE RAILS COME UP, THE WIRES COME DOWN

It doesn't take 20/20 hindsight to appreciate that Missouri's rural trolleys were viable only between 1890 when the electric car was perfected and 1910 when reliable and just-about-affordable automobiles arrived. It was obvious at the time. With rural trolleys (and indeed railroad branch lines) being built as substitutes for good roads, once such roads materialized for autos and motor trucks to run on, rural lines vanished with the morning mists. The consequences of a line's failure to the communities served were of no concern. No one stepped forward to help, no state or federal assistance was provided. Nor was it asked for. It was the end of the affair.

Highways had been a growth industry from 1910, a time when many rural trolleys were already in bankruptcy. By 1918, Federal officials were at a loss, overwhelmed by the

The Vandeventer car line, while not the first to be closed in St. Louis, was the first to be replaced by motor buses. Southbound Type 40 Yellow coach 603 of 1932 is crossing Lindell in September 1932.

blizzard of reports chronicling the industry's distress. Most frightening of all and utterly unforseen before 1910 was the terrifying prospect that almost all the nations's big city systems might go under as well, victims not just of jitneys and highways but of rocketing wartime inflation, loss of manpower, material shortages and increased demands for service at a time when the nickel fare remained enshrined in most franchises with no prospect of speedy change. Kansas City and St. Louis were among that number.

September 1917 was a time when the mind of David Francis, our man in St. Petersburg (U.S. Ambassador to Russia), was firmly focused on his mission. The Tsar and the Romanov dynasty had gone, Russia was collapsing at home and on the front lines, while the Bolshevik revolution in which he would play a heroic role defending our

In Kansas City, the Quindaro and Independence trolley lines were the first to be replaced by buses, in 1934 and 1935. Some of the first buses for the Independence line in late March 1935, with a group of Kansas City Public Service top brass including manager Fred Buffe (far left) and Powell C. Groner (third from left).

interests, was only weeks away. Yet in the little time he had for personal concerns, this former Mayor of St. Louis, former Governor of the State of Missouri, erstwhile U.S. Secretary of the Interior, one of the "Big Cinch's" leading lights in 1899's St. Louis street railway consolidation, head honcho and chief sparkplug of the 1904 World's Fair, was worrying over the United Railways nose-dive, declaring in a letter home that *"UR has not only cost us a great deal, but...(its) securities have been a pall over the (entire) St. Louis financial market." (D. R. Francis to J. D. P. Francis, September 21st, 1917, Missouri Historical Society, Francis collection.(Quoted in "The Big Cinch," by A. S. McConachie).*

Two years later, an army truck convoy, to which D. D. Eisenhower was assigned as a junior officer, made a coast-to-coast move over the (unpaved) Lincoln Highway from mile marker zero at the ellipse in Washington D. C. to San Francisco. It took 62 days to cover the 3,300-mile route, time mostly spent fighting intolerable road surfaces. While PR spin touted the trip as a success, it was in fact a fiasco that got political attention in a hurry. Elected officials and voters instantly realized subsidy was a powerful tool that could rapidly bring change for the better on America's highways. The 1921 Federal

A group picture of Springfield motorman and maintenance staff, Birneys and buses, on the last day, August 28th, 1937. STLMOT.

Highway Act shifted the nation's focus away from public transit's chronic problems to the coming nirvana of private transport on good roads. National, state and county highway systems were drawn up and most roads identified as part of a system were paved, widened and realigned. The Lincoln Highway Association led the way, sponsoring mile-long "seed" stretches of paved road

Even at the end of their days, old trolleys were still good publicity tools. This Kansas City car of the 220-259 series, originally built for and operated on the St. Louis World's Fair Intramural Railroad of 1904, is encouraging Depression era folks to do their 1936 Christmas shopping downtown and use a streetcar or bus to get there.

From 1938, ridership in St. Louis and Kansas City began rising noticeably and by 1941 the overcrowding and generally unpleasant conditions of the 1880-1920 period had returned. St. Louis "Witt" 971 is already full, yet many more are trying to board from this downtown safety zone. A late-model Packard squeezes by. STLMOT.

incorporating the latest technology, including road lighting.

With this the dominant mood in the country, big city systems too now slid into bankruptcy. United Railways went under in 1919, while Kansas City Railways was kept going into 1920 only by direct loans from the Armour family. ERJ noted that in 1917 *"the conservative financial department of the SaturdayEvening Post"* recommended the 5% bonds of the company—then selling at 98—as the best utility investment then in the market. Last December (1919) a block of 160,000 of these same securities changed hands at 36¹/², a...shrinkage of $18 million. In the blackest days of the old Metropolitan...when it was already in the hands of a receiver and the vigorous Colonel Nelson...was pummeling it morning, noon and night, it never defaulted on its interest...From its net earnings and by the terms of its franchise, Kansas City Railways is entitled to earn 6% upon its capital value. This is not a guarantee. The company must earn the money. And...it has not earned it— not at least for nearly three years, while

During World War II, most trolley-to-bus conversions were put on hold while old cars destined for the scrap-heap were instead remodeled and put back into service to join their newer brethren for a few years of the most intensive service of their lives, including promotion of the war effort, in this case the sale of War Bonds. St. Louis Mayor Becker cuts the ribbon for the inaugural trip of War Bond PCC car 1521 early in 1942.

While rural Missouri no longer rode the trolley, big-city Missourians had yet to use the bus to any great extent. But with new, sturdy examples coming onto the market in the late 1920s, that time would not be long delayed. Symbolizing the face of things to come is People's Motor Bus 600, an almost-new 35-seat Yellow Coach model Z-BM-617, posed facing north in a median gap of St. Louis's Forest Park Avenue, about a block west of Grand Avenue, early in 1930.

General Manager Kealy on Kansas City.
"We are now in good shape physically to serve Kansas City for twenty years to come...By providing good transportation to...outlying districts, we have brought about a condition where 70% ...own their own homes; not the Philadelphia narrow-fronted type of house... but homes with lawns and gardens, the sort of homes that invariably bring good citizenship in their train...

Ordinarily I am one of the most optimistic people in the business...Yet it looks to me as if the really big problem was not even reached as yet. Every large street railway across this land is in a growing community...Their transportation facilities are nowhere near keeping pace...Yet how can they be developed without capital? The industry is bankrupt. Its credit is nil. For the life of me, I cannot see how a bankrupt industry can respond to the growth needs of a community which it is supposed to serve.

Here is a problem that municipal ownership today cannot solve...American cities are already deeply in debt and petitioning their state legislatures for relief...Few of them can or will help their street railways...As for the general public, today the holder of traction securities feels stung to the limit...The whole structure of our rapidly growing urban centers is predicated upon adequate transportation. It forms their arteries, through which must move the...blood of their civic life. If there were anything else to replace this arterial structure, I should say 'discard it,' but we cannot... We must work out our own salvation with the material in hand...'"
(ERJ **May 1st, 1920 p.p. 884-888**)

Car maintenance became even more critical during World War Two. This is an inspection bay at St. Louis Public Service Company's 39th and Park shops around 1943, recently remodeled with interlocking pits for more efficient working conditions.

there is apparently little prospect of its reaching a dividend basis...Jitney and automobile competition...(won't) end quickly or ...easily. There are today some 30,000 automobiles in Kansas City as compared with 7,000 six years ago ...But the largest problem...is that of the huge physical bulk of the city itself... and its Kansas namesake across the Kaw.
(ERJ May 1st, 1920 p.p. 884-888)

At the time, Kansas City Railways was badly run down. A 1921 Chicago committee on local transportation, touring nine cities between March 4th and 26th 1921, was brief and damning. *"Service ...was confessedly inadequate, the equipment poor, the roadbed in bad condition and the wide ruts along the*

The Forest Park car line did rush-hour business all day on Easter Sunday April 6th, 1947, taking St. Louisans to the park, the Highlands and the Zoo. Car 1580 is westbound on Oakland at the Tamm Avenue stop. STLMOT

tracks in some of the main thoroughfares bore witness to the Company's failure or inability to meet the paving obligations...It has 95...(Birneys) on light...lines. Slow loading of these cars held back movement of larger cars."

So what chance had rural trolleys, now drowning in red ink? None. The country had highway fever. Billions in subsidies were available to pave roads and build new highways, but not a penny to rescue or rebuild big city mass transit or fragile rural rail lines. Rail was yesterday. Autos were today. The voting public reveled at the prospect of escaping train and trolley monopolies, while returning veterans jumped at the chance to go into business themselves with a few cabs or buses, perhaps a few trucks. After all, autos, trucks and buses ran on roads free of direct charge. Trolleys did not. A street railway paid annual property, franchise and other taxes and had paving obligations between and beyond its tracks, which had to be laid, fixed and lifted, all paid for out of the fare-box. Was it fair? Probably not. Were any attempts made to equal-ize the situation outside the transit industry? Certainly not. It was a non-issue.

There were no Federal, state or local subsidies and no coherent interurban network in Missouri as there was in Illinois, Indiana,

Ohio, or even Belgium, just a handful of rural lines of minimal benefit outside their immediate areas. Once the state and the Feds built hard-surfaced roads through subsidy (government handouts as many Missourians disgustedly described it until their own local highways were paved without having them dig into their own pockets), the need for rural lines evaporated and existing opera-tions withered. So it was that Missouri's rural trolleys ended up twisting in the wind, often running out their last miles hauling materials to pave a publicly-funded parallel road.

Still, the hard truth was that whatever their indirect social and economic benefits, and there were plenty, street railways were fiscal sinkholes that had swallowed billions since the 1890s with little to show for it, much less consistent and decent returns on investment. True, new suburban housing might be served by modernized trolley lines offering high-speed one-seat service to a big city. That happened in Los Angeles and Chicago. The potential was there in Kansas City and St. Louis. But there wasn't the imagination to develop the creative financing that might have allowed it to happen.

Instead lines struggled to stay alive, often with crippling fixed-

To The STOCKHOLDERS OF
ST. LOUIS PUBLIC SERVICE COMPANY

ST. LOUIS **Public Service** COMPANY

CITY TRANSIT
SAFETY COURTESY SERVICE

3869 PARK AVENUE   ST. LOUIS 10, MISSOURI

March 11, 1946

TO THE STOCKHOLDERS OF
ST. LOUIS PUBLIC SERVICE COMPANY

The year 1945 recorded the end of the world's major conflict and, with the return to peace, the transit industry was again faced with the prospect of declining revenues and increased operating expenses. Fortunately, through long-range planning which was inaugurated some time ago, our Company was prepared to meet the postwar competitive era.

Financially, our Company is in excellent condition. Our funded debt on December 31, 1945 was the lowest in the history of the Company. This means that our fixed charges are reduced to the lowest amount in the history of the Company.

We realize that our competition with the private automobile stems from the individualistic tendencies of the average American citizen who feels that, through the use of his private car, he can go when and where he pleases and return on the same basis. Recognizing this basic challenge, our Company, in 1944, placed large orders for new and modern equipment. Additional orders were placed in 1945. As a result, our Company received 99 new buses in 1945 and will receive, during the year 1946, 100 new streamlined street cars and 321 new and modern buses.

Every effort is being made to offer and maintain to our customers the most attractive service possible. During 1945, express service was added to several of our lines serving the downtown St. Louis area, which reduced traveling time for our customers as much as 34 minutes per day. Other changes which have improved and added to the attractiveness of our service have been made and will continue to be made as they are possible.

Going into 1946 we are pleased to say that, as a result of the measures which have already been undertaken, our gross revenue for the months of January and February, 1946, shows an increase over the corresponding period of 1945.

I want to express sincere appreciation to all of our employes for the loyal, earnest, intelligent service which they rendered through 1945. They are selling our service to our customers, the public, and with their continued cooperation and intelligent effort, I feel that our Company will be able to retain a large proportion of the increase in business which it received during the war period.

Respectfully submitted,

John Kurilson

Immediate post-war demand for new automobiles far exceeded supply but using motor flat car 139 to display a 1946 Ford must have seemed like a good idea at the time. It was chartered on October 26th, 1945 for a five-hour period to run between downtown St. Louis and Maplewood. With the imminent easing of wartime restrictions, autos (even if only warmed-over 1941/2 models) were on their way back and trolleys on their way out. STLMOT.

cost obligations. Within Kansas City, the MET and successors took 80% of the Clay County's revenue (though MET paid crew time and accident costs on its tracks), and sold it power at 1.2 cents per KW hour, high for the time. To cross the A-S-B bridge, the Clay County paid $1.00 per car. To run on 2.29 miles of St. Joseph trackage cost it a further three cents per head. But the Clay County was funded by outside investors and its failure in 1932 had little effect on the towns it served.

This was not the case with other rural trolleys and interurbans, which usually had a high proportion of local funds in them. Their failure financially embarrassed hitherto respected and honored members of the community, as exemplified by the Mexico, Santa Fe and Perry Traction. W. W. Botts, its secretary and a major stockholder, at the end of 1917 explained at length why the line could not continue.

"We have...been operating...from Mexico to Santa Fe for more than two years at a loss. It took a large part of the proceeds from sale of material in the south end of the road to pay the deficit in operating expenses and replace worn out equipment. There was no

The rise of the automobile and its effect on rural trolleys was obvious by 1915. John Beeler, author of this letter and already a respected transit consultant, suggested even more was going on.

Street and interurban railways have not been the only sufferers from increased…use of the automobile …Nearly every industry or enterprise not… connected with the automobile industry has suffered, and I believe that the…rapid growth of this great business has more to do in bringing hard times to the United States than the European war. According to the estimate made in Scientific American in June 1915, there were…in the United States 2 million automobiles. Their annual cost of operation was placed at $730 million. Add…the selling price of the year's output of new cars, viz: $450 million and…$1,108 billion results. This tremendous sum is not a permanent investment. On the contrary, it represents wealth put into one of the most rapidly depreciating devices that transportation has ever developed.

"Rubber tires, gasoline, machine and all are gone or worn out within a…short time. If the cost of building and maintaining garages…damages…from accidents and… expense due to wear and tear of roads and pavement were added, the…total would look like a war debt. According to the last census (1910) there were …92 million people in the U. S. A.. This, divided into $1,180,000,000, shows a present annual expense of approximately $13 per capita, and… increasing rapidly…The auto has proved a new and additional source of expense and to offset this, economies and curtailments have been necessary…Men buy caps or cheaper hats and inferior clothes as a good suit gets ruined more quickly apparently in an auto than a cheaper one…Women wear auto veils and cloaks and get along without so many good hats and dresses. Members of the family cut out the porterhouse steak and eat deviled-ham sandwiches out under a tree, or bean soup at home. They spend their vacations on nearby country roads instead of taking a trip on the train. Evenings are spent riding around instead of going to the theater… Practically every business man will tell you that he has felt the pinch of hard times…Almost invariably this pinch can be traced to the use of the automobile.

"The automobile has come to stay.It will be cheapened and continually perfected.Its life and service will be lengthened …its use will become…universal…It takes no prophet to foretell these conditions, which are virtually upon us now. The burning question is, what is it going to do with the railway? My firm belief is that in most communities the railway will be as necessary as ever…(though) business and conditions of traffic may change. These conditions must be met, how no one at present can say: (But)…one form of transportation must not be required to build and maintain its own…roadbed and also an additional roadway for its competitor to use practically free…The street railway that lays its rails for its own use and then paves the street around them for the use of the auto, must be relieved and the auto must bear its just share of such taxation." John A. Beeler, Denver CO. November 22nd, 1915. (ERJ (December 4th, 1915 p. 1125

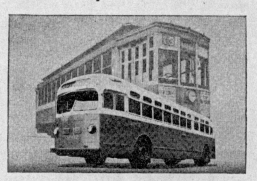

The first postwar streetcar to bus conversions in St. Louis were on July 16th, 1946, held over from their originally-scheduled 1942 conversion date because of World War Two.

balance…to pay taxes, interest or dividends. No stockholder…or officer received pay for his services except an occasional free ride…and no return on…investment. We see no prospect for improvement… Our experience has taught us…the only way to make the road self-sustaining is to extend it to Perry and operate with Keokuk power. We are sure that with such equipment, industries would soon develop along the line…It would be a permanent artery of commerce. But we have not the capital…to do this, nor can we get it.

Kansas City ridership in 1945 remained at an all-time high and the public was constantly exhorted to be careful. (The Railwayan, March 12th, 1946.)

"When this enterprise...started ten years ago, railroads were prosperous and railroad securities, even when...capitalized for twice their cost of construction, were regarded as good investments. At that time automobiles were not thought of as competitors...Now they have rendered short lines of little value to the public and of no value as an investment... The... $61,645 that the stockholders have in the road is held by seven parties: the Mar-

The steepest hill in Kansas City!

In his book entitled "Tom's Town," the author, William M. Reddig, formerly with The Kansas City Star, refers to Kansas City as the city of 77 hills. Steep hills in this community have always been a problem in transit operations, but the steepest one ever to face us is the hill down which our revenues are rapidly falling.

Down
Down
Down

During the first six months of this year, 26 of the 54 lines failed to pay their way!

And the reasons for that decline are simple. Transit fares are the same today as they were in 1932. *But the cost of providing service—just like the cost of everything else—has risen sharply.*

For example, a tabulation showing the *operating results by lines for the first six months of 1947* indicates that of the total of 54 street car and bus lines operating individually or in various combinations, *only 28 were in the black and 26 operated in the "red."*

Those results are *after* all proper operating costs, including the recent retroactive pay increases, but *before* deductions for income taxes, employees' participation and obsolescence.

Rail and trolley bus lines produced a small profit *before* those deductions, with motor bus operations on the losing side. *After* those deductions *the entire operation was at a loss.*

Some of those results will surprise you. The Troost Avenue line was the best line so far as revenue was concerned. That's no surprise, but do you know that the Independence-Kansas City motor bus line was the worst? The Country Club line, with the second highest mileage on the system, produced less than $3,000 and the Airport line $330.

Marlborough, Swope Park, Brooklyn-Sunset Hill, Rosedale, Haskell, Vine, Fairfax and North Kansas City were among the prize losers. The Prospect Avenue trolley bus line was also a loser.

In short, with 26 of the 54 lines operating in the "red," *the public received a lot of service below cost.*

That sort of a situation can't long continue. *We have no mysterious source of income.* Our ability to provide service is measured by what we take in in fares.

LINES WHICH OPERATED IN THE "RED" DURING FIRST SIX MONTHS OF 1947	
Name of Line	Amount of Deficit
RAILWAY	
Brooklyn-Sunset Hill (to June 8)	$ 54,597
Dodson	14,259
18th Street	3,142
Kensington	8,037
Marlborough (to June 8)	68,070
Rosedale	23,253
7th & Haskell	25,616
Swope Park (to June 8)	66,239
Swope Park-Minnesota (from June 8)	7,864
Vine Street-Observation Park	23,339
Woodland (to June 8)	3,471
Brooklyn-Woodland (from June 8)	3,102
Pratt & Whitney (shuttle)	4,909
MOTOR BUS	
Armour-Paseo	11,570
East 5th Street	4,406
Fairfax	13,416
Independence, Mo.-K. C.	108,590
North Kansas City	16,388
South Oak-Ward Parkway	12,418
South Rosedale	985
South Troost	9,178
31st Street-33rd Street	2,358
10th St.-12th St. (shuttle)	2,130
Broadway-Wornall - Sunset Hill (from June 8)	9,659
Marlborough - Brookside (from June 8)	3,142
TROLLEY BUS	
Prospect Avenue	5,390

However, by fall 1947, transit was on the skids in Kansas City (The Railwayan, September 27th, 1947).

shall Rust estate, W. W. Mundy, J. A. Botts, T. C. Bates, T. C. Botts, M. W. Beamer and W. W. Botts. We cannot afford to lose that sum...We are convinced...the road is not, under present conditions, of sufficient public utility to justify the expense of operation, maintenance and...interest on the investment. With the amount of business that we have had, rates would have to be almost doubled and we are sure that people would not pay such an increase. We are therefore forced to the conclusion that, unless the road should be wanted as part of a through line from Hannibal to Mexico, that the enterprise is a failure and ought to be abandoned." (Mexico Evening Ledger November 2nd 1917 p. 1.)

Tiny Santa Fe, which had enjoyed the blessings of electric trolleys for a scant 30 months, was furious about losing them so soon. Botts wrote the Santa Fe Progress on December 22nd 1917, ten days before the line quit, to make his case.

"Dear Sir, Am informed that some people, I don't know who, in the Santa Fe community, are making the charge that I have falsified the accounts of the railroad company so as to show that it is losing money and give an excuse for the discontinuance of operation. This charge, like most of such charges, is vague and hardly worthy of a denial, but for the information of the good people of the community who have sacrificed considerable sums of money to get this road, will make the following statement of receipts and expenditures during the first eleven months of this year.

"If anyone doubts the correctness of these figures, the books of our company are open...not only the books that I have kept, but the books that have been kept at the station... the daily reports that carmen have made, the accounts at the banks at Molino and Santa

Passenger interurbans were a lost cause. The only surviving system with Missouri passenger service after 1940 was the Illinois Terminal, which remained profitable because of its size and high-volume freight business. In the early 1940s it seemed that IT passenger service justified the ordering of three sumptuous new air-conditioned streamlined trains for St. Louis-Springfield-Peoria (and other) services in 1944. Strikes and materials shortage held up delivery until 1948.

These remarkable trains, the equal of any streamline passenger train on any Class 1 railroad in North America, were in service for just over seven years. They remained more or less intact in a St. Louis scrapyard under the McKinley Bridge until the early 1980s.

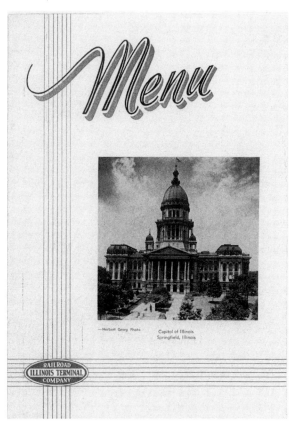

Food service on IT's streamliners was excellent. No other interurban serving Missouri ever offered meals, air conditioning, or cars with a build-date after 1927.

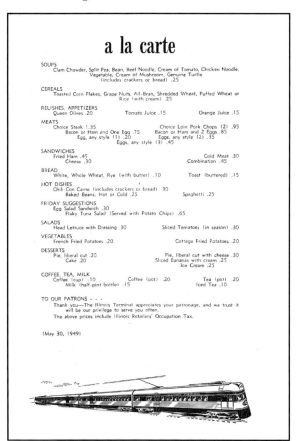

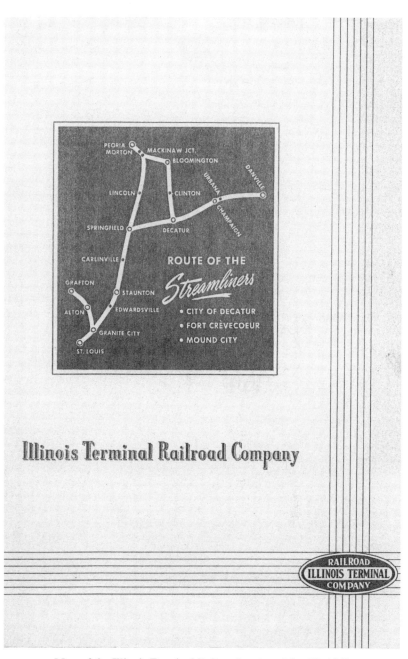

Map of the Illinois Terminal Railroad system, May 30, 1949.

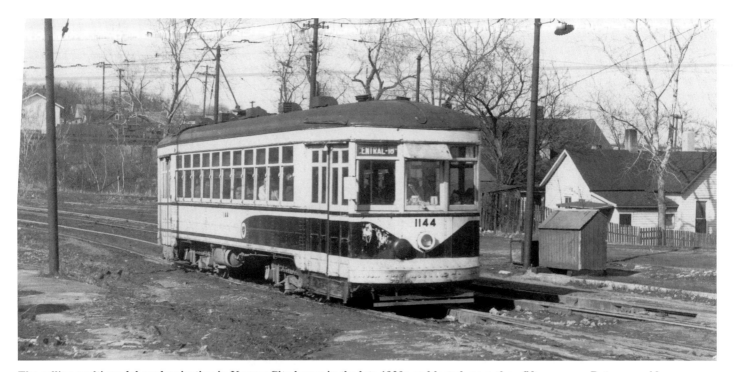

The rolling multi-modal modernization in Kansas City began in the late 1930s and lasted more than fifteen years. But many older cars survived World War Two and not even an up-to-date paint job could conceal the fact that they were looking desperately tired and out-of-date when compared to a new bus and especially a new family sedan. Car 1144 is on the private right-of-way on the Central Avenue line in KC KS in late 1948.

In this Kansas City street scene circa 1951, is it the trolleys on 9th Street or the stream of autos making an awkward turn out of Baltimore that clog up the intersection? STLMOT

Fe and all the vouchers and checks showing to whom money has been paid...In the above expenditures there is not a dollar of interest on the debts we owe, nor a dollar of dividends on the 60 odd thousand dollars that the stockholders have in the enterprise, nor any taxes. No stockholder...nor officer...received a dollar for his services..(or) ever received compensation for his services as officer of the company, except that we paid J. D. Bates $75.00 a month while he was manager ...that, by the way, is the highest salary ever paid any employee of the company.

"Our taxes for this year amount to over $700, now due, and we have no money...to pay them. We owe about $1,500 to banks, now due, and they want their money. There is a mortgage of $10,000 on the road past due and about 18 months interest due, which we cannot pay. We have been

Month	Receipts	Expenditures
January	$937.46	$1308.68
February	$814.31	$1592.51
March	$907.64	$1209.13
April	$769.30	$1136.16
May	$1173.82	$1152.29
June	$1127.28	$1218.42
July	$1286.09	$1211.84
August	$1255.45	$1347.68
September	$1022.04	$1279.95
October	$964.08	$1002.67
November	$981.13	$1030.82
Total	$11,238.60	$13,490.76
Loss		$2252.16

Mexico, Sante Fe and Perry Traction Company income and expenditure, 1917 (<u>Sante Fe Progress</u>, December 22, 1917).

Snow and ice were enemies to smooth operation of public transit. It's November 5th, 1951, the snow has arrived early, but the streetcar has not. How many of these poor souls waiting outside the St. Louis Public Library at Olive and 14th today will still be waiting for a car or bus in, say 1953? Not too many. The rest will be in their own autos, lost to public transit for good. STLMOT

St. Louis Public Service Company truck driver Paul La Greek waits for Joe Daloisi (raising the metal cover) and Nick Bonelli (with corncob pipe and a big bucket of salt) to de-ice a switch mechanism after a winter 1952 snow and ice storm, so next morning's rush-hour trolleys can flow through without problems. STLMOT

notified that we must pay these mortgages this spring.The Rust estate has about $23,000 in the road…His widow wants her money out of it. Some of the local owners of the road have been carrying a load of debt due to their investment in it that is very embarrassing to them; and for myself all that I have in the world is tied up in the enterprise. The statements herein made are the unvarnished truth and any statements that may be going the rounds contrary…are absolutely false. Mexico Evening Ledger *January 4th, 1918 p. 4.*

That was a rural project. The St. Louis and Jennings was a suburban project, built in 1912 to promote a new real estate venture. It went under early in 1923. The bankrupt UR couldn't help, so locals made the attempt.

"The two one-man cars that the City of St. Louis purchased several years ago to operate over the St. Louis Municipal Bridge…probably will roll over the tracks of the rehabilitated St. Louis and Jennings Railway.Plans are…for a complete reorganization of this line, which recently suspended operations because of

losses…in competition with jitneys. J. A. Jeorg, chairman of a committee of citizens …has prepared plans for community operation…$75,000 would be raised to refit the line. Of that, $35,000 would be paid…said Wayne J. Staedlin who bought the line at a bankruptcy sale last March. The balance would be used as follows. $5,000 for grading, $11,000 for rails, $3,000 for ties, $2,000 for car repairs, $5,000 for labor…$14,000 would be necessary to refit the Helen Avenue branch." (ERJ July 28th, 1923 p.158).

A few weeks later, residents of West Walnut Manor and Jennings *"at a mass meeting held at Owls Hall… appointed a committee to devise ways and means for having the former Jennings trolley line put back into service …29 merchants and manufacturers and professional men have interested themselves in the movement…."* (ERJ August 25th 1923 p.310). So far, so good. But within weeks the project foundered, never to be revived. Eighteen months later, UR was finally allowed to put on feeder buses from its Bellefontaine car line to replace the missing trolleys.

By 1926, towns like Hannibal, Cape Girardeau, Jefferson City and

Farewell to a Viaduct.

Last Friday the City council authorized the razing of the Eighth street viaduct, an object of great civic pride fifty-five years ago. With the old landmark removed, Kansas City can look for an improved, uncluttered Eighth street that will provide better access to the big North Side parking project.

The widening of Main street becomes possible and a short vehicular viaduct from Main over Delaware for through traffic is planned. How soon the razing can begin depends on the completion of the St. Louis avenue bridge rehabilitation. That will be part of the route for busses replacing the viaduct street cars.

Back in the late 1890s the old cable street cars traveling along Ninth street occasionally would run away with a resulting pile-up, usually at Ninth and Walnut streets. In 1899, after considerable civic argument, work was begun on the Eighth street viaduct with its "handsome landings" that was to carry the new-fangled electric trolley cars. By 1926 the Main Street Improvement association was demanding the removal of the "unsightly span" that "served no useful purpose."

A half century ago the construction of Kansas City's only elevated railway was a big improvement in the transportation system of that era. Today, its destruction will bring as big an improvement in the developing pattern for downtown parking and accesses to it.

Editorial page — KANSAS CITY STAR, August 22, 1955

FREE RIDES...

over the 8th Street Viaduct —through the 8th Street Tunnel

SUNDAY AFTERNOON, APRIL 29th

Work on demolishing the historic 8th Street Viaduct starts soon! The long streetcar tunnel sloping under Quality Hill will be closed after Sunday!

New bus service — more flexible and better suited to today's downtown transportation — will begin Monday in areas formerly served by streetcars using these long-famous tracks.

We view these changes sensibly, not sentimentally. Yet for old time's sake, we welcome you to join us in a fare-free farewell to those two 8th Street landmarks that spelled Progress when built... and whose going clears the way for new progress in the City which we serve.

Bring the whole family ... the ride is free for everyone! Streetcars will leave 8th & Grand every 15 minutes between noon and 6:00 p.m., Sunday, and will return from Central & James every quarter hour between 12:15 and 6:15 p.m. Come aboard! It's your last chance to ride this historic—and still exciting—route!

KANSAS CITY PUBLIC SERVICE CO.

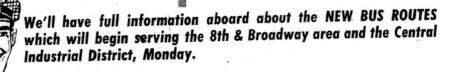

We'll have full information aboard about the NEW BUS ROUTES which will begin serving the 8th & Broadway area and the Central Industrial District, Monday.

With the end of trolleys in Kansas City in June 1957, most surviving cars or their components were sold for service elsewhere in the Americas and Europe. However, the 1941 cars on the left had been sold for scrap in 1955 and then leased back from the scrap dealer until the end of service. Car 795 on the low-loader is being moved to Swope Park for static display. Wrecked by vandals, it was scrapped in 1962. STLMOT.

Sedalia were a lost cause. Autos and paved roads had seen to that and industry executives knew it. <u>ERJ</u> April 24th, 1926 (p. 706) acidly noted their new habit of proclaiming the early and complete disappearance of trolleys, saying such remarks harmed the trolley and the bus side of the transit industry. *"The bus has a rapidly growing field of usefulness but its future is endangered by unwise attempts to apply it in service for which it is not adapted. Low-cost mass transportation is not the place for the bus."* It was no place for the trolley either, certainly not Missouri's few "Toonerville" or rural town-to-market lines still staggering through the 1920s, and judging from results in second-tier cities not there either. The Birney was no longer credible and the entire second-tier city trolley sector was under threat long before the Depression.

However, matters stabilized in the big cities from about 1924, usually when a system was acquired or refinanced by a deep-pocketed parent company and able to start again with more suitable equipment and infrastructure.Thus to <u>ERJ</u>, low-cost mass transportation by 1926 meant big cities exclusively, a position that implied buses *did* have a place almost anywhere else. Certainly, from then on the industry strongly advocated buses for almost universal use. In big cities, low-cost mass transportation meant multimodal. Interurbans, subways, streetcars, buses and trolleybuses

had specific niches to which they were best suited and if another mode could do the job more cheaply, the could and would be replaced. For example, interurbans soon disappeared from many big cities, replaced by long-distance buses often running from their downtown terminals, now recycled into new bus stations.

What was left unsaid by <u>ERJ</u> was that the auto was eroding all big-city transit, which was now increasingly focused on the journey to and from work and little else. But this was where buses gave fresh hope. Frank Buffe, the new Kansas City General Manager, experimented with nine new bus lines in 1925, five paralleling high-density car lines at premium fares on newly-built boulevards. Three others fed car lines and one was a new 39th Street crosstown line.

Kansas City...put a feeder line to...Leeds MO., in operation on July 20th. More than 600 passengers were carried by the two buses on the line during that day...Patronage...has increased daily and more than 7,000 passengers (were)... carried in the first 7 days...Much of this patronage means new business...since the workers who live in Leeds... employ(ed) other means...in getting to their work. Receivers for the company announced that all...buses will be thoroughly lighted on all lines at night and that 'petting parties will not be encouraged' ...One of the operators

stated that darkness within a bus tempts the younger passengers to spoon... Another said lights will not affect the petting parties since they go on 'in broad daylight—you can't stop 'em...'" (<u>ERJ</u> August 1st, 1925 p. 180).

In St. Louis, UR's Manager Colonel T. Perkins did something similar, first using buses to feed outer ends of car lines, then to serve new territory. In a statistical analysis for 1924 and 1925, <u>ERJ</u> (January 2nd 1926 p.2.) concluded that companies were happy with buses and were extending bus lines in an *"effort to provide high class modern transportation" without having to lay tracks."Encouragement for both the bus and the electric railway is to be found in this situation...not as competitors but as partners in a joint transportation enterprise."*

The next logical step was to use buses to replace weak car lines. St. Joseph's Grand Avenue line used just three cars. It was replaced in 1928 with one-man buses, the first since Frederick Avenue's State Hospital bus extension of 1916 went into service as a trolley feeder. The city then went multi-modal, trolleybuses replacing some car lines and motor buses the rest, the last streetcars running in January 1938. This course was also followed in Kansas City after the initial experiments of 1925/6. The 1930s was spent replacing weak car lines with buses and/or trolley buses.

In St. Louis, the Vandeventer line's tracks were at the end of their life, the paralleling Sarah line was close by and Vandeventer itself was due to be widened. New buses, larger and better-suited to intense city service than previous models, were now available and so Vandeventer was slated for conversion in 1929.

The trolley is about to vacate Vandeventer, the tracks will be ripped out of their stony embrace, the cars, thundering on iron (sic) wheels, will yield to the rubbered labor of the bus-and another landmark passes.This is Progress, whose imperious summons is entered proudly in the ledger,but surely it is permissible for gray-haired St. Louis to lift an unforgetting glass to the Vandeventer trolley...for many of us the Via Gloriosa which led to the enchanting land. In what jostles of expectancy we crowded thither to gaze in hero-worship at those invincible Browns who bore the fame of St. Louis across the world under the banner of Chris von der Ahe. This was the way, too, to the old Fair Grounds where annually were exhibited the valley's...fruits and grains and skill of husbandry...One recalls too, the gabled glory of Vandeventer Place, separated from the trolley by frowning gates of feudal aloofness... one sees again the stately carriages, the liveried grooms, the elegance of lavender and lace on all of which is settled now the palsy of the years...Steam-the dynamo-the gasoline engine. Each succeeding motive power is, so to speak, an impresario of mutation...skylines vary and settings change and the tempo quickens. Eheu Fugaces! From Vandeventer's ambrosial nights, the moons have vanished, the suns have set on her rubric days. (<u>P-D</u> editorial, July 20th, 1929.)

From replacing weaker lines with buses, it was a short step to replacing complete systems. On January 14th 1934 schedules for *"motor coaches,"* (effective that day) were published in the Jefferson City <u>Sunday News and Tribune</u>, next to a large dealer ad for new Ford V-8s. An accompanying featurette noted *"new buses...(are) scheduled to succeed the streetcars this week. The cars, looking more ancient and decrepit now that they have become little more than junk, have been pushed aside to rust and*

The St. Louis system carried on for another nine years. Car 1667 is westbound on Olive at Ewing in 1959, a century since the first animal cars first ran on the route. Ray Gehl/Mark Goldfeder collection.

MO-Picher OK) ran on or close to route 66 and the area's emptying out, together with the mine closures, was a body-blow. By 1933 most of the traditional half-hourly through services had become hourly. The last Joplin-Carthage cars ran in 1935 (there were attempts to wreck the last cars with dynamite) and from then until 1938 the once-great system quietly faded to black.

East St. Louis cars exited without comment in late 1935 but the company declined to run replacement buses. Losing up to $10,000 a month, with debts in the millions and being a wholly-owned subsidiary of Union Electric, it was happy to give the system away. Louis H. Egan, Union Electric's President, said as much in March 1935 to a Congressional investigating committee looking into Union Electric's activities. An agreement was reached with E. Roy Fitzgerald, President of the Rex Finance Company of Chicago, backers of a new "East Side Lines" bus company. It would run replacement buses at slightly cheaper fares, using men displaced from the trolleys. The last cars ran in October 1935. In December, equipment sales realized $65,000. It was distributed to former trolley staff for "years of faithful service."

Alton IL closed in August 1936, though the local papers noted that Henry A. Scovell, a former horsecar driver and motorman of the first electric car in 1895, would be motorman of a ceremonial last run with various city officials on board. Citizens' Coach Company ran the eleven replacing buses. Most stockholders were Alton employees of Illinois Terminal, which had owned and operated Alton's city cars for some time.

The mood changed in the later 1930s. Whenever a street railway system closed, one could now expect marching bands, speeches, last runs, parades and groups of railfans descending upon a town from everywhere U.S.A. taking pictures or color movies for old time's sake. The celebrations could last up to a week as ancient

Donald T. Scott, handling promotion for the St. Louis Post-Dispatch, devised a series of ads marking the end of streetcars in St. Louis. An uncorrected proof of one is reproduced here.

decay because there is no market for them." General Manager Beagle was negotiating with a firm owning Lake of the Ozarks shoreline property to buy the cars and use them for bungalows *"to shelter the overnight fisherman and hunter...(for) as a vehicle, they are through."*

By the 1930s, U.S. 66 from Chicago, via St. Louis, Springfield, Carthage and Joplin and into Oklahoma had become the escape route for the Midwest's displaced and desparate. Seeking work and shelter in California, they hit the highway en masse in their overloaded, ancient jalopies. Will Rogers dryly remarked this was the first time in history any country had ridden to the poorhouse in its own autos. The Southwest's main line (Carthage

The wires come down, and the rails will soon come up. This is Midland at Heman Park in University City St. Louis on the former line to Creve Coeur Lake in the Fall of 1950. Ray Gehl/Mark Goldfeder collection.

trolleys creaked and groaned under the weight of elderly folks taking young grandchildren on their first and probably last trolley ride. There's no real explanation for this, despite talk of changing times or trolleys symbolising a simpler, more optimistic age. Perhaps it was the Depression, a Depression ever more likely to be broken only by war. Springfield for example went all-out to mark the passing of their trolleys. August 28th, 1937 was declared a major shopping fest and fare-free day on all trolleys and buses. There was a carnival atmosphere downtown and the cars were jammed with riders. The day ended with a parade of cars and twenty-two new buses.

No ceremonies were held in St. Joseph when the city cars quit early on January 23rd, 1938, though hundreds took last rides. But when the St. Joseph-Savannah interurban closed on July 22nd 1939, it was given a rousing send-off. Dick Johnson, the first car's motorman back in 1911, drove the last car in 1939 and was scheduled to drive one of next day's replacing buses. Several of his passengers had also ridden the first Savannah car. Turnout was heavy, eighty on one car, over sixty on the other. They made a party of it, as did several hundred auto drivers on paralleling U.S. 71. Many rode in fancy-dress, including an otherwise proper bank liquidator, in his pyjamas on a bet. Savannah business folk served lemonade and wafers in the company's local office, there were speeches, gift exchanges, the local high school band and a salute to the trestle south of town, the cars slowing to a crawl to give riders a last look at the creek below. Scheduled to leave Savannah at 12:15 a.m., they were two hours late, not ending the run until 3:00 a.m.

On the last run, a boisterous crowd might well strip the car's interior for souvenirs. This was vandalism; anyone armed with a screwdriver, wrench and wire cutter who then spends a trip unscrewing, uprooting or cutting everything in sight, is a vandal. Some idiots pulled more dangerous stunts, such as tearing out light fittings or stealing controller handles while a car was on the move. On the Strang Line's last night in July 1940, the penultimate car's riders caused general mayhem from Olathe to Kansas City. On the return trip, things got worse, with smashed windows, broken phones, torn-out seats, dewired trolley poles and aggressive scuffles. At Overland Park, the revelers spotted the last through car of all come in from Olathe and made a dash to board it. Forseeing more trouble, officials terminated both trains on the spot, ejected the rowdies and sent the cars straight to the barns.

The line's electric freight continued, but a few weeks later, a run was halted when a train encountered a missing section of overhead wire. Copper wire was valuable. So, was it thieves or payback by vengeful revelers? The train returned to the barns and never ran again. No suspects were ever found.

From 1945 and seen through the rear-view mirror of a new family sedan, public transit became irrelevant to suburban Missourians, so closing ceremonies were quieter, often confined (as in KC) to riders saluting a regular motorman with gifts, tributes and farewell and perhaps a special railfan trip. St. Louis did merit a final run on May 21st, 1966 with a marching band and formal speeches as it was the last big city trolley system to close in North

America. Still, *"A little nostalgia, not much excitement at the Windup,"* claimed the St. Louis Post Dispatch, with some truth.

Only Boston, El Paso, Newark, Philadelphia, Pittsburgh, San Francisco and Toronto trolleys survived beyond that time with any intention of continuing. Some began upgrading their lines into Light Rail systems, using newly-legislated (1964) Federal aid as part of their capital funding. Bi-State too was interested, but St. Louis's mayor was opposed to trolleys on the one-way streets east of Twelfth. The few surviving lines closed instead, the last on May 21st, 1966.

In the 1920s and early 1930s the motor bus was the acme of modernity, as the electric trolley had been in the 1890s. Overcrowded 1940s transit changed that perception and by 1950 neither were a match for a comfortable sedan with a radio and climate control. No more waiting in bad weather on some bleak street corner for the chance to be crammed into an over-stuffed and underventilated vehicle with fifty or more others, no more odious strangers making a nuisance of themselves in a confined space, no more sweaty gropers, flashers, smelly drunks or pickpockets, no more fumbling for the correct change or fighting arrogant young hoods for a seat. Overcrowding may have been transferred to the highways, but your own well-ventilated box of steel and glass insulated you from the disagreeable. Fighting for a seat, fumbling for change was history. You only needed cash for parking, and not even then if you had a contract or a pass.

And there was something new. With memories of 1919's Lincoln highway debacle, the success of the U. S. highway system, and his experience of Germany in 1944/45 (hated the Nazis, loved the autobahns) President Eisenhower conceived the idea of a interstate defense highway system as the ultimate expression of America's return to the roads. A portion of I-70 in St. Charles was among the first built under this program, beginning in 1956. Rail and trolley lines traditionally collected people on a city's periphery and brought them in. The urban interstates had the opposite effect, efficiently draining population out of an inner urban core and practically abolishing mass transit in the outer suburbs.

By the 1960s, all buses except intercity vehicles were an endangered species outside Missouri's big towns. The few bus systems that survive still provide needed service in second-tier towns such as Springfield, Jefferson City and Columbia. But smaller Missouri settlements are completely off the intercity bus map and no form of public transit has made it from the farebox in decades. The automobile is king. It has been since 1910.

A last run

"It was a gay and chummy occasion yesterday (Sunday) afternoon for the passengers who took the last streetcar ride and photographed one another all the way from 48th and Harrison streets to Waldo and back again. What a delightful experience a streetcar ride can be when there's a seat for everyone, no one is in a hurry and an operator has not a thought in his mind except keeping his passengers happy! If there should be melancholy days ahead for the Public Service Company it can always look back upon and savor with pleasure the memory of its finest hour—the afternoon that last streetcar in Kansas City made its final run and nothing but good cheer and fellowship prevailed.

"No fares were collected…Persons stood out in their yards to wave friendly greetings as the car moseyed along. There was a guide aboard to comment on the passing scene and offer advice on light readings and settings for the camera. The car (No. 778) like all others of the PCC type, has 51 seats. As it clanged grandly out of the 48th and Harrison division point there were perhaps 45 people aboard…Across the street stood a solitary figure, disdainful of the rain… beating down on his coat collar, and snapping pictures with a 3-dimensional color camera. He was L. P. Cookingham, city manager, one of the better amateur photographers and a man with a deep and abiding love for a streetcar.

Edward F. Bowman…persuaded Mr. Cookingham to come in out of the rain. Then everybody got aboard with Mr. Bowman acting as tour guide and general impresario. Just before the stop at 43rd and Main, Mr. Bowman announced that he would introduce the distinguished guests…Mr. Cookingham, W. L. Galey, superintendent of transportation for the Public Service Company, G. V. Cannon, division superintendent, and the operator Mr. Hood. Each appeared gratified by the round of applause which followed his introduction…There was a welcoming delegation at Waldo station. The car turned around and Mr. Cookingham took the operator's seat…The city manager displayed a sure and steady hand at the controls. He eased the car back as far as Meyer Boulevard with professional skill before giving way to the regular operator. For this intrepid exploit, he received another round of applause.

"Among the passengers was James N. Spencer, Los Angeles, a Union Pacific fireman on the Los Angeles-Las Vegas run, and a man who just happens to love streetcars. He arrived here three days ago…and had put his time to good use by walking up and down the right of way taking pictures. At last count, he had made 118 photographs. He was to be off to St. Louis last night, to take more streetcar pictures. Back at 48th and Harrison, the passengers stepped off reluctantly. So now it's all over, and a generation will grow up knowing nothing but busses. The Public Service Company has a contract with a salvage company to take over many of the cars. A salvage company deals in—well we might as well face it—it deals in salvage…" (Kansas City Times June 24th, 1957 p.1, story by Bill Moore).

MISSOURI'S TROLLEY TOWNS
AVA

Line 1 Ava. Line 2 Mansfield

1880	**1890**	**1900**	**1910**	**1920**	**1930**	**1940**	**1950**	**1960**	**1970**	**1980**	**1990**	**2000**
1. –	–	–	1713	845	1,041	1,393	1,611	1,581	2,504	2,761	2,938	3,021
2. –	300	494	477	757	861	922	963	949	1,056	1,423	1,429	1,349

Ava, the Douglas County seat, is 65 miles southeast of Springfield and 15 miles south of the Frisco at Mansfield. Originally a Union Army camp, it became a civilian settlement in 1871. SRJ April 7th, 1900 (p. 389) reported a plan for a twelve-mile Ava-Cedar Gap interurban in this remote Ozark area costing $10,000 a mile (M. C. Reynolds President, H. S. Williams Secretary). SRJ October 26th, 1901 (p. 660) said the **Ava Northern Railroad Company** would build north from Ava to Cedar Gap on the Frisco's Memphis Division but SRJ November 9th, 1901 (p. 733) noted this line would be steam, not electric. Nothing happened.

SRJ (May 2nd, 1908, ad p. 35) noted a **Kansas City, Ozarks and Southern Railway** had surveyed the line and grading would start April 15th. It was incorporated on June 27th 1908 with $300,000 capital as an Ava-Mansfield project. There was talk of extending beyond Ava to Mountain Home AR along Big Creek and Baxter County AR to Leslie, Heber then south to Little Rock AR to serve a fruit-growing area and several zinc mines. Later reports refer to the company (not always consistently) as the **Kansas City Ozarks and Mansfield Southern Railway** and the **Kansas City, Ozark and Southern Mansfield Railway.** However, American Street Railway Investments 1909 (p. 180) calls it the **Kansas City, Ozarks and Southern Mansfield Railway.** So did Poor's Manual. Neither talked of a line to Little Rock.

The most surprising thing about this unpromising project was that it was completed, but J. B. Quigley, the chief engineer and promoter, had Sedalia and St. Louis investors rather than locals behind him. Track laying began August 24th 1909, Mansfield marking the occasion with a golden spike and "*general jollification.*" The Douglas County Herald ("*A Republican Newspaper devoted to the interests of Douglas County,*") said on November 4th, 1909 (p. 1) that Springfield's Colonial Motor Car Company had contracted with Quigley for storage-battery cars. "*Two...are to be put on the road next Saturday (November 6th) and each...is to make three trips a day for three days as a test. If they are satisfactory...larger cars will be placed on the road (and) make the trip every hour or so.*"

ETW (November 27th 1909 p 1317) noted the line "*was recently opened to traffic*" as the first Ozark interurban and that the battery cars would run "*until the passenger cars had been completed.*" This is the only evidence so far that this line had anything other than steam traction and the first to suggest it opened (if only partially) as early as 1909. How long the battery cars operated, where they came from and what happened to them subsequently, isn't known.

The first freight train steamed in on February 13th, 1910. Quigley, "*a man who in the face of abuse and discouragement had pegged away for two years until he had made his dream come true,*" (Douglas County Herald February 17th, 1910 p. 1.) rode in an open gondola and about froze to death. The first passenger train arrived on February 25th, Ava's mayor presenting Quigley with a mortgage release, a $20,000 construction bonus from Ava and a welcoming address. Quigley said he'd been better treated by Ava than any place he'd done business with and he would electrify the line using hydro power. The 14.25 mile line may have begun passenger services with the three battery cars, or possibly with gas-electrics supplemented by two steam locomotives. No overhead wires were ever strung.

Receivership began in March 1913 on application of the Ozark Construction Company, still unpaid for building the line. Quigley ran it during the receivership but its subsequent history once the bankruptcy ended on August 5th 1922 isn't clear. It was reorganized as the **Ozark Southern Railway Company**. Poor's 1920 (p. 2118) calls the line **Ozark Southern Railway**, successor to the Kansas City, Ozarks and Southern (sic), implying an even earlier reorganization and name change. This 1920 incarnation, owned by St. Louisan Claude E. Vrooman, had offices at 108 North 8th Street, St. Louis. Earlier offices were in Ava.

Though passenger and freight services continued, Vrooman sold it in August 1922 to a local consortium in a $65,000 time payment deal. $15,000 was paid in cash, the rest in ten payments of $5,000, the balance due in five years at 6% interest. $7,500 was set aside for new rail, ties and reversing Y's at each end (Douglas County Herald, August 3, 1922, p. 1.). Except for local Ava shipments, the line had not run for a while. Former customers were shipping by truck, a fact not lost on the new owners who bought a 5-ton truck and resumed freight service on September 18th, 1922, a two per day round-trip schedule. They also bought a Shay (geared) steam locomotive from an Atlanta GA broker but the Frisco embargoed passage until October 7th. Overheated bearings stretched delivery to three weeks and this unsuitable locomotive was never used. The gas-electric combine "Bluebird" had a broken wheel but resumed service October 1st, implying that while rail freight service had stopped, the line still ran passenger and express services.

Its 1930 MOPSC report spoke of a 14.70-mile long freight line with offices at Jefferson Street in Ava, ten employees and three passing sidings. An 0-6-0 Baldwin steam switcher made a daily trip (except Sundays) "*unless there is nothing to haul.*" The gas-electric combine made two daily trips between Mansfield and Ava (trains 1 and 3) and from Ava to Mansfield (trains 2 and 4) while "*a number 15 Baldwin Locomotive is kept in emergency reserve.*"

Prospects were grim. The new owners were in arrears with property tax, Vrooman couldn't get them to pay installments owed him and the Ava-Mansfield highway, paved in the late 1920s, had creamed off the freight business, hence the almost universal use of the combine on the two daily trains. Vrooman decided to force the issue, but rather than foreclose the mortgage he instead sued on the original contract; foreclosure meant he'd have to run the railroad himself or junk it, neither of which he wanted to do. When, however, in June 1933 the road was to be sold by the county to pay back taxes, Vrooman changed his mind. He took over the tax liability, got it cut by a third and paid the rest, after which he foreclosed. The sale was on June 17th, Vrooman paying $25,000 for it. He believed further operation was impractical and sold the line for scrap. The date of the last train is unknown, but it was sometime in spring 1933.

BEDFORD

Bedford is about 10 miles southeast of Chillicothe in Livingstone County. The <u>Chillicothe Constitution</u> (January 7th, 1930) ran an article on the "Bedford Short Line," built in 1877 by Ed Austin and R. F. Davis as a one-mile station-to-village horse line. Soon after, it was bought by James H. Houx who coined the tongue-in-cheek name and reinforced the joke by sending passes to every railroad president. The courtesy was reciprocated, though the Wabash Railroad President, who actually rode the line, felt he'd been scammed. There was little traffic and it closed in 1882.

BEVIER

(Notes compiled with the help of Lowell H. Rott)

1880	**1890**	**1900**	**1910**	**1920**	**1930**	**1940**	**1950**	**1960**	**1970**	**1980**	**1990**	**2000**
867	876	1,808	1,900	1,868	1,229	1,105	838	781	806	733	643	723

Bevier is in Macon County, 180 miles northwest of St. Louis and 5 miles west of Macon. In 1898 a <u>Kansas and Texas Coal Railway</u> was built from the CBQ at Bevier south to Ardmore. Merged into the <u>Missouri and Louisiana Railroad,</u> in 1914, the coal-hauling line was renamed **Bevier and Southern Railroad**. Two daily passenger trains carried miners and mail for Ardmore until 1926. In 1945 a five-mile Ardmore-South mine (Darksville) branch was built by the Binkley Coal Company, new owners of the South Mine (but not the Bevier and Southern). It was electrified with materials and locomotives removed from their Binkley mine rail spur (once part of the Indiana Railroad interurban) near Terre Haute, closed in 1943 when the mine was exhausted. Electric operation on the Darksville branch ended in 1947 (date unknown) and the mine sold to Sinclair coal. The electrics were sold to the Kaw Valley. The branch closed in 1950 with the South Mine. The <u>B&S</u> survived into the 1960s, Missouri's last steam-operated railroad.

Incomplete Roster notes

Locomotive 200 (home-built 1927 by Terre Haute, Indianapolis and Eastern Traction Company) was Indiana RR 753.

Locomotive 201 (home-built 1928 by Union Traction Company of Indiana) was Indiana RR 787.

Locomotive 202 (home-built 1920 by Terre Haute, Indianapolis and Eastern Traction Company) was Indiana RR 752

Locomotive 202

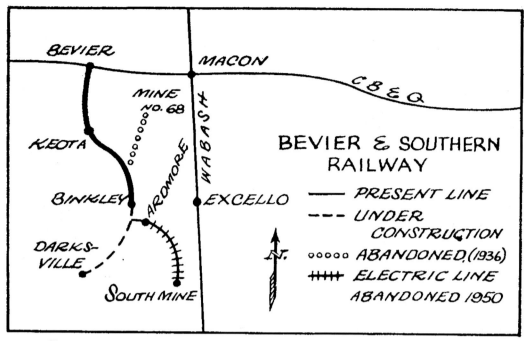

Map, circa 1955.

CAPE GIRARDEAU
Line 1, Cape Girardeau. Line 2, Jackson

1880	1890	1900	1910	1920	1930	1940	1950	1960	1970	1980	1990	2000
1. 3,889	4,297	4,813	8,475	10,252	16,227	19,426	21,578	24,947	31,282	34,361	34,475	35,349
2. 795	941	1,658	2,105	2,114	2,465	3,113	3,707	4,875	5,896	7,827	9,256	11,947

The Cape, 117 miles downstream from St. Louis, was a rock promontory overlooking the Mississippi later destroyed by railroad construction. Girardeau was Jean Baptiste de Girardot, a French marine stationed in Illinois territory who either got into a fight or deserted in 1733, crossed to Missouri, discovered the rock and began a trading post before moving on. Incorporated as a village in 1806, the county seat was at Jackson for the Cape did not blossom until 1835 when steamboats made it the busiest port between Saint Louis and Memphis. It became a city in 1843. Railroads and the Third District Normal School of 1873 (now Southeast Missouri State University) solidified its economy. Direct trains to Memphis and St. Louis came in 1904, a 24-hour riverboat trip to St. Louis becaming a three-hour jaunt.

1. Cape Girardeau Street Railway. This 3-mile 3' 6"-gauge animal line opened January 12th 1893 and by 1896 had 5 cars (at least 3 from Cairo IL)and 10 horses. $5,500 of locally-raised capital in 1892 was $10,000 by 1895 ($5,350 paid-up). Board and management were local. In the late 1890s, horses were replaced by mules. The line looped round Jackson (Broadway), Spanish, Sprigg and Good Hope. A later spur went up Pacific to the Normal School. An 1899 reorganization led to a **Citizens' Street Railway**, but it ceased operation around 1900.

2. Cape Girardeau and Jackson Railroad Company. SRJ October 12th, 1902 (p.636) said this company was set up by St. Louisans to absorb the dormant Citizens, electrify, run city lighting and extend to Jackson. Building began on August 14th 1905 when left-over rail from the mule car loop was removed. Test runs were made on December 15th 1905 but leakage from poorly-bonded track joints delayed opening to December 27th on Good Hope Street north to International Shoe. Two days later, cars ran on Broadway and down Broadway Hill. From the Main Street barns tracks ran south, west on Broadway, north on Henderson, west on Normal, south on West End Boule-

Car 103 outside the Boston grocery and rooming house circa 1910

Broadway circa 1910.

Open car 100 runs past acres of parked Fords in and around the old St. Charles Hotel and the new J. C. Penney store circa 1920.

vard, east on William, south a block on Pacific, east on Good Hope, north on Spanish, east on Independence a block to Main, then north on Main to Broadway. A Frederick Street branch to Mill Town closed when the Frisco shops moved in 1906. Circa 1908 extensions created a loop from Main west on Broadway, then via Henderson, Normal, West End, William, Pacific, Good Hope, Spanish, Independence and Main to Broadway. Two blocks of new track were added on Spanish south from Broadway to Inde-

pendence, then a block east to Main, avoiding Broadway hill (ending up in the river was an apocalyptic vision shared by many). Capaha Park (Fairgrounds) was now served.

3. Cape Girardeau-Jackson Interurban Railway Company. The company reorganized under this name in late 1909, with the same folks in charge. As in animal days, the routing was adjusted to best serve riders and company finances. In November 1910, for example, rather than proceed one-way around the loop, rearrangement of track and passing sidings made it possible to transit the loop in both directions. After a 1913 barn fire, the company was sold to Light and Development Company, a subsidiary of Community Power and Light of St. Louis, part of North American's Union Electric of St. Louis, as well-heeled a parent as any in the utilities industry. But plans to build 18 miles of line in Cape Girardeau and Jackson were shelved.

Services were reduced, tracks crumbled and by October 1921, city commissioners had condemned all but one car until repairs were made. Not until new Birneys arrived did things improve. Light and Development in 1924 was renamed Missouri Utilities Company but then the decline resumed. In one month of 1925, ridership tumbled to about 25% of the same month in 1924. Floods, particularly that of 1927, washed out tracks and it is surprising the cars continued. Yet a 1930 community straw poll suggested the public wanted them kept. The end came in 1934 after a petition noted cars were not covering expenses and were a hazard to road traffic. The Southeast Missourian (August 11th, 1934 p. 2) reported daily receipts of $10.00 and for much of 1934 just $5.00. The last run was on Friday August 10th 1934. Car 101 reached the barn at 9:30 p.m. five minutes early. The motormen got a week's paid vacation and were then assigned other duties, a welcome change for at least one man for whom the cars had been "pretty lonesome" of late. There were no direct replacements. Cape Transit's buses didn't roll until 1941 and bus service ceased in 1969. Most disused tracks were visible until the 1970s.

Incomplete Roster notes

Three or more animal cars with wood-burning stoves came used from Cairo IL.

Three single-truck closed cars on Brill 21-E trucks, possibly numbered 1-3 (circa 1905).

Electric 105 was a closed car on a Brill 21-E single truck.

One single-truck 26' closed city car (Brill, 1909), number unknown.

One single-truck 35' open car (Brill, 1909), number unknown.

Two single-truck 34' open cars (St. Louis 1909?), numbers unknown.

Two single-truck 35' open cars (Brill, 1910), numbers unknown.

Six 30' 1" closed city cars (Brill, 1910), numbers unknown.

One Brill single-truck "combo" city car (Brill, 1910), number unknown.

On January 3rd 1913, a barn fire destroyed most cars. Later in 1913, four closed cars went one-man.

McGraw 1918 reported 4 closed cars, 3 opens and 3 miles of track.

In 1921 Birneys 101-3 came from American on time payments.

Two lightweight cars (Southern Car, 1915) were bought from Natchez MS in 1921 and were overhauled and repainted by December. It isn't known if safety equipment was fitted. Cape Girardeau Southeast Missourian (December 17th, 1921 p.1.) quoted Hart saying they'd be as good as new, and that he'd do the same for the two native "summer cars," to make five closed and two open cars in total. By 1924, there were seven one-man cars. The Birney paint job was yellow or orange-yellow, probably the vivid "Traction" orange then in vogue on traffic safety grounds. Birney 103 was single-end, the others double-end. No buyer could be found and they were scrapped with the four other surviving cars in 1934.

CARROLLTON

1880	**1890**	**1900**	**1910**	**1920**	**1930**	**1940**	**1950**	**1960**	**1970**	**1980**	**1990**	**2000**
2,313	3,878	3,854	3,452	3,218	4,058	4,070	4,380	4,554	4,847	4,700	4,406	4,122

The Carroll County seat, about 75 miles north-east of Kansas City, was the site of 1723's French Fort Orleans. Permanent settlement began in 1818 when Americans from North Carolina moved in. The town and county were named for Charles Carroll of Carrolton MD, a signer of the Declaration of Independence. Local businessman Frank V. Crouch, who lived uptown, promoted a rail line to the station (the third or fourth time such a project had been mooted since 1880) applying for franchise on August 17th, 1888. This may have been the **Carrolton Belt Railway Company**, which withdrew early in 1890, but more likely the **Carrolton Rapid Transit Company**. Surprisingly, the Wabash provided enough rail and ties to build a line from the South Carrollton Freight Depot to town. While the city wanted the connection, shopkeepers felt tracks circling the square would hurt them and applied for an injunction to prevent this.

Crouch ignored the injunction, began laying track and was jailed for contempt. On release, he modified the route so it began in the Square, ran west on First to North Folger, then south to the end of Folger and onto right-of-way, gradually working its way close to the present US 24-65 while crossing Wakenda Creek on its own bridge before turning into the Wabash station. So began the Carrollton steam dummy on September 1st, 1893, usually hauling two 12-passenger cars.

Amazingly, it was a success, and Crouch decided to electrify. At six p. m. on Monday August 30th, 1897, the new **Carrollton Electric Railway**

Car 2 crossing the line's private Wakenda Creek bridge. No date.

Company's first car, with Crouch at the controls, ran over the dummy's tracks. Power shortages were rectified by installing ground wires and bonding track joints. Full service began September 1st, fare one dime. Car 2 was tested September 3rd (with passengers) and soon cars met all trains, at one time as many as thirty-six daily. A half-hour before a train's scheduled arrival, a car would leave the Square and run to the station, an extension circa September 20th 1897 taking cars right to the platform. Soon after, a stockholders' meeting in St. Louis voted to reorganize. Crouch stayed as secretary and manager, J. L. Minnis became President, George S. Grover Vice-President and F. L. O'Leary Treasurer, the latter pair being the Wabash's St. Louis attorney and treasurer.

Tickets could now be sold to anywhere on the Wabash by the CERC and CERC tickets were sold from all Wabash stations. But Crouch had begun investing in mines and zinc smelters in north-east Kansas and was promoting a street railway in Iola KS. In 1899, he sold the CERC to Carrollton men and to the Iola line's building contractor George Baumhoff of St. Louis, who brought ex-St. Louis streetcar men with him to run Iola's cars. Crouch spent the rest of his career promoting street railways and interurbans in and around Iola, (and Fulton MO) with limited success.

Car 2, outside Carrollton "Opera House," then under construction.

In 1902 CERC merged with local electric and water utilities as the **(Carrollton) Water Light and Transit Company.** Poor's 1901 reported two miles of standard-gauge track, three cars and $25,000 capital, $10,000 paid up. After the merger, capital was $100,000, increased 1907/8 to $150,000. In 1902/3 a spur was built into the Carroll County Courthouse grounds. Talk of extending southeast to the County fairgrounds and Bowdry Lake went nowhere. A December 10th, 1905 barn fire was suspicious (phone lines were found to be cut), but if this was an "insurance" fire, it didn't do the job as scorched cars were rescued from the barn. In 1909, Company brass formed the **Carrollton, Missouri River and Northwestern Railroad Company**, capitalized at $150,000. ERJ July 10th, 1909 (p. 95) said it would build 10 miles south from Carrollton to the Missouri and from Carrollton north-west to an unspecified Carroll County destination. ERJ July 24th, 1909 (p. 164) said preliminary surveys

had been made, but the promoters were put off by the results and couldn't raise the needed $150,000.

Around 1915, owner-operated Model T Fords began whisking riders from the station for a "jitney" or a nickel. The trolley ride was a costly dime. In 1922 ownership of Water Light and Transit passed to Kansas City Power and Light. Jitneys had killed ridership, but freight revenues too now began to fall and when in 1924 the U. S. mail contract which had sustained the line since 1893 was not renewed, KCP&L had had enough. Nothing could persuade them otherwise, certainly not the delegation of locals who suggested the line be run on an as-needed basis for freight only. At closure on August 1st, 1924, there were two passenger and two freight cars plus a trailer freight car. Sporadic operation may have continued until 1928 as KCP&L brought in carloads of supplies needed to build a regional electrical grid. Whether these were hauled by the electric freight car or a small railroad locomotive isn't known.

Incomplete Roster notes

Car 1 was single-truck, Car 2 double-truck, Car 3 (St. Louis Car, 1899) a double-truck baggage/express, Car 4 (1903) on Brill 27-G trucks was half enclosed and half open, Car 5 maybe was similar.

Car 7 (St. Louis 1915) was a Pullman green interurban combine on St. Louis Car 23-A trucks. It went back to St. Louis Car at the end of 1919 for repairs. Local claims that the line was the fifth built in the United States or that this was the smallest town ever to have streetcar service are unsustainable. Keytesville was smaller and its horse line opened before Carrolton's. Farmington's electric line opened in 1904, passenger trolleys quit in 1927, electric freight trolleys quit about 1948. It too was smaller.

Car 4 and crew, no date. (Mayor Sharon E. Metz, Carrollton)

CARTHAGE
(See also Joplin/Webb City. For population statistics, see Joplin).

Carthage is the Jasper County seat, named for the ancient city when platted in 1842. In the 19th century its prosperity came from a fine grade of locally-quarried marble, examples of which grace the Missouri and U. S. Capitols and the White House. Proximity to lead and zinc mines after 1873 tied its fate to Joplin and Webb City. Myra Belle Shirley was born and raised here. An 1860s graduate of the Carthage Female Academy, the Civil War turned her Confederate family's life upside down. After leaving Carthage, she was better known as Belle Starr.

1. **Carthage City Railway Company** Opened October 17th, 1883 as the **Carthage Railway Company**, it ran a block east from Courthouse Square then north to the Frisco station at Elm and Vine, also west on Oak from Courthouse Square, then north and west to the MoPac station on Vine, plus south on Main from Courthouse Square to Carter's Park. It was renamed **Carthage Horse Railway Company**, later in 1883 or 1884 after a reorganization. Service ceased January 24th 1885 when a barn fire destroyed all cars and killed horses and mules. Months later it resumed under the CCRC name. By 1889, the 3.25 mile 3' 6"-gauge long line had three cars and 16 mules. It was sold in August 1891 to a J. Guinney, possibly a front for E. Z. Wallower of Harrisburg PA, then building a downtown Joplin hotel and one of an investment syndicate funding local mines. Guinney was an electrical engineer and this may have been a preliminary to electrification. The name **Carthage Street Railway Company** may have been a mis-reporting by SRJ February 1891 (p. 100), which noted a new two-mile extension.

2. **Jasper County Electric Railroad Company** This company, promoted by Fred H. Fitch, was formed with Chicago money (from whence Fitch had recently arrived) to build a 12-mile Carthage-Carterville electric line. Organized November 8th, 1893 and capitalized at $150,000, Carthage and Carterville franchises were obtained but the Chicago backers pulled out during 1894, leaving Fitch to carry the can. He lost a $3,000 deposit,

but supported by local pride (it was locals who paid up the $150,000 capital) he kept going, incorporating November 12th, 1894. His was one of several groups aiming to link the two towns. 1891's Rapid Transit Corporation planned a Carthage-Carterville electric line with a Joplin extension. So did E. J. Spencer and associates in 1894 and of course Rogers and Wallower's Southwest. But only when nearing Carterville from Webb City in September 1894 had Southwest then applied for a Carthage franchise. The mayor considered them late and refused, awarding it to Fitch instead.

JCERC construction began in January 1895. The first test car ("Orlana"), piloted by motorman Henry Long, carried 94 people between Carthage and Carterville on Saturday afternoon August 24th, 1895, a big day for Carthage which turned out in huge numbers, spirits undampened by a thunderstorm that bubbled up during the trip. Full 1/2-hour service began on Monday from the square in Carthage with five motors and trailers, each named for a director's wife and painted a dazzling white with a gold band, hence the "White Line" nickname. Its Carterville terminal was at Hall Street near the Carterville Hotel on Fountain Street where riders for Webb City, Joplin and Galena transferred. The prime destination en route was company-owned Lakeside Park whose 42 acres and dance hall were popular for years. When animal services ceased, the old cars were used as playhouses there.

Local runs beyond the Square to the Carthage railroad depots lost money and ceased until 1896 when smaller electric cars were bought. But Fitch and his cohorts, having made their point, were now willing to sell when Rogers of the Southwest once again came calling. White Line cars went into Southwest's fleet on August 21st, 1896 (the merger date) and Fitch himself became a senior Southwest officer. Southwest now controlled all car lines in Carthage, Carterville, Webb City and Joplin. For Carthage transit history from 1896, see Joplin.

AMERICAN CAR COMPANY.

1895 American Car catalog photo of Jasper County single-truck open car "Waukina."

AMERICAN CAR COMPANY.

CARTHAGE, CARTERVILLE, WEBB CITY.

ARCADIA.

JASPER COUNTY
Electric Railroad

No. 133.

Length of car body, 25 feet.　Seating capacity, 36 persons.

1895 American Car catalog photo of Jasper County closed car "Arcadia."

"Arcadia" interior.

CASSVILLE

Line 1 Cassville. Line 2 Exeter.

	1880	1890	1900	1910	1920	1930	1940	1950	1960	1970	1980	1990	2000
1.	–	626	702	781	845	1,002	1,215	1,441	1,451	1,910	2,091	2,371	2,890
2.	–	244	438	375	399	323	249	355	294	434	588	597	707

Incorporated in 1846, the Barry County seat is 50 miles southeast of Joplin and 12 miles north of the Arkansas state line. A Missouri Confederate center, Civil War battles fought in the area included Wilson's Creek in 1861 and Pea Ridge in 1862. Union victory in the latter removed the rebel threat to Missouri for the rest of the war, but Cassville was physically destroyed and, expecting to be on the Pacific Railroad, was psychologically destroyed a few years later when it was bypassed. Not until 1896 was the **Cassville and Western Railroad Company** conceived by locals, but by June the first rails were laid at Exeter, the Frisco interchange. The five-mile line opened on July 4th and had two spurs, one to the Cassville Roller Mill. Passengers rode in a combination passenger/baggage car, freight in a box car. There was a 240' difference in elevation between the termini. The grade was continuous and Cassville-bound trains coasted in from Exeter. Fortunately there were no serious accidents.

SRJ (March 28th, 1908 ad p. 20) reported sale to a syndicate out of Eureka Springs AR who planned to electrify and extend to Roaring River and a new quarry. The Cassville Democrat April 3rd, 1909 reported it as the **Ozark Traction Company**, but described it as the **Ozark Traction System**, headed by S. M. Mitchell of Cassville, president of the C&W, which would electrify a part of the 28-mile interurban. Other segments would be fed from a new hydro-electric project on the White River, six miles from Eureka Springs AR. Ultimately it would be a Cassville-Joplin interurban, the company supplying all towns en route with cars, light and power. The owner of the Arkansas, Oklahoma and Western Railroad, about to run between Eureka Springs and Rogers, was interested, saying if the hydro-electric plant was built he would electrify. Various Southwest Missouri Railroad notables drove in from Joplin on April 19th *"in a 90 HP automobile"* to inspect the project. They didn't invest.

American Street Railway Investments 1910 reported (wrongly) four cars and five miles of electric standard-gauge track as of April 1909, claiming **Ozark Traction Company** of Eureka Springs was owned by the same interests that controlled the C&W (i.e. the Eureka Springs syndicate), building north from Eureka Springs AR into Missouri to link with the C&W. Lack of money stalled the project. In summer 1911, a contract was signed for cars and equipment to be delivered by October 6th. They didn't arrive. At the end of October G. M. Sebree (the line's general counsel) went to

New York to either remove the road block or cancel the contract and get trolleys from elsewhere (Springfield Republican November 1st, 1911 p. 10). Nothing happened and soon after, Sebree was appointed C&W's receiver.

McGraw 1918 wrongly claimed two motor and two "other" cars, but the line's 1917 MOPSC report calls it a *"steam carrier operating in the State of Missouri."* David Dingler and Clint Ault rescued the line in 1919. Ault was the money man, Dingler the mechanic with railroad experience. Aided by their families, they then ran the road between them. The **Cassville and Exeter Railway Company** came out of receivership in 1923, now owned by Mr. and Mrs. Dingler with Ault family members as officers. Freight was steam-hauled but passengers rode a one-man Edison storage-battery car at 35 cents a trip. Whether this exotic and fragile conveyance came new or second-hand isn't known. All other electrification plans were extinct. The battery car ran the 4.7 miles twice daily (except Sunday).

After that, the line was reported as a human-interest "curiosity" in places such as the Springfield Press (May 1930), Ripley's "Believe it or not" strip in 1931, the New York Times (December 12th, 1936) and the St. Louis newspapers. It even inspired *"Clem and Martha,"* a syndicated radio show. What intrigued journalists and their readers was the idea it was a one-man show—Dingler. He was the locomotive engineer, maintained the track, ran to time and made extra trips if a load was waiting. In fact several worked the line, but as mere employees they didn't count for story purposes.

Dingler died in November 1939, but the line continued. By 1945 the locomotive was worn out, local roads were paved and service had declined to a daily mixed train. Yet the family persevered. Some repairs were made and a replacement locomotive was bought, but the bad winter of 1948/9 prompted them to call it a day, selling the line as a going concern. The new owner repaired loosened fills and weak trestles, then resumed service in July 1949. There was no schedule, trains ran as needed. From 1952 to 1956 one paid employee wore every hat from general manager and locomotive engineer to switchman and track hand. But the last empty boxcar was moved from Cassville to the Frisco on September 11th, 1956, an event noted across the state. Even the St. Louis Post-Dispatch marked its passing with a lyrical editorial.

CHILLICOTHE

1880	1890	1900	1910	1920	1930	1940	1950	1960	1970	1980	1990	2000
4,078	5,699	6,905	6,265	6,772	8,177	8,012	8,964	9,236	9,519	9,089	8,799	8,968

The Livingston County seat, Chillicothe (incorporated 1855) is 123 miles west of Hannibal. A 4'-gauge mule line opened in February 1891 though a line may have run in 1885 and not survived. Poor's 1896 reported four miles and three Laclede-built cars. In 1897 it carried 124,480 passengers at a nickel fare, earnings were $62,764, expenses and taxes $60,613, profit was $2,151. Cars served Public Square, Walnut Street, the Leeper (Lambert) Hotel, Fairgrounds, Fair Street and the Normal School (now Chillicothe business college). It met all trains at the depots. A 6% five-year deed for $2,000 was due in 1901 but not redeemed and the line closed late in the year. It was sold for $2,500 on November 21st, to Clark and Peatman of Centerville IA, its original owner and builder. The Chillicothe Constitution (November 22nd 1901 p. 2) said Peatman, seeing its

run-down state, blasted the cars as traveling billboards none would ride and that he'd fix them. Poor's reported it running until 1904, but it almost certainly never reopened.

SRJ February 1897 (ad p. 122) said Elmer Moorman was interested in an electric line from Chillicothe southeast to Avalon and Hale City and north from Chillicothe to Trenton. The Chillicothe Constitution (November 22nd, 1901 p. 1) noted John Doll and P. A. Gibson of Erie PA in town to inspecting the city electric plant, the roadbed of the old Chillicothe and Des Moines Railway (a steam railroad grade established in 1877 but never built) and getting a franchise for a 24-mile electric line to Trenton. SRJ May 3rd, 1902 (ad p. 77) noted surveyors working, but no more was heard.

CLINTON

1880	**1890**	**1900**	**1910**	**1920**	**1930**	**1940**	**1950**	**1960**	**1970**	**1980**	**1990**	**2000**
2,868	4,737	5,061	4,992	5,098	5,744	6,041	6,075	6,925	7,504	8,366	8,703	9,311

The Henry County seat, Clinton is 78 miles southeast of Kansas City and 71 miles northeast of Nevada. The **Clinton Street Railway Company** opened in fall 1888 with 2 miles of 4' gauge track (one Poor's directory suggests 4' 1") three cars and nine mules (A. P. Frowein President, J. T. Ruffin Vice-President, H. P. Faris Secretary and treasurer). It began at the Burrell Hotel (southeast corner of Second and Franklin, near the MKT crossing and the Cozart Hotel), ran west on Franklin round the square, south on Washington, west on Ohio, south on Orchard to Allen and the north entrance to Artesian Park, built around the *"Great Artesian White Sulphur Springs,"* discovered in 1883. It ended at the park's 1892 White Sulphur Springs Hotel. By 1896 there were three miles of track, five cars and eight mules.

In 1897 the Faris family took charge. Their franchise allowed them to change to cable or electricity at will, but there was no incentive to cable and with capital of $12,000, electrification was unlikely. Not that they didn't hope. SRJ (January 18th, 1902 ad p. vii) dryly observed *"the owners of this animal line want someone to electrocute it."* They were now down to a monthly franchise run. The Clinton Daily Democrat (March 25th, 1903 p. 2) noted the city suing in Sedalia's Pettis County Circuit Court to vacate the franchise. Within days that was done, by which time there was a gap of a city block where locals had ripped out rails "obstructing" Orchard Avenue and thrown them into the nearest ditch.

Several "hot-air" interurbans included Clinton in their plans, the biggest being the **Kansas City, Lee's Summit and Eastern Electric Railroad**. Grading began in the Kansas City area (Raytown) in 1908, by which time the project was known as the **Kansas City and Southeastern** but money ran out before surveying was done in Clinton (See Sedalia)

Western Missouri Interurban Railway ERJ February 27th, 1909 (p. 165) reports a Clinton franchise application. Its 75-mile line would run from Odessa in Lafayette County (40 miles east of Kansas City) southeast and south to Clinton via Warrensberg, then south from Clinton to Greenfield in Dade County just south of the present Stockton Lake.

COLUMBIA

1880	**1890**	**1900**	**1910**	**1920**	**1930**	**1940**	**1950**	**1960**	**1970**	**1980**	**1990**	**2000**
3,326	3,985	5,651	9,662	10,392	14,967	18,399	31,974	36,650	58,812	62,061	69,133	84,531

Midway between Kansas City and St. Louis, Columbia (in Boone County) is home to the University of Missouri. It had no trolleys but has had motor buses since 1915. One of the few Missouri cities to develop away from a river, it was on the Boone's Lick Trail from St. Charles through central Missouri to Independence. But in the railroad age, the trail and Columbia were both by-passed. The MoPac took a southern route between St. Louis and Kansas City while the North Missouri (Wabash) took a northern route. Columbia languished at the end of a Wabash branch from Centralia and was an intermediate point on a backwater MKT branch meandering down to Jefferson City. Both gave poor service.

In the 1890s, rebuilding began following the burning down of the University. This kicked off a civic revival in which good streets and roads were a high priority (this was the height of the bicycle craze). By 1910, long before the railroad age ended, road-oriented Columbia was Missouri's best-paved city, stunting all trolley proposals. Yet between 1908 and 1914 Columbia was the focus of three overlapping but abortive interurbans: the **North Missouri Central Electric Railway**, the **Mexico Santa Fe and Perry Traction** and the **St. Louis-Kansas City Electric Railway**. Only the Mexico company built, petering out six miles south of Mexico. Columbia had three good gravel highways, south to Ashland, west to Rocheport and the Missouri and east to the county line towards Fulton. But the town yearned for restoration of direct east-west road links with St. Louis and Kansas City. In 1911, Columbia hosted a Missouri "good road" convention, where a group was formed to push for adoption of the old Boone's Lick Trail (or Central Missouri route) as the first St. Louis-Kansas City trans-state highway. Public enthusiasm for the project was easy to generate now it was clear the automobile was here to stay. After war delays, the road was built in the 1920s as U. S. 40, a long-delayed extension of the National Road from Vandalia IL to Kansas City via St. Louis. It was mostly upgraded in the late 1950s as I-70.

ELDORADO SPRINGS

1880	**1890**	**1900**	**1910**	**1920**	**1930**	**1940**	**1950**	**1960**	**1970**	**1980**	**1990**	**2000**
–	1,543	2,137	2,503	2,212	1,917	2,342	2,618	2,864	3,300	3,868	3,830	3,775

Eldorado Springs was incorporated in 1881 and is 75 miles southeast of Kansas City in Cedar County. SRJ August 1892 p. 499 noted a mass meeting of citizens was to investigate the cost of a steam dummy line to Nevada, about 18 miles west. A Committee of five was appointed, including a C. A. Edgar.

Eldorado Springs, Tiffin and Monegaw Springs Electric Railway SRJ December 7th, 1907 (ad p. 35) reported a 12-mile line would be built northeast between the points in its title, powered from the Osage River. C. A. Edgar was president, John Harrison General Manager. ERJ January 2nd 1909 p. 49 reported a renaming to **Eldorado Springs, Tiffin, Monegaw Springs and Lowry City Railroad**, a 30-mile long standard-gauge line which would build by April. Dr. (sic) C. A. Edgar of Eldorado Springs and John Harrison of Tiffin retained their posts. No more was heard.

EXCELSIOR SPRINGS

Line 1 Excelsior Springs. Line 2 Liberty.

	1880	**1890**	**1900**	**1910**	**1920**	**1930**	**1940**	**1950**	**1960**	**1970**	**1980**	**1990**	**2000**
1.	–	2,034	1,881	3,900	4,165	4,565	4,864	5,888	6,473	9,411	10,424	10,373	10,847
2.	1,476	2,558	2,407	2,980	3,097	3,516	3,598	4,709	8,909	13,679	16,251	20,459	26,232

Originally named Viginti, its name was changed when iron-manganese mineral springs were found bubbling up from 1300 feet underground. It was Missouri's first spa town, incorporating in 1881. Located in Clay and Ray Counties, about 30 miles northeast of Kansas City, it was a tourist magnet. Many classy hotels, pools and support facilities were built and the town still retains much of its glory. From 1913, it was the terminus of the Kansas City, Clay County and St. Joseph Railway Company branch via Liberty, whose last cars ran March 10th 1933.

1. Excelsior Springs Railroad Company SRJ 1896 directory said this company was in receivership. While this implies a line may have been built, no further information has come to light.

2. St. Joseph, Excelsior Springs and Lexington Railway Company SRJ (September 7th, 1907, P. 40) reported incorporation (capital $200,000) to build a ten-mile long interurban to Hibbard, crossing the Missouri at Lexington on a new bridge. *This would give an electric line from Kansas City to Lexington...(via) the proposed Heim line, making direct connections at Excelsior Springs...Promoters are Dr. G. P. Lingenfetter of Denver...the largest stockholder, C. D. Wade...(and) S. S. McIntire of Excelsior Springs, D. C. Finley of Kansas City.*

3. Excelsior Springs and Suburban Railway Company Incorporated May 21st, 1908 with $50,000 capital and a 30-year franchise, this would be a 3 car, 2.5-mile long standard-gauge line from the Milwaukee Road tracks via Kennedy to Marietta and Hillside, with a branch from Marietta over Wert Street west to the Dry Fork of Fishing River and an alley between lots 3-10 in Block 23, Northern addition. Promoted by Henry J. Arnold, W. A. Bell of London (UK) was President and W. A. J. Bell of Excelsior Springs Vice-President, a father-son team better known for developing the Excelsior Springs Golf Club. Work would start within ten days. It didn't because insufficient money was subscribed despite application blanks being placed at all town banks. ERJ April 17th, 1909 (p. 755) reported Arnold buying controlling interest from the Bells.

"If the electric line...falls through, it is probable a company will be organized to operate...motorbuses between the depot and different points in town...A bus line...can be put in operation at a tenth of the cost of an electric line, do just as much business, and at a profit...An electric line would not be a paying proposition for at last five years...Completion of the Dunbar Avenue paving will make a motor bus line easy to operate, as there is no grade...of more than six per cent." (Excelsior Springs Daily Call, April 2nd, 1909 p. 1.) Nothing was done.

4. St. Joseph, Excelsior Springs and Lexington Railway Company Incorporated during summer 1907 (ERR September 7th, 1907 p. 289) and capitalized at $200,000, this project for a 6-mile standard-gauge electric line from Excelsior Springs northeast to Vibbard got nowhere. The grandiose title reflected its ultimate ambitions.

FARMINGTON

1880	**1890**	**1900**	**1910**	**1920**	**1930**	**1940**	**1950**	**1960**	**1970**	**1980**	**1990**	**2000**
608	1,394	1,778	2,613	2,685	3,001	3,738	4,490	5,618	6,590	8,270	11,596	13,924

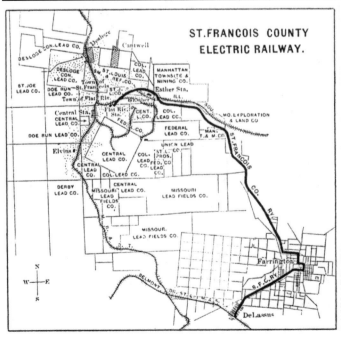

ST. FRANCOIS COUNTY ELECTRIC RAILWAY.

Incorporated in 1836, Farmington is the St. Francois County seat, 70 miles south of St. Louis. Miles from a railroad, a Farmington-St. Louis trip meant taking a stagecoach to the Iron Mountain RR at Pilot Knob before riding the rails. The solution? Link town and railheads with an electric line. The project was discussed in 1900 and a September 3rd 1901 promoters' meeting fixed a route and capitalized the line at $150,000 plus issuance of $100,000 in bonds. SRJ September 14th (p. 325) and October 12th 1901 (p. 584) reported the **St. Francois County Electric Railway Company** (Peter Giessing president, J. P. Cayce secretary, W. H. Hipolite chief engineer) would run from Flat River to Farmington and De Lassus. Right-of-way was paid for, five motors and two trailers would run and building would start in 30 days.

There was a reorganization at one point but grading was done by 1903, the route interchanging with the Iron Mountain Railroad at De Lassus. Farmington-De Lassus opened July 22nd, 1904, Farmington-Hurreyville-Flat River December 22nd, 1904. The 1.3-mile Esther-Flat River section had trackage rights over the Illinois Southern Railroad. Farmington was the area's shopping and administrative center, with a state hospital, a courthouse and a small park. A convoluted route through city streets took it to Courthouse Square before turning southwest for De Lassus. After a slow start, ridership from both ends into town was heavy for years despite the 25 cent fare—in Kansas City or St. Louis one could ride the same distance (and more) for a nickel. From Farmington, there were ten daily runs

Combine 102 and passengers pose for the camera at what is believed to be the De Lassus Station circa 1908. An engraving of this car graced all company letterheads, envelopes and checks for the first years of the line's existence. State Historical Society of Missouri.

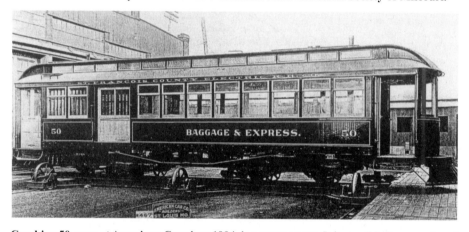

Combine 50, seen at American Car circa 1904, is a mystery car. It is possible it was ordered but could not be paid for, but more likely it was delivered and operated before either being destroyed in a wreck or sold to raise some cash; there is at present no known record of its existence on the St. Francois.

The Farmington station building and company headquarters was still in immaculate condition at the end of electric operation. It is November 16th, 1947, the new diesel locomotive has arrived and the electric cars will not be running for much longer. All the same, car 54 appears to be positioned for another assignment. Willis Goldschmidt.

to Flat River and seven to De Lassus. The section between Missouri State Hospital #4, just beyond Farmington on the De Lassus line and the Power House two miles north of Farmington on the Flat River line, had its own schedule.

SRJ January 18th 1908 (p. 102), reported a new 2000' spur on the De Lassus line and a 2600' extension at the State Hospital to the Mississippi River and Bonne Terre Railroad, which in 1912 became the line's new owner. Expansion plans, including a Bonne Terre extension and electrification of the Crawley spur to give a Flat River entry, came to nothing. In 1924 the company was sold to a local syndicate. In 1925 Flat River-Esther-Hurreyville closed. The northern division was now Farmington-Hurreyville only. All passenger runs ceased early in 1927. Its 1927 MOPSC report stated Hurreyville-Farmington-De Lassus was 7.56 miles long, with 2.74 miles of sidings, three closed motor cars, a motor freight and an unmotored work car. In 1945, there were 10 miles of 600V D. C. (550V D. C until 1940) standard-gauge tracks, two motor cars and two freight cars. In October 1947 a diesel was bought and St. Louis trolley fans chartered car 54 on November 16th for a last run. This was probably the last electric movement though wire, power and cars remained until 1948. Money was lost in every subsequent year except 1951. In 1957 the State Hospital switched to natural gas and the last diesel coal train from De Lassus to the hospital ran on November 15th.

Incomplete Roster notes

This list is based on the line's 1913-14 MOPSC report. The 1904/5 fleet seems not to have been included. A builder's photo of St. Francois County #50, a combine lettered "Baggage and Express" (American order 467) can't be reconciled with this list, nor a similar photo of a box motor lettered "Electric Locomotive #1" (American order 462).

50. Express Motor (McGuire-Cummings, 1908). Built 1908 for Fort Dodge, Des Moines and Southern as express car

100. Rebuilt 1911 as center-entrance branch line car #50. Sold to St. Francois County Electric RR in 1927 as car 50 and either delivered as or converted to express motor.

54. Combine (McGuire-Cummings 1916). Built 1916 for Fort Dodge, Des Moines and Southern as center-entrance branch line car

54. Sold to St. Francois County in 1932.

99. Trailer (unknown builder, circa 1907).

100. Combine (unknown builder, circa 1903)

101. Freight car (unknown builder, circa 1904)

102. Combine (unknown builder circa 1904)

103. Combine (unknown builder, circa 1905)

Line car at Farmington Station, November 16th, 1947. Willis Goldschmidt.

Car 54 out on the line towards State Hospital, November 16th, 1947. Willis Goldschmidt.

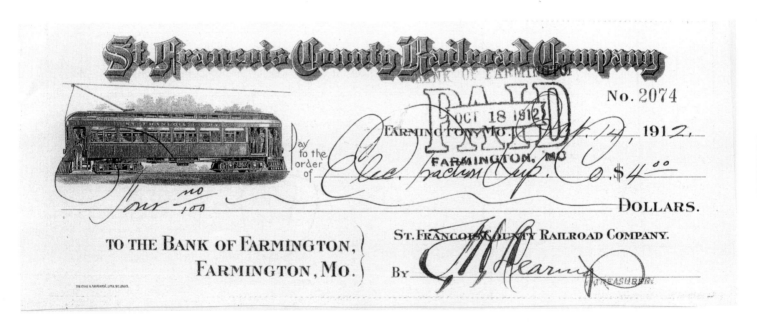

Car 54 circles Farmington's courthouse on November 16th, 1947. Willis Goldschmidt.

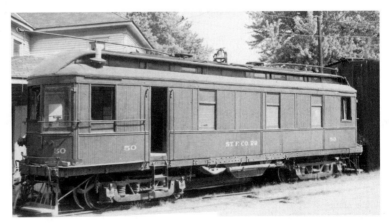

This is the second car 50, seen at Farmington on November 16th, 1947. Notice the railroad bell on the roof and the all-steel underframe.

FULTON

1880	**1890**	**1900**	**1910**	**1920**	**1930**	**1940**	**1950**	**1960**	**1970**	**1980**	**1990**	**2000**
2,400	4,314	4,883	5,228	5,595	6,105	8,297	10,052	11,131	12,248	11,046	10,033	12,128

About 120 miles west of St. Louis in Callaway County, the State Hospital and the Missouri Institute for the Deaf were established in Fulton in 1851. William Woods College for women followed. The town was a center for corn, hay, horse, mules and fire-bricks. Westminster College (established 1841) was the site of Winston Churchill's 1946 "Iron Curtain" speech. A 17th-century Wren Church, a casualty of the London blitz, was later rebuilt on campus, the nucleus of a Churchill memorial for which the college received his moral support in 1962. In 1992, a piece of the Berlin wall was added, personally dedicated by former President Gorbachev just weeks after the collapse of the USSR.

It comes as a surprise to list Fulton in the "never had streetcars" category, but so it was. A transfer service was begun in the 1890s by John Jameson with two-horse 10-seat wagons (referred to as "busses"), with roof racks for baggage. They ran from the railroad depot to the Fulton Hotel at Sixth and Court, to the Palace Hotel and to Fifth and Market. Freight was carried on separate trips. The business was sold to J. Roy Tucker in 1906/7. He ceased taking passengers around 1920, but hauled freight until 1942. His son took over but closed it down in 1946.

Talk of trolleys (*SRJ* June 1899 ad p. 69) was attributed to Frank V. Crouch of Carrolton. However, his interest in Fulton was ephemeral. No more was heard until 1909 and the trumpeting of the **North Missouri Central Electric Railway** to link Jefferson City and Hannibal via Columbia, Mexico and Perry, plus branches to Fulton and other Calloway County points. When that project died, an F. S. Mordaunt plan emerged to use a Chicago and Alton branch for a Mexico-Jefferson City interurban, serving Columbia and Fulton. Another project, based on the Mexico, Santa Fe and Perry Traction, was the **Keokuk-Jefferson City Electric Railway,** which surfaced as late as 1915.

HANNIBAL

1. Hannibal. 2. Palmyra

	1880	**1890**	**1900**	**1910**	**1920**	**1930**	**1940**	**1950**	**1960**	**1970**	**1980**	**1990**	**2000**
1.	11,074	12,857	12,780	18,341	19,306	22,761	20,865	20,444	20,028	18,609	18,811	18,004	17,757
2.	2,479	2,515	2,323	2,168	1,964	1,967	2,285	2,295	2,933	3,188	3,469	3,371	3,467

Hannibal is a Mississippi river town in Marion county, 117 miles upstream from St. Louis. A trading post since the 1790s, in 1818 Moses Bates surveyed the junction of Bear Creek and the Mississippi for a town site. Platted in 1822, growth began in the late 1830s when steamboats began making regular calls. By 1840 there were 1034 residents, mostly from Virginia, Kentucky and Tennessee. The first railroad (the Hannibal and St. Joseph) came in 1859 when the volume of lumber coming downriver was growing. Lumber was big for decades, as was agricultural processing, especially tobacco. At its peak, Hannibal had twelve tobacco and cigar factories. There's no consensus on why it was so named but in its 1840s/50s incarnation Hannibal is the world's best-known American small town, thanks to Mark Twain (Samuel Clemens), a resident from the age of four until seventeen (1839 to 1853.

In Twain's later years, Hannibal was a modest streetcar town. While his reaction to the cars isn't known (nor to the fact the company owned a "Mark Twain Cave" yet never built a line to it), he did say on his last visit in 1902 that Hannibal hadn't much changed since he was a boy. Many say the old town by the river hasn't changed much since. Surviving photos suggest they're all of them right. There were streetcar proposals in 1866, 1870 and 1873. All failed until the **Hannibal Street Railway**

Wood engraving of Hannibal Union Depot with a passing horse car on Main Street circa 1885.

Company began pick-and-shovel grading of Market Street (Broadway) after a modest "first spike" ceremony on June 4th 1878. Two cars came early in July and the first run was made on July 8th. Mules were the motive power and the first line ran south from North Main (at Hill Street) to Broadway (Market) and west on Broadway to the "wedge," just beyond Maple Avenue. It wasn't speedy; one could walk the route faster. Its income reflected that.

The company was bought in 1882 by James O'Hern and Mike Doyle. No immediate changes were made, *SRJ's* 1886 directory noted two miles of standard gauge track, six cars and 23 horses. By 1889, there were two and a half miles, reflecting an extension to Union Station on South Main (Main north of Market was closed at this time) and an extension from the "Wedge" west to Houston. Return trips ran from Houston via Lyon to Maple Avenue, then north to rejoin Market. Electric cars began on July 15th, 1890 (*SRJ* August 1890 p. 393). This may have been a test run as the opening date is usually given as August 1st. Initially, three cars towed three trailers, all re-worked horse cars. In 1891, there were five trailers. By December 1896 the western line ran to Smith Park, the southwest line to Minnow Branch plus a line to Indian Mound Park at St. Mary's Avenue and Pleasant.

Car 5 at the end of the Fulton Avenue tracks circa 1909.

Former horsecar as electric car 3 at the 500 block of Broadway on what's believed to be the inaugural trip on August 1st, 1890.

Poor's 1898 (p.1015) noted a December 14th, 1897 sale to John H. Garth of Hannibal for $13,500, the Indian Mound Park line being cut back to Hill Street on St. Mary's Avenue. Renamed **Hannibal Railway Company**, Doyle, O'Hern, four cars and a trailer remained. On May 1st, 1899, the HRC was sold to "Haines Brothers, New York City," (Poor's 1899 p. 1008), emerging on May 15th as **Hannibal Traction Company** with $75,000 capital. It was sold on to the Sutherland Construction and Improvement Company of New York (June 1st, 1899). O'Hern now left the board, Doyle having been gone for some time. Capital was increased to $100,000, the company taking out a 5% bond for that sum.

Whether the **Hannibal Railway and Electric Company** was new or a renaming of the Traction Company isn't clear but Poor's 1903 (p. 980) claims HR&EC began in 1899 as HTC's successor and this may not have been so. By 1901, the company was the property of the Mainland family, remaining with them until around 1926. It's not clear when the south line to Fulton Avenue and Mount Olivet cemetery began, but it was after the Main Street Bridges opened on November 5th, 1902. 1907's planned extensions to company-owned Mark Twain's Cave and the Altos Portland Cement plant (each 3 miles long) were never built, but two miles to Oakwood (Robal Park) opened in 1906 after a bridge was built over Minnow Branch on Market Street. All lines were single track and cars ran every fifteen minutes.

In 1909, HR&EC switched to three cents a kilowatt city power, but from 1913 bought cheaper power from the Keokuk dam. Relations became prickly as a result, especially when the city began insisting cars stop not only at every block but also mid-block. One-manning, rush-hour cars and track realignment also became issues. MOPSC (as arbiter) declared mid-block stops were redundant in so small a town and settled everything else by the end of 1915. But paving obligations remained con-

tentious (especially Broadway) until the mid-1920s when HR&EC got a 20-year franchise extension and a paving waiver provided it paid the city $16,101.82 (time-payments at 5%). Licenses and occupation taxes were replaced by a 1% franchise tax levied on gross receipts. Real estate, including the Mark Twain Cave, was sold to pay back taxes. Fares went to six cents in February 1924 and eight in 1926.

Four Birney cars came in 1924 and another two (double-ended) in 1925, Hanibal's first one-man cars. There was a radical recasting of operation and it is thought the St. Mary's Avenue line was extended several hundred yards during 1923 in anticipation. All base service was now run by Birneys, older cars ran as extras in one-man and two-man form. In 1925, a **Hannibal Transportation Company** began bus service in and around Hannibal. In 1926 its stockholders bought a controlling interest in HR&EC and took it over on January 1st, 1927.

Open car 21 and trailer 212 at the end of the Oakwood line circa 1918.

In 1926, HR&EC talked of cutting back the Mt. Olivet Cemetery line to the CB&Q shops and closing the St. Mary's Avenue line, leaving a line from the CB&Q shops through downtown and out to Oakwood. This wasn't done. Instead, on October 10th, 1927 it filed for bankruptcy. Liabilities were $200,000, including $16,000 owed to the city for paving. Allegations HTC had taken HR&EC into bankruptcy to eliminate debts taken over on acquisition were not true but clearly there was no long-term future for the trolleys. By 1928 HTC had eight city and three interurban buses on 118 miles of route. The trolleys ceased October 28th 1930, minutes after the company was sold at foreclosure for $4,725.

A subsequent MOPSC hearing was held on the complaint of Oakwood residents who alleged the foreclosure sale and immediate cessation of trolleys, especially the Oakwood line *"was the culmination of a conspir-*

Open car 21 descending Broadway circa 1912, Mississippi River in the background.

Main Street bridge over Bear Creek looking north, circa 1910. Tower of Union Station on right.

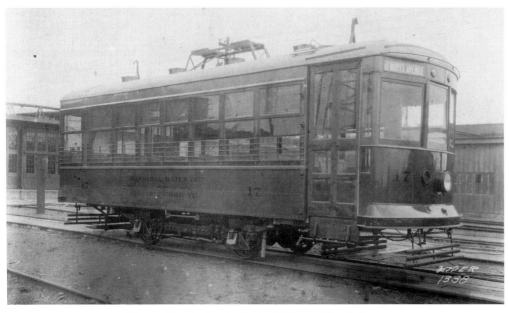

Birney 17 at St. Louis Car in 1924, awaiting delivery.

acy by the owners of the Hannibal Transportation Company to eliminate a competitor to its..bus system." They'd given money for the Oakwood trolley extension, made their homes there because of it and felt a new company could still operate cars profitably. MOPSC disagreed. The cars had lost money for years and no convenience or necessity would be served by resumption since HTC's buses ran on all trolley routes and served areas never reached by the cars. *"To resume ...would require reconstruction of practically the entire system... Acquisition of...cars and equipment would call for the expenditure of large sums...with no prospect of return."* (Hannibal Railway & Electric Co. Records 1917-1913, Western Historical Manuscripts collection C577, Hannibal Railway and Electric Company papers-Missouri Public Service Commission case #7322). HTC subsequently ran Hannibal's buses for years.

Incomplete Roster notes

The Hannibal fleet is confusing and details are lacking. 1890's three electric cars (#1-3) were probably converted horse cars. A photo of car 3 has the legend "August 1st, opening day" on it, conflicting with <u>SRJ's</u> report. A photo of car 5 shows a seven-window deck-roof vestibuled car with platform doors on an early single truck. Cars 21, 22 (St. Louis, 1902) were 10-bench opens on St. Louis Car #34 trucks. In 1903, there were eight cars and three trailers, in 1904 twelve cars (the trailers had been retired) and a 1/2-mile more track. The 1909 fleet of 8 closed and 7 opens were Jones and St. Louis cars. Car 1-3 (second) may have been from St. Louis's <u>UR</u> 743/799, 900-907 series (St. Louis, 1895/6). A 1910 photo of an eleven-bench single-truck Hannibal car looks like UR's 600-699 series (St. Louis, 1902).

In 1914 there were eight closed and five open cars, a snow plow (a horse-drawn road scraper) and a work car, 36 employees and 61/2 miles of track. In 1928 there were Birneys #14-17 (St. Louis, 1924), 18, 19 (St. Louis, 1925) plus four obsolete cars including opens 21 and 22 and a work car. The bankruptcy court ordered the Birneys to be returned to St. Louis Car, who held trust certificate and title to them. They were set out on a spur next to the Hannibal and St. Louis Railway on the morning of October 30th and a Car Company representative picked them up and shipped them out of town.

Car 10 eases its way along the 200 block of Broadway during the 1913 Labor Day festivities.

Car 8 poses outside Southside school on Fulton Avenue

Cars 8 and 21, seen in other photos, here have collided. Car 8's platform bearer has collapsed, taking the entrance steps and platform with it, and the car's windshield has been pushed in. It is not known if there were casualties. Circa 1912. George Schwartz.

A posed picture, perhaps for insurance or training purposes, showing part of car 8 with the motorman at his post. Other crew members "ride the cushions" before their next assignment. There is little protection for the motorman in the event of a collision, the entrance step are steep and there is little room on the platform. This is clearly a car unsuited to heavy city service, but fine as a small town trolley. George Schwartz.

Power was then cut off. The two remaining work cars were valued at $100 each but weren't fit to run.

Hannibal Interurban Proposals

1. Hannibal and Jefferson City Interurban Traction Company (North Missouri Central Electric Railway Company) See Jefferson City and Mexico.

2. Hannibal and Northern Missouri Railroad. ERJ March 27th, 1909 (p. 572) reported Henry Funk proposing a 110-mile Hannibal Kirksville via Palmyra line plus branches and a powerhouse on the Salt River. ETW June 19th, 1909 (p. 652) reported incorporation for $2 million as the **Kirksville and Hannibal Interurban Company**. ERJ July 10th 1909 (p. 95) said surveys had begun. ERJ December 10th 1910 (p. 1176) noted grading west of Bethel (Shelby County). Later reports claimed progress, including Palmyra franchises, but by 1911 it was bankrupt. Funk bought it (including 12 miles of completed bridges and grades) in March 1912 for $12,500, and that was that.

3. Hannibal, Palmyra and Suburban Traction Company SRR August 1898 (p. 189) reported incorporation for $275,000. It would run Hannibal's trolleys and build extensions to South Hannibal, the cemeteries and Hannibal Cave (2 1/2 miles), to Oakwood (1 1/2 miles) and to Palmyra (10 miles), plus a steam-heating plant fed by exhaust steam from the traction power plant to heat downtown Hannibal.

4. St. Louis, Terre Haute and Quincy Traction Company An abortive interstate interurban project, SRJ July 6th, 1907 (ad. p. 37) noted a *"conference at Hannibal last week with a committee of the Commercial Club...to put up $1,500 for the Pittsfield-Hannibal survey."* At $38,000 a mile it would run from Quincy IL to Pittsfield IL and to Hannibal, with a steel bridge over the Illinois River at Montezuma. SRJ September 21st, 1907 (ad p. 24) said from a connection at Marshall IL and building southwest, it would parallel the Vandalia Railroad from Pocahontas, then go west to Edwardsville, IL with connections to St. Louis via trackage rights over Illinois Traction and the planned McKinley Bridge. Branches would run from Pittsfield IL to Hannibal and from Hannibal south to Louisiana MO. Capitalized at $2 million, construction would not exceed $1/2 million. No more was heard.

INDEPENDENCE
(Also see Kansas City)

1880	**1890**	**1900**	**1910**	**1920**	**1930**	**1940**	**1950**	**1960**	**1970**	**1980**	**1990**	**2000**
3,146	6,373	6,974	9,859	11,686	15,296	16,066	36,963	62,328	111,630	111,806	112,301	113,288

Independence, the Jackson County seat (twelve miles northeast of Kansas City) began circa 1825 as a port of entry for Mexican goods and a supply and base station for hunters and trappers, indeed "Prairie Schooners" and heavy freight wagons were built there. But the landing was some miles away and river freight soon left the town. In the 1830s the region was seen by the new Mormon church as its promised land, but Mormon settlers were soon forcibly expelled by locals, mainly Kentucky, Virginia and Tennessee frontiersmen. Soon after, Independence became a jumping-off point for the California, Santa Fe, and Oregon Trails. The first overland mail coaches began their runs in Independence, as did '49ers headed for California who meanwhile made Independence notorious as a hell-raising western town.

Its name may commemorate the signing of the Declaration of Independence, (there are other, less exalted stories) but it wasn't on the national map until 1944 when Missouri Senator Harry S. Truman became President Roosevelt's vice-presidential running-mate. The Trumans' preference for life in Independence was uindisguised, Bess Truman often returning with relief to their home at 219 North Delaware (once her parent's house) throughout his Washington career. The couple returned permanently in 1953, living out their lives as the town's most famous son and daughter.

Kansas City & Independence Rapid Transit Railway Company steam dummy "John" circa 1888.

1. Kansas City, Independence and Park Railway. Built in 1886, later known as the **Kansas City and Indepdence Rapid Transit Railway,** this was the first of Willard E. Winner's real-estate lines. In the early 1890s six Baldwin-built steam dummies ran trains to Independence on a route memorialized by the present Winner Road. He owned 2,400 acres of forest between Independence and Kansas City, damming several streams in 1887 to form a lake and Washington Park, a suburban housing and park development. He reorganized the line as the KC&IR. Locomotive smoke contravened KC by-laws, so his line ended at 15th and Askew Avenues, giving easy transfer to KC cable cars. In 1895, the line was bought by the Metropolitan Street Railway and electrified in 1896. Washington Park closed in 1900, 400 acres being bought by the Mount Washington Cemetery Association. The line ran until March 1935, when KCPS, declining to pay its share for a new viaduct over the Blue River Valley, substituted buses.

2. East Fifth Street Railway Company Another Kansas City steam dummy that started some time in the 1880s, this five-mile line penetrated Independence for a short distance and maintained offices there.

The **Citizen's Street Railway**, was noted in SRJ September 1892 (p. 555) as losing its franchise due to poor service. Being told to remove itself or be removed, its tracks were lifted by Independence City Council order.

Incomplete projects included the **Independence Suburban Railway** of 1890 and **Independence Railway Company**. These were sucked into the Kansas City system. SRJ July 29th, 1904 (p. 354) said a **Kansas City, Independence and South Eastern Electric Railway** would build from Independence to Holden (probably via Blue Springs), 30 miles southeast in Johnson County and surveys had begun. ERJ November 6th, 1909 (p. 1003) said it now planned to reach Warsaw in Benton County, a further 50 miles. No more was heard.

A more modest project was the 1½-mile long **Independence and Sugar Creek Railway**, noted in ERJ June 15th, 1918 (p. 1172.). By private subscription, the city was said to be arranging an electric line from Independence to Sugar Creek *"a small industrial settlement with a cement plant and refinery."* $13,000 of the estimated $50,000 costs had been raised and Kansas City Railways would build and operate it. Though the company was incorporated, it went nowhere.

Kansas City & Independence Rapid Transit Railway Company steam dummy 5 and train, 15th and Askew, Kansas City September 30th, 1890.

JEFFERSON CITY

1880	**1890**	**1900**	**1910**	**1920**	**1930**	**1940**	**1950**	**1960**	**1970**	**1980**	**1990**	**2000**
5,271	6,742	9,664	11,850	14,490	21,596	24,268	25,099	28,228	32,407	33,619	35,517	39,636

The Missouri state capital and Cole county seat, Jefferson City is on the Missouri, 120 miles west of St. Louis. St. Charles was the state's first capital, Jefferson City only became so in 1826. Originally named Missouriopolis, that clumsy appellation was dropped in favor of commemorating President Jefferson and the 1803 Louisiana Purchase. Horse bus services began in 1857 but beyond fables and legends, little is known. At least two bus lines met trains at the stations when the Jefferson City Daily Tribune (February 8th, 1887 p. 2) first reported an ordinance allowing S. W. Cox to *"construct, maintain and operate a street railway."* Cox was front-man for promoters H. Clay Ewing and Judge A. M. Hough. They were given a forty-year franchise and allowed to build single or double track. As Judge Hough recalled in 1905 they couldn't raise the money nor interest the *"right persons."* The writ-

ten papers were filed by the Judge, who re-discovered them in 1905 and wrote the Tribune thinking they might be interested in this old project.

High St looking west from Monroe

High St. Looking West from Monroe, Jefferson City, Mo.

Jefferson City Bridge and Transit Company was set up on January 29th 1894. It was a horse-bus operation with unfulfilled trolley pretensions, linking the town with North Jefferson station via the Fred Kay ferry. In bad winters it crossed the frozen Missouri on its own wheels. When a new river bridge opened in May 1896 services were transferred to it, the "ark" connecting with all trains to and from the Chicago and Alton depot in North Jefferson. The JCB&TC was sold on April 2nd, 1910 for $250,000 to a group of St. Louisans headed by George D. Rosenthal, local manager for General Electric of New Jersey. The bridge was needed to get the proposed North Missouri Central Electric Railway into Jefferson City from

Mexico, Fulton and Columbia, but Rosenthal made it clear no Jefferson City-St. Louis division was presently contemplated, though maybe later. (Jefferson City Daily Democrat-Tribune April 2nd, 1910, p. 1.)

In October 1910 the JCB&TC received its city franchise and began building at the end of November. The Capital News (November 24th, 1910 p. 1) talked of extensions once cars ran, east to Houchin's Park and west to the Country Club. The first test run was conducted in the presence of the Mayor, City Councilors, invited guests and gentlemen of the press and left the West Main and Mulberry barns on Saturday afternoon, April 1st, 1911. Regular service began April 5th, every 30 minutes from the transit office at Madison and Main downtown to the MKT/C&A station over the bridge in North Jefferson. Red cars went to the station, blue cars only as

far as Bolivar. The one-mile Houchins Park line opened at summer's end. It ran on Main, Cherry, High, Ash, McCarty and Clark Avenue to the park. In August 1911 a two-block extension opened on West Main Street from Bolivar to Fulkerson.

On February 7th, 1912 Jefferson City Light, Heat and Power was bought by McKinley interests which consolidated isolated small town systems such as this into its **Western Railways and Light Company**, believing these properties, earmarked for linkage with the main system, would meanwhile benefit from unified management and access to a large company's resources. But, as other IT properties in Iowa and Nebraska had already discovered, automobile growth in Jefferson City made it clear that money spent on new interurbans was wasted money.

Jefferson City car lines.

1. Jefferson City to North Jefferson, from the downtown loop northwest via High Street to Broadway, northeast on Broadway to Main, northwest on Main to Bolivar and across the Missouri River toll bridge into Calloway County via the hamlet of South Cedar to North Jefferson station. 3.112 miles. This met the few trains serving the station. By 1919 this line ran from the Madison Hotel and past the other hotels before heading out to North Jefferson.

2. As line 1 to Main and Bolivar, then west to Fulkerson (2 blocks). By 1914 this line was extended on Main from Fulkerson with a one-block jog onto Brooks and back onto Main

to end just short of the west city limits between Ware Street and Price Street. 1.037 miles.

3. Jefferson City to the east end, from the downtown loopsoutheast via High Street to Ash Street, southwest one block on Ash to McCarty Street, McCarty to Clark(e) Avenue, three blocks southwest on Clark(e) to end one block along Fairview Boulevard at Church, a block from Houchins Park. 2.098 miles. By 1919, this line ran further along Clark(e), across the city line and on Moreau Drive to Moreland Avenue, a further 0.5 miles.

All served a downtown loop circling Madison, Main, Monroe and High Streets.

On September 10th, 1915, the Democrat Tribune reported six cars were on order, claiming *"growth of the city and the increase of business"* were behind the purchase. General Manager Snyder claimed *"these cars are up-to-date in every particular…and may be operated as pay-as-you-enter,"* but their initial use was as two-man cars, one-man service beginning only on January 16th, 1916. Given the blizzard of adversity crippling the industry, radical economies of this kind were welcome, but without bridge tolls and the security of being part of a regional utilities group, the system could not have survived long on the nickel fare that continued to the end of operation. By 1917, the six one-man cars, plus a single two-man car together were daily averaging 585 miles, with only 2,000 riders (ERJ September 22nd, 1917 p. 530).

Illinois Traction sold the company at the end of 1924 to **Missouri Power and Light** of Kansas City, a North American Light and Power of Chicago subsidiary. The company's first new buses, 25-seat Macks with leather seats and air-cushion springs, began runs to Washington Park in September 1925. Even on the rough roads of the day, they rode better than the Birneys and always had higher fares than the cars, initially a dime. There were no complaints. By 1927 the bridge line to North Jefferson was closed, buses replacing it temporarily, permanently from 1929. As the system slipped into the 1930s, it became increasingly decrepit and should have been replaced years before it was.

More buses arrived at the start of 1934 and the last car returned to the barns unnoticed, probably late on January 14th, but the date is unrecorded. The new buses ran from East Circle Drive to Moreland Avenue via Fulkerson, Monroe and Miller, and vice versa. Missouri Power and Light ran them until at least 1942 and **Jefferson City Lines** continued until 1966. There have been several owners since then, but remarkably for so small a town, bus service continues.

Incomplete Roster notes

Little is known of Jefferson City's cars. An opening-day picture shows car 10, a 6-window deck-roof car. The Capital News November 24th, 1910 (p.1.) said cars on order (quantity unspecified) were all "pay-as-you-enter" and painted blue and white. On July 29th, 1912 Philadelphia 547 (American, 1894), a closed single-truck car with an 18' body, was shipped to Jefferson City. In 1914 there were 6.2 miles of track, 0.3 miles of sidings and turnouts, six cars and one baggage car. Six one-man cars (one numbered 8) came late in 1915, bringing the fleet to 13. It isn't known if these were new or used. By 1918, there were 12 cars. Two cars were scrapped in 1923. In 1925, Galesburg (IL) Birneys 2, 3 and 14 (American, 1920) were bought. A 1934 photo at High and Monroe Streets shows Birneys 20 and 24, suggesting they were given even numbers only. In 1928 there were ten cars (nine one-man, but only seven in service), four service cars and two buses. By 1930, there were seven cars, one freight motor and two buses.

Jefferson City Interurban Proposals

McKinley was not the only promoter to envisage Jefferson City as a hub or junction for a state-wide system of interurbans. Others had the same idea. None made it into operation.

1. **Kansas City and Southeastern** See Kansas City.

2. **Keokuk-Jefferson City Electric Railway** ERJ September 26th, 1914 p. 591 mentions H. W. Knight of Chicago as interested. ERJ April 24th, 1915 (p. 822) said the line would run from Keokuk IA to Jefferson City crossing the Des Moines River into Missouri near Kahoka, then southwest via Williamstown, La Belle, Newark, Bethel, Shelbyville, Shelbina, Paris and on **Mexico, Santa Fe and Perry Traction Company** tracks

Car 10 and an appreciative crowd, believed to be on opening day. Missouri State Archives.

(not the first time this line was proposed as a bridge) to Fulton and Jefferson City, plus a Williamstown-Canton (on the Mississippi) branch. ERJ September 18th, 1915 (p. 612) said surveys were done and right-of-way bought as far as Shelbyville. SRJ October 19th, 1915 (p. 788) said a committee was soliciting surveying funds through Shelbina.

3. Missouri Interurban Electric Railroad Company SRJ March 24th, 1906 (ad page 37) said 200 attended a March 14th meeting of folks living on a proposed 80-mile Jefferson City-Sedalia line via Centertown, California, Prairie Home, Bunceton, New Lebanon, Otterville and Smithton. A committee was appointed to raise money. An April 2nd meeting of backers and city heads hired H. B. Colby (former St. Louis Sewer Commissioner) and H. H. Humphrey to survey and report in 60 days. Other than awarding building contracts in April 1907 and announcing work would begin in both directions from Otterville on May 15th, the project fell out of sight. ERJ January 24th, 1914 (p. 214) noted this company (or a separate project with the same name) had completed surveys for forty miles between Sedalia and Prairie Home via Smithton, Otterville and Bunceton, but construction wouldn't begin until the right of way and financial backing were firm. The president was now A. W. Nelson of Bunceton, but H. B. Colby remained one of the engineers. They were still active in 1915, but nothing was done.

4. North Missouri Central Electric Railway Company When first noted (ERJ October 24th 1908 p. 1304), this was to be a 30-mile Mexico-Columbia interurban. O. W. Spaete of St. Louis and V. M. Dissaffrey of Buffalo NY were the promoters, though this was thought (wrongly) to be a project backed by Jefferson City interests. Promotion began in 1908 and was met with skepticism. A Columbia franchise bid of January 1909 was refused and the company withdrew to regroup. It surfaced again (ERJ July 24th, 1909 p. 164), as a 65-mile Mexico-Columbia- Jefferson City

Birney 24 headed for Clark Avenue passes Birney 20 on one of Main Street's three passing sidings, shortly before the system closed. Missouri State Archives.

line, interchanging with the C&A at Mexico and the MoPac at Jefferson City. But finances were shaky. ERJ July 31st 1909 (p. 197) reported just $6,000 had been raised with another $10,000 as a bonus, when estimates called for at least $200,000 to be available before building could start. Yet surveys continued on the Mexico-Jefferson City via Columbia and Ashland route, beginning with Columbia-Ashland.

The company incorporated early in 1910 increasing capital from

$600,000 to $2.5 million. Getting this paid up was problematic, however, and O. F. Spaete resigned as President at a July 15th St. Louis meeting, replaced by M. M. Stephens, former mayor of East St. Louis. ERJ August 27th, 1910 (p.164) said Stephens asked Mexico, Columbia, Ashland and Jefferson City to raise $1/2 million for stock or 2nd mortgage bonds to begin construction. That didn't happen and while there was talk of adding a 39-mile Columbia-Moberly branch, only reorganization held out promise of forward motion. This was done in September 1911 (ERJ October 21st, 1911 p. 932), the name being changed to **Columbia and Northern Electric Railway Company**, with a second branch to Fulton one of its goals. Even less happened in this incarnation. The last heard was that in 1914 (ERJ November 4th p. 1014) it had capital of $1.5 million, authorized bonds of $1.5 million and would build in 30 days. (See also Columbia, Mexico)

5. Oklahoma and Golden City Railway Company
ERJ January 2nd 1909 (p. 49) reported a proposed interurban from Jefferson City SW to Springfield and on to Oklahoma, ending 50 miles west of the Missouri-Oklahoma state line at Pawhuska, 12 miles west of present-day Bartlesville. Headquartered at 717 Dwight Building in Kansas City MO, Winfield S. Pope of Jefferson City was President, E. W. Dempsey of Pawhuska OK Vice-President, F. W. Griesel of Golden City MO General Manager and W. K. Palmer Chief Engineer.

6. Ozark Transit Company SRJ December 8th, 1906 (p. 35) reported incorporation with $50,000 capital of a 65-mile interurban from Waynesville in Pulaski county north through Miller and Cole counties, to Jefferson City, with a 65-mile south extension from Waynesville through Texas and Wright counties to Mountain Grove. A J. Burns of Webster Groves (St. Louis) owned all but four of the 1,000 shares.

Replacement bus schedule as published in the Sunday News and Tribune January 14th, 1934.

MISSOURI POWER & LIGHT CO.

ANNOUNCES TIME SCHEDULES

FOR THE NEW

MOTOR COACH SERVICE

Effective Sunday, January 14, 1934

EAST BOUND

East Cir. Drive	Fulkerson St.	Monroe St.	Miller St.	Moreland Av.
5:30 A. M.	5:33 A. M.	5:37 A. M.	5:41 A. M.	5:45 A. M.
	Coach every 15 minutes thereafter until 7:00 A. M.			
7:00 A. M.	7:05 A. M.	7:10 A. M.	7:15 A. M.	7:20 A. M.
	Coach every 10 minutes thereafter until 9:00 A. M.			
9:00 A. M.	9:05 A. M.	9:10 A. M.	9:15 A. M.	9:20 A. M.
	Coach every 15 minutes thereafter until 11:00 A. M.			
11:00 A. M.	11:05 A. M.	11:10 A. M.	11:15 A. M.	11:20 A. M.
	Coach every 10 minutes thereafter until 1:00 P. M.			
1:00 P. M.	1:05 P. M.	1:10 P. M.	1:15 P. M.	1:20 P. M.
	Coach every 15 minutes thereafter until 4:00 P. M.			
4:00 P. M.	4:05 P. M.	4:10 P. M.	4:15 P. M.	4:20 P. M.
	Coach every 10 minutes thereafter until 8:00 P. M.			
8:00 P. M.	8:03 P. M.	8:07 P. M.	8:11 P. M.	8:15 P. M.
	Coach every 15 minutes thereafter until Midnight.			

WEST BOUND

Moreland Av.	Miller St.	Monroe St.	Fulkerson St.	East Cir. Drive
5:30 A. M.	5:34 A. M.	5:37 A. M.	5:41 A. M.	5:45 A. M.
	Coach every 15 minutes thereafter until 7:00 A. M.			
7:00 A. M.	7:05 A. M.	7:10 A. M.	7:15 A. M.	7:20 A. M.
	Coach every 10 minutes thereafter until 9:00 A. M.			
9:00 A. M.	9:05 A. M.	9:10 A. M.	9:15 A. M.	9:20 A. M.
	Coach every 15 minutes thereafter until 11:00 A. M.			
11:00 A. M.	11:05 A. M.	11:10 A. M.	11:15 A. M.	11:20 A. M.
	Coach every 10 minutes thereafter until 1:00 P. M.			
1:00 P. M.	1:05 P. M.	1:10 P. M.	1:15 P. M.	1:20 P. M.
	Coach every 15 minutes thereafter until 4:00 P. M.			
4:00 P. M.	4:05 P. M.	4:15 P. M.	4:15 P. M.	4:20 P. M.
	Coach every 10 minutes thereafter until 8:00 P. M.			
8:00 P. M.	8:03 P. M.	8:07 P. M.	8:11 P. M.	8:15 P. M.
	Coach every 15 minutes thereafter until Midnight.			

*On Saturday night 10 minute service will be extended until 10:00 P. M. instead of changing to 15 minute service at 8:00 P. M.

On Sunday, from 5:30 A. M. until midnight, coach service will be each 15 minutes throughout the entire day.

JOPLIN

Line 1 Carthage. Line 2 Joplin. Line 3 Webb City. Line 4 Carterville. Line 5 Galena KS. Line 6 Pittsburg KS.

	1880	**1890**	**1900**	**1910**	**1920**	**1930**	**1940**	**1950**	**1960**	**1970**	**1980**	**1990**	**2000**
1.	4,167	7,981	9,416	9,483	10,068	9,736	10,585	11,188	11,264	11,035	11,104	10,747	12,668
2.	7,038	9,943	26,023	32,073	29,902	33,454	37,144	38,711	38,958	39,256	38,893	31,175	45,504
3.	1,588	5,043	9,201	11,817	7,807	6,876	7,033	6,919	6,740	6,923	7,309	7,538	9,812
4.	483	2,884	4,445	4,539	2,434	1,600	1,582	1,552	1,443	1,716	1,973	2,013	1,850
5.	–	–	10,155	6,096	4,712	4,736	4,375	4,029	3,827	–	–	–	–
6.	–	6,697	10,212	14,755	18,052	18,145	17,571	19,341	18,678	20,171	18,770	7,789	19,243

"Get your kicks on route six six," advises Bobby Troup's song. Joplin was one place to do it. Founded in 1840, it sprang to life in 1869 with railroads and mines. Webb City followed when John C. Webb unexpectedly harvested lead as well as corn, opened a mine and platted a town. Soon Joplin and Webb City were centers for every political and recreational vice known to humanity. For Joplin, this was ironic; it was named for the Reverend Harris G. Joplin, founder of Jasper County's first Methodist congregation in 1840. In the early 1900s the mines migrated west to Kansas and Oklahoma. The bars, brothels, honkytonks, soiled doves and hustlers followed. Remaining citizenry embraced family, respectability and religion, though Ma Barker's gang and Bonnie and Clyde were active in the 1920s and early 1930s. Designation of U. S. Highway 66 in November 1926 and its paving and development, extended the area's life into the 1960s after which the commercial centers shifted towards the new I-44 and suburban shopping malls.

1. THE SOUTHWEST MISSOURI AND ITS ANTECEDENTS

(Maps courtesy of Edward A. Conrad)

1. Joplin Street Car Company In the early 1880s, John B. Sergeant, newly-enriched from his mining interests, decided to invest in Joplin's growth. On November 15th, 1882, with a streetcar franchise and $20,000 capital, he organized the JSCC. Opened early in 1883 it ran mule cars from East Broadway via Broadway, Main and 9th Streets to the zinc works in West Joplin. It may have become the **Joplin Street Railway Company** but little is known of the JSCC except it was 4' gauge and had six miles of track, four cars and 26 mules.

2. Twin Cities Railway Company. Based on Webb City, the TCRC was opened early in 1890 as a 2.75-mile mule line from Webb City's western limits to Carterville's eastern. Its original 16 mules and five cars soon became 28 mules and ten cars (four closed, six open). A. H. Rogers took over on September 1st, 1890.

3. Joplin Electric Railway and Motor Company Organized in August 1890 with $100,000 capital, this was a project of J. N. Bofinger, B. F. Hammett, Henry Newman (of the Joplin National Bank) et al to bring trolleys to Joplin. On December 4th, 1890 a noonday opening banquet was held in the powerhouse and next day cars began service on 2.64 miles of track from College Hill (East Joplin) to 10th Street on Main. A 2.4 mile Blendville extension opened August 21st, 1891 running south on Main, west on 19th, south on Byers, west on 21st and south on Murphy to 26th. The line's success led to the annexation of Blendville by Joplin in 1892.

4. Joplin and Galena Electric Railway Company Little is known of this except that from at least 1895 it was leased and operated by the Southwest though it had only five miles of track. The Southwest took it over in 1896.

5. Southwest Missouri Electric Railway. Alfred Rogers came to Joplin from Springfield MO and stayed the rest of his life. He and E. Z. Wallower were introduced and soon Wallower and his Harrisburg PA investment syndicate bought the Twin Cities Railway Company and its 1890 Carterville mule line.The Southwest was formed in 1892, took over the Twin

Cities and built a trolley line from Webb City to Carterville. In February 1893, a two-mile branch opened from Carterville south to the Prosperity mining camp. On July 4th 1893 the main line was extended southwest six miles from Webb City to Joplin's city limits. Initial Webb City franchise problems, tied to retailer fears that Joplin-bound riders would desert the town's stores, were addressed when Webb City's mayor added a franchise condition that Southwest be based there, not in Joplin. So it was done.

In January 1893, Rogers made a pitch to the Carthage Commercial Club regarding a Carterville-Carthage line but waited until 1894 to ask for a franchise. The Carthage mayor instead awarded a franchise to Fred Fitch's rival group, who formed the Jasper County Electric Railroad Company (see Carthage), and opened a Carterville-Carthage line in August 1895. Southwest's main line through Joplin (via Blendville) to Galena KS opened early in 1896, with Galena's local trolley service. Its cars replaced Fitch's "White Line" cars on August 21st, 1896, after the Southwest Missouri Electric Railway, Jasper County Electric Railway and Joplin and Galena Electric Railway merged as the new Southwest Missouri Electric Railway.

Joplin began losing ground in 1903 when zinc was found in Cherokee City KS, probably the reason Stone and Webster Corporation of Boston, a major utilities and traction management company, decided in November 1902 not to pick up an option for 8,000 Southwestern shares it had held since September. In 1903, Southwest built a new power house and shops just north of the old, and opened a 2½ mile extension (the Duenweg loop) to Smelter Hill in East Joplin and a one-mile extension from there to Blendville and Chitwood.

A new 2000' double-track viaduct carrying the line over railroads between Webb City and Carterville opened in mid-1905 and the new **Webb City Northern** subsidary built a 9-mile Webb City-Oronogo line north via Neck City, Purcell and Alba (small zinc mining towns). Two

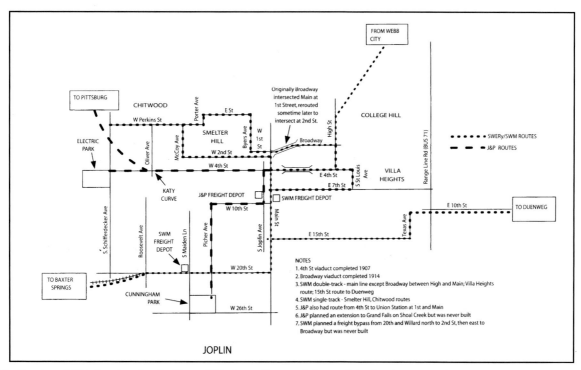

Map of Joplin circa 1915, showing the Joplin and Pittsburg lines and those of the Southwest within the city limits. Edward A. Conrad.

Car 30 at the Jackson and Sharp plant in Wilmington DE, awaiting shipment to Joplin during 1898.

Heights), making a belt line round the Joplin/Webb City mining district. Years of prosperity followed. In 1917, a westerly Galena-Baxter Springs KS-Picher OK extension was built. For this, Rogers by-passed Galena (another franchise dispute) by running two blocks south of the city limits, the new extension leaving the main line a mile east of town. Most was a former steam railroad (the Oklahoma, Kansas and Missouri).

The Picher line opened June 10th, 1918, though Baxter Springs-Hockerville opened earlier. Southwest cars now ran through from Carthage MO in the east to Picher OK in the west (about 40 miles), by-passing Galena whose local line, running south on Galena's main street, was not extended to meet the new main line until 1919. Rogers's health now declined and he died in March 1920 at age 62. His son Harrison was elected to the board in June 1920. But the local economy was on the skids. Lead prices fell, replacements pits were being sunk further away and unrestricted jitney competition in Carthage, Webb City and Joplin wrought havoc. Though new Birneys were bought for the Chitwood, Smelter Hill, Broadway and Villa Heights local lines in Joplin, lines to Alba, Duenweg

miles to the Yellow Dog Mine opened February 28th, 1906, the year Carterville-Lakeside Park was double-tracked. A new **Southwest Missouri Railroad Company** took over the old Southwest and Webb City Northern as of September 1st 1906, capital increasing from $1,150,000 to $5 million. Incorporation as a railroad gave it the right of eminent domain, which it didn't have as a street railway.

J. J. Heim was a Kansas City brewer who since 1903 had been trying to build a Joplin-Baxter Springs (KS) line (with a Galena KS extension), a Joplin–Duenweg line and a connection in downtown Joplin for an as-yet unbuilt Pittsburg-Joplin high-speed (or "Air Line") interurban. Southwest already had ten miles of Joplin tracks, but its proposed Joplin extensions clashed with its franchise, which didn't allow local car operation. When Heim applied for a Joplin franchise, Rogers asked for 3 blocks on East 15th Street, a key part of its proposed Joplin-Duenweg service. Heim claimed that if those blocks went to Rogers, his "Air Line" plan would collapse. The city agreed. Heim's "Air line" passenger and freight trains began running to and from Joplin on March 19th 1908.

Southwest's new Duenweg service east from Joplin opened in 1908, as did a northern link to the Prosperity branch (via Villa

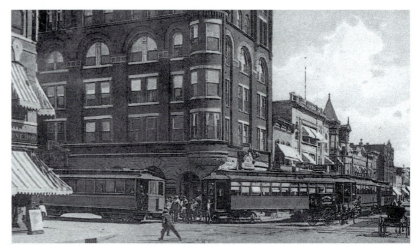

Cars on Main Street, Joplin circa 1910.

Webb City carhouse circa 1910. Earl E. McMechan.

and Prosperity were slated for closure, their earning potential gone. A last dividend was paid in 1921, followed by a 10% pay cut and a long, hard look at local lines and staff levels.

ERJ August 29th, 1924 p. 205 reported a citizens group volunteering to pay increased fares if Southwest would keep cars running to Alba and Duenweg, arguing that service was needed for miners, workmen and school kids in rural areas. This sentiment was voiced again in a 1926 MOPSC hearing on an application to close the lines. They were reprieved for 60 days but fares were raised, Alba going from 15 to 25 cents, on the understanding that no opposition would be made to junking the six miles from Duenweg north to Prosperity immediately. If Alba and Duenweg still showed a loss at the end of 60 days, they would go. They did and were soon gone, Duenweg before year's end, Alba early in 1927. Rail was picked up to avoid paying property tax, and was relaid elsewhere.

Base fare on Joplin trolleys and buses went from 5 to 8 cents early in 1926, Webb City-Joplin from a dime to 13 cents in late spring and Carthage-Joplin from 35 to 38 cents. It didn't help.

<u>ERJ</u> July 3rd 1926 (p. 41) reported that in a letter to Joplin's mayor, Southwest had suggested closure of lines in Main Street plus all Joplin city service. Main line cars would be re-routed over West Fourth to McKinley Avenue, then south to connect with the Southwest main line in Joplin Heights, allowing Southwest to remove tracks on Main and West 20th Streets *"on account of the inability of the...Company to pay for a proportionate part of the repaving of Main Street in Joplin,"*

A proposal to reinstate nickel-fare Joplin local cars was approved by a 6-1 majority in a September 1926 special election. A counter-proposal to again allow jitney service was defeated by the same margin. The nickel fare began immediately, but within a month Southwest

Right of way past mine tailings west of Galena KS circa 1910.

declared bankruptcy on the petition of E. Z. Wallower who still owned 12,000 shares and $400,000 in bonds on which interest hadn't been paid for years. Other creditors too threatened legal action. By Fall 1927 it was clear nothing could save Joplin local services and Southwest began closing everything except the main line. The mines had now migrated almost beyond Southwest's reach. Yet paradoxically freight traffic was growing, 30 to 40 cars daily by 1928, mainly ore and gravel.

New lightweight interurban cars were bought and a three-mile extension built from Baxter Springs OK south into the Quapaw Indian reservation. Passenger and freight service began in mid-1927. A new January 1929 freight line ran north from Picher OK to the Golden Rod and Blue Mound mines over the border in Kansas. A third extension was proposed; a 20-mile interurban running south to Neosho from the end of the Joplin County Line trolley route at 32nd Street. Right-of-way was bought and grad-

ing began but it was never finished. A belt line to get freights off Joplin streets was to run from 20th and Willard in West Joplin to 2nd Street and then east to rejoin the main line. But there was no money and freights avoided Joplin by interchanging west of town.

When the Depression hit, mines closed and a drought began, creating dust-bowl conditions which in turn led to migration from the area. The last Carthage-Joplin car ran July 21st, 1935, replaced next day by four new Twin Coach buses. F. C. Wallower, as receiver, drove the final interurban on July 21st and the first bus next day (<u>Joplin Globe</u> July 21st, 1935 p. 4). Many locals were unhappy and three unsuccessful attempts were made to wreck the last cars (<u>Joplin Globe</u> July 23rd, 1935 p. 2). The Smelter Hill line also went and Lakeside Park closed at the end of 1935. However, Webb City-Joplin-Galena cars continued for a few more months. Carthage-Webb City tracks were lifted as part of a WPA project. By 1936, buses ran Carthage-Galena, cars Galena-Picher.

Two cars then served the 11.5 mile Galena-Picher run until May 7th 1938. They were replaced next day by home-built motored rail buses, which ceased on April 26th, 1939 when Southwest ran its last electric freights. Anxious to ditch bus operation as well, Southwest's Joplin-Galena buses quit June 2nd, 1939 and its Carthage-Joplin bus line was sold for $2,000 to the new Joplin Public Service Company, which had no buses to its name for months. Jopliners were served through an arrangement between the JPSC and former Southwest drivers who used their own autos (for a fee) to provide transit. These men were then hired to run Joplin's new buses. The Baxter Springs KS-Picher OK rail segment was sold to the Northeast Oklahoma Railroad which continued Miami-Picher passenger service until December 1939 and trolley freight to June 1940 when the line

Car 18 on Main Street Webb City, circa 1918. Earl E. McMechan.

Car 61 going south on Madison Avenue in Webb City, January 1919. Earl E. McMechan.

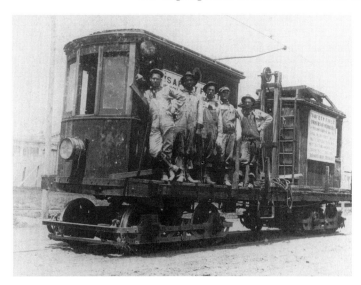

Repair car 11 at an unknown location circa 1918, with "Safety First" posters exhorting automobile drivers not to take chances by driving on car tracks. Earl E. McMechan.

was dieselised.

The Southwest now led a ghost existence, continuing to liquidate assets until wound up in 1941. In the 1940s, JPSC was a subsidiary of the Bangert-owned St. Louis County Bus Company, which often moved buses between its properties. JPSC was sold in 1951 to Joplin Transit Company who transferred services to the Ozark Leasing Company in 1960. In 1964 the Joplin-Carthage Bus Company took over, the Crown Coach Company from 1969. By 1979 there were no Joplin buses, a situation that continued for some time.

Roster notes

SRJ directory March 1897 notes 25 motor cars and 7 trailers (American, St. Louis and Laclede). SRJ May 1899 notes former Twin Cities and

Car 70, at its terminal on Carthage Public Square prior to running through to Picher OK. Earl E. McMechan poses with the car in June 1920. Earl E. McMechan.

Car 90 was built by American Car in 1927 and is seen northbound on Main turning east onto Fourth Street in Joplin during May 1934. Five similar but slightly longer cars were home-built in 1927. Earl E. McMechan.

Carthage mule cars used as passenger shelters/stations, a shoe-maker's shop and a newstand. There were 10 single-truck, 12 double-truck, 11 double-truck opens and 3 trailers. New 2-motor Jackson and Sharp cars held down "Empire County Express" service. No car had air-brakes initially. After a fatal collision between cars 29 and 30 in 1903, most were upgraded with new Taylor trucks, GE type M control and Westinghouse air brakes.

Little of this agrees with Conrad's roster, based on company records (since destroyed) and Official Railroad Equipment Register entries which, for example, show no American Car vehicles in the 1890s. From 1903 to 1917 Southwest built 44 passenger cars, mostly with steel frames. Each batch was slightly different. Most had 11 or 12-window bodies, deck roofs and Brill 27 or 27-G trucks. They included 12 (#2), 14 (#2 of 1912, 15-19 (1903/4), 20-23 (1910), 24-28 (1905), 29-32 (1905/6), 33-38 (35-38 #2 of 1911/12), 39-41 (#2) of 1913, 44 (built 1906 as a parlor car), 45 (built 1906 as a funeral car), 46-50 (1906/7), 51-55 (1907/8), 56-59 (built as steel cars 1916.) Also built were 3 steel baggage/ express cars, 2 double-truck line cars and 4 single-end locomotives, run back-to-back as two units. Southwest's home-built cars looked like typical city cars and lacked interurban accoutrements such as toilets and drinking fountains. They had spartan seats typical of city cars, many of them with bench (longitudinal) seats and smoking sections originally.

Between 1905 and 1910 about 45 cars were in service, but new home-built vehicles replaced older units on a one-for-one basis, often taking the same number. Orders for 12 city cars (60-71) were placed with American in 1916 and 1917. A Brill magazine article (February 1917) claimed Southwest sometimes ran two and three-car trains so these cars had "more steel" in their construction than previously, while the "no smoking" compartments were eliminated. Nine single-truck Birneys (81-88) came from Cincinnati Car in 1921, a General Electric locomotive (#2) in 1924, four (#4-7) home-built locomotives between 1927 and 1930 and six light-weight double-truck cars (#90 from American, 91-95 home-built) in 1927. Two locomotives were sold to the Joplin and Pittsburg after Southwest freights ceased in 1939. Preserved Southwest car 62 runs annually

Twin Coaches Replace Street Cars

- On Monday, July 22, twin coaches will replace the street cars between Joplin and Carthage with a faster, more frequent service schedule.
- Coaches leave Fourth and Main, Joplin, for Carthage at 5:30 a. m. and every thirty minutes thereafter until 11:30 p. m.
- Coaches leave Union Bus Terminal, Carthage, for County Line, Joplin, at 5:45 a. m. and every thirty minutes thereafter until 12:15 a. m.
- Running time Joplin-Carthage—45 minutes.
- Twin coaches replace Smelter Hill street cars. No change in time schedule.
- Ten-minute schedule to Blendville, via Main and Twentieth streets, until 7:45 p. m. Then 15-minute schedule. (10-minute schedule Saturday and Sunday nights.)
- 6:15, 8:15 and 10:15 to Picher. Only cars west of Joplin on week nights. (7:15 p. m. west to Iron Gates only.)
- No street car service east of Webb City.
- No street car service east of Joplin after 7:45 p. m. on week nights. (11:50 p. m. to Webb City, barn and 12:15 a. m. to Main street, Webb City, excepted.)
- No change in street car schedules on Saturday and Sunday nights. (30-minute service Joplin-Webb City until 12:15 a. m. Hourly service to Picher until 10:15 p. m. 11:15 p. m. Galena only, Saturday and Sunday only.)
- Coaches leave Webb City for Joplin at 10 and 40—street cars at 25 and 55 minutes after the hour.
- With the exception of the above mentioned changes all service will continue as at present.
- For information call Joplin 290.

SOUTHWEST MISSOURI RAILROAD CO.

Replacement bus notice from the Joplin Globe, July 21st, 1935.

on "Mining Days," powered by an automobile motor, on freight tracks in King Jack Park, Webb City. (These notes were compiled with the help of Edward A. Conrad)

2. JOPLIN AND PITTSBURG

Pittsburg KS saw its first electric cars in late 1890. Of the several companies, the **Pittsburg, Frontenac and Suburban** emerged as top dog in 1895. By July 1901, the PF&S was **Pittsburg Railway Company,** later **Pittsburg Railway and Light Company**. In 1905, the PR&LC was bought by Guy Walker of New York and Fred Fitch, who since 1896 had been Southwest's superintendent. Fitch now quit Southwest to promote extension of the PR&LC 21 miles south from Pittsburg to Columbus KS, the Cherokee County seat. Northern extensions to Crawford County KS coal mines were announced in 1906 by which time Fitch and others had bought out Guy Walker. Another merger formed a **Joplin and Pittsburg Railway Company**, comprising Heim's proposed high-speed Joplin-Pittsburg "Air Line", Fitch's PR&LC now running to Scammon and Columbus KS, plus a Scammon-Mineral branch.

The J&P incorporated on June 10th, 1907 for $5 million, though only $2.3 million of common stock was issued. Heim had the majority interest and ran the company. Fitch and associates invested $2 million and Rogers of the Southwest (hedging his bets) took a minority interest. Between 1907 and 1910 the J&P took over Pittsburg Railway and Light, Joplin and Pittsburgh Street Railway and Pittsburg and Kansas Railway (owners of the Girard Coal Belt Electric Railway. The "Air Line" was complete by March 19th, 1908, four months ahead of schedule, opening in October 1908.

In 1910 all underliers were merged in an enlarged J&P, now the biggest interurban system in Kansas. A crucial twelve miles was in Missouri. Besides locals, the "Air Line" ran a four-stop "Limited" and heavy freight trains.These too were speedy, had to be so as not to delay the Limiteds. All cars carried express, while a freight/express car made a daily round trip on every division. Joplin city service was every ten minutes, Pittsburg city service every fifteen, "Air Line" cars hourly. There was through Joplin-Pittsburg-Mulberry service. The J&P interchanged with the MoPac, MKT, Kansas City Southern and Santa Fe railroads, its freight depot was at 110 W. 7th Street (moved a block south in 1914), the ticket office and waiting room at 640 Main. The Joplin car house was at 4th and Maiden Lane and it ran a couple of Joplin local services including a line on West 4th Street to Schifferdecker Park, and a short line into South Joplin.

Labor relations were the J&P's Achilles heel. There were constant disputes and walkouts and an 80-day strike in 1914. Issues were always working conditions and wages. The ease with which the railroads picked up the slack during a strike was a measure of just how marginal J&P's lines were. Settlement costs, jitney competition and the war fatally undermined the company and when depression hit the mines from 1920, there was a risk it might go under, idling 200 men and over 100 miles of track. Short-term hopes were on one-man operation and wage reductions but the J&P posted losses for 1921 and 1922. Extensions were put on hold (none were contemplated in Missouri), including a 12-mile Columbus-Picher OK line intended to meet the Southwest, newly extended to that point.

Some right-of-way had been bought, but the Northeast Oklahoma was building from its northern Lucky Jew Mine terminal in Oklahoma to Picher and Columbus, (opened October 1923) and the J&P was relieved of the burden. Still, it went under on September 18th 1924 and Heim interests ceased. On October 16th, services were cut system-wide and track repair

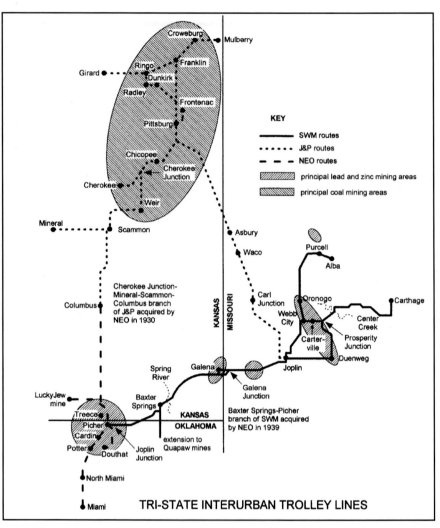

Map showing the relationship between the Southwest, Joplin and Pittsburg and Northeast Oklahoma (NEO) interurban lines in Missouri, Kansas and Oklahoma at their maximum extent. Edward A. Conrad.

ended. In Joplin track was so bad by the end of 1928 the J&P was told to fix it or leave. It left.

The last "Air Line" run was May 31st, 1929. Two weeks previously, the bankrupt company had been sold for $115,000 to a Pittsburg group and renamed **Joplin-Pittsburg Railroad Company,** capitalized at $200,000. The new name was misleading as May 31st also saw the last Joplin freight. The "Air Line" was cut back to Chitwood, a quarter-mile inside Joplin city limits. Pittsburg and Frontenac KS passenger cars ran to 1932 but tracks south of Cherokee Junction were sold to the Northeast Oklahoma in 1930, which maintained service to Scammon (south of Cherokee) until 1933. Freight service also continued, giving the smelters a through rail route to railroad interchanges on the Northeast Oklahoma.

The Air Line was pruned from Chitwood to the Missouri state line at Waco at some point but the Croweburg line was extended four miles in the 1930s to a new mine. All wires came down in 1936, and freights were run by gas-electric locomotives, later by diesels. The J-P shrank as it lost customers and rights of way were condemned for highway widening. With less than a dozen employees, coal and mine chat loads tailing off and just 38 miles of track, it filed for abandonment in 1953.The last freight ran March 1954.Trains ran until fall, picking up tracks to vacate the right-of-way.

Incomplete Roster notes

In 1908 the fleet included 14-bench opens 41 and 42, closed cars 51-66, except 53, (St. Louis, 1905), 60-66 (1906, on St. Louis 23-AE double trucks). Combines 201-205 and express 251 (Jewett, 1908) were "Air Line" cars on Baldwin 78-30 double trucks with 4 75 HP WH 112B motors. There were also six closed cars (Jewett 1908) on Brill 21-E single trucks (numbers unknown). Another express car came later, (Jewett, 1912), also on Baldwin 78-30 trucks. Car 201 was sold to the Northeast

Oklahoma circa 1922 and rebuilt as steeple-cab locomotive 402 in 1929 (scrapped 1940). ERJ March 13th, 1909 (p. 454) motes five Jewett combines, two express cars (one numbered 254),15 double-truck passenger cars, four double-truck 84-seat open cars, seven single-truck closed cars, twelve single-truck open cars, two line/ wrecker cars, ten flat cars, three ballast cars and sixty coal cars. 1913 saw six 40-seat closed cars (Brill, 1900) on Brill 27-G double trucks, formerly Philadelphia 1633/46/48/82/89/90, part of a batch of 771 almost identical cars.

3. JOPLIN INTERURBAN PROPOSALS

For a town so well endowed with street railway and interurban services, it is remarkable that more were proposed.

1. Joplin and Monett Interurban Railway ERJ June 20th, 1908 (p. 138) notes this company's Joplin-Neosho proposal with a possible extension from Neosho (Newton county) east to Monnett (Barry county). Neosho citizens had subscribed $40,000 in bonds and hoped to get $80,000 from Joplin residents.

2. Joplin, Neosho and Pierce City Interurban Railway Company SRJ December 26th, 1903 (ad p. 24) reported its incorporation for $50,000,

half of which was paid up. It would build through Jasper, Lawrence, Newton and Barry counties, linking Joplin, Sarcoxie, Pierce City, Scott City, Newtonia, Granby and Neosho. Incorporators were all St. Louisans, including Charles Benjamin Cinliffe, William S. Brawner, John Kimpel and John Weathers.

3. Joplin, Oklahoma and Western ERJ January 21st, 1911(p. 143) reported surveys completed and that building of a Joplin-Corman (OK) line would begin February 11th. F. M. Overlees of Bartlesville OK was interested.

KANSAS CITY AND NORTH KANSAS CITY

Line 1 Kansas City MO. Line 2 Kansas City KS. Line 3 N. Kansas City MO. Line 4 Lawrence KS.
Line 5 Leavenworth KS. Line 6 Olathe KS. Line 7 Overland Park KS.

	1880	1890	1900	1910	1920	1930	1940	1950	1960	1970	1980	1990	2000
1.	55,785	132,716	163,752	248,381	324,410	399,746	399,178	456,622	475,539	507,330	448,159	434,159	441,545
2.	6,149	38,316	51,418	82,331	101,177	121,857	121,458	129,553	121,901	168,210	161,087	151,521	146,866
3.	–	–	–	–	870	2,574	2,688	3,886	5,657	4,507	4,507	4,130	4,714
4.	–	9,997	10,862	12,374	12,456	13,726	14,390	23,351	32,858	52,738	52,738	65,608	80,098
5.	–	19,768	20,735	19,363	16,912	17,466	19,220	20,579	22,052	33,656	33,656	38,495	35,420
6.	–	–	–	–	3,268	3,656	3,979	5,593	10,998	37,258	37,258	63,402	92,962
7.	–	–	–	–	–	–	–	–	21,110	81,784	81,784	111,790	149,080

1. KANSAS CITY CITY STREETCARS

An elegant new 8-bench open summer trailer 368 of Kansas City's Metropolitan Street Railway, seen in 1886 at Laclede Car of St. Louis before delivery.

Cable train on Main Street circa 1887.

and downs of the stockyards. Transit began November 1st, 1870 with Nehemia Holmes's **Kansas City and Westport Horse Railroad Company** running from City Market east on 4th, south on Walnut, east on 11th and south on Grand to 17th. It had three cars, two usually in service. An extension and gauge change to 3' 6" took it further south to the town of Westport (39th Street) on April 26th, 1872.

In that year, a new **Jackson County Horse Railroad** built a line from Independence Avenue to City Market. On completion of a new Union Depot in 1874, a **Union Depot Horse Railroad Company** began serving it and the West Bottoms. Wyandotte KS had its own horse line, the 1872 **Kansas City and Wyandotte Horse Railroad Company**, which met Union Depot cars at 9th Street and State Line in the West Bottoms. Holmes died in April 1873, at age 47, His cars continued, intially without family participation, but by the early 1880s his sons ran the business.

Brothers and railroad contractors Bernard and Thomas Corrigan began their **Corrigan Street Railway Company** in the mid-1870s by taking over the competing Jackson County and Union Depot lines. By 1876, they were kings of KC transit. In ferociously protecting their interests, brother Tom crafted a reputation as a "fixer" of his own projects and later (for a fee) of other movers and shakers needing a smooth road to civic approval. In that role, he was "Boss" Corrigan and "fixing," (i.e. bribing) elected representatives became his thing.

In the early 1880's, the Corrigans were singled out by the Kansas City Star and its owner William Rockhill Nelson, the start of the paper's anti-streetcar campaign that lasted into the 1940s. They were an appropriate target. Their influence on Kansas City street railway matters was notorious, stifling progress in many areas, mechanization for example, a capital-intensive exercise that could yield rich rewards to those who could afford to take the risk. Most could not. The Corrigans could but didn't, and opposed anyone else who tried. Robert Gillham, an engineer in KC for the first time, was astounded by the bluffs

Though organized in 1850 and chartered in 1853, Kansas City did not really exist before 1860. After that, real estate, railroads, grain and meatpacking fueled an intense demand for residential and commercial property, especially after the first bridge over the Missouri opened in 1869. Horse, cable, electric, elevated, trolleybus, bus, KC had them all at one time or another. It was the usual story of competition, expansion, greed, graft, overcapitalized consolidations and bankruptcies, linked to the ups

The 9th Street roller-coaster of the Kansas City Railway Company circa 1890 A two car train begins its ascent from the terminal building in the West Bottoms (right center). Union Depot is in the center of the photo.

Summit Street Viaduct, April 1903.

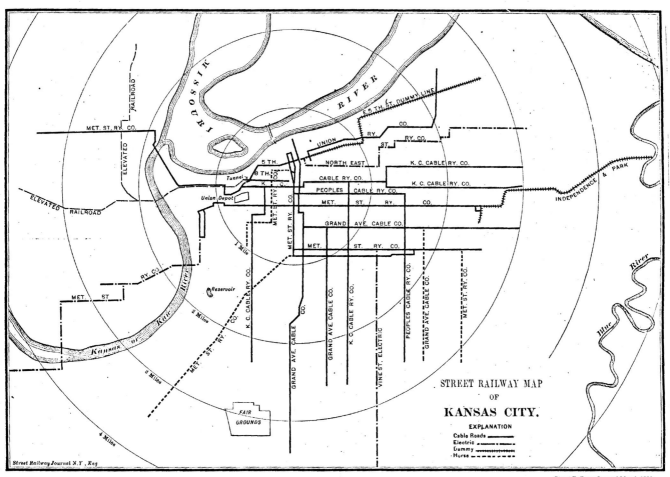

Car 662 at the Vine and 31st terminal in the new southern suburbs October 19th, 1903 offers civilized, smooth, weatherproof transport over the otherwise horrendous unpaved roads.

east of Union Depot; downtown was up there? Foot-loose, he decided to stay and see if he could do something, maybe an inclined plane from the station up to downtown, or perhaps a cable line.

By 1883, his project had gelled as the **Kansas City Cable Railway Company**. The Corrigans threw up roadblocks, fixing the council so that nothing Gillham proposed was passed. But Nelson's KC Star was an ally and since the council was elected annually, administrations hostile to Corrigan often got in with Nelson's help. At such a time, Gillham got his franchise. Beginning at a Union Depot elevated terminal, KCCRC cars

crossed the railroads on a truss bridge, climbed the bluff on a lofty 18.5%-graded trestle to 9th Street, made two difficult 90-degree turns onto Grand and then east on 8th, to end at Woodland Avenue. It should have opened before June 15th, 1885 but tracks were an inch over gauge, car wheels a half-inch under and both had to be corrected.

As Gillham had given the project close daily supervision, this glitch probably happened during his enforced absence, caused when a cable grip he was adjusting in a pit came loose and smashed him in the head. He'd fallen back onto a brick wall, banged his head again and was lucky to sur-

The original east entrance to the 8th Street tunnel circa 1903.

The 8th Street tunnel was lowered, the old 9th Street viaduct abolished and cars were sent through the remodeled tunnel and over the rebuilt and realigned 8th Street viaduct from April 6th 1904. The tunnel and realigned viaduct now did double duty for the previously separate 8th and 9th Street cars. One of the modifications to the viaduct was at Union Depot, seen here on April 26th, 1904.

vive. He didn't work again for a year. The KCCRC eventually had a 2.3 mile branch south on Troost from 8th to 33rd Street, a 2.4 mile branch from 9th and Washington south to 13th, west to Summit and south on Summit to 29th Street and a branch east on Ninth and Independence to just east of Spruce.

The Corrigans also blocked the Union Depot-Wyandotte (InterState) elevated line, while regrouping in 1884 as the **Corrigan Consolidated Street Railway Company,** ($3,600,000 capital) to consolidate a mixed bag of properties (many not yet standard-gauge) with differing franchises which they needed to harmonize. Later, they asked for (and got) a universal 30-year franchise, approved in circumstances that left KC voters incandescent with rage at the eight councilmen who had swung the deal. Corrigan of course had bought their votes, just as he had the votes that rejected the Wyandotte elevated. A backlash spawned a series of indignation meetings and only deft footwork saved the octet from a lynch mob. The mayor immediately convened a special session, vetoed the franchise, defeated an override and approved the long-blocked InterState elevated to Kansas, which opened October 17th, 1886.

InterState Consolidated Rapid Transit Railway Company was the transit arm of Colonel David W. Edgerton's InterState Investment Company real-estate firm. It included 3.75 miles of steam railroad with two Kansas branches, two miles of elevated tracks across the West Bottoms to Union Depot, 0.8 miles of cable line from there up another elevated section and into a tunnel to downtown KC (opened 1888),

The Twelfth Street cable lasted until October 12th 1913 as the 20% grade was too fierce for electric cars. This is the last day of the cable, with car 3, a trailer, company officers and staff plus a group of passengers posing for a souvenir photograph.

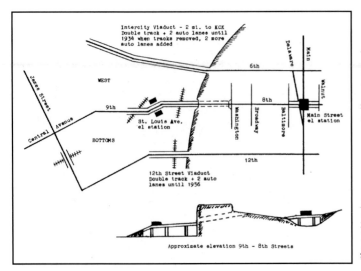

The Twelfth Street cable cars were partially replaced by an electric route over the new 12th Street viaduct. This simplified map sketches the street railway layout around the Bluffs and West Bottoms between 1934 and 1956. Henry Elsner.

Interurbans of Kansas City present and future. May 4th, 1913. The Kaw Valley line from Bonner Springs is shown as "planned" but opened 1914. The rest of the projects, shown as dotted lines, remained pipe dreams.

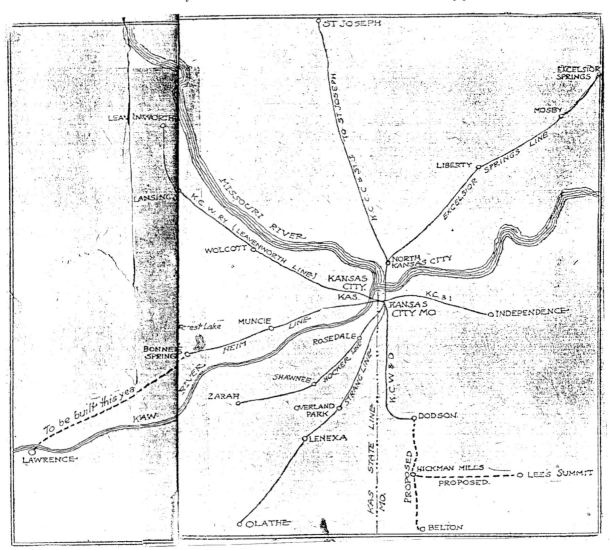

By 1915, things had changed on the interurban front. Under the title *"The interurban arms will have a longer reach at the end of 1915,"* this <u>Kansas City Star</u> map of January 2nd 1915 was said to show the 69 miles of *"trolley railway now radiating out of Kansas City, with the Heim line extension to Lawrence to be built this year"* (it wasn't) *"and the projected line to Belton and Lee's summit, which its promoters claim is not far from realization"* (untrue). *"Other interurban lines are proposed whose financing is awaiting the war's cessation."* None materialized.

plus 1.6 miles of cable line in Kansas (Riverview line) by 1890. The tunnel's costs broke the company in 1889 and cable cars were soon replaced by steam dummies. An 1892 reorganization renamed it **Kansas City Elevated Railway.** Its cable and steam lines went electric March 1st, 1893.

Meanwhile, without the 30-year franchise, the Corrigans' lines were no good to them and were sold to a new **Metropolitan Street Railway Company** in July 1886. The pair were paid off with $1 million in cash and securities. The MET was owned by a loose confederation of oddfellows, including an Armour or two (the meatpackers and a major force in Chicago and KC), John Adams (scion of the presidential family), and a syndicate of Boston investors with a controlling interest in KC's stockyards. However, the Corrigans remained minority stockholders, retaining some influence over the MET in its relations with the city. MET also inherited the Corrigans' blanket franchise, allowing use of any street in Kansas City KS until 1893. All parties saw bringing cars to the West Bottoms as crucial.

The merits of cable and electric traction were yet to be settled, but the MET's rag-bag collection of animal lines was no match for InterState's steam dummies nor Kansas City Cable Railway cars. That had to be fixed. The old Union Depot line from City Market was cabled and extended into Kansas City KS via Minnesota Avenue in 1887. A new 12th Street cable opened in May 1888, with a trestle on a 20% grade taking the line down to a stockyard owned by MET backers. Its eastern terminal was at Cleveland Avenue. Finally a cable line from 9th and Main, south on Main to 18th and 19th Streets, then east to Cleveland Avenue, opened in October 1888.

Car 1102, one of 75 lightweight city cars ordered in 1916 for the new Kansas City Railways, seen at St. Louis Car on a CBQ flat car, about to leave for KC.

"AIN'T IT A GRAND FEELIN'"

The <u>Kansas City Star's</u> attacks on the trolleys and general sleaze in Pendergast's city government, continued well into the Prohibition era. Not surprisingly, the new <u>Kansas City Railways</u> was unhappy about this, making its point with this editorial cartoon in its in-house magazine on February 11th, 1921.

St. Louis and Kansas City were heavily polluted places until the 1940s. This is Main Street Kansas City, looking north from 24th Street on November 2nd, 1926. Downtown (up the hill) can barely be seen. STLMOT

The former Westport company remained a Holmes family venture. In 1886, it reorganized as the **Grand Avenue Railway Company** and cabled three lines; the original Westport via Grand and Main, a new line east on 15th from Grand to Kensington and on Holmes south from 15th to 31st Street, all this while the Henry experiment continued. Its failure, however, was a hiccup, a result of technological immaturity that time soon fixed. The Armourdale line was double tracked in 1888 between Sixteenth and Bell in KC MO and Fourth and Kansas Avenue in Armourdale, with an extension to 12th and Osage. In 1889 it was extended again, to Third and Metropolitan in Argentine KS. The entire 4.11 miles was electrified in December 1889, the first permanent trolley line in the two Kansas Cities.

In 1894, the MET absorbed the now-electrified InterState Elevated. In May 1895 it paid $4.4 million for the KCCRC and $2.4 million for the Grand Avenue's four cable lines (15th Street, Westport, Holmes Street and Walnut Street) the Prospect Avenue horse line and the Rosedale Avenue Motor line (steam dummies). Except for the People's, the MET now owned every cable line in KC. MET also took over Winner's steam **Kansas City, Independence and Park**, now the **Kansas City and Independence Rapid Transit Railway** (see Independence) in 1895. By mid-1897, the MET had 136.5 miles of track. 63 miles were cable, 16.1 miles elevated, 54.6 miles electric and 2.98 miles animal, the last of which (Broadway and Madison) ran on August 7th. By 1899, most KC lines were in MET hands. Half were electrified. The People's cable was acquired in that year but stockyard expansion required its realignment from Bell to Wyoming. As existing plant was in poor shape, MET called in consultants. *"Electrify now"* was their advice. The last People's cable ran July 15th, 1899, electrics began December 14th.

In 1899 the J. Ogden Armour family bought out all Boston interests to take sole control of the MET and the KC electric utility. More expansion was expected after franchise issues were settled and more working capital raised. This was necesaary since franchises on underliers were coming up for renewal, the city was disenchanted with MET's monopoly and MET's board had concluded there'd be no chance of franchise extensions for cable services. So opening new negotiations was a way to get civic approval for their commitment to speedy total electrification.

The RAILWAYAN

KANSAS CITY PUBLIC SERVICE COMPANY
Kansas City, Missouri

Vol. 27   KANSAS CITY, MISSOURI, JULY, 1943   No. 6

In 1902, Bernard Corrigan ("Boss" Thomas, had died at age 59 in 1894) was hired by the Armours to run MET and negotiate terms with the city. A so-called May 1903 "Peace agreement" ordinance obliged MET to replace all cable lines, pay 8% gross earnings to the city, close the 9th Street trestle, and revamp the 8th Street tunnel at a lower grade, on the basis of a nickel fare and free transfers. For this, the city would consolidate all franchises and extend them to 1925. Since this "Peace agreement" would strain MET finances, a new **Kansas City Railway and Light Company** was registered on May 8th, 1903, to buy and hold MET and Kansas City Electric Light Company stock (another Armour investement). It was capitalized at $25 million. Poor's 1905 said $19.157 million had been paid up by 1904.

The great Kansas City Flood of 1903, one of the many Missouri and Mississippi River valley "floods of the century," swept away more than a dozen bridges around May 31st. The MET alone lost four, plus a temporary trestle. Flooded power stations halted trolleys for over a week. Cable cars fared even worse. Grand Avenue cable lines were electrified within weeks (15th, Holmes and Walnut), followed early in 1904 by the Summit cable on the opening of the Roanoke electric line, the last of the old KCC cables and the ninth Street trestle closed on April 6th, 1904.

However, Washington from 9th to 12th and down the West Bottoms to 16th via Genesee (southbound) and Wyoming (northbound) went back to cable in 1906 when the MET's 12th Street cable was electrified and cut back to 12th and Washington. This was because 12th Street's fearsome grade out of the West Bottoms was impossible for electric cars. Once the MET put in a new viaduct on a suitable grade, the last KC cable cars ran early on October 13th, 1913.

Between 1903 and 1908 Corrigan's focused on raising new money. He had a hard time of it, for while the franchise now ran to 1925, potential new

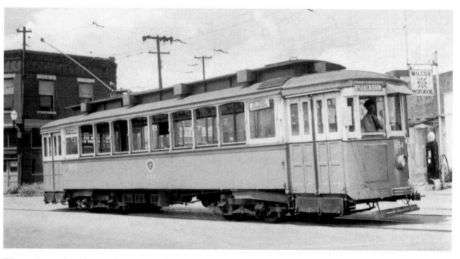

Though modernized as one-man front-entrance, rear exit cars, turn-of-the-century trolleys such as 654 were geriatric by the 1940s. Ironically this veteran sports a banner in the front side window exhorting riders to "Try Troost streamliners," meaning the 24 new PCC cars that went into service on Troost during July 1941.

The Scout, seen here with roof canopy attached circa 1943, was originally passenger car 136.

investors were doubtful it would again be renewed. MET had never been able to retire its bonds, was determined to pay dividends and had an apparent death-wish when it came to setting aside money for depreciation (it didn't). This spooked existing bondholders, yet MET couldn't issue new bonds to pay off its debts and those of its underliers (some going back to the late 1880s) without the guarantee of an assured future a franchise extension would give. Moreover, poor earnings and miserable relations with the city would make it impossible to negotiate reasonable sale terms for new MET bonds even if they could be issued, since these would have to mature by the end of the franchise in 1925, insufficient time for investors unless brokered at a huge discount. A new franchise would allow fresh bonds to be issued that could refinance the whole system.

This seemed odd to the City Council and the <u>KC Star</u>, for the "Peace Agreement" ordinance had been hailed as MET's salvation only six years before. But in April 1909, at the MET's suggestion, the City Utilities Commission imported auditors to examine MET finances, identify what was spent on operations and what was needed for new equipment and other necessities for the comfort and convenience of the riding public. After that, the franchise might be renegotiable. The electorate smelled something rotten and MET's franchise extension was voted down late in 1909.

Corrigan then quit and the Armours were left to carry the can. The MET took voluntary bankruptcy during 1911 in the expectation a receiver could do what it had been unable to do; get the franchise extension, negotiate with creditors, raise confidence, then issue and sell new bonds based on

those changed expectations. But by the time creditors and the city were placated two, more years had passed and the reform and franchise extension wasn't put to the vote until a 1914 referendum approved it in the traditional manner; a fix enforced by the massed cohorts of Thomas J. Pendergast, "Boss" Corrigan's successor as King of Kansas City. Who knows what the terms of the deal were, who was paid off by whom and by how

Car 1231, heading south on Main to Country Club and 75th in the mid-1940s, has just passed 24th Street.

PCC car 717 is southbound under Troost viaduct on a pre-opening inspection trip over the Dodson line, newly double-tracked from 75th to 87th and Euclid (approximately). This work was done in connection with a new 1/2-mile spur track to the Pratt and Whitney aircraft motor plant near 79th and Troost, which opened December 18th, 1943.

Cars 1223 and PCC 717 at the Pratt and Whitney plant loop and loading platforms.

Car 1223 is entering the new Pratt and Whitney spur on the same pre-opening inspection trip.

With delivery of the first postwar PCC cars in 1946, several older cars were given similar paint jobs with streamline swoops and swirls, modeled here by car 682. It did nothing to improve their antiquated appearance.

Once assigned to appropriate lines, the Birney cars did yeoman service for decades in Kansas City. This is 1544, still running in the late 1940s on the 39th Street line.

much. But the local papers saw that booze, bribes (if not broads) and fists had been thrust into many a voter's face, encouraging an enthusiastic response to the old slogan *"Vote early, vote often, vote for us."*

Whatever. MET's franchise now extended to 1944, in return for which the city nominated five of the eleven directors, and had one seat on a new two-member board of control, set up to run day-to-day operations. Old securities were replaced, most underlying debt was gone and on February 15th 1916 the electric light company was cut loose. Both companies were renamed, the MET becoming the **Kansas City Railways Company**. (A sanitized, account of this seven-year fight is in ERJ September 30th, 1916 p.p. 666-670).

ERJ April 19th, 1913 (p. 716) noted MET with 182 track miles in Kansas City MO, 58 in Kansas City KS. 5.26 miles in Independence MO. 9.73 miles in Jackson County MO and 4.37 miles in Rosedale KS. The **Kansas City and Westport Belt Railway Company** had 16.87 miles of track in Kansas City MO and 4.23 miles in unincorporated Jackson County. Begun in 1870 as the narrow-gauge Kansas City and Clinton branch of the **Tebo and Neosho Railroad Company** and later called **Kansas City, Memphis and Mobile Railroad Company**, money ran out at Dodson. In 1880 it was sold to the **Kansas City Southern**, who sold it in 1886 to the **Kansas City and Southeastern Railway** who laid new standard-gauge tracks. In 1897, it was bought by the **Kansas City and Westport Belt Railway** as a freight and switching line, with a Westport terminal at 40th and Summit.

The MET's parent (Kansas City Railway and Light) bought and electrified it in 1905 and MET ran cars over it from downtown to 47th Street (from 1907 to 51st Street). MET took ownership of the line July 7th, 1914 and extended tracks on to Waldo. It ran until 1957 as the Country Club line. Electric freight outlived the streetcars, as did the 40th and Summit yard which doubled as a materials yard.

March 4th 1916 saw extension of the 31st Street line from Indiana to Brighton Avenue, a Broadway extension from 14th to 25th Streets and a 24th Street extension from Brighton to Hardesty Avenue. Two hundred new cars were bought between then and 1920 and more were remodeled with pay-as-you-enter facilities, folding doors and steps and motor upgrades. It was a good start but timing is everything and KCRC's could not have been worse. From the get-go, it was enfeebled by inflation,

Cars continued to run to the Pratt and Whitney plant for years, as witness 1161 en route in July 1948. STLMOT.

Southbound PCC 546 swamped by traffic at Main and Delaware on a summer Saturday in 1951. STLMOT.

unregulated jitneys and catastrophic labor relations. Three strikes between 1917 and 1919 idled operations despite importation of strike-breakers and hiring of permanent replacements (possibly 2,400).

The December 1918-May 1919 strike was especially bitter. The Militia (National Guard) was called out to deal with riots and property destruction. Several were killed and cars were dynamited but the strikers lost. A company-sponsored "brotherhood" took the broken union's place, drawn largely from Camp Funston, then standing down veterans of Pershing's army. Men who didn't come back instead went out and bought automobiles, setting up competing jitney routes that cut deeply into KCRC's revenues and needed no city franchise to operate. Fare increases, from six to seven and by 1920 to eight cents, pushed more KCRC customers to their own transport, while Pendergast's grip on Kansas City (at the height of its reputation as a "wide-open" town) capped the situation.

It was clear the new extensions served areas of such low density that they could not pay, this at a time when despite competition and higher fares, ridership was the highest ever, with 740 cars running on 319 track miles. Economies were vital and 95 one-man-operated Birney

Car 131 rolls off the 8th Street elevated at Baltimore in 1949. The Main/Delaware station is in back. STLMOT.

Southbound auto traffic battles the snow on Delaware, March 3rd, 1952. The 8th Street elevated is right center and the Kansas City Public Service offices are behind that. STLMOT

cars were bought to cut costs on the worst-paying lines while maintaining the level of service the public expected. It was not enough. In 1920 over 400 jitneys creamed off 10% of KCRC's riders on heavy downtown routes. No relief was in sight, <u>KC Star</u> hostility intensified and the public remained indifferent. After failing to pay bondholder interest in mid-year, KCRC in September went into a receivership that lasted until 1926. Only later was it discovered 1919's payments had been made from private loans raised from the Armour family. The receiver moved on the jitneys immediately, authorities in Missouri and Kansas finally being "persuaded" to pass jitney-regulating ordinances. By 1922, they were no longer a factor. In 1920, consultant John A. Beeler was hired to advise how best to unclog downtown. Most of his recommendations were phased in over the next year. Skip stops were introduced, "double berthing" of cars at downtown stops was set up, parking restrictions imposed, on-street fare collection from waiting passengers was begun, plus re-routings and through routings of lines previously terminating downtown. The result? Average rush-hour speed increased and major savings were achieved.

In 1922 a loop was laid at the end of the 15th St. line and in 1924 South Prospect was extended from 72nd to 75th and Fairyland Park. But the 8th Street tunnel and elevated was decrepit. Initial suggestions were to tear down the elevated across the West Bottoms, divert tracks onto Ninth Street and build short lengths of new elevated to the tunnel at one end and the Central Avenue bridge at the other. Nothing was done.Despite remedial work in the form of new braces and trusses, the support beams were rotting. A broken beam over Santa Fe Street ended it all, happily without mishap. An inspection found the entire structure unsafe and the line closed (for nearly six years) on December 29th, 1922.

PCC 560 on 8th at Baltimore on March 3rd 1952 is the only vehicle other than for the wrecker that's coping with this late snowstorm. STLMOT

Serious motor bus competition now began, mainly from a new **Kansas Cities Motor Coach Company.** While the receiver saw off this threat, to prevent others making a similar nuisance of themselves, KCRC went into the bus business. Five of the nine lines authorized were high density, premium fare routes paralleling trolley lines but running on KC's famed

PCC 512, Main and Pershing, 1953. Cliff Scholes

Repair of infrastructure and tracks began and in the next decade over $11 million was spent, $1.5 million on car refurbishment alone. More trolleys were readied for one-man operation with "safety" equipment, heavier-duty controllers, line-switches, linoleum floors, better seating air doors and bright lighting. It was hoped this would bring back old riders and attract new. The first seventeen, in a new apricot and orange color scheme trimmed with plum (the Municipal Arts Commission's choice) were welcomed by a July 1927 downtown parade, musical accompaniment coming from the KCPS brass band riding an open-top double-deck bus. The power plant was sold to Kansas City Power and Light for $2.5 million, commercial power now being bought.

Finally, the Eighth Street tunnel and viaduct were rebuilt, the latter a new structure from the tunnel's west end spanning Bluff Street, the railroads (Mopac and Wabash) and Union Avenue to end at Santa Fe Street where a ramp took tracks down to the east line of Mulberry. The old El structure from the tunnel to the state line was removed and in its place a surface line ran to the Central Avenue Bridge and over the Kaw River. The entire project cost $1/4 million and the first car ran on February 21st, 1928 with (a nice touch, this), the same crew that made the last run in December 1922.

Between 1929 and 1932 annual ridership declined from 113 million to 67 million. More cost-cutting was vital. KCPS decided that since buses and their routes were experimental, if they didn't pay, they would go. Car lines, except high-density routes such as Troost and Country Club, would also go, replaced by buses initially, totally closed if buses couldn't hack it. In 1933 the cross-town car line from Troost to Summit via 33rd, 25th and 24th Streets was replaced by buses. KCPS then decided to convert all but the 12 heaviest lines to buses within ten years, scrapping the most unserviceable cars. In mid-1933, there were almost 750 cars, by early 1934 there were 623, with a further 50 slated for withdrawal that year.

boulevards. Three other lines were feeders and one was a new cross-town 39th Street line, long proposed for trolleys but never built. The buses went into service between July and November 1925 but had mixed fortunes. The premium-fare routes served affluent suburbs but despite the "parlor-car" fittings of vehicles assigned to these routes, few were tempted from their autos. The feeder routes, however, were a solid success.

Kansas City Public Service Company took over from KCRC on October 15th, 1926, with a new thirty-year franchise and new money from New York and New Orleans investors, including J. K. Newman of New York's Newman-Saunders and Co. Armour involvement now ceased.

PCC 510 heading south on Main Street for Country Club. Top right is the Junction, (Delaware and Main) circa 1952. STLMOT

Conversion of Kansas City streetcar lines

(*=initially converted to trolleybus).
Route numbers were not assigned until 1940. This list is not exhaustive; it deals only with the principal lines.

July 1st, 1928.	Sixth Street (KC KS).
November 22nd, 1930.	Broadway-33rd. The north end continued as part of another line. The south end was combined with the 25th Street line to form a new 25th-33rd Street line.
August 16th, 1933.	25th-33rd Street.
July 1st, 1934.	Quindaro, Third Street (KC KS).
March 3rd, 1935.	Fairmount Park.
March 31st, 1935.	Independence (KC-Independence plus Independence city line)
September 1st, 1935.	East Twelfth Street.
November 10th, 1937.	South Fifth Street (KC KS)
February 1st, 1938.	Hardesty-Jackson.
May 29th, 1938.	Independence Avenue,* Northeast.*
June 26th, 1938.	Thirteenth Street (KC KS).
July 2nd, 1938.	Holmes. (line 31st to 33rd Street abandoned, rest incorporated into revised Woodland line).
August 31st, 1939.	East Fifth Street.
March 17th, 1940.	Prospect,* South Prospect, Fifteenth Street.*
April 16th, 1940.	Argentine.
January 1st, 1941.	Twenty-Seventh Street.
September 23rd, 1941.	Tenth Street north of Central Avenue.
December 17th, 1944.	Tenth Street south of Central Avenue.
June 8th, 1947.	Marlborough, Sunset Hill.
June 23rd, 1947.	Seventh & Haskell-Stockyards.
November 30th, 1947.	Eighteenth Street (KCKS)
December 14th, 1947.	Brooklyn,* Woodland,* North Prospect.
December 28th, 1947.	Indiana.*
July 1st, 1948.	Rosedale, Vine Street, Eighteenth Street (July 3rd?).*
November 28th, 1948.	Observation Park.
May 1st, 1949.	Thirty-Ninth Street
August 22nd, 1949.	Kensington.
March 13th, 1950.	Roanoke.
October 4th, 1950.	Kansas Avenue*, Central Avenue.
July 13th, 1951.	Minnesota.
February 15th, 1953.	Chelsea (later known as Parallel). (KC KS)
October 3rd, 1954.	Swope Park.
October 2nd, 1955.	Thirty-First Street.
April 29th, 1956.	Eighth Street Tunnel.
July 8th, 1956.	Jackson, Twelfth Street.
October 28th, 1956.	Troost Avenue.
February 22nd, 1957.	Pratt & Whitney/Westinghouse Spur.
June 23rd, 1957.	Country Club, Dodson, Rockhill.

This was no hardship. At best only 463 were needed for peak-hour runs.

By now, the Intercity Viaduct linking Missouri and Kansas, was in urgent need of repair. Rather than pay its share, plus rent for using the structure, KCPS instead replaced its Quindaro-Main car line with buses from July 1st, 1934. Similarly with the Independence line. $225,000 was KCPS's share of the cost for a new viaduct over the Blue River Valley. From March 31st, 1935, new buses were used instead; a cheaper solution.

The mid-30s saw partial recovery. In the hope this would continue, KCPS in summer 1937 announced a $3.35 million modernization, calling for 34 buses, 100 trolleys and 106 trolleybuses, all new. $1.77 million would come from a ten-year Reconstruction Finance Corporation loan. New trolleys would serve the heaviest routes, (the system's backbone) and buses the light urban, suburban and feeder lines plus new express routes. Trolleybuses were experimental, for use on intermediate lines where operating conditions dictated neither streetcar nor motor bus. In part the idea was to use existing electrical infrastructure rather than junk it prematurely. The trolleybus experiment began in 1938 with delivery of thirty-four Mack 40-passenger units soon after KCPS managed to lower the interest rate on its (refinanced) debt.

The Northeast and Independence Avenue car lines were converted on May 29th 1938, the 15th Street and Prospect Avenue car lines on March 17th, 1940. By 1941 the four lines and 78 trolleybuses had generated almost half the year's operating revenue for all of KCPS and the effectiveness of this multi-modal approach was the foundation for the company's success over the next decade. In addition to new buses, 24 new PCC streetcars were delivered in 1941 and but for World War Two the rest of the scheduled 100 units would have arrived by 1943. As it was, orders were deferred and more new cars did not arrive until 1946.

By January 1942 there were 194 miles of track, 412 passenger cars, 68 work, freight and utility cars, two electric locomotives, 86 trolleybuses on 25 miles of route and 260 motor buses on 100 miles of route. On December 18th, 1943, a trolley extension opened to the Pratt & Whitney aircraft engine plant, made by double-tracking the Dodson line south and east from 75th and Wornall to a junction in line with Euclid where a new right-of-way to the plant was built. In 1945 KCPS had roughly 206 miles of tracks, 390 cars, 60 work and miscellaneous cars and 2 locomotives, plus 96 trolleybuses on 50 miles of route and 302 buses on 106 miles of route.

The multi-modal modernization resumed in 1946 with delivery of more PCCs and trolleybuses. The Troost line was extended from 55th to 63rd Streets in 1947, Missouri's last street railway extension, except for a 1956 off-street loop in downtown St. Louis. But KCPS's multi-modal policy was based on revenues from stable or growing ridership, which couldn't be sustained indefinitely given national trends. In fact ridership declined quickly. Trolleys were less profitable than diesel or trolleybuses and from 1948 were gradually phased out. Worse, the Kaw River flood on Friday July 13, 1951, which just about ended the meat packing industry, devastated all KCPS Kansas operations. The two remaining Kansas car lines (Minnesota and Parallel) were replaced by shuttle buses, Minnesota permanently, parallel for a short period. The Jackson and 8th Street Tunnel lines were cut back to a newly installed loop at Central and James, just over of the Missouri-Kansas line.

Nothing could be done about the city's low-density territory and suburban expansion. By 1955 KCPS ridership had declined over 50% from its 1946 peak. Most PCC cars were sold and June 22nd 1957 (early a.m. June 23rd) saw the last car on the 56 Country Club-Dodson line. A special car ran next afternoon. Trolleybus conversion continued into the 1950s but declining revenues saw them make their last run on January 4th, 1959. Trolley freight (south of 43rd Street) continued until turned over to an independent operator who ran diesels from July 29th, 1957, though sporadic electric operation continued for weeks. The line was embargoed in 1968 and sold on October 27th, 1981 to the Kansas City Area Transportation Authority for $1.5 million as the city was trying to preserve the right-of-way for Light Rail. However, KCATA in August 2005 replaced the #56 bus with an experimental express service to downtown to see if installation of Bus Rapid Transit might speed up the process.

West entrance of 8th Street tunnel with PCC 772 circa 1955.

Incomplete Roster Notes

Kansas City had a large and complex fleet of animal, cable and electric cars. No attempt has been made to compile notes: readers are referred to ERA Headlights February 1943, which contains a 1929 KC roster. PCC cars came in 1940 (701-724), 1946 (725-799) and 1947 (501-585). 40 of the 1946 group were sold to Philadelphia in 1955, 27 of the 1946 group and three of the 1947 group went to Toronto in 1957, going elsewhere in the 1970s and 1980s. Seven of the 1946 group and three of the 1947 group went to Tampico, Mexico in 1957. 80 sets of trucks, motors and equipment from the 1947 cars went to Brussels Belgium and were used with new bodies (7081-7155). A few remain (2006) in service. At least eleven of the Philadelphia cars are owned by a private individual and stored in Windber (Johmstown) PA.

2. NORTH KANSAS CITY

In 1883, Willard E. Winner bought land north of the Missouri in Clay County, planning a new city, bridge and roads. In 1887, he began (it didn't get far), subdivisions and utilities before running out of cash. Decades later, the Armour, Swift and Burlington companies built Armour, Swift and Burlington Streets. Their A-S-B Bridge was based on Winner's abandoned work and was a crucial piece of the Clay County interurban's route.

1. North Kansas City Street Railway Company Little is known of this mule line beyond entries in Poor's. It opened September 13th, 1889 and was a Willard E. Winner operation with eleven mules, four cars and two miles of standard-gauge tracks. It was not heavy-duty, costing just $14,563 to build. It grossed $2,318 in its first year, but only $61.53 net. It still ran in 1896, possibly under new ownership, but probably closed before 1900.

2. Union Depot Bridge & Terminal Railroad Company Created in 1901 to continue work on Winner's bridge, it was headed by Theodore C. Bates. In 1903, control passed to the Armour and Swift Packing Companies and the Chicago, Burlington and Quincy railroad, each with a 1/3 share, who later finished the 5000'-long double-deck steel A-S-B bridge and began developing 3,200 acres through the North Kansas City Development Company. The UBD&T was a subsidiary, a local trolley line that ran over the bridge into Kansas City proper and also owned a terminal and

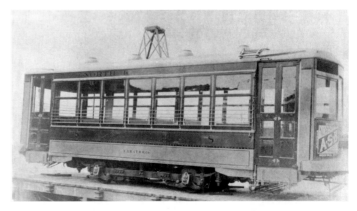

Car 8, ready for delivery from American Car in 1919. The card on the dash reads A-S-B North Kansas City, Armour Swift Burlington Industrial City.

North Kansas City Bridge & Railroad Company

General Offices—Railway Exchange, Kansas City, Mo.

EXECUTIVE COMMITTEE

J. S. PYEATT, Chairman, Kansas City, Mo.

F. G. GURLEY, Chicago, Ill.   JAMES S SIMRALL, Kansas City, Mo.

J. S. PYEATT, President, Cleveland, O.

A. W. ZIMMER, Vice-President.   Kansas City, Mo. | N. M. FITCH, Chief Engineer.   North Kansas City, Mo.

JAMES S SIMRALL, Treasurer.   P. B. WILLIAMSON, Superintendent.

A. L. LINCK, Secretary.

JAMES S SIMRALL, General Attorney.

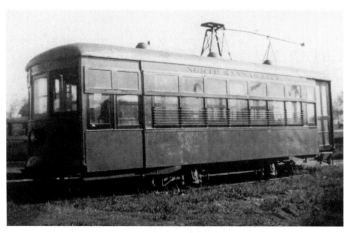

Industrial Railroad Mileage ...... 20.00 Miles
Electric Railroad Mileage 12.78
Total Mileage .... 32.78 Miles
Industrial Railroad Mileage Operated by Chicago, Burlington & Quincy R.R

NORTH KANSAS CITY, MO.

Birney 3 at the end of its life circa 1937.

railroad switching operation, conducted by the CB&Q.

The bridge went into limited use on January 1st, 1912, but wasn't completed until June 30th, 1914. Clay County interurbans began using it in January 1913 but it isn't known if UDB&T cars began earlier. A 50-year contract gave the Clay County trackage rights over the bridge and the UDB&T to access Kansas City (Jackson County), paying UDB&T $1 for each crossing, a minimum of $25,000 annually, increased by $1000 p.a. for ten years, then capped at $35,000 for the duration of the contract. Line voltage was 600V D.C and the interurbans used this on MET and UDB&T tracks to the beginning of their right-of-way, which was powered at 1200V D. C.

It was expected the new bridge would help the A-S-B syndicate sell industrial lots in North Kansas City around which UDB&T tracks formed a large loop. It interchanged with the MET at Third and Cherry in KC, crossed the bridge, ran north on Burlington Avenue, east on Armour Boulevard, south on Linn Street and west on 14th to Burlington. A line

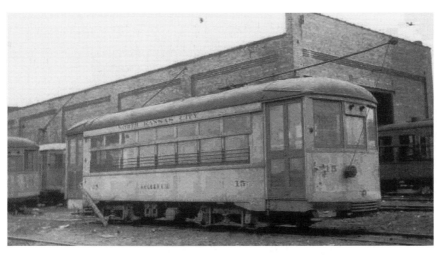

Double-truck car 15 circa 1937.

3. North Kansas City Bridge & Railway Company

On July 24th, 1927, the A-S-B bridge and approaches were sold to Kansas City (Jackson County) and North Kansas City (Clay County). The UDB&T name change dates from this sale. Road tolls were abolished but not the Clay County's bridge contract. The interurban defaulted in September 1930, inability to renegotiate the contract during the receivership being one factor that led to its ending rail service in 1933. However, the NKCB ran until May 15th, 1937. The OK railroad survived to 1938. NKCB's switching tracks, used by the CB&Q, were acquired by that railroad circa 1940.

Incomplete roster notes

There is no information on equipment. The UDB&T possibly leased cars from MET until enough traffic built up to buy their own. Five single-end lightweights #1-5 (American, 1917) had no safety equipment, and seated 36 plus 28 standing. They had a rear door on the left side, double-folding front doors and replaced cars weighing 56,000lbs. Birney "Safety" cars 6-8 (American 1918) followed and later five more Birneys (#9-12/14, Cincinnati, 1920) plus at least two double-truck Birneys. McGraw 1924 lists 13 passenger cars. By 1930 there were thirteen passenger cars, a freight motor and a service car which survived to the end of the line's life.

also ran south on Howell from Fourteenth to Tenth. The Clay County used the same bridge tracks from Kansas City, then went north on Swift from Armour and onto its own right-of-way. Its Excelsior Springs branch continued on Armour through Avondale to its right-of-way. In all, the Clay County used about 5 miles of the UDB&T, of which 2 miles was double track.

3. KANSAS CITY SUBURBAN AND INTERURBAN LINES

(Roster notes for this section were compiled with the help of Lowell H. Rott)

Kansas City's five interurbans reached downtown Kansas City MO over MET tracks at some point in their lives. The **Kansas City Interurban Freight Terminal Company**, jointly owned by the local interurbans, opened a Union Freight Station on October 10th, 1917 at Fourth and Wyandotte, other freight stations in town being closed. In 1918, KC set up a Central Interurban Station Company to build a $3 million interurban union station at the northeast corner of Tenth and McGee, but inflation and changing conditions stalled the project. Land was bought but was rented as a pay parking lot to meet interest payments and property taxes.In February 1926 the franchise was cancelled.An intercity bus terminal for Pickwick Greyhound lines was later built on the site (ERJ February 20th, 1926 p.339)

1. Kansas City, Clay County and St. Joseph Railway Company (the Missouri Short Line). Between 1899 and 1910, there were several attempts to link Kansas City and St. Joseph by trolley using a short and direct route over the hills. This would have been impossible as a steam line, wnhich is why the many railroads meandered through the river valley taking up to 3 hours to run the 60-plus miles. An electric interurban would have no such problem. It could give low-fare, high-speed local service and cut the journey time by a third. The **St. Joseph, Parkville and Kansas City Railroad** planned such a route via Parkville, Platte City,

Beverly, Weston and Dyer, plus a Leavenworth KS branch, (SRJ February 22nd, 1902 p. viii). But the company, an MET subsidiary, failed to act, as did J. J. Heim's **Kansas City, St. Joseph and Excelsior Springs Electric Railway** circa 1906/7.

The Clay County was incorporated March 22nd, 1911 to build a 51-mile main line and a 29-mile Excelsior Springs branch. ETW December 11th, 1911 p. 1623 said Boston's Tucker-Anthony bank was managing the project and New York's National City Bank had either put up money direct or brokered the line's paper. Soon after (ETW February 10th, 1912 p. 172), capital went from $720,000 to $10 million, $5 million coming from the New York and Boston bankers who then sold the bonds in America and Europe. A Kansas City, Clay County and St. Joseph Corporation was set up in Maine as a holding company for the Clay County plus a **St. Joseph Electric Railway Company**, this last to take the interurban through St. Joseph streets to meet local car tracks.

The A-S-B bridge eliminated the Missouri barrier at little cost to the Clay County. But to make money without profitable on-line stops, the interurban had to provide frequent, rapid, low-cost service on a straight route, ignoring rocks, creeks, forests and gullies.Yet its route north of the bridge

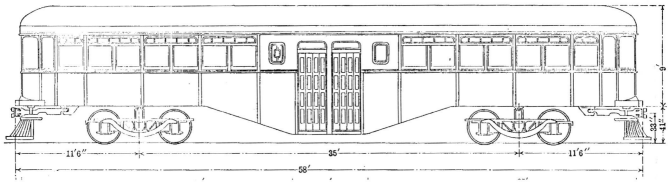

Kansas City and Clay County & St. Joseph Interurban car.

One of Sixteen Cars for the Kansas City, Clay County & St. Joseph Ry.

This 80-mile line, recently completed, is one of the best built and equipped electric railways in the Central West.

The initial equipment consists of sixteen Cincinnati cars of the type illustrated. This car is built of steel practically throughout and in general is designed for single-end operation.

The road being a new one, had no precedent to follow in choice of equipment and was therefore free to adopt the most efficient equipment the country offered.

A description in detail of the construction of the cars was published in this Journal and clearly shows the ability of The Cincinnati Car Company to produce construction of the highest order.

Designs and specifications of any type of car for electric or steam railway service will be furnished upon request.

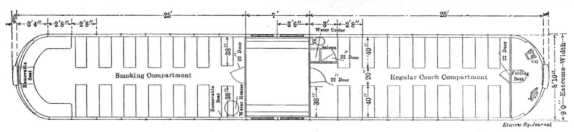

The Cincinnati Car Company

Winton Place   **Cincinnati, O.**

ERJ advertisement for the first cars, August 1st, 1914.

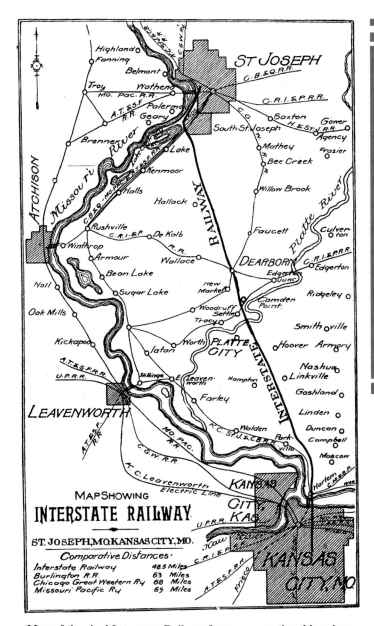

Map of the rival Interstate Railway from a promotional brochure issued circa 1907.

Kansas City, Clay County and St. Joseph car lines circa 1918

1. 45.70 miles of track from North Kansas City to St. Joseph city limits.
2. 22.94 miles of track from North Kansas City to Excelsior Springs.
3. 1.09 miles, plus 1.09 miles of second track—trackage rights in Kansas City.
4. 4.87 miles, plus 2.28 miles of second track-trackage rights over the Union Depot Bridge and Terminal Railway Company and the A-S-B bridge, from Kansas City to North Kansas City.
5. 0.53 miles, plus 0.8 miles of second track-trackage rights over the St. Joseph Electric Railway Company, a wholly-owned subsidiary of the Clay County.
6. 2.29 miles, plus 1.70 miles of second track rights in St. Joseph over St. Joseph Railway Light Heat and Power Company.

Express and LCL freight cars were added to passenger runs, or scheduled as needed. However, the line's freight locomotives could manage no more than six cars. Additionally, the passing tracks were 300' long dead-end sidings rather than loops, ostensibly on safety grounds. This made for slow operation as a freight train switched to a siding had to back out again before resuming its journey. However, automatic block signalling was installed by 1914.

From the Kansas City terminal at 13th and Walnut, Clay County cars ran a block west on Thirteenth, north on Walnut, east on Fifth, north on Grand, east on Third to Cherry (and its freight house). This 1.1 miles took twenty minutes and was the slowest part of the trip. Once across the A-S-B bridge, the line ran north on Burlington and east Armour. The main line then almost immediately turned northwest onto its right-of-way. Camden Point and Dearborn were served but Platte City was by-passed. The Excelsior Springs branch ran east on Swift before turning northeast on its right of way. Avondale, Liberty, Mosby were served. Two stops beyond Avondale was the stop for Winnwood Lake, beach, zoo and dance hall. The line's shops and barns were at Armour and Burlington in North Kansas City

Car 66 in dead storage at the North Kansas City shops on January 1st, 1935

was infested with such obstacles, including rock that yielded only to blasting, acres of trees and underbrush to be removed (with crosscut saws), and creeks and gullies to be bridged. Still, this Missouri River bluffs route was nine miles shorter than railroad routes through the river valley, and the Clay County's proposed (and realized) 2-hour schedule was superior to their almost three hours. The railroads had no reason to cooperat, pelting the interurban with lawsuits citing safety concerns. The interurban responded by building six steel bridges and many reinforced concrete arches. Local farmers were more receptive, selling land and helping build the line, or hiring out their horses and mules for that purpose.

Excelsior Springs service began without ceremony in January 21st, 1913. Cars simply set off at 6:00 a.m. from both ends. The opening had been postponed so often it was felt the best publicity would be cars in regular service. Initially every 90 minutes, cars soon ran hourly. The only size-able town en route was Liberty, the Clay County seat and home to William Jewel College, 16 miles northeast of Kansas City. The 51-mile St. Joseph line began restricted service on April 29th and full service May 5th. Three extra St. Joseph trains were limiteds, stopping only at Dearborn and Camden Point. Two daily round-trip freights ran on each division, plus extras as needed.

Clay County car 26 in a special three-car train, location unknown circa 1914.

The St. Joseph entry was on the 11th Street extension of the St. Joseph Electric Railway Company whose 0.53 miles met St. Joseph Power & Light tracks at Eighth and Edmond, over which the Clay County continued to a terminal loop serving the Robidoux Hotel at 5th and Francis. The St. Joseph passenger depot, (8th Street across from the Post Office), was shared with the St. Joseph and Savannah. It was later the Trailways Bus Terminal.

Cars on both branches often reached 70mph. Initial annual gross revenues were $400,000 to $600,000 and the interurban service prompted the Rock Island to kill its Kansas City-St. Joseph passenger trains. But the Milwaukee Road and the Wabash responded by cutting fares and adding trains with new equipment.

Clouds were soon on the Clay County's horizon. The **Interstate Railway Company**, one of many Kansas City-St. Joseph interurbans that hadn't built, still had live options on several routes including the Clay County's. Seeing a chance to recoup their losses, the Interstate in May 1915 filed a $2 million damage suit against the Clay County for ignoring their still-valid option. They were awarded $1.5 million damages. KCCC&STJ appealed, but before the Missouri Supreme Court would hear the case, the company had to post a $3 million appeal bond and it had to go into receivership. The October 1917 appeal resulted in a reduction of damages to $250,000.

This wasn't the only claim against the Clay County by those who'd failed

to build, but it was the only one to result in such a verdict. By the time the receivership was lifted, auto and truck competition was endemic and delays in downtown KC had become intolerable. In 1920 a new KC passenger terminal opened in the Railway Exchange Building at Seventh and Grand and cars were cut back from 13th and Walnut to this point. (ERJ July 17th, 1920 p. 141) But nothing changed things for the better, not 1922's "luxury plus" services (quick, reversible conversions of vehicles to carpeted "business class" parlor cars at premium fares), not fare increases, not even its own bus line.

1923's receipts exceeded $1 million, but once the Liberty-Excelsior Springs road was paved, an alignment that curved and weaved as country roads do, yet roughly paralleled the interurban, ridership dropped 19% in early 1924. Robert Woods, the line's engineer and manager since 1919, blamed competing buses on the newly-paved road for the decline (ERJ December 26th, 1924 p. 959) but in reality private automobiles were responsible.

The **Kansas City, Clay County and St. Joseph Auto Transit Company**, the new bus subsidiary, allowed the company to halve the number of rail trips, saving money while giving similar service. Miss Liberty, Miss Excelsior and Miss Clay were 26 seat Fageol 6-cylinder parlor buses, which from August 7th, 1924 traveled the highway to Excelsior Springs every two hours. As a result, one competitor went out of business and two others were taken over, with at least one former owner hired to manage the bus fleet. "Blue line" buses were extended over all the Clay County's routes on January 20th, 1925.

Car 22 circa 1905 probably in Leavenworth KS.

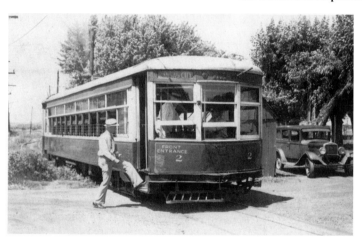

The Leavenworth's four new lightweight cars held down most passenger services after 1927. Car 2 "Quindaro" takes on a couple of passengers at an unknown location in the mid-1930s. This car fell into flooded Maltby Creek on August 19th, 1937 after a rain-weakened trestle collapsed under it. No one was seriously injured.

<u>ERJ</u> January 26th, 1924 (p. 148) noted general superintendent C. W. Ford saying at the Midwest Electric Railway Association's January 17th Springfield MO meeting, that with handling costs of 40-41 cents a mile, 85% of the line's freight was LCL, carried in 60' motors and special trailers, *"clearances not being sufficient to accommodate standard railroad boxcars."* That was odd since the line had supposedly been engineered to fit such vehicles. But it was academic as by 1927, all LCL business had gone, customers using motor truck lines or setting up their own. But car-load haul increased and the Clay County began increasing its rates to match the steam railroads. It also tried to get industries capable of generating freight to locate on the line, which now interchanged with the CBQ, Rock Island and Chicago Great Western. All of this might have made a difference given time, for the road was meeting operating expenses and its fixed charges might have been reduced by negotiation.

But the Depression blighted everything. By August 1930, Woods was in New York, seeking financial relief. He didn't get it. On September 1, 1930, the line defaulted on payment of semiannual and fixed charges including the 50-year A-S-B contract, and a receiver was appointed. As the line's securities had been sold in the east, it was eastern stockholders who pressed for rapid liquidation, hoping to salvage as much as possible. On December 1932 the receiver was ordered to file for abandonment and on March 10, 1933, the last cars left Kansas City for St. Joseph and Excelsior Springs. Both lines were replaced by Clay County buses and rerouted to the Tenth and McGee bus terminal, though Seventh and Grand continued until the end of March. The Excelsior Springs Terminal closed, the buses looping downtown to serve the principal hotels. Several attempts were made to refinance and revive rail operations, but the system was sold for scrap to Hyman-Michaels of Chicago and lifted in 1935. The twelve buses served 103 miles of route (about the same as the rail lines) but were sold to the Union Pacific Railroad's subsidiary **Interstate Transit Line** around August 1934.

Incomplete Roster notes

(All Cincinnati-built cars had Baldwin double-trucks)
In 1926, there were 31 passenger and baggage cars, 24 freight cars, 6 work cars and 2 locomotives. Car 1 was a ditcher supplied by American Hoist & Derrick Co of St. Paul MN in 1915.
Cars 2, 3 were wooden flat cars of unknown origin.
Car 12 was a wood combination car of unknown origin.
Cars 14 and 15 were steel passenger cars of unknown origin.
Cars 20-27 were Cincinnati-built steel center-entrance passenger cars of 1912/13.

Strang line gas-electric demonstrator "Irene" at the Brill plant, Philadelphia, before delivery.

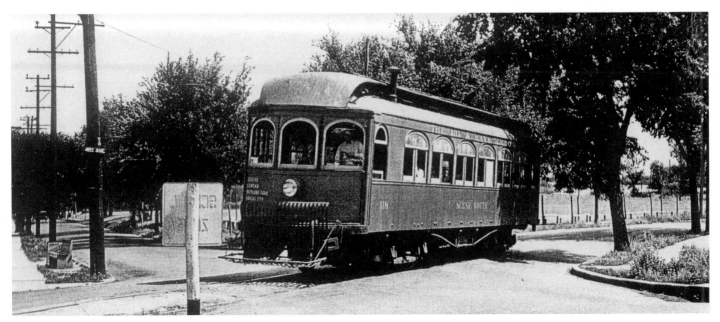

Missouri and Kansas (Strang line) interurban car 118 entering private right-of-way at 41st Street, Kansas City circa 1940.

Cars 30-33, 40-43 were Cincinnati-built steel passenger combines of 1912/13.

Cars 50-54 were Cincinnati-built steel express/freight motors of 1912/13.

Cars 60-62, 63-66 were Cincinnati-built steel passenger cars of 1915 (60-62) and 1920 (remainder).

Car 90 was a Cincinnati-built line car of 1912.

Cars 98, 99 were steeple-cab locomotives built in 1916 and 1918

Cars 100-104 were ACF-built wooden box cars of 1912.

Cars 300-305 were wooden box cars of unknown origin.

Cars 400, 401 were wooden refrigerator cars of unknown origin.

Cars 600, 601 were Rodgers ballast Gondolas of unknown origin

Cars 900/01/03/11-14 were wooden gondola cars of unknown origin.

Cars 1000, 1001 were Oliver Air dump gondolas of unknown origin.

Car 1100 was a steel flat car of unknown origin

Car 1200 was a tank car of unknown origin.

Most cars survived the March 1933 closure, stored complete at the company shops in working order until well into 1935 when track-lifting was complete and all hope of selling them other than for scrap had gone.

2. <u>Kansas City-Western Railway Company</u> As the **<u>Kansas City and Leavenworth Traction Company</u>** of 1897, this was an outgrowth of Leavenworth's city system. <u>SRJ's</u> March 1897 directory lists 30 miles of track and five cars. Trolleys came to Leavenworth in 1892, several local companies then competing to get a line through to Kansas City. The KC&LTC line opened January 6th, 1900 after earlier incremental openings. It paralleled the Kansas City-Leavenworth highway (such as it was), later known as Kansas route 5. Its Kensington branch in Kansas City KS was subsequently taken over by Kansas City Railways. Eventually it was to connect with the Kaw Valley line at 13th and Oakland in Kansas City KS, but its main line ended at MET's Grand View line in Kansas.

<u>SRJ</u> September 21st, 1901 (p. 352) said all competitors had merged to form the **<u>Kansas City-Western Railway Company</u>**. Plans to enter Kansas City MO via a new river crossing and ascent of the bluffs were announced in October 1901. A $1/2 million Kaw River bridge would be the centerpiece, with an elevated line and tunnel from Third and Minnesota in Kansas City KS to 6th and Bluff in Kansas City MO. However, the bridge and its Kansas approach tracks were MET property when built and once KC-WRC's line to Missouri began on November 11th, 1904, an extra nickel was collected by MET in each direction. MET motorman ran all cars in Missouri and on the Kansas bridge approaches. The terminal was at 8th and Grand in Kansas City MO. Once in Kansas, the line ran on on the Missouri's west bank via Walcott and Lansing to 3rd and Delaware in Leavenworth.

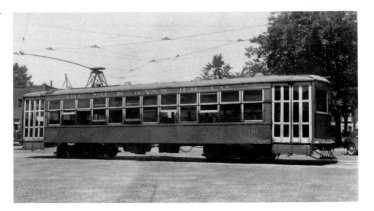

Strang line lightweight car 116 near Olathe circa 1940.

The Kaw Valley's first passenger interurban cars of 1914 were if anything even more magnificent in their green with white trim colors than the Clay County's similar cars in their dark red.

In March 1905, the line was sold it to an eastern group headed by Clarence A. McClellan of Mount Vernon, New York, with interests in the new Intercity viaduct. From June 1905 freights went from 2 to 4 daily runs and a new freight terminal opened at Second and Wyandotte in KCMO. The stockyards provided most freight business. Armour, Swift, Cudahy, Wilson all used local interurbans, though not exclusively. Lansing-Fort Leavenworth tracks were doubled in 1907, a new Walcott cut-off eliminated grades and curves and through passenger service became hourly (1/2 hourly in rush hours) with a 2-cents-per-mile fare. Leavenworth was a prime source of traffic, the Penitentiary and Soldier's Home

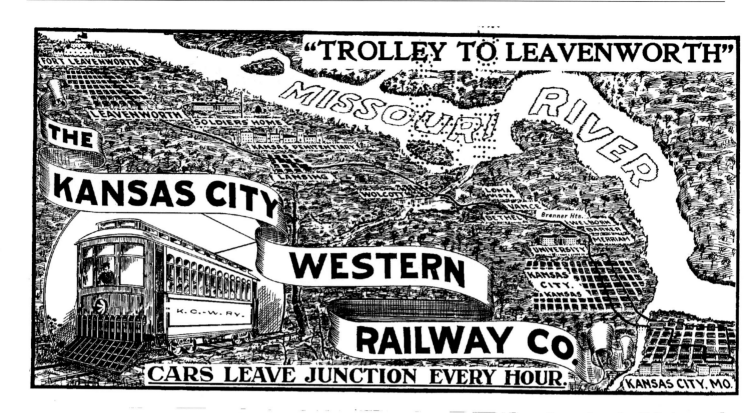

Map circa 1905

Four Interurban Units Ordered by Kansas City, Leavenworth & Western

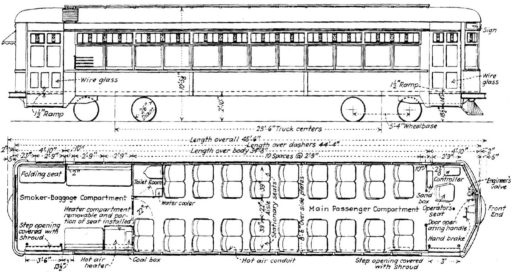

Following are specifications, seating plan and elevation for the four one-man, interurban, semi-steel cars ordered on July 20 for the Kansas City, Leavenworth & Western Railway, Kansas City, Kan. This order, which was placed with the American Car Company, St. Louis, was announced in ELECTRIC RAILWAY JOURNAL for Aug. 13. The cars will be painted in a color scheme of blue, ivory and red, the colors to be used on the roof, center, bottom and letter board respectively. Four GE-247 inside-hung motors will furnish the power and the bodies will be mounted on Brill 177-E-1 trucks. A spacious smoking compartment of observation car design will be one of the outstanding features of these cars.

Number of units	Four
Type of unit	One-man, motor, passenger, single end, double truck
Number of seats	47
Builder of car body	American Car Company, St. Louis, Mo.
Date of order	July 20
Length over all	45 ft. 6 in.
Length over body posts	34 ft. 8 in.
Truck wheelbase	5 ft. 4 in.
Width over all	8 ft. 8½ in.
Height, rail to trolley base	10 ft. 8 in.
Window post spacing	33 in.
Body	Semi-steel
Roof	Arch
Air brakes	G. E. straight
Car signal system	Faraday
Compressors	CP-27
Conduit	Flexible
Control	K-75
Couplers	American Car Co.
Curtain fixtures	Curtain Supply Co.
Curtain material	Pantasote
Destination signs	Hunter
Door mechanism	American Car Co.
Doors	End
Finish	Enamel

Floor covering	Rubber tiling
Gears and pinions	G. E.
Glass	D. S. A.
Hand brakes	Brill vertical
Heaters	Hot air
Headlights	G. E. luminous arc
Headlining	Agasote
Interior trim	Mahogany
Journal bearings	Plain
Lamp fixtures	American Car Co. indirect lighting
Motors	Four G E.-247, inside hung
Painting scheme	Blue roof, ivory center, red bottom, and letter board
Roof material	T. & G. board
Sash fixtures	Schechter post casing
Seats	Brill bucket type
Seat spacing	33 in.
Seating material	Leather
Steps	Stationary
Step treads	Kass safety
Trolley catchers	Eclipse
Trolley base	Ohio Brass
Trolley wheels	Ohio Brass
Trucks	Brill 177-E-1
Ventulators	American Car Company
Wheels	26-in. rolled steel
Wheelguards	Steel pilot

Drawings and specifications of 1927 cars (SRJ November 7th, 1927)

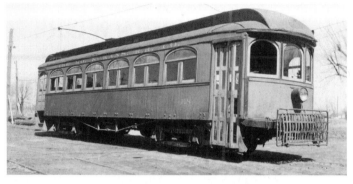

Strang line interurban 118, Overland Park KS circa 1938.

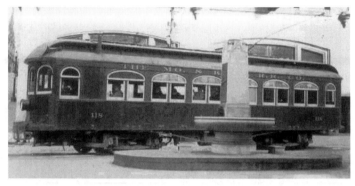

Strang line car 118 in downtown Kansas City, 1937. Bill Volkmer collection

DETAIL of DOWNTOWN SECTION, KANSAS CITY, MISSOURI
✦ Where to Board Cars and Busses in the Downtown District ✦

(Reading on destination signs shown in italics)

STREET CAR LINES

CENTRAL AVENUE—ROUTE 60—ON 8TH STREET
E. B. sign reads, "*McGEE-10th*"
W. B. sign reads, "*CENTRAL-18th*"

COUNTRY CLUB—ROUTE 56—ON MAIN ST.
N. B. sign reads, "*56-Main-3rd—COUNTRY CLUB*"
S. B. sign reads, "*56-75th St.—COUNTRY CLUB*" or "*56-63rd St.—COUNTRY CLUB*"

PARALLEL-JACKSON—ROUTE 59—ON 12TH ST.
E. B. sign reads, "*59-24th St.-Hardesty—JACKSON*"
W. B. sign reads, "*59-Parallel-33rd—PARALLEL*"

ROANOKE—ROUTE 57—ON MAIN ST.
N. B. sign reads, "*57-10th St.-Main—ROANOKE*"
S. B. sign reads, "*57-State Line-45th—ROANOKE*"

SWOPE PARK-MINNESOTA AVE.—ROUTE 53—ON GRAND AVE.
N. B. sign reads, "*53-Minnesota-19th—MINNESOTA*"
S. B. sign reads, "*53-Swope Park—SWOPE PARK*"

31ST STREET—ROUTE 55—ON MAIN ST.
N. B. sign reads, "*55-Main-9th-31st STREET*"
S. B. sign reads, "*55-31st St.-Van Brunt—31st STREET*"

TROOST AVE.—ROUTE 50—E. B. ON 10TH ST. OR W. B. ON 8TH ST.
E. B. sign reads, "*50-Troost-63rd—TROOST*" or "*50-Troost-48th—TROOST*"
W. B. sign reads, "*50-8th St.-Walnut—TROOST*"

12TH ST.-KANSAS AVE.—ROUTE 58—ON 12TH ST.
E. B. sign reads, "*58-12th St.-Jackson—12th STREET*"
W. B. sign reads, "*58-Kan.-18th-Stock Yards—KANSAS AVE.*" or "*58-Genesee-16th-Stock Yards—12th STREET*"

MOTOR BUS LINES

ARMOUR-PASEO—ROUTE 3—N. B. ON BALTIMORE OR S. B. ON WYANDOTTE
N. B. sign reads, "*3-Union Sta.-Main-9th—ARMOUR-PASEO*"
S. B. sign reads, "*3-Union Sta.-Paseo-Meyer—ARMOUR-PASEO*" or "*3 Union Sta.-Paseo-49th—ARMOUR-PASEO*" or "*Union Sta.-Paseo-39th—ARMOUR-PASEO*"

BROADWAY-WORNALL-WARD PKWY—ROUTES 4 & 5—N. B. ON BALTIMORE OR S. B. ON WYANDOTTE
N. B. sign reads, "*5-Main-9th—BR'DWAY-WORN'L*"
S. B. sign reads, "*5-Wornall-Meyer Blvd.—BR'DWAY-WORN'L*" or "*4-Belleview-Meyer Blvd.—BROADWAY-WARD PKY.*" or "*5-C. Club Plaza—BR'DWAY-WARD PKY.*" or "*4-Belleview-Ward Pky.—BROADWAY-WARD PKY.*"

EAST 5TH ST.—ROUTE 22—N. B. ON GRAND, W. B. ON 5TH ST. OR S. B. ON OAK ST.
Both directions sign reads, "*22-10th-Grand-Monroe-Gard'r—EAST 5th ST.*"

KANSAS CITY-INDEPENDENCE-FAIRMOUNT—ROUTE 1—W. B. ON 11TH ST., E. B. ON 10TH ST.
E. B. sign reads, "*1-Lex'ton-Mein—INDEP., MO.-K. C.*" or "*1-Claremont—INDEP., MO.-K. C.*" or "*1-Mt. Wash'ton—INDEP., MO.-K. C.*" or "*1-Lex'ton-Mein—EXPRESS*" or "*10-Fairmount Ph.-Mt. Wash'ton—FAIRMOUNT*"
W. B. sign reads, rush hours only. "*1-11th-Grand—INDEP., MO.-K. C.*"

LINWOOD-BENTON—ROUTE 2—ON GRAND AVE.
N. B. sign reads, "*2-Grand-11th—LINWOOD*"
S. B. sign reads, "*2-Benton-46th—LINWOOD*" or "*2-Benton-35th—LINWOOD*"

MUNICIPAL AIRPORT—ROUTE 18—N. B. ON MAIN, S. B. ON WYANDOTTE OR W. B. ON 9TH ST.
Both directions sign reads, "*18-13th-Main—MUNICIPAL AIRPORT*"

NORTH KANSAS CITY—ROUTE 24—S. B. ON GRAND, W. B. ON 11TH ST., OR N. B. ON MAIN
Both directions sign reads, "*24-11th-Main-Armour—NORTH K. C.*"
N. B. side window card reads, "*Tancy*" or "*Burlington*"

QUINDARO—ROUTE 6—E. B. ON 10TH ST., W. B. ON 11TH ST. OR ON BROADWAY
E. B. sign reads, "*6-Main-11th—QUINDARO*"
W. B. sign reads, "*6-Min'sota Ave.-Quindaro-22nd—QUINDARO*" or "*6-Min'sota Ave.-Quindaro-9th—QUINDARO*"

ROSEDALE-VINE—ROUTE 32—N. B. ON GRAND, S. B. ON WALNUT, N. AND S. B. ON BROADWAY
E. B. sign reads, "*22-Woodland-Linwood—VINE ST.*"
W. B. sign reads, "*32-S. W. Blvd.-10th—ROSEDALE*"

SUMMIT ST.-OBSERVATION PARK—ROUTE 30—ON 10TH ST. E. B., 11TH ST. W. B., BETWEEN WYANDOTTE & WASHINGTON
Summit St. sign reads, "*30-10th-Wyndt.-S. W. Blvd.—Summit—SUMMIT ST.*" Observation Park sign reads, "*30-10th-Wyndt.-Mercier-20th Ter.—OBSERVATION PK.*"

27TH STREET-STOCKYARDS—ROUTE 19—ON 27TH ST., PERSHING RD., OR 23RD ST. TRFY.
E. B. sign reads, "*19-Union Sta.-Van Brunt—27th STREET*"
W. B. sign reads, "*19-Union Sta.-B'lway-S. W. Blvd.—27th STREET*" or "*19-Union Sta.-Stock Yards—27th STREET*"

TROLLEY BUS LINES

BENTON-INDIANA—ROUTE 45—N. B. ON McGEE, S. B. ON GRAND, OR ON 15TH ST.
N. B. sign reads, "*45-9th-Grand—BENTON-INDIANA*"
S. B. sign reads, "*45-Benton-Swope P'hway—BENTON-INDIANA*" or "*45-Benton-39th—BENTON-INDIANA*"

BROOKLYN-WOODLAND—ROUTE 44—ON GRAND AVE.
N. B. sign reads, "*44-Grand-10th-Br'klyn-44th—BROOKLYN*"
S. B. sign reads, "*44-Grand-15th-W'dland-47th—WOODLAND*"

18TH STREET—ROUTE 46—ON 18TH ST. OR S. W. BLVD.
Both directions sign reads, "*46-18th-Jackson-Kans.-Berger—18th STREET*"

15TH STREET—ROUTE 42—ON GRAND AVE. OR 15TH ST.
N. B. or W. B. sign reads, "*42-Grand Ave.-3rd—15th STREET*"
S. B. or E. B. sign reads, "*42-15th St.-Crystal—15th STREET*"

INDEPENDENCE AVE.—ROUTE 41—ON GRAND AVE. OR 8TH ST.
N. B. or E. B. sign reads, "*41-Indep. Ave.-Hardesty—INDEPENDENCE AVENUE*"
S. B. or W. B. sign reads, "*41-Grand Ave.-Union Sta.—INDEPENDENCE AVENUE*" or "*41-Grand Ave.-15th—INDEPENDENCE AVENUE*"

NORTHEAST—ROUTE 40—N. B. ON GRAND, S. B. ON WALNUT
N. B. sign reads, "*40-St. John-Belmont—NORTHEAST*"
S. B. sign reads, "*40-Walnut-13th—NORTHEAST*"

PROSPECT—ROUTE 43—N. B. ON GRAND, S. B. ON WALNUT, OR ON 15TH ST.
N. B. or W. B. sign reads, "*43-Walnut-7th—PROSPECT*"
S. B. or E. B. sign reads, "*43-Prospect-75th—PROSPECT*" or "*43-Prospect-43th—PROSPECT*"

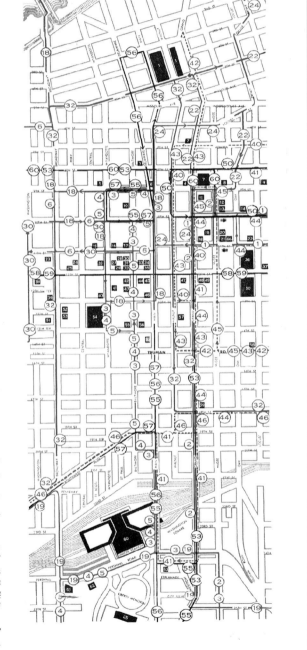

Downtown Kansas City, September 1949

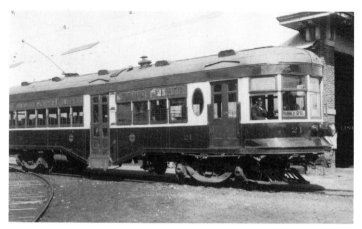

Even after more than twenty years of service, the Kaw Valley's interurbans remained imposing cars. Car 21 outside the Bonner Springs car house in January 1935.

being served. The line ended at Fort Leavenworth, in the center of the post.

A planned Leavenworth-Topeka extension was not built and from 1914 auto and truck competition, inflation, and the war crushed the company. In 1919 it defaulted on bond payments. It was reorganized in 1920 as the **Kansas City, Leavenworth and Western Railway**, issuing $1million in 6% bonds, $1/2 million in preferred stock and $1/2 million in common stock. It used the next few years to retrench and refocus, vacating its Missouri freight terminal in 1922 and retreating to Fourth and Minnesota in Kansas City KS. Soon after, its trucks took over LCL trolley freights. But suburban traffic was growing. By 1923, the KCL&WR had spent over $100,000 to upgrade. In the next few years it would spend as much again, including four new lightweight cars in 1927.

In February 1925, Leavenworth city cars were replaced by buses, The interurban's tracks were relaid, roadbed and ties elsewhere were refurbished and new freight switches to the Kansas City Outer Belt system installed. The Wolcott connection with the MoPac increased in importance as efforts were made to expand carload freight business. However, efforts put into reviving trolley freight were futile and the company soon switched to trucks. In the late 1920s the line on State Street in KCKS was lifted to make room for U.S. route 24.

In 1937, Wyandotte County planned the rebuilding and widening of Marshall Creek Dam to create a lake, a county park and picnic ground. It condemned the line, which went through the planned lake.There was no money to build a diversion nor to bridge the lake, while South Fourth Street in Leavenworth needed repaving. The company did the only thing it could and in March 1938 declared bankruptcy. But the Cleveland Trust Company, (its owner) was unwilling to see its investment go for nothing now there were signs ridership was recovering and set up a new **Kansas City and Leavenworth Transportation Company**. Cars were replaced on April 1st, 1938 by KC&LTC 24-seat buses, using Kansas Route 5 between Leavenworth and Kansas City. They were extended to Topeka for some years but ceased after a 1951 bankruptcy.

Incomplete Roster Notes

Little is known of the 1899 interurbans 21-24 (21-25?). Their numbers continued on from Leavenworth city cars and they were painted fern green. In 1906 four 60-seat cars with smoking compartments, Brill semi-convertible windows, four 75HP motors and Brill 27-E11/2 double trucks arrived. In 1910, two nearly-new 60-seat center-entrance cars 25/6 (Brill 27-E11/2 trucks, four 75HP motors) came from the South Fork-Portage Ry (Johnstown PA). One was destroyed by fire on a Leavenworth street in 1920, the other became a freight motor in 1927. Twin City (Minneapolis/St. Paul) 610, 622/3 (American, 1892) on Bemis double-trucks, came in 1916. There were also some single-end semi-convertible cars on Brill 27-E trucks, four 75HP motors, multiple-unit equipment and 60 seats. Normal schedules required six cars, but 18 were in stock. A 1925 fire destroyed many of them. In July 1927, four one-man lightweight 52-seat interurbans (1-4) came from American. ERJ March 3rd, 1928 p. 355-6 said they would furnish all regular service and old equipment would be retired, except for a small reserve fleet.*"We cannot continue with the equipment and methods of twenty years ago."* The cars had leather bucket seats and "pneumatic" cushions, rubber-tiled floors, two-tone mahogany interiors, indirect lighting, Brill 177 E-1 trucks, 4 GE 247 45HP motors and a red with cream trim and blue roof paint job.

3. Missouri and Kansas Interurban Railway The "Strang" line, was named for promoter William B. Strang, a railroad builder and real estate man with acres of homesites in Johnson County KS and no link to either Kansas City or the Johnson County seat at Olathe. So he built his own. Rather than cross into Missouri over the flood-prone West Bottoms and then charge the bluffs, he built to KCMO over high ground. He was reluctant to electrify until the rival **Kansas City, Olathe, Lawrence and Topeka Electric Railway** proved itself. His line opened in November 1906, gas-electric railcars running from downtown KC MO to 39th Street and state line, where it went on its own tracks to reach Overland, Overland Park, Rosedale, Lenexa and Olathe (about 20 miles).

Strang was caught in the 1907 slump. Housing lots were not selling and the gas-electric cars, each with a motor and generator designed by his chief engineer Lars Nilson, were unreliable. He decided to electrify in March 1908. There was a receivership from June 6th, 1908 until October 24th, 1909, but electric service began January 1st, 1909 from 7th and Walnut in Kansas City MO. The line then stabilized. The eleven daily runs of 1909 were stepped up to 18 by World War One, limiteds taking 75 minutes and locals 90 minutes. The new subdivisions eventually did well and Overland Park commuters, for whom this was essentially another KC car line, paid the 25-cent fare without complaint. This gave them the right to travel a distance equal to or shorter than its MET equivalent, for which

Kaw Valley Express car 108 switches a railroad box car at Bonner Springs 1949.

Kaw Valley locomotive 504 hauling a short freight at an unknown location in 1949

they would have paid a nickel and whined unmercifully had it gone up to 7 cents.

Strang died in 1921, but the line ran as usual until 1925. Then two things happened; highway paving between Kansas City and Olathe and a 1925 fire at the Overland Park car house which destroyed all but two cars. These were replaced by new lightweights just at the time affluent residents of the Strang subdivisions were leaving the line for their own autos and the paved highway. Receivership came soon after and years were spent in a fight between bond and stockholders wanting to liquidate as much cash as they could, and employees who needed regular paychecks and took voluntary pay cuts to protect their jobs and keep the cars going.

The line's superintendent and a group of businessmen, shopkeepers and traders bought the company in 1937, but couldn't buy out the bondholders and didn't do well enough to avoid foreclosure in 1940. Had they been able to hold out, the line might have survived. Instead, the last car ran on July 9th, 1940. Electric freight continued, but the first train of July 25th 1940 was stopped mid-trip when a thousand feet of copper trolley wire was found missing, stolen in the night when power was off. The train returned to the barn, never to run again.

Incomplete Roster notes

Four Brill-built gas-electric cars came in 1905. One, named "Ogerita" for Strang's niece, was bright red. "Marguerite" was named for Strang's wife. "Rosamund" and "Geraldine" were built in 1908 as steam railroad demonstrators, the latter an observation car on Brill 27-E3 and 27-E2 trucks (one each),lettered for the "Strang Gas-Electric Car Company. They were never delivered, going instead to the Minneapolis St. Paul, Rochester and Dubuque Electric Traction (Dan Patch lines). All had two 50HP electric motors and made about 2 miles to the gallon on their own but not when hauling trains of up to three trailers, often double-truck 12-bench opens. "Ogerita" and "Irene" were also sold to the Dan Patch Lines. "Geraldine" became electric car #101, "Marguerite" freight motor 107. Poor's 1908 says there were seven electric cars. Brill Magazine February 15th, 1909 (pp 32-39) describes new 52-seat single-end interurbans 102-104 (American, 1908) on Brill 6' wb 27-E-11/2 trucks. 104-5 came circa 1909. 115-117 were lightweight 53-seat one-man interurbans (American, 1925, Brill 77-E-1 trucks, 4 35HP motors). Rebuilt interurbans 118, 119 remained to the end.

4. Kansas City-Kaw Valley Railroad The Kaw Valley line, originally the **Kansas City, Kaw Valley & Western** was the last KC-based interurban built, opening in 1914. Its complex pre-history is punctuated by false starts and competition from others quicker off the mark. It originated in the **Kansas City and Bonner Springs Railway**, an 1899 Willard E. Win-

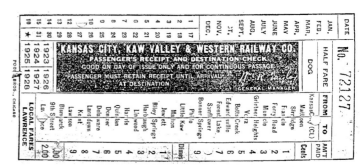

Passenger receipt and destination check, 1923.

ner project. Much had been graded when in February 1900 he sold it to the **Kansas City, Mexico and Orient Railroad**, a line fated never to leave the state of Kansas. The KC&BS was chartered in September 1902 but didn't get a KC MO franchise until 1904. Construction then began.

Money troubles forced a three-year hiatus and a 1908 reorganization.The new treasurer was J. D. Waters, founder of 1905's Bonner Springs Oil and Gas Company who had just begun the Bonner Springs Portland Cement Company. A trial run was made from Bonner Springs KS east one mile to the cement plant on April 27th, 1908. By June 4.9 miles was open from to Lake of the Forest. In 1910 the line was heading east to Kansas City along the Kaw (Kansas) river's north bank in Wyandotte County KS when it ran out of money. Bonner Springs-Lake of the Forest closed and the Hocker line (the Kansas City, Lawrence and Topeka) began making noises about building northwest from Zarah KS to Bonner Springs and perhaps absorbing the KC&BS. This didn't happen and by 1913, Kaw Valley seemed dead until Waters got J. J. Heim to buy the line, reorganize and resume the Kansas City extension, under the name **Kansas City, Kaw Valley and Western**.

It opened on July 20th, 1914, connecting at KCKS with MET tracks at City Park.Trackage rights took cars to Riverview Station (Fifth and Central Avenue) in KCKS. The route into KCMO was shared with Kansas City, Leavenworth and Western interurbans, running over MET's EL and 8th Street tunnel to a station at 907 Main Street. West of Bonner Springs, the line aimed for Lawrence & Topeka. However the UP objected to the upstart crossing its tracks east Lawrence. The Kaw Valley's contractors took matters into their own hands, laying the crossing one night and defying the UP to do anything about it. No more was heard.

The first Kaw Valley car entered Lawrence around June 1st, 1916. University of Kansas sports events in Lawrence attracted huge crowds and

Kaw Valley service would be extended two miles over city tracks from the Lawrence interurban depot to the Mount Oread campus. Freight cars served on-line industries and farms and by 1917 there were two electric locomotives, a line car, eight box cars, four flat cars and three refrigerator cars. Carload freight was taken from railroad interchanges to on-line industries and the locomotives ran 24/7 hauling 100,000lb sand cars and night freights. Typical loads included crushed rock and cement, cattle, wheat, potatoes and farm produce The connection to South Lawrence was not used because of clearance problems on the Kaw River bridge.

Surveying west of Lawrence to Topeka continued until World War One made the project impractical, but a greater priority was independent access to Kansas City. All railroads interchanged through the Kansas City Terminal, wartime freight loads taking up to five days to transit its two routes. The old **Kansas City, Mexico and Orient Railroad** would have been a third. Over $2 million had already been spent on right-of-way, grading and construction and the line was almost finished. Unfortunately, so was the company, having spent huge sums to remove 600,000 cu. ft. of material to make a cut at the peak of the divide between the Kaw and Missouri river valleys.

The Kaw Valley bought the KCM&O's Kansas City terminal facilities and much of its right-of-way, prompted by the Heim interests, which still had a controlling interest. At the same time, it began a protracted purchase of the Kansas City Outer Belt from Emil Metscham which he'd earlier bought at foreclosure (<u>ERJ</u> August 25th, 1923 p. 313). The Outer Belt was conceived around 1903 by Arthur E. Stilwell and would have circled both Kansas Cities with an electric railroad. By 1920 seven miles of rail had been laid, while real estate had been bought for terminal and switching purposes. It was to run from a connection with the Kaw Valley to a point near the Kaw River's mouth. The purchase was split between the Kaw Valley and the KCS and a jointly-owned **Kansas City and Missouri Railway and Terminal Company** was set up. Progress, however, was slow and ICC approval only came on February 16th, 1924, with several caveats against the financial package the two roads set up via their subsidiary.

But the Kaw Valley now had the green light to complete the KC Outer Belt, using its Terminal Company subsidiary to do the job. All Outer Belt

Kansas City, Kaw Valley & Western Railway

Between Kansas City, Mo., 10th & Main and
Lawrence, Kans.
Leaves Kansas City, Mo.

6:30 A. M.	2:30 P. M.
7:30 A. M.	3:30 P. M.
8:30 A. M.	5:00 P. M.
9:30 A. M.	5:30 P. M.
10:30 A. M.	6:30 P. M.
11:30 A. M.	7:30 P. M.
12:30 P. M.	9:45 P. M.
1:30 P. M.	11:30 P. M.

4:30 P. M. and 8:30 P. M.
Bonner Springs only.
Double Daily Express Service at Freight Rates.
Connections with all Lines at
Kansas City, Kansas and Kansas City, Mo.
For any other information
Call

Fairfax 3922   Fairfax 3855

Kaw Valley schedule from the Official Guide to Kansas City, 1920.

bridges were in and 80% of the line was graded but while the original ruling grade was 1/2%, to speed construction and reduce costs the Kaw Valley left a 11/2% grade for 1,000 feet to get over the hump of unexcavated material in the cut at the peak of the valley divide. At the south end, a two-mile extension linked the Kaw Valley with the Rock Island, KCS and KC Terminal RR tracks. This went into service first. By May 1924, a single-track electric line ran on the entire eight miles. There were few grade crossings, most streets being bridged. Four miles of industrial sidings were laid and an effort was made to get industries to locate on-line.

This remarkable investment was made at a time the company was wilting due to bus and automobile competition It formed a protective committee in July 1924 to set up a reorganization plan to protect its first mortgage 6% ten-year gold bonds. Though passenger business had fallen off, freight was poised for growth and the committee saw the line's future in heavy-haul rail freight, considering the tripling in size of the biggest on-

Kaw Valley locomotive 507 and a box car at flag stop 14, east of Edwardsville KS. January 7th, 1961

"Betsy," the Blue Valley's open car heading to Swope Parkway circa 1930.

line shipper, the Kansas Portland Cement Company at Bonner Springs. There was however the tricky business of negotiating the fiscal hurdles and that couldn't be done without a receivership, which began in mid-1925.

On September 12th, 1927 the Kaw Valley was sold to a new **Kansas City-Kaw Valley Railroad Company**, part of the protective committee' reorganization plan. The new company claimed 11,000 carloads of freight were annually interchanged with the railroads in addition to on-line haulage and that freight interchange could only increase as the Kaw Valley effectively by-passed the bottleneck throttling the rest of KC's railroad system. With the Depression, business went into free-fall and the line was in receivership again by September 1932. Passenger service from Bonner Springs west to Lawrence ended June 10th 1935, east from Bonner Springs to Kansas City June 27th, replaced by company buses running Kansas City-Bonner Springs-Lawrence. The cars were stored disused for years.

Trolley freight continued and as late as 1944 the rickety trestle linking the Kaw Valley with KCPS in KCKS (the old passenger route) was still used to reach a customer. In 1945, there were 45 miles of 650V. D. C. standard-gauge tracks, ten passenger cars, six trailers, four express cars, two locomotives, a work car and nine freight cars plus an unknown number of buses on 35 miles of route. Trolley freight continued until December 22nd, 1949, when the 22-mile Bonner Springs-Lawrence section closed. The company declined to accept further LCL freight on the Bonner Springs-Kansas City segment and became a short-line railroad, shipping and interchanging railroad cars only.

The Lawrence closure was due to city authorities wanting tracks off the streets, but dismantling didn't begin until 1951 and the Kaw Valley held on to the right-of-way for years, hoping for a buyer. Eventually the Kansas Highway Commission bought over eight miles to widen Highway 32. The bus line was sold to the Kansas Trails Bus Company in 1956 and the Kaw Valley finally quit the passenger business. The KHC later bought the KCKS-Bonner Springs right-of-way for $120,000 to continue widening of Kansas Highway 32. The last freight ran on September 30th, 1961 from the west limits of KCKS to Bonner Springs KS. Most of the line then closed. At Bonner Springs some segments were incorporated into the Union Pacific RR after relaying with heavier rail. To assist, UP leased a Kaw Valley locomotive for use around Bonner Springs until November 17th. The original 1909 segment between Bonner Springs and the cement plant survived to early 1962, no longer under wire.

Incomplete Roster notes

Twin City (Minneapolis/St. Paul) 611/14/15/17 (American, 1892) on Bemis double-trucks were bought in 1914.

Center-entrance cars 20-27 (Cincinatti 1914/1916), Baldwin BLW 28-22 double-trucks, 4 WH 306CV 65HP motors. Cars 30 and 31 existed but there is no information.

Poor's 1918 records nine passenger cars, four Cincinnati-built express cars (probably #107-110), one other motor car, nine miscellaneous cars, double-end line car #100 on Standard MCB trucks and locomotives.

Locomotives 201/2, (American Car, 1917) on Baldwin 73-22K trucks. 202 sold to the Petaluma and Santa Rosa Railroad (CA) 1920 as their #502, 201 sold to Interstate Public Service Corporation (IN) as their #605, later Indiana Railways 750. From 1941 it was owned by American Aggregates Corporation who rebuilt it as a diesel locomotive.

In 1945 American Aggregates sold three former Indiana RR locomotives to the Bevier and Southern Railroad. The B&S re-sold them to the Kaw Valley in 1947/48. Two ran, the other was used for parts. They kept their B&S numbers.

Locomotive 200, (home-built 1927 by Terre Haute, Indianapolis and Eastern Traction Company) was Indiana RR 753.

Locomotive 201, (home-built 1928 by Union Traction Company of Indiana) was Indiana RR 787.

Locomotive 202, (home-built 1920 by Terre Haute, Indianapolis and Eastern Traction Company) was Indiana RR 752.

Locomotives 501/2 (BLW class B, 1919). 50 scrapped 1956. 502 sold 1944 to Cornwall (ON) as #6, scrapped 1973.

Locomotive 503, (BLW 1912) was Connecticut Co. 028, #1054 in 1916 sold 1937 to Fort Hancock at Sandy Hook NJ, later to Transit equiupment Co. Passaic NJ, to Kaw Valley 1943, scrapped 1956.

Locomotive 504, (BLW class B, 1917) was Chicago North Shore and Milwaukee #10002, sold 1919 to Monongahela-West Penn (later City Lines of West Virginia) as #2000, to Kaw Valley in April 1948, then sold on in 1953 to Texas Transportation Co, San Antonio TX as locomotive #1 (fourth), where it is preserved.

Locomotive 505, 506 BLW class B, 1921, 1919) were Northeast Oklahoma #2 and #1 sold 1940 to Cedar Rapids and Iowa City as #57, #56, sold to Kaw Valley in 1954, sold 1963 to Iowa Terminal (Traction) of Mason City as #51, #52. #501 burned in carbarn fire January 1967, 52 still operates.

Locomotive 507 (BLW class B, 1920), was Washington & Old Dominion #50, sold 1948 as Cedar Rapids and Iowa City #58, sold 1956 to Kaw Valley, sold 1963 to Iowa Terminal (Mason City) as #53, became 50 in 1964. It still runs.

5. **Kansas City, Lawrence and Topeka Electric Railroad Company (The Hocker Line)** Another line with unfilled Topeka ambitions, 1901's **Kansas City-Olathe Railway Company** was to build a KCMO-Olathe KS via KCKS, Rosedale, Merriam, Shawnee, Lenexa and Pleasant View. Promoters were William Lackman (an Olathe farmer) and David B. Johnson (ex-treasurer of Johnson County KS). SRJ December 26th, 1903 (ad p. 24) said it would open on April 1st 1904 and that fourteen miles of grading had been done, largely following Turkey Creek to Merriam KS. I would carry passengers, freight, dairy and garden produce and join MET tracks at Rosedale.

Little grading had been done whe it failed in 1904. A December 17th 1906 foreclosure satisfied a loan from the Fidelity Trust Company of Kansas City to build southwest of Rosedale. R. W.Hocker, a real estate promoter in the Willard Winner mould, now became interested, joining Johnson and other holdovers as directors. A new **Kansas City and Olathe Electric Railroad Company** resumed building Rosedale-Olathe. Service began on the completed portion with a single-truck car leased from the MET. From Main and Third (City Market) in KCMO, it ran to Main, 19th and Southwest to its own tracks and then to Rosedale. As building progressed, service was extended to the railhead, reaching Merriam KS by December 1907. From here, the line was to go south to Olathe via Lenexa. But the board instead chose a 36-mile western extension to Lawrence, leaving Merriam by crossing Turkey Creek, passing the new

Hocker Grove amusement park in mid-1908. The line opened to Shawnee on September 1st.

The **Kansas City, Lawrence and Topeka Electric Railroad** sprang from a 1909 reorganization, which in addition to the main line now contemplated a 28-mile extension to Lawrence and Topeka, a branch to Osage City KS (south of Topeka) and an Olathe branch. The branches were dropped when the Strang line electrified its own Olathe via Lenexa route and only six miles of the Topeka extension was built, ending west of Shawnee at Mill Creek, just east of Zarah, though right-of-way was acquired as far as Lawrence and some grading was done. A Zarah-Bonner Springs extension was considered in 1910, $25,000 in bonds being raised from locals, but was cancelled when estimated costs for bridging the Kaw River came in too high. Bonner Springs was left to the Kaw Valley.

During 1910, Kansas City-Zarah cars ran hourly, half-hourly between Rose Hill and Rosedale in the morning and evening rush. An all-day Rose Hill-East Zarah (five miles) local service was also run. In 1912 a block-long spur was built in Merriam to connect with the Frisco, making interchange freight shipments possible, generally lumber, food for local distribution and coal. There was milk service to Kansas City, which from 1919 was run by a converted former MET single-truck car. Brill Magazine (January 1917) said the line was 13 miles long, (17 miles City Market to Zarah), with a mile of double-track and 52 miles of single-track under construction between Zarah and Topeka. This was wishful thinking, but clearly the dream of getting to Topeka was still alive.

Within a year, however, it was clear this wouldn't happen. The usual suspects (automobiles and wartime inflation) were implicated and cost-cutting began when a flanged-wheel Model T truck was experimentally used on Rose Hill-Zarah locals, after which a single-truck car was leased from Kansas City Railways. Hocker, who still owned almost all stock and securities, died on December 28th, 1918. Soon after, the line defaulted on bond interest payments and a receiver was appointed on January 30th, 1919. ERJ April 16th, 1927 (p. 128) reported negotiations to sell the line to KCPS but this went nowhere and the line quit July 21st 1927, being sold for scrap at public auction.

That upset Shawnee and Merriam suburbanites, who on October 20th agreed to raise money to buy the line, giving themselves a January 1928 deadline. Arrangements were made for KCPS to run it as a feeder to their own lines. ERJ January 28th, 1928 (p. 175) claimed four cars would be leased from KCPS, that KCPS officers estimated the line would cost $16,000 to refurbish and cars would run from downtown KCMO to Rose Hill KS. From March 1928 it was renamed **Kansas City, Merriam and Shawnee Electric Railway**, with seven miles of track from Rosedale to Rose Hill KS, a mile west of Shawnee. The Zarah section did not reopen. ERJ May 19th, 1928 (p. 832) reported a May 12th opening parade of eight cars hauling dignitaries and the 30-piece KCPS band from Ninth and Wyandotte in KCMO to Rose Hill, with a barbecue and picnic in Shawnee Park. All went well until well into the Depression and by 1934, less than 20,000 rode monthly. The line closed March 30th, 1934.

Incomplete Roster notes (Kansas City, Lawrence and Topeka Electric Railroad Company (The Hocker Line) Every car was leased or bought used. Early services used single-truck cars leased from the MET. Two brown-painted St. Louis Car single-truckers (50, 52) were used on local and rush-hour services. Cars 101-104 came in 1908 from UR of St. Louis (probably 900-series cars), with four 35HP motors, olive green paint and mahogany interior finish. In September 1910, UR 762 and 962 (St. Louis Car 1895/6) came (numbers unknown in Hocker line service), In 1917, Twin City (Mineapolis/St. Paul) 613/16/20 (American, 1892) on Bemis double-trucks, were bought used from St. Louis Car. They replaced earlier cars and were painted red. McGraw 1918 said the line was 12.75 miles long, with ten motor and three other cars. Power was now bought from Kansas City Railways.

6. **Blue Valley Railroad** In 1907, Jackson County Court granted rights-of-way to the BVR for a trolley line on Blue Ridge Road from 49th and Swope Park Highway to *"a point east of the Blue River."* (SRJ November 23rd, 1907 ad. p. 20). It's not known when the 1.5 mile line opened, but it ran from MET's Swope Park line (Swope Parkway) to Chelsea Avenue. By the 1930s, its track ran down the center of the newly-paved 50th Street to serve its two termini. One car was an ancient ten-bench open named "Betsy," the other a closed car named "Nancy." Both were of equally dubious ancestry. Whatever car was in service stood at Swope Parkway. At any point on the line, an intending passenger could push a button on one of the poles supporting the overhead. This rang a bell at Swope and the car would run out to pick the rider up. The line closed in September 1931, after sale to the Kansas City municipality for $5,000. An independent bus company running old school buses replaced it for a time.

4. KANSAS CITY AREA INTERURBAN PROPOSALS

1. **Interstate Railway Company** Set up February 23rd 1904 to build a 48.5 mile standard-gauge Kansas City-St. Joseph electric railroad or interurban (a rival **St. Joseph, Albany and Des Moines** project planned electric pass- enger trains and steam-hauled freights), the Interstate's capital was about $4 million. It soon developed delusions of grandeur, talking of a 600-mile line to Duluth MN. SRJ September 3rd, 1904 (p. 356) claimed contracts had been let on the first 400 miles north of KC, bringing it close to Minneapolis. *"The consolidated Trust Company was recently formed to finance this company and...$2 million of French money is in it."* Gould money too was in it and F. S. Mordaunt of Chicago would promote the project. SRJ August 25th, 1906 (ad. p. 7) talked of the line entering Buchanan County near Dearborn and St. Joseph, at the foot of King Avenue Hill.

It then slipped below the radar. ERJ April 3rd, 1909 (p. 666) said it would now be a double-track third-rail line to St. Joseph only. Building began in October 1909 about 2½ miles south of St. Joseph, but litigation between the Interstate and its rivals killed it and the Interstate went dormant circa 1910/1911. It did, however, still exist in May 1915, having outlived all rivals except the Kansas City, Clay County and St. Joseph. The Interstate felt it still had live options on many routes, including the Clay County's. Seeing a chance to recoup its losses, it filed a $2 million damage suit in Jackson County Circuit Court against the Clay County for ignoring their options and building on the same route. The Interstate was awarded $1,500,000 damages, reduced on appeal in 1917 to $250,000.

2. **Kansas City and St. Joseph Electric Railroad** Between 1905 and 1911 Poor's said this company proposed 47 miles of line and 2300' of sidings, via Platte City, Dearborn and Faucett to St. Joseph and noted that thirteen miles was already operating by May 1905, with twelve cars and four freight cars. This was not so, though building did begun north of Dearborn and the line was slated to open December 1st 1905. Twenty-five miles of its right-of-way south of St. Joseph may have been used by the Clay County to jump-start its own project. The KC&SJER certainly believed this and in 1914 sued the Clay County for $200,000, ERJ July 17th, 1915 (p.119) saying the suit was based on the latter *"having taken possession and...using land on which (the KC&SJER) had active options."* Rather than chance the outcome, the KC&STJ sold its rights to the Interstate which rolled them into its own claim against the Clay County, based on the 25 miles of right-of-way north of Kansas City, so giving it a *"presumptive series of options on the entire KCCC&STJ right-of-way between Kansas City and St. Joseph."*

3. **Kansas City and Southeastern Railroad** This was an ambitious project with some potential. SRJ March 21st, 1908 (p.474) reported chief engineer J. C. Herring had surveyed a 30-mile line southeast from Kansas City to Leeds, Raytown, Lees Summit, Cockrell and Lone Jack. Gas-electric cars would handle passengers and freight. Officers were mainly

Kansas City men, Charles A. S. Sims (President), Howard. W. Gibson (Vice-President), B. F. Shouse (Treasurer) and G. P. Norton (Attorney). Building would begin September 1st 1908 and include an amusement park near Little Blue. Capitalized at $880,000, ($180,000 issued), ETW October 24th, 1908 (p. 1136) said the line would be built alongside existing country roads, rather than on right-of-way. ERJ January 30th, 1909 (p. 214), reported lack of funds, reorganization and renaming as **Kansas City and South Eastern Traction Company.** Kansas City-Lone Jack would now be the first division of a Kansas City-Jefferson City interurban as follows;

A. Main line running 125 miles from Kansas City east to Leeds, Ray town, Little Blue, Lee's Summit, Lone Jack, Warrensberg, Knob Nos ter and Sedalia to Jefferson City.
B. Branch from Lee's Summit south to Greenwood, Pleasant Hill and Harrisonville (15 miles).
C. Branch from Pittsfield south to Holden and southeast to Clinton (24 miles).

Construction would be incremental, Kansas City-Lone Jack (30 miles), Lone Jack-Warrensberg (24 miles), Warr- ensberg-Sedalia (30 miles) and Sedalia-Jefferson City (40 miles). The promoters said it was already financed. ERJ March 6th, 1909 (p. 446) noted a February 17th, 1909 capital increase from $180,000 to $5 million after which a $5 million mortgage was taken out with New York's Carnegie Trust Company to build 125 miles of main line and 65 miles of branches. The Clinton branch was now to be provisional. A large force was working on rock excavation 2 1/2 miles north of Raytown. More would be done once the weather cleared. No more was heard.

4. Kansas City and Southwestern Railway Company ETW October 24th, 1908 (p.1133) said this would be a Kansas City-Topeka line, with a Lawrence-Independence KS branch, *"tapping the gas, oil and cement districts,"* recently financed in Europe by Whitsed Laming and Charles Gould (who until lately been company president).

5. Kansas City & Tiffany Springs Railway ERJ January 22nd 1916 (p. 183) reported Clay and Platte county granting franchises for this project. The next step would be a MOPSC hearing to allow a bond issue. This may have been a renaming and pruning of an earlier Kansas City-Parkville proposal, with a branch to Campbellton and an interchange with the Quincy, Omaha and Kansas City Railroad. The KC&TSR was interested in the latter's closed ten-mile Gower-Trimble segment. February 1916 estimates were based on an electric car at two cents per mile with frequent stops as compared to a steam train making few stops. But MOPSC didn't believe an electric line could be profitable on a rural line a railroad had already abandoned and the project died.

6. Manufacturers Electric and Terminal Railway Company This was conceived as late as 1926 by Willard E. Winner, who convinced eleven Liberty investors (including the mayor, city engineer, a grocer and a bookseller) it was feasible. Articles of association were granted in February 1927, capital being $300,000. The Kansas City Star (February 14th, 1927) noted that *"Mr. Winner has been an enthusiast over electric lines from the day he rose to a success some forty years ago...Since the collapse of Mr. Winner's development plans after many of his comp- anies failed thirty-six years ago, he has undertaken several electric line developments, but has not gone through with them. However civil engineers have always agreed that Mr. Winner's schemes were practical and, in fact, many of the projects conceived by him have been carried out subsequently by others."*

The line would run southwest from Liberty (Clay County) to cross the Missouri on its own bridge, reaching Washington Park Boulevard and Blue Ridge Road just east of KC. Winner claimed the right-of-way was under option and building would begin in May. A short branch three miles south of Liberty would serve Atwood quarries, where a cement plant would be built. The double-track line would be laid in the median of a new divided highway, the right of way being 150' wide in Clay County and 100' wide in Jackson County. No more was heard.

7. Pittsburg and Kansas City This project is a mystery. It isn't known if this was to be a Kansas line or go through to Kansas City MO. If the latter, by what route? Its existence went largely unnoticed, though ERJ March 6th, 1909 p. 445) talked of a 50-mile line to Burgess MO. But a company was capitalized at $500,000 and investors included Fred Fitch. Builders' photos of two cars lettered for the company exist, baggage/express 107 (Danville, circa 1909) and passenger 108 (American order 814, dated June 30th, 1909). Their subsequent history is unknown.

8. St. Louis-Kansas City Electric Railway Company (See Columbia)

KEYTESVILLE

1880	**1890**	**1900**	**1910**	**1920**	**1930**	**1940**	**1950**	**1960**	**1970**	**1980**	**1990**	**2000**
737	819	1,127	963	872	738	854	733	644	730	689	564	533

Keytesville in Chariton County, some 65 miles west of Moberly, is named for James Keyte, an English immigrant who built a log cabin that served as a post office from 1831. The Wabash, in its original guise as the North Missouri Railroad, built a station about 1 1/2 miles south of the post office and the town was established in 1868. The station's location was an unpleasant reality for those pinning their hopes on growth, as the original survey had tracked the railroad through the town. Instead, from 1869 to 1889, passengers either walked to the station or risked health and well-being in the rickety horse bus that occasionally put in an appearance. Freight traveled by wagon.

An animal streetcar line to the station began in 1889, established by partners Hugo Bartz (a Prussian born in 1838, who settled here in 1867 and set up a mill) and J. J. Moore. It had no name and had a net worth of $10,000 with 1.5 miles of track, two passenger cars, a freight/baggage flat car and a car barn. It began at Walnut and ran east on Bridge (Main) Street to Ash. *"The track is divided and spurs (sic) run close to the sidewalk on each side which enables the conductor and general passenger agent to unload his freight on the walk. Unfortunately, what was the busiest block is not the busiest any more and the principal stores are in the next block east."*

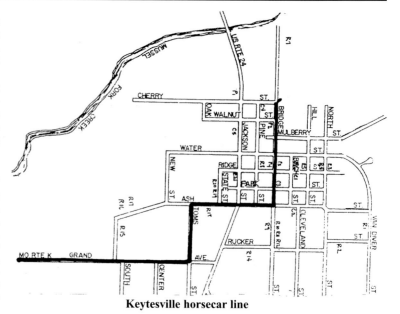

Keytesville horsecar line

"The old flat car of the Keytsville line." Kansas City Star, August 14, 1910.

(Kansas City Star August 14th, 1910.)

The line then turned south on Ash and ran five blocks, turning east on Toms Street for a block, then south on Grand through the cornfields to the station. The entire trip took twenty minutes. The "freight" (flat) car was in daily use, usually carrying mail between the station and Keytesville. It had benches for passengers if needed. Freight was also carried on the front and rear platform of the passenger cars. By 1914, there was one passenger car, one flat car and no schedule, but a vehicle met every passenger train religiously, running on sleds in snow and ice.

The 1914/15 MOPSC report claimed 23,280 passengers at a 15 cent fare yielded $3,492, the mail contract $420, express $450, baggage $133 and general freight $1048.64; a total gross revenue of $5,543. Expenses included $840 for driver and conductor wages, $263 for track hands, $400 for track repairs and $330 on unexplained fees leaving $3,710 profit. But *"No accurate accounts have ever been kept, numbers of items being paid and charged as one. Hereafter, such accounts will be kept as will conform to the requirements of the MOPSC as nearly as can be done. The owners... are J.J. Moore and George West, successors to J. J. Moore and Hugo Bartz of Keytesville."*

Horse car and flat car at Keytesville Station, date unknown

In summer 1919, the road between Keytesville and the station was paved. Passengers began switching either to their own autos or to cabs and freight was moving to motor trucks. In the summer of 1919 the partners planned to replace the line with a motor bus, but whether this happened isn't known and it faded without trace.

LEBANON

1880	**1890**	**1900**	**1910**	**1920**	**1930**	**1940**	**1950**	**1960**	**1970**	**1980**	**1990**	**2000**
1,419	2,218	2,125	2,430	2,848	3,562	5,025	6,808	8,220	8,616	9,507	9,983	12,155

Set up as a trading post in 1849, Lebanon was bodily moved a mile south of its original site in 1869 when the Frisco Railroad arrived. The Laclede county seat, Lebanon incorporated as a city in 1874. It became an Ozarks spa destination in the 1890s thanks to the presence of the newly-dug "MagneticWell" whose water, besides being pure and thus medicinally desireable, was said to have beneficial magnetic properties for rheumatism sufferers. A St. Louis syndicate bought the Lebanon Light and Water Company for its well and in 1890 built the new Gasconade hotel, complete with resident physician, bath-house and gym. A one-car electric trolley line opened in1890 from the Frisco Depot (Laclede Hotel), south on Commercial Street to the Gasconade after Light and Water received a street railway franchise on July 5th, 1890. The exact route is not definitively known and it is possible that at some point the line ran on Van

Buren Street. There was also a competing horse bus line from the station to the Gasconade. The car barn was on Commercial Street, next to the railroad tracks and Jefferson Street. The hotel and spa did not thrive, the car was used less and less and by 1896 had ceased running. On November 2nd 1896, the line's franchise was voided by the Light and Water Company. The hotel building became a college but burned to the ground on September 21st, 1899.

In 1895 meetings were held to promote an electric interurban from Lebanon to Bagnell via Linn Creek and Ha Ha Tonka in Camden county, to be funded by a Des Moines IA syndicate (Jefferson City Daily Tribune, September 28th, 1905 p.4) who planned a southern extension "through the richest timber country of the state." The project soon fizzled.

LEXINGTON

1880	**1890**	**1900**	**1910**	**1920**	**1930**	**1940**	**1950**	**1960**	**1970**	**1980**	**1990**	**2000**
3,996	4,537	4,190	5,242	4,695	4,595	5,341	5,074	4,845	5,388	5,063	4,860	4,453

The Lafayette County seat, about 60 miles east of Kansas City, Lexington (named for its Kentucky sister) was settled in 1822 and incorporated in 1845. Early in the Civil War there was a major battle and the town didn't thrive until the railroads came. Its streetcar history is fragmentary and confusing. On April 20th, 1884 William Ewing, Alfred Leard and John C. Young Sr. got a franchise for a horse line, which opened in late 1884 or early 1885. SRJ's January 1886 directory lists a **Lexington Street Railroad Company** with two miles of 4' 1"-gauge track, eight mules and two cars. SRJ's 1890 directory lists a **Lexington and Kansas City Land and Investment Company** with 2.5 miles of 4' 4"-gauge track, two cars and eight horses (R. G. Estell President, W. Z. Hickman Vice-President). Poor's 1890 lists both companies, but only one in 1896, a 4' 4"-gauge line named **Lexington Street Railway** and owned by Smith T. Benedict. Poor's 1898 claims three miles of track and J. S. Borland as "Sole Owner."

Lexington's "Sesquicentennial Commemorative book, 1972" (p. 45) identifies neither company, disagrees with the trade directories, claims the franchise was dated April 2nd 1884 and that the line first ran from the *"Nickel Home (hotel), via Main, Franklin and South Streets to the old Missouri Pacific RR freight and passenger station."* It said the rails were second-hand from a defunct Lexington-Kansas City railroad and the route ran from *"Highland Avenue below the Elizabeth Aull Seminary on Third Street, to Main Street, east on Main to 13th, south to Franklin, east on Franklin to 20th, then to South and back east on South to the Old Fort, the eastern terminus, returning via South and Main Streets."* The line was unprofitable, NIMBYS moaned ceaselessly about street damage and the city, wanting evenly graded streets but not itself prepared to pay for them, ordered the line to cease because of the "tow path" in the road created by the mules hauling the cars. Closure was September 30th-October 1st, 1899. It was replaced by a "hack' line.

Interurban proposals

Kansas City and Lexington Electric Railway SRJ May 3rd 1902 (ad p. 77) says articles of association were filed April 17th. Capital would be $500,000. Incorporators included Walter B. Waddell of Lexington and. E. J. McGraw.

LOUISIANA

1880	**1890**	**1900**	**1910**	**1920**	**1930**	**1940**	**1950**	**1960**	**1970**	**1980**	**1990**	**2000**
4,325	5,090	5,131	4,454	4,060	3,549	4,669	4,389	4,286	4,533	4,261	5,571	3,863

In Pike County, about 90 miles up-river from St. Louis and 40 miles down-river from Hannibal, Louisiana was founded circaa 1820 and incorporated in 1848. This charming Victorian riverboat town never had street railways nor any proposals beyond **Louisiana Light Power and Traction Company** circa 1906 line to Bowling Green, about 12 miles west. Incorporated for $200,000, D. Turnbolt was President/General Manager, F. E. Murray of Louisiana, Secretary.

MACON

1880	**1890**	**1900**	**1910**	**1920**	**1930**	**1940**	**1950**	**1960**	**1970**	**1980**	**1990**	**2000**
3,046	3,371	4,068	3,584	3,549	3,851	4,206	4,152	4,507	5,301	5,680	5,571	5,538

The Macon County seat, about 65 miles west of Hannibal and 22 miles north of Moberly, Macon was only briefly the subject of interurban proposals. SRJ May 1893 (p. 334) noted locals talking of a steam dummy to link Macon, Bevier and Ardmore to the west of town. In 1906, SRJ March 31st (ad p. 40) noted an entirely different proposal, an interurban running south via College Mound to Huntsville, northeast of Moberly. A College Mound committee was appointed on March 21st to consult with Captain C. J. Dubois, who was also the chief engineer of a proposed "motor" line from Shelbina to La Belle. The Macon line was promoted to serve Darksville, College Mound and the mining town of Keota (long-gone from Missouri's map), ending at interchanges with the Wabash at Huntsville and the CBQ at Macon. (See Bevier, Huntsville and Shelbina)

MEXICO

1880	**1890**	**1900**	**1910**	**1920**	**1930**	**1940**	**1950**	**1960**	**1970**	**1980**	**1990**	**2000**
3,835	4,789	5,099	5,939	6,013	8,290	9,053	11,623	12,889	11,807	12,276	11,290	11,320

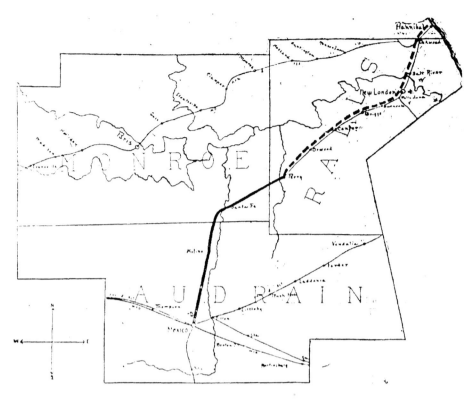

Map of proposed line to Perry and possible extension to Hannibal. (Audrain Historical Society)

Mexico Street RR ticket circa 1889.

The Audrain County seat, Mexico is 110 miles northwest of St. Louis. It was established in the 1830s during agitation over the Mexican war but was put on the map with the arrival of the Northern Missouri Railroad in 1858. In late 1889, an animal streetcar began running from town via Clark Avenue and the military academy to the Fairgrounds. Its badly-laid track caused derailments, riders refused to repeat the experience and it closed within a year. No trade directories list it and nothing more is known, except that in February 1910 William M. Garland, one of its promoters, was charged with grand larceny in Seattle in connection with a stock brokerage business he then ran.

By 1907 several interurban proposals had been floated including one from S. L. Robison of Belleville IL who talked of a Mexico-Perry line (25 miles), interchanging with the Wabash and Chicago and Alton railroads. (SRJ March 30th, 1907 ad p. 25). The **Mexico Perry and Santa Fe Traction Company** incorporated in April 1907, was grading within a year. A Perry-Hannibal extension would come later. Mexico would have a town system plus a line south to Fulton and Columbia. Capital was $850,000 but only $60,000 was subscribed and by May 1908 grading ceased.

After an October 1908 reorganization, Robison became secretary and Judge Mathias Crum President. Judge W. W. Botts, later an Audrain county state representative, was also involved. Their thoughts turned to Columbia and Jefferson City. A rival **North Missouri Central Railway** presentation to the Columbia Commercial Club on October 10th left the

members believing its bond issue was water and its earning potential dubious. The same people took a later MSF&PTC presentation at face value, several subscribing for $10,000 of stock. Why the Mexico line was taken on board so unquestioningly by the Columbia people, is odd. With 20/20 hindsight, its claims seem naive given the 1907 slump, that existing interurbans were mostly unprofitable and that Columbia was red hot for highways. Yet Crum predicted every share sold would yield at least 12% annually. *"We have…procured a good portion of the right of way south of Mexico and have also interested persons along that route in a financial way. We have assurances of franchises for Columbia, Boone and Callaway Counties…"* (UM October 12th, 1908 p. 1, 4).

Botts added they'd build the Mexico-Molino-Perry section first, having already spent $40,000 to grade a third of it. Mexico-Molino was slated to open late in 1909 with five gas-electric cars. It didn't and work ceased until March 1st, 1910, which for some reason rated a golden spike ceremony held at approximately the site of Mexico's present West Shopping Plaza. A new $1½ million deed with Fidelity Trust of Kansas City financed further building north and south from Mexico. Once another mile of the north line was done, the first mile of the south line would begin. It was noted (probably incorrectly) that the money was also earmarked for building 100 track miles (Mexico-Hannibal, Mexico-Columbia, plus a Fulton branch). The Mexico Evening Ledger (March 12th, 1910 p. 1.) said 37 miles was financed from Hereford via Mexico to Santa Fe and that Hereford-Fulton and Hereford-Columbia branches were planned.

On April 26th 1910, work began on the south line, from *"Liberty Street to the Alton branch line, crossing it near the stock pen…follow(ing)*

The only known (and very poor) photo of 1889 Mexico horse car 7, believed to be the line's only car.

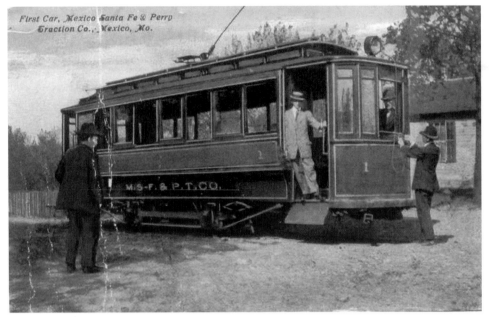

First Car, Mexico Santa Fe & Perry Traction Co., Mexico, Mo.

Postcard of Car 1, circa 1911.

the branch railroad south to the southwest corner of Charles Dean's farm and then southwest ...About 50 men will be kept at work until the road is completed 17 miles south. It is the intention...to construct about four miles of road a month" (Mexico Evening Ledger April 27th, 1910 p.2). Originally, the south line was to leave Mexico via Liberty Street to the cemetery before reaching its own right-of-way. Two days later the paper reported completion of the south lines's second mile, noting a car was operating on the first mile, with another on order.

The two lines remained disconnected. The railroad tracks were the obstacle and a grade crossing was out of the question. A subway (underpass) was needed, and it was not yet built. Judge Botts explained:

"We have not commenced on the subway for several reasons. One is that we have not yet arrived at terms with but one of the (rail) roads. Another is that we need miles of road in the country even worse than we need the subway. The subway and paving will cost us from $10,000 to $15,000. The only way we can get money for this is by selling bonds. We can't sell bonds except as the road is completed, a mile at a time. We have issued $60,000 in bonds...That is all we can issue until at least five miles of road is constructed. So at present we have available only $60,000 in

bonds.$13,000 of these are deposited in the banks for the subscribers. That left us only $30,000... The first mile and power plant cost more than that. The subscribers have only paid in...$7,000 and hold $30,000 of our bonds. The other fellows have paid in...more than $30,000 and have $30,000 in bonds.This makes it clear we must build in the country in order to get a surplus of bonds...(and) our subscribers should pay up promptly." (Mexico Evening Ledger, May 20th, 1910, p. 2.)

In 1910, the board pondered the merits of the Edison-Beach battery car. Edison "nickel" batteries were lighter, stronger and more powerful than their wet-cell ancestors of the late 1880s and such cars were a modest success on rural lines, in small Florida towns and on Manhattan's quiet cross-town lines, previously animal operated, which the Third Avenue Railway was not prepared to electrify. But there was little cost advantage and Mexico stayed with overhead wire.

By now, four miles of the south line had been built and about to be used to run passengers and schoolkids to and from Mexico. A daily workmans' car had run for some time (UM November 6th, 1910 p. 1.). Another mile south to Champ was graded by December, but Boone County and Columbia remained out of reach.Money was the problem.Subscribers were slow to pay or wouldn't pay. In November 1910 the North Missouri Central (with money problems also) sounded out the MP&SFTC about a merger. That went nowhere. So did a suggestion the Chicago and Alton take over the south line and build on to Columbia. But pile driving on the Molino line was doing fine and track would soon go down. It was built close to the present Missouri 15 and Sunrise Road, entered Molino from the west, and opened April 7th, 1911. At the February 5th, 1912 board meeting Botts seemed pleased with the Molino line's performance. Passengers and mail were carried, plus agricultural freight and package express. All were confident the line could make it on its own, for at this meeting negotiations were broken off with C. Porter Johnson for sale of the south line to the Columbia-Northern. But the Molino line, though busy, did not generate

Car 1 outside the power house circa 1911. This facility was on present highway 15 (east side) on the north side of Davis Fork, north of Mexico.

Schedule circa 1912.

Poor photo of car 2 said to be at Santa Fe circa 1916.

Car 1 at unknown terminal. This may have been a staged first-car run. Note the primitive platform.

much profit and soon defaulted on the $55,000 owed Fruin-Bambrick for construction. The directors had over $53,000 of their money invested and other stockholders an equivalent sum, lost in the May 1913 foreclosure to pay the Fruin-Bambrick bill. Service ceased for about a year.

Botts and others paid all debts personally and the corporate shell became theirs. Renamed **Mexico Investment and Construction Company** it still planned to extend north from Molino to Santa Fe. Plans to link the north line with the C&A on temporary track via Olive and Promenade were not acted on, but in 1914 a spur was built east on Jackson from the C&A to the north line's railhead, to aid material delivery (Mexico Evening Ledger June 9th, 1914 p. 1.)

In early 1914, Robison induced Chicago's F. Mordaunt and a colleague to look at the south line, already graded to Champ. Four miles was running for workmens' transport. The company took some heat for refusing an offer of $10,000 for the south line, especially from

Club used it to make several "booster" trips.

"Mexico produce men should get in communication with the people of Santa Fe and compete with Perry," said Judge Botts… *"Perry merchants are sending wagons down to Santa Fe and buying all the poultry, butter, eggs and other produce in the vicinity. I would like to see produce brought to Mexico over our line."* (MWI November 16, 1915 p.3.)

The extension was a popular Sunday excursion, but facilities were crude. Typical stops included a pine tree on the east side of today's Missouri route ZZ a mile southwest of Santa Fe, and stock pens in a corner of a farm outside Molino. But despite derailments, bad weather, cows on the tracks, problems in loading grain and hogs into the sole freight car, erratic power and army worms eating the wooden ties, the line was warmly received. Shopping, visits and business trips became possible, as did picnics, out-

M.S.F.&P. Traction Company

PASS

GOOD FOR ONE PASSAGE ON ANY MEXICO, SANTA FE & PERRY TRACTION COMPANY RUN.

the bonus subscribers who felt the Molino line hadn't performed. Botts however, claimed the materials alone were worth more than the offer. This was no fire-sale, he knew nothing of Mordaunt and saw no reason this stranger shouldn't pay more than they could get by selling the south line for scrap. *"We have offered it to them for…$12,500 cash. If they won't give that for it, then in our opinion they don't intend to try and build a railroad. We think it is their time now either to put up or shut up."* (MDI June 4th, 1914 p. 1.)

Nothing daunted, Mordaunt moved on to Columbia where he hoped to interest them in city trolleys and an interuban to Jefferson City, Fulton and Montgomery City. Columbia was more interested in the Mexico company than in Mordaunt, but would not put money into the south line until it got closer. It never did, though Mexico-Molino resumed in 1914 and the Santa Fe extension opened in August 1915, tracking through Santa Fe on the north side of the schoolhouse to a depot behind the "Christian Church." Despite a population of just 135 and a fare to Mexico of 45 cents for the 16 miles, initial ridership was promising. The Mexico Commercial

ings, ice-cream socials and chautauquas. It was even used for daily travel by students at Mexico's McMillan High, Western Avenue station being closest to the school.

In 1916 there was talk of a 10-mile Santa Fe-Perry branch (ERJ January 8th, 1916 p. 108) and lines to Calloway and Monroe counties (ERJ February 5th, 1916 p. 294). So divorced from reality were things now that Mexico's Commercial Club, a bunch who surely should have been more on the ball, resolved to offer $7,500 to reopen the south line and extend 12 miles to Poram's Corner, within reasonable distance of Fulton (ERJ April 29th, 1916, p. 843). The board, however, knew better. Seeking to cut costs, they solicited Illinois Traction to help them get cheaper power or even take over the line. Cars were still running in late 1917 in the hope such a deal would be made. It wasn't. Then the Missouri Highway Commission gave Audrain county a 50/50 grant to hard-surface existing roads. That was the final blow.

MWI October 25th, 1917 (p. 1) reported without comment that the stockholders *"voted at an October 22nd, 1917 meeting to dissolve the corpo-*

ration. In the meantime, until court permission is given, they will experiment by increasing fares three cents per mile as a possible remedy for (its) financial status." Columbia's Evening Missourian (January 2nd, 1918 p. 4.) noted that even with increased fares, the line still lost money and December receipts did not pay fuel bills. Yet it had been *"an excellent trade feeder for Mexico and its discontinuance will work a hardship on many."* The last car ran on January 3rd, 1918.

A proposal that new interests take company stock, hold over 3 former directors, elect new officers and run the line, was rejected later in January as it took care only of one-third of outstanding debts and ignored the $30,000 advanced by stockholders to build Molino-Santa Fe. It was felt to be wrong that owners of an $80,000 investment should surrender control to unnamed parties who would contribute just $5,000 of capital. So, after foreclosure on May 18th, the tracks came up, the wires came down (with the help of a steam locomotive) and the recovered metals were sold for $37,000 to Uncle Sam for the war effort. After all this, ERJ May 31st 1919 (p. 1077) briefly noted an I. S. Fisher of Moscow Mills MO was proposing construction of an electric line from Mexico to Perry!

Incomplete Roster Notes

Poor's wrongly reported five gas-electric cars in 1908 and 1909. A 1910 tinted postcard shows electric car 1 in green on a Brill 21-E truck, but contemporary reports say the line's two cars were yellow and gray. Car 2

was a used St. Louis vehicle on St. Louis #13 double-trucks.

Mexico Interurban Proposals

SRJ June 7th, 1902 (ad p. 92) in reporting that *"the electric railway to Paris MO was now almost a certainty"* claimed that once built, trains would leave Paris early in the morning *"to stop at each farm and gather all milk, vegetables, fruit etc."* then take them to connect with the Wabash and Chicago and Alton railroads in Mexico MO. and elsewhere and have the produce reach morning markets in St. Louis. This line was not built and its official name is not known.

Iowa-Missouri Power and Traction Company SRJ November 17th, 1906 (p. 32) says this company was financed and ready to build a 52-mile interurban from Fairfield IA to Memphis MO in Scotland County via Keosauqua and Milton IA, with a southern extension from Memphis to Mexico and a northern extension from Fairfield to Cedar Rapids IA. SRJ April 27th, 1907 (p. 30) reported a mortgage to secure an issue of $1 million 5% gold bonds had been made to the Knickerbocker Trust Company of New York. The first 52 miles was not ready for construction.

St. Louis, St. Charles and Northern Traction Company (See St. Charles).

MOBERLY

1880	1890	1900	1910	1920	1930	1940	1950	1960	1970	1980	1990	2000
6,070	8,215	8,012	10,923	12,808	13,115	12,920	13,115	13,170	12,988	13,418	12,839	11,945

Moberly is in Randolph County, about 155 miles northwest of St. Louis. Huntsville is the Randolph County seat, about 8 miles west of Moberly. Neither had street railways or interurbans. SRJ November 9th, 1907 (ad p. 20) noted right-of-way on the Moberly-Hunstsville road awarded for an electric line. ERJ (April 10th, 1909 p.709) said *"Moberly and Huntsville have accepted a proposition made by Manning and Wellman of Ottumwa IA to build a street railway in Moberly and an interurban between Moberly and Huntsville."* If this was a revival of the 1907 proposal or a new idea isn't known, but it would run close to the Wabash Railroad. ERJ April 24th, 1909 (p. 802) said Charles A. Wellman, the promoter, already had $40,000 and needed another $40,000 to complete it.

By early June 1909, the 71/2 mile **Moberly, Huntsville and Randolph Springs Railway** had been franchised. ERJ November 27th, 1909 (p. 1121) reported the **Moberly and Huntsville Electric Railway** with five cars, $100,000 capital and a line to Radium Springs and Randolph Springs. ERJ (January 18th, 1913 p. 135) reported incorporation (capital

$500,000), with W.T. and C. H. Dawson plus W. M. Evans of Huntsville in charge. Three steel bridges were needed. In April the A. J. Jennings Construction Company of Joplin began work, pausing late in early 1914, after a fire destroyed the springs hotel. Soon after, one of the promoters took off for foreign parts with what was left of the money.

After reorganization, (probably under the name **Moberly, Huntsville and Randolph Springs Railroad Company**), ERJ March 27th, 1915 (p. 654) noted Charles H. Dameron as president and that grading would resume when the weather allowed. The only grading left to do was completion of work within Huntsville city limits, the rest having been finished and concrete abutments installed in summer 1913. Nothing happened. Much of the work survives to this day.

North Missouri Central Railway See Mexico MO. A branch was to run from Columbia north to Moberly-why isn't known as it would have been cheaper to run direct from Mexico via Centralia.

NEVADA

Line 1. Nevada. Line 2 Jerico Springs.

	1880	1890	1900	1910	1920	1930	1940	1950	1960	1970	1980	1990	2000
1.	1,913	7,262	7,461	7,176	7,139	7,448	8,181	8,009	8,416	9,736	9,044	8,597	8,607
2.	–	486	443	395	262	247	254	235	179	188	208	247	259

Nevada, the Vernon County seat, is 95 miles south of Kansas City, 64 miles north of Joplin and 20 miles east of Fort Scott KS. It was destroyed by Union troops in 1863. Coal and zinc were found and mined in the 1880s. The MoPac and MKT railroads each had division headquarters in Nevada and a joint Union Station. Little is known of the street railways, but a mule line ran from about 1887 until the 1890s, serving Lake Park Springs. Poor's 1896 reported a **Nevada City Street Railroad** with 4.5 miles of track and eight horse cars.

Colonel Harry C. Moore incorporated the **Nevada Electric Railway, Light and Park Company** on September 16th, 1895 as Manager and Treasurer. Arthur S. Partridge (a nationally-known street railway equipment broker of St. Louis) was President. The NERL&PC owned Lake Park Springs (later renamed Radio Springs Park), a 130 acre property with medicinal springs, an electric light plant franchise and a ten-year contract with Nevada for 50 arc lamps at $90 per year. They would electrify the line to the park and build a two-mile northern line from Plaza Square on North Washington past the County Fair Grounds, then west to

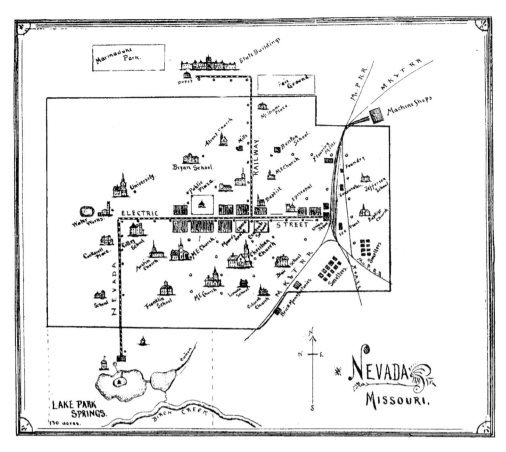

Map 1895.

ital funds to get it built. Nothing happened.

The 3-mile standard-gauge main line and the new northern branch cost $325,000 to build, had four motor and four trailers and was in trouble from the start. It spent years trying to sell $100,000 of 6% 5 to 20 year bonds and a further $125,000 in 5% 5 to 20 year bonds. A February 1907 receivership saw $100,000 of stock still outstanding. Sam A. Mitchell of St. Louis, one of the trustees in bankruptcy, bought the company on May 15th, 1909, brokering a deal to set up a new **Nevada Water, Light and Traction Company.** This new entity began on June 15th 1910, with $350,000 capital. It did even more badly and ERJ March 16th, 1912 (p. 440) reported appointment of a temporary receiver when the company defaulted on $140,000 of its bonds. It was bought by (and renamed) the **Fort Scott and Nevada Water, Light and Traction Company**, controlled by the Ohio and Western Utilities Company and run by National Utilities Company of New York. In 1915 tracks were extended several blocks along South College (ERJ April 15th, 1915 p. 696), but the cars still did poorly and in 1923 it was decided to replace them with two Dodge 20-seat buses.

An October 16th Council meeting ended with a unanimous vote that this be done within 30 days and that the streets be paved. In an October 30th special session, Colonel Moore argued the cars should be kept but could not counter the reality asserted by the company's president who said that since 1918 dividends were 1% and sometimes º%, despite heavy spending on gas and electric equipment. Formerly they'd charged higher water, gas and electric rates to balance streetcar losses, but MOPSC had outlawed this practice and they were now accounted for separately. The session adjourned with no action taken, but clearly it was a done deal. Colonel Moore was furious.

the State Institutions and Marmaduke Park. At the same time, Moore was heavily involved as stockholder and promoter of the **Nevada and Eldorado Springs Railroad Company**, a proposed 20-mile steam branch line that was never built.

In March 1899 the **Missouri Water, Traction and Light Company** was chartered with $100,000 capital. Moore left and J. B. Quigley of Sedalia became President, though Partridge remained for a time. Nevada Daily Mail June 4th, 1900 (p. 1.) reported delivery of two 75-passenger summer cars on Saturday evening June 2nd. They were tested on Cherry Street next day at about 2:00 a.m, the first electric runs. Later, they ran over the lake line as far as the park gates. At day's end, a phone wire fell across the overhead, the telephone switchboard caught fire and equipment in the power house was damaged. Testing was suspended until repairs were made.

The line as built went west on Cherry from the railroad depots, through the square, south on Austin and then west to Cotty College, ending at the park gates, for Quigley was unable to get a right-of-way within. But he assured the public the northern branch would be built. *"Just as soon as the city pays me for the lights, I will…build the line to the Asylum. As you see, I have the ties on the street and everything else ready to put the line in. I have charged the city $175 per month for 30 lights while formerly they paid $210 a month for 21 lights."*

There was talk of a 13-mile interurban southeast to Montevallo and on to Jerico Springs in Cedar County. A group from Nevada and the two towns lobbied for it, unsuccessfully riding the wave of optimism following the Nevada opening. The line had the potential to open up the region and Quigley was interested but was frank about the fact he couldn't afford it to do it himself. However, he did know how to access cap-

Car "Nevada" date 'and location unknown. This car looks to be one of the St. Louis United Railways 743-799, 900-907 series (St. Louis Car 1895 for Union Depot RR), all of which were out of St. Louis service by 1910.

Open cars "Rockwood" and Stratton" at the car barns, date unknown.

"The people have been paying increased utility rates 37 years for the streetcars. If they voted the contract in...they should have the opportunity to vote it out...I had breakfast at the Mitchell Hotel the other morning and sat beside the president of this utility company...When I tried to engage him in conversation about streetcars he was as cold on the subject as a frog on ice." (quoted in "An era that vanished," by Betty Sterett,

Vernon County Historical Society/ Bushwhacker Museum, Nevada MO pp-126-130 circa 1973.)

His fury changed nothing and there was no further point in opposing the closure. The new buses arrived November 14th, 1923, MOPSC approved cessation on November 17th and the line faded out in the next few days, unnoticed. What did attract attention was track-lifting on College and repaving of the pot-holed road to Radio Springs. One could now drive an auto there unhindered marveled a reporter. (Southwest Mail and Daily Post December 14th, 1923 p. 3). Buses ran to the park, station and State Hospital until franchise expiry at the end of 1927.

Incomplete Roster Notes.

Nevada began in June 1900 with two 75-seat open cars. The Nevada Daily Mail (June 5th, 1900 p. 1.) said that *"next week, 3 more cars will come from Brooklyn and 2 more will follow them, making 7 cars to be used here."* By 1903 there were six cars. Two open cars came circa 1904 from St. Louis, either from the Intra-mural Railroad or UR. Another car came in 1908, possibly from St. Louis United Railways 900-907 series. Former Philadelphia People's Traction Company cars 247 and 343 (St. Louis, 1894) on Peckham 6E single trucks were bought in September 1913. Nevada car numbers are unknown and surviving photos suggest all the cars had names. A Nevada car survived as a shed at a private house until the late 1960s, but its survival (or location) since then are unknown. For years there were nine vehicles but by 1918 there were five passenger cars and two others.

OREGON

1880	**1890**	**1900**	**1910**	**1920**	**1930**	**1940**	**1950**	**1960**	**1970**	**1980**	**1990**	**2000**
862	948	1,032	1,002	904	922	978	870	887	789	901	935	935

Oregon is the Holt County seat, northwest of St. Joseph and began in 1841. SRJ May 1890 (p. 246) reported plans for an Oregon-Forest City electric line, backed by Judge George Anderson and Lewis L. Moore. SRJ April 1896 (ad p. 69) noted the **Oregon and Forest City Electric Railway Company** incorporation by J. E. Cummins and R. C. Benton of Oregon and F. C. Oakley of Wyandotte KS, capitalized at $60,000. This was

a non-starter. But the **Oregon Interurban Railway Company** (SRJ November 23rd 1907 ad p. 20) did get built—as a 4¹/₂-mile long rural branch railroad. It was never electrified. Freight was interchanged at Forest City (CBQ) from February 1909. A gas-electric passenger car made six daily runs from April 1909.The line survived to the early 1920s.

ROLLA

1880	**1890**	**1900**	**1910**	**1920**	**1930**	**1940**	**1950**	**1960**	**1970**	**1980**	**1990**	**2000**
1,582	1,592	1,600	2,261	2,077	3,670	5,141	9,354	11,132	13,571	13,303	14,090	16,367

The Phelps county seat and home to the University of Missouri's mines and engineering schools, Rolla was established in 1861. The only credible trolley proposal was the **Missouri Inland and Southern Railway Company**. ERJ April 10th, 1909 (p. 709) said E. E. Young and associates would build a 75-mile standard-gauge line from Cabool in Texas County northwest to Rolla. ERJ May 15th, 1909 (p. 931) said the line (via Houston, Raymondville and Licking to Rolla) had raised $100,000 in subscriptions under the MI&SRC name. Promoters were from Licking including E. E. Young and A. H. Bradford, though Albert Campbell and C. H. Evers were from Spokane WA. Young, now General Manager and President, in a letter to ERJ (June 19th, 1909 p. 1146) said they would use gas-electric

cars on a 40-mile Licking-Rolla route via Lenox, Anutt and Lecoma (essentially today's Missouri Highways C and O in Texas, Dent and Phelps counties) rather than the more direct route that became U. S. 63. Capital was $400,000; $40,000 had been issued. It would serve 200,000 acres of farmland and 100,000 acres of pine timber, all 25 miles from a railroad. It didn't.

Rolla, Ozark and Southern Railway Company ERJ (May 9th 1914 p.1063) noted this proposal to build a steam or electric line 18 miles from Rolla to Anutt.

ST. CHARLES

1880	**1890**	**1900**	**1910**	**1920**	**1930**	**1940**	**1950**	**1960**	**1970**	**1980**	**1990**	**2000**
5,014	6,161	7,982	9,437	8,503	10,491	10,803	14,314	21,189	31,834	43,551	50,634	60,321

In 1767, the Spanish built a fort at "Les petits cotes" (Little Hills). Abandoned after a year, French settlers set up a small town nearby, calling it San Carlos after the Spanish king's patron saint. The name was gradually elided to St. Charles. It incorporated in 1809, became the St. Charles County seat and, for a few years, Missouri's first capital. In 1900, **St. Louis, St. Charles and Western** interurbans from Wellston (St. Louis),

The German Protestant Orphans' Home Station was an elaborate affair, in keeping with the nature of the home and the station's public relations function; putting on its best face for visitors. St. Louis, St. Charles & Western car 15 heads west from the station circa 1902. STLMOT

Eastbound car 4 at Busch's Beer Garden (right), St. Charles Rock Road circa 1903.

Another view of Home Station, with a car awaiting departure circa 1902. STLMOT

Missouri River Bridge looking east from St. Charles, shortly before completion in 1904. STLMOT

terminated on the St. Louis County shore, the final leg of the trip to St. Charles being by company-owned steamboat. A bridge opened in 1904 and the line was extended to St. Charles (Second Street). UR took over from 1905, creating a new **Missouri Electric Railway** subsidiary to run the line. It closed January 17th, 1932, but the terminal building, complete with tracks, stands to this day. A rump of the line continued from Wellston Loop to Woodson (Edmonson) Road until December 1948.

St. Louis, St. Charles and Northern Traction Company On April 28th, 1910 a company was set up "*of sufficient size and capital to promote a line of electric railway from St. Charles... northwest... through Troy, Olney, Marling, Middletown, Mt. Carmel, Laddonia, Mexico, Paris and points west...a modern high-speed road with first-class equipment... (which) will open up the vast prairies east of Mexico with the St. Louis market. Handsomely equipped offices have been opened at Middletown.*" (Mexico Evening Ledger April 29th, 1910, p. 2)

On May 23rd 1910, the Troy Free Press noted field manager R. E. Race visiting Troy, saying the seventy-seven mile line would enter from the northwest, serve the business area (route unspecified), go east near the fairgrounds and head to St. Charles, probably via old Monroe. Engineers were at work in two places and expected to get the Mexico division done in a few weeks. The St. Louis Republic (June 3rd, 1910) reported engineering at St. Charles, Laddonia (Audrain county) to follow during June. On November 7th 1910 the P-D reported incorporation for $900,000.

St. Charles station building circa 1912, with an express car at the loading platform, a passenger car peering out under the tower and the Missouri River bridge into St. Louis County in the background. STLMOT

No more was heard.

SRJ (August 6th, 1910 p. 244) noted an O. J. Martin asking for a franchise to build 5 miles on St. Charles streets, either in connection with the **St. Louis, St. Charles and Northern** proposals or the **Kansas City-St. Louis Electric Railway**'s attempts to get into St. Charles and over the Missouri into St. Louis County. This too was a non-starter.

ST. JOSEPH

Line 1. St. Joseph. Line 2. Savannah.

1880	**1890**	**1900**	**1910**	**1920**	**1930**	**1940**	**1950**	**1960**	**1970**	**1980**	**1990**	**2000**
1.32,431	52,324	102,979	77,403	77,939	80,935	75,711	78,588	79,673	78,230	76,691	71,852	73,990
2. 1,206	1,288	1,886	1,583	1,831	1,888	2,108	2,332	2,455	3,324	4,184	4,352	4,762

A Lewis and Clark camp in 1804, St. Joseph (the Buchanan county seat) was founded in 1826 on the banks of the Missouri as an Indian trading post by Joseph Robidoux and named for his patron saint. The site was Indian Territory until transferred to Missouri by the 1836 "Platte Purchase" in return for cash plus land in Kansas territory for displaced tribes. Also known as Blacksnake Hills, St. Joseph incorporated as a city in 1843. Growth was fueled by the Gold Rush and thousands of '49ers took the overland trail west to California. But many stayed and when the Hannibal and St. Joseph Railroad opened in February 1859, fifteen months before the Central Overland California and Pike's Peak Express ("Pony Express,") began, the place was sizeable. By the 1870s, it was second only to Kansas City in meat packing and the stockyards survived until the 1960s. Grain processing was a staple and Quaker Oats a major employer.

A Major Holman and a Samuel Jerome gave the city its first regular transit in the early 1860s. The **St. Joseph Omnibus Line** linked the station and the city. It had decades of ups and downs, but horse buses ran throughout. For example, in 1867 it was owned by Thomas Christopher, who ran five buses, one carriage, four buggies and 36 horses. Joseph A. Piner bought the line in 1871 and ran buses until 1894 when it was bought by Brown Transfer Company.

1. ST. JOSEPH STREETCARS

Citizens' Railway Company On December 21st 1866 the CRC tested cars on a line from Market Square (Pacific Hotel) to the Hannibal and St. Joseph Railroad depot at Mitchell and 11th Street and south to the city limits. Barns were at Eighth and Senaca. It opened on December 25th and was backed by two city grocers; Richard E. Turner (president) and Thomas J. Chew, who extended it in 1881 via 11th Street to the Exhibition Grounds at Atchison Street, making it 1.1 miles long. SRJ's 1886 directory says that Citizens had three miles of standard-gauge track, 14 cars and 52 mules.

Union Railway Company was chartered in June 1876, and from July its cars ran 21/2 miles from Market Square to New Ulm Brewery and park via St. Joseph Avenue, extended to Sixth Street and south on sixth to Atchison in 1880. Backed by the Krugs and Adolph Steinacker, it was better equipped than the Citizens and its cars were "heated" in winter. In April 1881 it was extended south from Market Square to the Kansas City, St. Joseph and Council Bluffs Railroad shops. SRJ's 1886 directory entry lists 27 cars, 110 horses and five miles of track (Seymour Jenkins President, H. Lewis Superintendent, Adolph Steinacker Secretary and Treasurer).

SRJ April 1887 (p.84.) reported Adolph and Theodore Steinacker visiting New York to buy electric motors. *"After inspecting the various systems...they contracted with the Sprague Electric Railway and Motor Company ... (They) expect to surpass results reached by any of the electric roads so far built, including the lighting of cars by electricity and...run (at)...10-12mph."* The first Sprague-motored car was tested on September 6th, 1887 to great acclaim. *"The motor worked to a charm and is one of the greatest inventions of the age,"* marveled the St. Joseph Daily Gazette (September 7th, 1887 (p. 4.). Initially the wires went a mile from Highland and St. Joseph Avenue to New Ulm Park.

Incremental revisions were made and the wires were extended to Market Square on July 5th, 1888. This split the Union system, which was animal-powered south of Market Square (where passengers changed from the electrics), running on Second Street to Charles, then east to 5th Street. By the end of 1888, eight electrics served the northern section, each with two 71/2 HP Sprague motors. They made 10 mph in the city and 15 mph in the

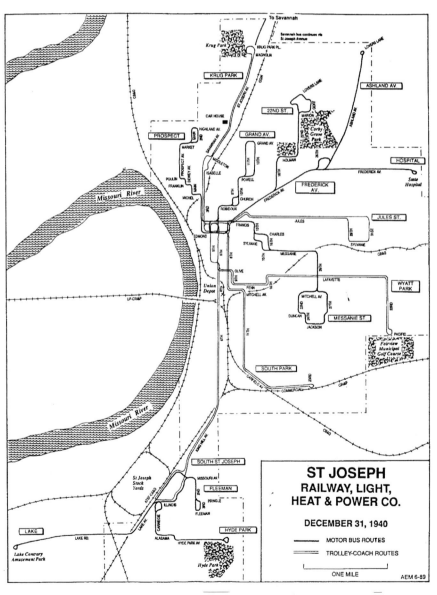

ST JOSEPH RAILWAY, LIGHT, HEAT & POWER CO.

DECEMBER 31, 1940

MOTOR BUS ROUTES
TROLLEY-COACH ROUTES

ONE MILE

AEM 6-89

No street railway map of St. Joseph has emerged so far; this is the position in 1940 when replacement bus and trolley bus lines still closely resembled the trolleys they replaced between 1929 and 1938. Mac Sebree/Motor Coach Age.

E.H.HARRIMAN, PREST.   CHAS.C,TEGETHOFF, SECY.& TREAS.   W.T.VAN BRUNT, VICE PRES.& GEN'L MANAGER.

St. Joseph Railway, Light, Heat & Power Co.

St. Joseph, Mo. July 8 1900

suburbs and averaged 110 miles daily on a line that included two lengthy 5% grades. By 1891 SRJ's directory listed the Union with eight miles of electric line, 45 horses, 36 cars and four other vehicles. Horse cars were towed by the electrics as trailers.

St. Joseph and Lake Narrow Gauge Street Railway.Using materials from an unsuccessful Penitentiary line in Leavenworth KS, Augustus Kuhn and Charles A. Perry laid 3'-gauge tracks from Eighth and Edmond and up Frederick Avenue to their carbarn. Bankrupt soon after its 1878 opening, it was bought by Thomas E. Tuttle and others who extended it to Market Square. In 1881 its six cars ran from Market Square to Twentieth (about 11/2 miles). In 1885 it was the **Frederick Avenue Railroad**, running to 25th Street. It was bought by and merged with the Citizens in 1887.

St. Joseph had no cable lines. The **St. Joseph Circle Railway** and the **Wyatt Park Railway** planned them but while various components were delivered, neither line was built. St. Joseph Circle's two routes were to leave Union Station via Fourth and Sixth Streets (one way in each direction) to Francis and Jules and out to 22nd Street. The Wyatt Park was to run from Edmond and Seventh, east on Edmond, south on Nionth and east on Lafayette to 28th, returning to Seventh Street westbound on Olive (St. Joseph Daily Gazette, September 6th, 1887 p. 4).

10-bench open car 112 circa 1912 at unknown location.

A bad winter, a difficult 5-mile route, a 200-yard 71/2% grade and the impressive performance of the Union's Sprague motors prompted the Wyatt Park to junk its cable project in July 1888 and electrify. Six cars ran east on Lafayette to the city limits near 33rd from January 3rd, 1889. Each had two 71/2 HP Sprague motors and ran 115 miles daily. Later, the Wyatt Park built a line on Jules Street.

But now things get confused. A new **People's Street Railway Electric Light and Power Company** popped up in 1889, and without a franchise or an inch of track began making takeover noises. New York venture capital was behind it, represented by R. B. Newcombe and Company. Joseph Van Brunt and his brother W. T. came to St. Joseph with the new company, a merger of the enlarged Citizens Traction and St. Joseph Electric Light and Power Company. W. T. became general manager and electrified the Citizens and Frederick lines by September 1889. ERJ, June 29th, 1918 (p. 1125) claimed J. H. Van Brunt began his career with Newcombe in 1885 in New York City. *"When…(it) in 1889 took over various St. Joseph companies, Van Brunt was sent to St. Joseph to take charge of the receipts."*

SRJ May 1890 (p. 250) reported People's wanting access to Union Depot on South Sixth Street. It was blocked by the Union's tracks, that company claiming sole rights by priority of occupation. People's claimed a franchise allowed them trackage rights over the Union down 6th Street. The Union counter-claimed that such a franchise would destroy their business. By May 1890, there was a standoff. Meantime, People's ran cars south on Eighth Street to a terminal two blocks east of the train station, at the same time stringing wires over 22nd Street. Their first cars ran on May 17th.

SRJ May 1890 (p. 250) noted *"Samuel Allerton and E. H. Fudge of Chicago, representing a syndicate, are negotiating for the purchase of the Wyatt Park and Union electric railways. $800,000 is demanded for the 2 roads."* SRJ July 1890 (p. 360) incorrectly reported People's buying a controlling interest in the Wyatt Park. This in fact was a 49-year lease and it was the Union (with the Wyatt Park line) which in fact was taken over. SRJ August 1890 (p. 397), noting that People's already owned Citizens and Frederick Avenue said the Union had been added on July 2nd for $400,000.

The united company's first action was to close the gap on Seventh Street between the Wyatt Park and Jules Street lines to make a city belt.The People's got a franchise extension and six months to build from Lake Boulevard to the stock- yards. Messanie was relaid in 1892, and a new car house replaced the old Union barn at St. Joseph and Fillmore. A new line ran east on Mitchell Avenue to Vineyard Heights soon after, but this and the belt line ceased in the early 1890s for lack of revenue as did a former Citizen's extension of 1890 to South Park and Gladstone Heights, cut back to South Park by 1896. A new line from Frederick Avenue north on 22nd Street to Highland lasted longer.

In the summer of 1892, People's defaulted on bond interest, with foreclosure in 1893. A new **St. Joseph Traction and Lighting Company** made the most attractive bid. Essentially it was a reorganized People's as almost all its directors were on the new board. Not a good move; it was in receivership by 1895. The **St. Joseph Railway Light, Heat and Power Company** was set up on November 17th, 1895 to take over all car lines plus city light and heat. Capitalized at $3.5 million, Edward H. Harriman was president. He talked of a new line to Lake Contrary where a park and race track were planned, an extension from Sixth Street to the stockyards and electric heaters on all cars. The best paying of all its utilities, however, were the new downtown steam heat circuits.

12-bench open car 169 seen at American Car in 1907 awaiting delivery.

Harriman resigned in 1901, selling the company in 1902 to E. W. Clark and his Philadelphia syndicate, owners of the East St. Louis and Suburban. Both Van Brunts stayed, W.T. becoming president, J.H. General Manager, but in 1903 W. T. moved back to New York. Poor's 1905 lists 40 track miles and 132 cars. Talk of an extension from Lake Contrary to Atchison KS as a 17-mile interurban (SRJ June 8th, 1907 p. 30) went nowhere. A 11/2-mile extension opened in October 1908 from Krug Park to the Industrial Development Company. By then, there were 178 cars and 44 miles of track. Only 50 were needed for daily use yet by 1910 there were 196 cars, of which 137 were motored and 59 were trailers.

ETW September 9th 1911 (p. 1049) talked of a union open shop in St. Joseph while on February 3rd, 1912 (pp. 115-121) it ran an article, perhaps a reworked company PR piece, describing "welfare work" at St. Joseph similar to St. Louis and Kansas City. It glowingly describing facilities including a barber's shop, restaurant, club-rooms and an in-house newspaper, but buried in the article was an admission that relations hadn't always been good. Clearly the "welfare" policy was a ploy to buy off the men and avoid unionization, a recipe for future instability.

While the Clarkes continued ownership and development of the East St. Louis and Suburban, they were more than willing to accept an offer for St. Joseph. In spring 1913, Henry L. Doherty's Cities Service Company took over. Doherty had a large portfolio of street railway properties in small towns (St. Joseph was one of the largest), but already made more money in gas and electric utilities. Ultimately oil and gasoline dwarfed his other ventures. Under Doherty, trolleys and utilities were marketed aggressively. *"Pile 'em high, sell 'em cheap"* was the mantra and power prices were cut as the company pushed its new irons, toasters, coffee per-

Pay-as-you-enter Car 82, November 25, 1912 at American Car, awaiting delivery.

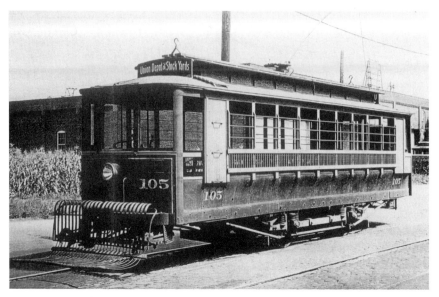

Convertible car 105 circa 1918, outside the carhouse.

revenue gain resulted and power savings exceeded 50% (SRJ June 14th, 1919). Maintenance arrears were tackled from 1919 and until 1924, up to 0.75 miles of track were relaid annually. 1922 was an exception (ERJ January 6th, 1923 p. 49) as 2.92 miles of track was relaid. However, 1.13 miles was abandoned that year; where and when is not known. Other problems were not as easily fixed.

Between March 1917 and April 1918 there were three wage increases but fares were increased only in December 1919. STJHP&L originally wanted six cents, then upped it to 8 cents to back a further wage increase. The MOPSC would only allow seven cents as that was *"about all the traffic will bear. All...lines of the St. Joseph Railway, Light, Heat and Power Company are short. An increase in fares over the above... would only result in decreased net revenue."* (ERJ December 20th, 1919 p. 1021). This fare allowed a 5.9% annaul return on current values after taking a 3% depreciation.

This was a trolley system with solid financial backing. If the MOPSC felt this way about St. Joseph, what hope was there for smaller systems? The company went ballistic and matter became a Federal case when the company sued in 1920, claiming the ruling was flawed being based on original cost and 1913 replacement prices. The Federal Court reversed the MOPSC ruling, saying a present-day fair value had to be used, a figure nearly double MOPSC's and based on 1920 reproduction costs without depreciation. STJHP&L interpreted this liberally, assuming they could now collect not seven but ten cents, and this fare was announced for November 18th, 1920. That irked the city, already hostile to the company on general principle. A restraining order was issued, resulting in a long-term stalemate. Eventually, an eight cent fare was settled upon and this prevailed for some time.

colators and fridges. Not yet hooked up? How about us wiring up six rooms (plus bath, lamps and brass light fixtures) for just $28, with 10% discount for cash?

Money was spent on overdue capital improvements to the trolleys, but the system was marking time when it should have been expanding. In 1916 the Frederick Avenue line was to be extended to the State Hospital, a mile beyond the 26th Avenue terminal. Instead a feeder bus was put on, initially a jitney, later a White 2-ton truck chassis with a 14-seat body. This was the first authorized motor bus in Missouri city service. As for unauthorized buses, St. Joseph suffered from the same jitney plague that hit the rest of the country in 1914. In 1917 an ordinance was passed to protect trolley services. It required jitney operators to furnish a $3,000 indemnity bond. They disappeared virtually overnight.

The Messanie line switched to Birneys in November 1918. An initial 25%

A city demand that the company pave between all tracks in addition to replacing worn-out rail and switches proved hard to implement. Though sales of appliances and domestic current were fine, the company could not cross-subsidize the trolleys. So what to do? Cars and tracks could be sold to the city, but that might raise a municipalization issue regarding the steam heat loops and electrical business. Motor buses could be run, but

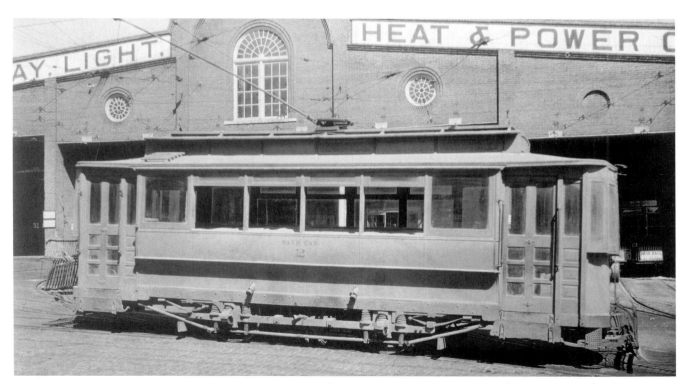

Sand Car 2 was a converted passenger car, and is seen outside the car house circa 1930.

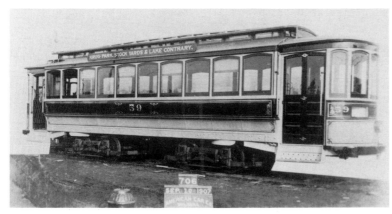

Car 59, September 10th 1907 at American Car, awaiting delivery.

Birney 308, May 20th, 1918, at American Car awaiting delivery.

the anti-jitney ordinance was still in force. Profitable extensions might be made, but only with buses. Finally, labor costs had to be reduced.

That was tackled in 1925 when cars were made one-man. Next, the jitney ordinance was repealed and the city agreed buses should run *"as coordinate units of the railway system."* The short Grand Avenue car line, due for track renewal, was converted in 1928, buses following the car line to Tenth and Powell and then re-routed to give wider distribution of service.The Messanie line followed in 1929 and the Hyde Park and Lake Contrary lines in 1931. But the company was hesitant to write off the trolley's electrical system. The trolleybus had evolved from its "trackless trolley" origins (solid tires, low capacity, heavy power-to-weight ratio) and was now a modern electric bus. In 1932 a test began on the four-mile Jules Street line, the public liked the new vehicle, and on August 1st, Jules street went trolleybus.

Road-widening hastened conversions and the last St. Joseph city car left downtown at 1:00 a.m. on January 23rd 1938, replaced by eight new trolleybuses on a through Krug Park-South Park run. There was a partial fleet renewal in the late 1940s and used trolleybuses were bought until 1959. Ridership drop in the 1960s robbed the service of profitability and the last trolleybus ran November 22nd, 1966. Most were sold to Mexico City where they ran for a further decade. Many car tracks remained visible until the 1970s. Today, city buses run under the St. Joseph Transit name.

Incomplete Roster Notes

Nothing is known of the animal cars but many were "bobtails." Electric cars were constantly renumbered. Six Brill closed cars ordered August 1st, 1888 for the Wyatt Park, may have been electric. Three more were ordered January 29th, 1889. An overheated stove sparked a barn fire on November 30th, 1891 and burned 35 cars, which were only partly insured. Cars 23 and 34, said by the St. Joseph Gazette to be comparatively worthless, were saved.

Electric car 22 of circa 1890 had six-windows and (later) a motorman's windshield.

Electric car 30 of circa 1890 was a former mule car.

At the end of 1891, 16 electrics came "from Minneapolis," possibly for the People's. 12 opens came from St. Louis Car in June or July 1893. SRJ directory March 1897 said there were 49 motors and 12 trailers, built by Brill, Brownell, Gilbert, Lewis and Fowler, St. Louis and Stephenson.

Cars 82-92 (St. Louis, 1899) were 10-bench single-truck opens. 82 and 83 (Danville, 1909) had arch roofs.

Cars 50-53, 54-57 (St. Louis, 1899, 1900) were closed single-truck city cars.

Six single-truck 10-bench opens (possibly 93-95) came from St. Louis Car in 1900.

Four 11-bench opens (St. Louis, 1902) possibly numbered 96-99 on St. Louis 46 single-trucks

Eight 11-bench opens (St. Louis, 1903) possibly numbered 100-107. May also have been convertible to closed cars.

Cars 7-12 (St. Louis, 1903) were closed city cars on St. Louis 25 single-trucks

Cars 17-20 (St. Louis, 1905) were closed city cars on St. Louis 46 single-trucks.

Cars 53-58 (St. Louis, 1905) were closed double-truck city cars.

Six 11-bench open cars (numbers unknown) came from St. Louis Car in 1906.

Car 59-68 (?) (American, 1907) were closed double-truck city cars.

Car 160-169 (American, 1907) were 12-bench open cars (Brill 22-E trucks, 2 50HP motors) for the 71/2 mile Krug Park-Lake Contrary route. They could be run multiple-unit with a single-truck car.

Car 69-73 (St. Louis, 1909) were closed double-truck PAYE city cars.

Cars 77-81 (American, 1909/10) were closed city cars on Brill trucks. A later #77 was a double-truck maximum-traction closed city car.

Cars 114, 165 and one other were sold to Sedalia in 1913.

Cars 112, 121 were early 9 or 10-bench single-truck open cars.

Single-truck snow sweeper 12 (McGuire-Cummings, 1910).

The numbers of six closed city cars (American 1912) on Brill trucks, plus two more (American, 1914), are unknown.

Conversion of St. Joseph streetcar lines
(*=initially converted to trolleybus).
This list is not exhaustive; it deals only with the principal lines.

Date	Line
July 4th, 1928.	Grand.
October 27th, 1929.	Messanie.
May 17th, 1931.	Hyde Park (branch of Union line).
July 31st, 1932.	Jules Street* (partly worked by trolleybus since March).
August 26th, 1934.	South Park.*
July 5th, 1936.	Twenty Second Street.
July 5th, 1936.	Frederick Avenue.
August 30th, 1936.	Wyatt Park.*
December 9th, 1937.	Prospect Avenue.
December 12th, 1937	Union (south).*
January 23rd, 1938	Union (north).*
January 23rd, 1938	Lake Contrary.*

Birney 323 unknown downtown location, September 1936. Bill Volkmer

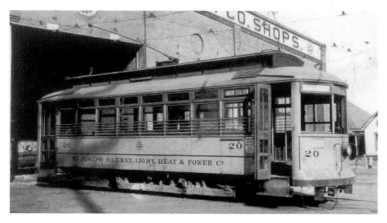

Car 20 at the car house on the last day January 16th, 1938. Bill Volkmer.

McGraw 1914 says there were 48.71 miles of track, 145 cars and 41 trailers. ERJ August 1st, 1914 (p.221) described a 15' wb. radial truck (sub-truck type within a 22'5" frame) developed by company Master Mechanic Fred Steffens. It made a trial trip under car 12 on April 30th, 1914, was in service next day and ran until July. The car had 2 GE 80 25HP motors and National straight air brakes. Previously it was on an 8' wheelbase St. Louis 25 single truck and suffered from overhang and oscillation problems, eliminated with this new truck.

The numbers of eight closed city cars (American, 1917), which may have been single-truck lightweights of Birney appearance but without the safety apparatus, are unknown.

Cars 301-312 (American, 1918) were Birney "Safety" cars.

Cars 313-324 (American, 1923) were Birney "Safety" cars.

McGraw 1924 claimed 43.44 miles of track, 16.45 miles of second track, 103 cars, 38 trailers, 5 motor freight cars, 4 freight trailers, 6 motor service cars and 1 bus. In 1926, 36 cars were scrapped, followed by a further nine in 1928.

2. ST. JOSEPH INTERURBANS

Preliminary discussion on interurbans north to Savannah and south to Kansas City began in 1903. For the Clay County line, see Kansas City interurban entries.

St. Joseph and Savannah Interurban Railway Company This 13-mile interurban competed with the Chicago Great Western Railroad. Construction began July 5th, 1910 and it opened April 3rd, 1911 with hourly cars and a 25-cent fare. It was a separate entity (J.H. Van Brunt held one-third of its shares in his own name), but had links to StJRLH&P and in 1912 merged with it. Cars left St. Joseph's interurban depot at Eighth and Edmond, (shared with the Clay County from 1913) ran north on Eighth, west on Francis, north on St. Joseph and via the Krug Park line to the city limits. Its own tracks ran from there on the roadside for 1½ miles to just south of the Country Club where a single-track fenced right-of-way began, mostly paralleling U. S. 71 north to Savannah. In Savannah, the line ran north on First to Main, then west on Main across the square to Tenth. Talk of pushing on to Fillmore, (11 miles northwest) went nowhere. Many used the line to access Savannah's cancer hospital (Dr. Nichols Sanatorium), near Hall Street and Park Avenue.

To maintain a 2% ruling grade, ten trestles, rock cuts and a fill

over 300' long and 57' high were needed. A wood trestle a mile south of Savannah near the present water treatment plant, was recalled as *"kind of weird ...At the bottom was a little creek and a spot of pasture between the interurban tracks and the CGW tracks—a mighty good place for a small picnic and close enough to walk to...That trestle was HIGH... the cars came often, and it was exciting to see it go across weaving from side to*

Combine 3, December 28th, 1910 at American Car, awaiting delivery.

side...*You wondered how it kept its balance."* (Andrew County; a community p.76)

A CGW injunction prohibited the SJ&S from crossing its Savannah tracks and cars ended just east of them until the injunction was lifted on April 19th, 1911. A freight and express car made two daily round trips out of St. Joseph once the new freight house opened in September 1911, generally following a regular passenger car. After the city cars closed in January 1938, the interurbans were cut back to their Krug Park barns, running on until July 22nd, 1939. Replacement buses resumed the through route to downtown St. Joseph (Eighth and Francis) and the company ran them until 1958.

Incomplete Roster Notes.

Interurbans 1-3. (American, 1911). Cars 1 and 2 were 46-seat passenger cars with a smoking compartment, Car 3, otherwise identical, had a baggage rather than a smoking compartment and seated 32. It later became a combine. All had rattan-upholstered seats, full-length railroad roofs and later renumbered 21-23. Brill Magazine February 1911 (p. 40, 41) said they were air-braked, had Brill 27-MCB1 trucks and 4 GE 216 50HP motors. Freight/express car 404 (home-built, 1911) was two St. Joseph single-truck car bodies spliced, an ungainly vehicle that sat high off the ground. Its home-built double trucks had 4 GE 800 25HP motors.

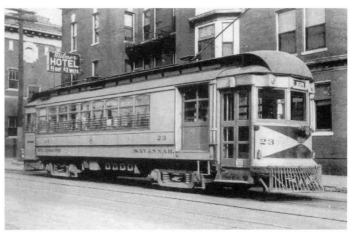

Combine 3, now numbered 23 outside the Milner hotel ($1.00 a day, $3.00 a week) St. Joseph, January 1938.

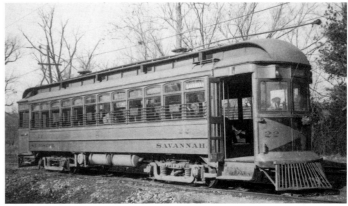

Combine 3, in the snow at stop 24 on the Savannah line circa 1912.

Car 22, at an unidentified location, January 16th, 1938. Bill Volkmer

3. PROPOSED ST. JOSEPH INTERURBANS

1. SRJ August 54th, 1906 (p. 71) noted an un-named Iowa syndicate working on a St. Joseph-Sioux Falls SD line via Bedford, Corning, Adair, Carroll, and Cherokee IA. Though a wheat and corn belt, coal fields in Adams County IA, would be served, some miles from any other railroad. *"Work on the new line is to begin in St. Joseph just as soon as Mrs. Alice M. Butler, promoter of the **St. Joseph, Stanberry and Northern**, complies with the contract she has made with the interurban syndicate."* Nothing more is known and this project vanished.

2. **St. Joseph Belt and Interurban Railroad** Incorporated in November 1906 to build a double-track St. Joseph-Savannah line and capitalized at $1.5 million, this St. Joseph and Savannah ancestor was backed by local men. SRJ June 22nd, 1907 (p.23) noted the **St. Joseph and Nodaway Valley Interurban Company** (building to Tarkio in Atchison County) merging with the St. Joseph Belt, the latter to build a St. Joseph belt line

to link with the former which would now extend to Graham, (Nodaway County) via Savannah. Nothing happened.

3. **Missouri Valley Traction Company** Chartered in 1907, this was a St. Joseph-Excelsior Springs line, with a branch to Mirabile in Caldwell County. Capitalized at $6,000, it would increase to $1½ million once grading began.(SRJ November 9th, 1907 ad p. 20). By December, when ten surveyors were at work, it changed its name to **St. Joseph-Excelsior Springs-Mirabile Interurban Railway Company.** The route surveyed now ran via Saxton, Garrettsburg, Starfield and Lathrop, where the Mirabile line diverged. The main line would go via Lawson (Ray County) and south to Excelsior Springs. Originally to serve Plattsburg (the Clinton County seat), the revised route took it 5 miles south. (SRJ December 7th 1907 ad p. 36).

St. Louis, St. Louis County,
Adjacent Illinois Towns

<u>Missouri</u>. Line 1 St. Louis. Line 2 Clayton. Line 3 Kirkwood. Line 4 Maplewood. Line 5 University City. Line 6 Webster Groves.
<u>Illinois</u>. Line 7 Alton. Line 8 Belleville. Line 9 Collinsville. Line 10 E. St. Louis. Line 11 Edwardsville. Line 12 Granite City.

	1880	1890	1900	1910	1920	1930	1940	1950	1960	1970	1980	1990	2000
1.	350,518	451,770	575,238	687,029	772,897	821,960	816,041	856,796	750,026	622,236	453,085	396,685	348,189
2.	–	402	–	–	3,028	9,613	13,069	16,035	15,245	16,100	14,219	13,926	12,825
3.	1,280	1,777	2,825	4,171	4,422	9,169	12,132	18,640	29,421	31,679	27,987	28,318	27,324
4.	–	–	–	4,976	7,431	12,657	12,875	13,416	12,552	12,785	10,960	9,962	9,228
5.	–	–	–	2,417	6,792	25,809	33,023	39,892	51,249	46,309	42,738	40,087	37,428
6.	–	1,783	7,895	7,080	9,474	16,487	18,394	23,390	28,990	27,457	23,097	22,992	23,230
7.	8,975	10,294	14,210	17,528	24,682	30,151	31,255	32,550	43,047	39,700	34,171	33,060	30,496
8.	–	15,361	17,484	21,122	24,823	28,425	28,405	32,721	37,264	41,223	42,150	42,806	41,410
9.	–	–	4,021	7,478	9,753	9,235	9,767	11,862	14,217	18,224	19,613	22,424	24,707
10.	–	15,169	29,665	58,547	66,767	74,347	75,609	82,295	81,712	70,169	55,200	40,944	31,542
11.	–	–	4,157	5,014	5,336	6,235	8,008	8,776	9,996	11,070	12,460	14,582	21,491
12.	–	–	3,122	9,903	14,757	25,130	22,974	29,465	40,073	40,685	36,815	32,766	31,301

1. St. Louis City Streetcars

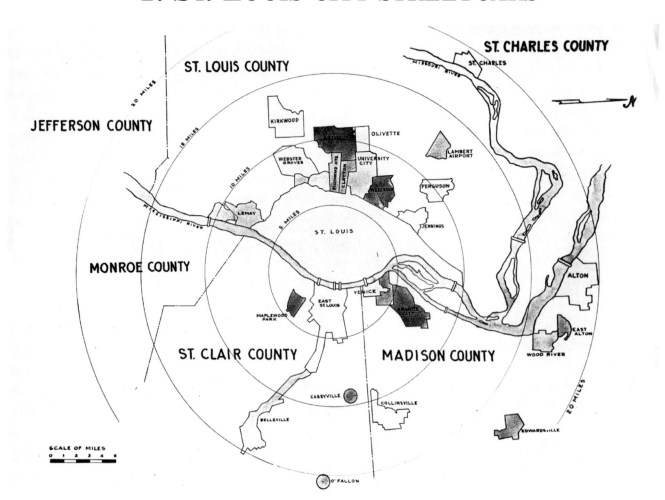

Map of St. Louis Metropolitan area circa 1930

St. Louis RR cable train-grip 39, trailer 239 in the 3700 block of South Broadway, 1890.

Broadway at Washington, looking north. On left, Lindell Railway electric car 201 and trailer, on far right Lindell Ry. horsecar 154. It's a warm day in 1892, all car windows are open. Far in the distance on Broadway, St. Louis RR cable car 314 (northbound) passes a southbound car.

St. Louis was settled in 1764, a year after the French ceded jurisdiction west of the Mississippi to the Spanish. It was 1770 before the Spanish took physical possession and most inhabitants came from French settlements in Illinois. The symbolic French name honors King Louis IX, the patron saint of King Louis XIV. St. Louis County was formed in 1812. The affluent city was its main component but seceded from the hard-scrabble rural county in 1876. Transit began in 1843 with horse buses. By the 1850s, there were over a dozen lines. In 1859, Erastus Wells's **Market Street Railway** opened an Olive Street car line from 4th to 12th Street (and soon to Leffingwell), to replace his horse buses on the same route. It was one of North America's early street railways. Others followed, initially running on separate streets, later competing for downtown terminals.

The first cable line came in 1886, an addition to the **West End Narrow Gauge** steam railway, running from Grand to downtown., the company being renamed **St. Louis Cable and Western Railway. Citizens' Railway,** another 1859 entrant, in 1887/8 cabled some of its lines after losing traffic to the Cable and Western. The **Missouri Railway** followed with an Olive Street cable. The **St. Louis Railroad** cabled its heavily-traveled line on Broadway in 1890. A ban on downtown overhead wires was lifted by the Board of Aldermen in March 1890 in sleazy circumstances but the cable was still considered necessary as electric traction was considered too fragile for Broadway's heavy traffic. The **People's Railway**, serving Lafayette Square and Tower Grove Park was the last to cable.

Missouri RR trailer 274 and unidentified cable grip car at the Maryland and Kingsshighway terminal in the Central West End circa 1896.

Lindell Railway Car 3 on Mississippi Avenue at Lafayette Park St. Louis, circa 1896.

The St. Louis transit strike of 1900 was long and bitter. Debris and household articles dangle from the wires, while a man hung in effigy bears the label "This is a SCAB." Photo taken at 19th Street looking north from O'Fallon. The state of the roadway is appalling; the man seen driving a horse wagon fitted with seats (center background) is using the car tracks for smooth passage; his wagon wheels are just about the right gauge. He may be looking for riders in the absence of trolleys. STLMOT.

The **Lindell Railway** of 1864 (which never ran on Lindell), was the largest St. Louis system and in 1887 began experiments with battery-powered electric motors. The motors worked well, but the limited life and range of the batteries pushed the Lindell to overhead wires. The first overhead wire line, however, was the St. Louis Railroad's Seventh Street branch on November 1st 1888. From 1891, electric lines were extended into the county to Clayton, Creve Coeur Lake, Florissant, Kirkwood, Maplewood and elsewhere. Some were interurbans or rural farm-to-market lines and offered limited freight service. They stimulated residential growth and soon became suburban lines.

Consolidation as **United Railways** was largely achieved by 1899 and completed in January 1907 when the **St. Louis and Suburban** joined. There was little expansion after 1899 except for a few county lines and cross-suburban links, plus electrification of the last cable lines in 1902. Initially, service was poor and UR was mired in labor unrest, mostly caused by autocratic management anxious to cut costs. An entirely avoidable strike in 1900 lasted six months, with several dead and hundreds injured. It was a poor start for a new company. But after 1905, when North American assumed ownership, service became fast, frequent and efficient, with over 1600 (at maximum) large, wide cars. UR was determined to build up a standard fleet of new cars and rebuild its best older cars to the same standards, which it did from 1900 to 1920, mostly in its own shops. Hundreds more older cars were remodeled and sold for service elsewhere. When the Suburban became part of UR in 1907, the same treatment was accorded most of their cars.

UR went bankrupt in 1919 for the usual reasons: inflation, underlying debt and the war. Though many county lines were expensively rebuilt, often on new alignments, no new lines were built after 1917. The **People's Motor Bus Company** in 1922 partly filled the gap. A corporate relation to New York's Fifth Avenue Coach Company, Hertz, Yellow Cab and General Motors' Yellow Coach Company, it was franchised to use streets with car tracks to access new suburban areas beyond the trolley's reach, often on a more direct route from downtown. Car fare now was eight cents; protests brought it back to seven and even six cents for a short time. But people lined up in droves, eager to ride a People's bus for ten cents. UR was finally allowed by the bankruptcy judge to run feeder buses from outer car line terminals in 1924 and soon began crosstown links and lines into new territory.

In late 1927 **St. Louis Public Service Company** took over UR's system. It expanded bus service and made noises about taking over People's, which after a few good years was faltering. A working arrangement was reached late in 1929 and full consolidation in 1934, though the People's green double-deck buses lasted until 1944. Soon after, SLPS buses began replacing existing rail lines. Trolleybuses were not considered, though there was an early trial in 1903 and St. Louis Car demonstrators were sometimes displayed in the late 1920s. St. Louis was early with high-capacity (40 seats plus) double-truck trolleys in the 1890s and was so again when high-capacity one-man city buses appeared in the late 1920s. They were used for the 1929 Vandeventer conversion, and lines such as St. Charles, Market and Natural Bridge between 1932 and 1936. Most were enforced road-widening evictions,

Night in St. Louis. City Hall and Municipal buildings circa 1910.

Night in St. Louis. Olive circa 1910.

but buses also replaced no-hope shuttles, such as Midland, Marcus, Spalding, Meramec Highlands, Jefferson Barracks and Florissant between 1930 and 1937.

A 1939 multi-modal modernization program saw new buses replace more car lines but two hundred PCC cars were bought in 1940 and 1941 for the heaviest routes following SLPS's refinancing after a 1933-1939 bankruptcy. These vehicles, plus hundreds more new buses and elderly trolleys (some from 1895) got the city through the war and the 1940s ridership peak. In 1945 there were 358 miles of 600V D. C. 4' 10"-gauge tracks, 762 motor cars, 15 trailers, 74 work cars and two locomotives, plus 793 buses on 334 miles of route. Modernization continued into the 1950s but ridership decline threatened profitability. SLPS sold its assets to the Bi-State Development Agency on April 1st, 1963, which also took over East St. Louis and thirteen other bus companies. Initially, Bi-State looked to keep surviving lines as the nucleus of a light rail system, but was discouraged by cost and by the mayor's hostility to rail on one-way streets east of 12th. The last car ran on Olive and the Hodiamont right-of-way to Wellston on May 21st, 1966.

In the 1920s, subway and rapid transit lines were planned from the riverfront through downtown to the suburbs using dedicated right of way and the Eads Bridge rail tunnel under Washington and 8th Streets. But except for the grade-separated realignment of Illinois Terminal in 1931 (with a "subway" terminal at 12th Street), nothing had been done; there was no money. In the 1980s, Bi-State revived the idea of using the 1874 rail tunnel, which had closed in 1974. A deal was arranged giving the railroads ownership of the Municipal Bridge and Bi-State's MetroLink project ownership of the Eads Bridge and tunnel. Opened June 30th, 1993, MetroLink was extended from North Hanley to the Airport on June 25th, 1994, to Belleville May 4th, 2001, to Scott-Shiloh June 23rd, 2003 and Forest Park - Clayton-Shrewbury August 26, 2006.

Incomplete Roster Notes

A D. Young's book "Street cars, Light Rail and Utility cars of St. Louis 1899-2003" provides an exhaustive analysis. Some information on cars prior to 1899 is at the St. Louis Museum of Transportation's Library and Archives at 3015 Barratt Station Road, St. Louis. MO 63122. However it is incomplete and remains to be analyzed.

Other than for passenger cars of the St. Louis and Suburban, the only trolleys that moved in St. Louis city for the strike's first few weeks, were utility cars and their crews, picking up the debris. STLMOT

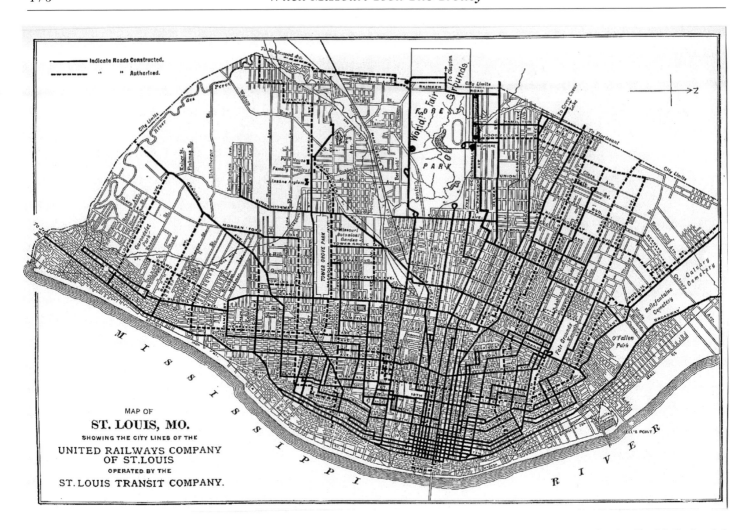

United Railways system map circa 1903, showing proposed extensions, almost none of which were made othe than for the City Limits (top left from Maplewood). The line on Morganford Road from Gravois to Wyoming Street was built by 1899 by the Lindell Railroad, but never used.

Car 635 on the Hodiamont line at Newstead Avenue circa 1920. This line began life in 1875 as a narrow-gauge steam railroad; today it is a paved busway. STLMOT

Old Manchester (Vandeventer) and Tower Grove grade crossings. Car 2053 turns right onto Old Manchester (Vandeventer), car 2476 makes the opposite turn, heading for Wellston. The MoPac Tower Grove railroad station is at the upper right. Street traffic is light. Several groups of people are clustered around street corners, just hanging out. These crossings were bridged by a complex series of overpasses by 1916.

(Above left) De Baliviere at Pershing in 1920, looking south to Forest Park and the Jefferson Memorial building of the Missouri Historical Society. The entrance to today's Forest Park MetroLink station is just beyond the buildings on the left, but at that time there was a Wabash railroad grade-crossing with De Baliviere, not today's underpass and tunnel. Part of the proposed Delmar heritage trolley's tracks will go straight on to loop the Jefferson Memorial building. One of the two cars for this project is presently (2006/7) displayed at the left of the building. STLMOT

(Above right) The same location and date as the previous picture but now looking west across De Baliviere at Pershing. Two cars climb the ramp to the bridge spanning the Wabash RR (MetroLink) to access the line to Skinker, Big Bend and Clayton. STLMOT

The fall in ridership and the 1933 bankruptcy saw hundreds of cars placed in open-air storage, mainly those built prior to 1907, the trailers and the Birneys. They were not scrapped until the late 1930s since they were part of the bankrupt Company's assets. Judging from their sorry state in this 1935 picture at the former Kraft Avenue car house storage yards, their value as assets must by now have been debatable. Surrounded by trailers on the left and older cars on the right, Birney 500 rests by the fence, all window glass shattered, stripped of useable parts and its doors ripped out.

(Above left) An eastbound car ascends the trestle to cross Wabash (MetroLink) tracks to access De Baliviere and Pershing. The view looks west on what today is Forest Park Expressway, now shared with MetroLink's Clayton-Shrewsbury tracks. STLMOT

(Above right) A westbound car about to cross Wabash (now MetroLink) tracks circa 1910. STLMOT

Some days after St. Louis's unveiling ceremony for the new PCC streamliners, the Baden Chamber of Commerce held a dedication of its own. Car 1526 stands outside the Treit building on North Broadway just before breaking the ribbon. June 21st, 1940.

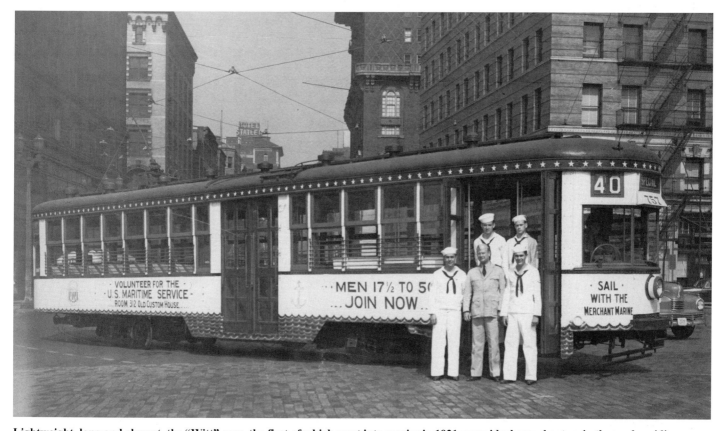

Lightweight, long and elegant, the "Witt" cars, the first of which went into service in 1921, were ideal crowd-eaters in the modern idiom, even when converted to one-man operation. "Peter Witt" car 757 as a recruiting car for the Merchant Marine in 1943, seen at the 3rd and Washington loop. STLMOT

Conversion of St. Louis Streetcar lines.

Route numbers were not assigned until 1928.
This list is not exhaustive; it deals only with the principal lines.

1897.	Fourth Street and Arsenal.
November 5th, 1912.	Seventh Street between Cherokee and Chippewa.
July 21st, 1929.	33 Vandeventer.
March 15th, 1930.	71 Fourteenth Street.
June 21st, 1930.	07 Spalding, 34 Marcus.
June 29th, 1930.	03 Midland.
April 8th, 1931.	66 St. Peter's.
August 15th, 1931.	67 Bridgeton.
November 14th, 1931	02 Florissant (Berkeley-Florissant only).
January 17th, 1932.	64 St. Charles (Woodson-Road St. Charles only)
March 16th, 1932.	43 Barracks.
April 17th, 1932.	56 Osage Hills/Meramec Highlands (Woodbine & Magnolia-Meramec Highlands). Line resumed from May 14th 1933 to October 8th, 1933.
July 25th, 1932.	Tenth Street between Cass and Hebert, due to bad track.
August 10th, 1932.	Market Street (Broadway to 21st, Laclede to Vandeventer) due to road widening. Cars re-routed to 52 line.
September 18th, 1932.	31 Natural Bridge (Grand to Kingshighway) due to road widening.
May 27th, 1933.	51 Market, 52 Laclede, merged next day into new 51 Forest Park line.
February 7th, 1934.	44 Chippewa (Shuttle from Kingshighway via Chippewa to Broadway). Tracks kept for non-revenue access to South Broadway car house, but 44 line resumed July 9th, 1940 as a through route from Kingshighway via Chippewa and Broadway to downtown.
August 1st, 1936.	31 Natural Bridge (from downtown to Grand).
May 15th, 1937.	83 Thirty-Ninth Street (a.k.a. Tiffany).
January 14th, 1939.	20 Cherokee.
August 31st, 1940	01 Kirkwood-Ferguson. Cut back next day from Ferguson to Big Bend. Tracks closed between Big Bend and Hodiamont Avennue via Maple Avenue in University City.
November 2nd, 1940	21 Tower Grove, 41 Lee (south of Walnut), 80 Compton.
June 15th, 1946.	13 Union, 18 Taylor, 42 Sarah.
July 6th, 1946	41 Lee, 72 Eighteenth Street belt.
May 24th, 1947.	17 Page.
July 12th, 1947.	30 Cass, 73 Bellefontaine.
February 21st, 1948.	02 Berkeley, 16 City Limits-Ferguson.
December 28th, 1948.	12 Maryland, 65 Woodson Road.
January 29th, 1949.	57 Brentwood.
February 10th, 1949.	44 Broadway-Chippewa.
March 12th, 1949.	04 Clayton.
April 2nd, 1949.	53 Manchester-Maplewood, 54 Manchester-Webster, 55 Manchester-Kirwood (Clay and Adams), 56 Manchester-Kirkwood (Woodbine and Magnolia).
July 25th, 1950.	05 Creve Coeur Lake.
August 2nd, 1950.	01 Kirkwood-Big Bend.
August 13th, 1950	51 Forest Park (Euclid and Laclede to Dale Avenue).
December 16th, 1950	51 Forest Park (downtown to Euclid and Laclede).
June 6th, 1951.	50 Southampton, 81 Park.
August 19th, 1956.	40 Broadway.
October 12th, 1958.	22 Jefferson.
January 3rd, 1960.	70 Grand.
Febraury 3rd, 1963.	14 University-Clayton , 11 University (from De Baliviere to Big Bend loop).
July 28th, 1963.	32 Wellston.
April 19th, 1964.	10 Delmar, 11 University (from downtown to De Baliviere).
May 21st, 1966.	15 Hodiamont.

There's A Friendly Message In The Flash Of Our Amber Light

The amber light, that you sometimes see flashing on the front of a Public Service street car or bus, is a friendly message from the operator to folks waiting to get aboard.

The blinking light says: "Sorry, neighbors, but my car (or bus) is filled to capacity or out of service so I'm going to pass you by. But there's another vehicle right behind me that has plenty of room. It will pick you up. You won't have long to wait."

Not all of our vehicles have these special lights to flash the "filled-to-capacity" message to you. So there are times during rush hours when vehicles without the blinking light will pass you.

But any time we pass you up, you may be sure another car or bus will reach you soon.

ST. LOUIS PUBLIC SERVICE COMPANY
Helping Greater St. Louis To Help Win The War

St. Louis Globe-Democrat April 14th, 1944

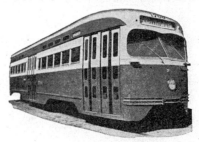

50 NEW STREAMLINERS GO INTO SERVICE TODAY

Delmar and University Routes to be completely equipped with Streamliners

Beginning Sunday, October 27, the Delmar, University and University-Clayton lines will be completely equipped with streamlined street cars to give faster, better service. The arrival of 50 of 100 modern, smooth-riding streamliners makes this improvement possible.

At the same time, 17 streamliners will be worked into the schedules of the Wellston line. As soon as the remaining 50 new street cars are received, the Grand line will be completely equipped with streamliners and a group of the new cars will be placed in service on the Jefferson line. As the modern streamliners are added, older type yellow cars will be retired.

In outside appearance the new streamliners are a great deal like the streamliners which have been serving the community as well for several years. However there are many important interior

changes to make riding more comfortable, more pleasant. A new seating arrangement provides more aisle space in the front of the cars. This allows a freer movement of passengers from the front to the exits. Improved ventilation and lighting, leather-upholstered seats and easier window operation add to your comfort.

The purchase of these new, better, more comfortable street cars costing $2,000,000 is in keeping with the Public Service policy of investing a large part of its income to make America's best city transit system even better. The cars are a part of a $9,000,000 order for new street cars and buses to be delivered during 1946 and 1947.

Watch for the new streamliners on the Olive lines. Their numbers start at 1700. You'll enjoy the extra comfort, the smoother ride, the safety and service they give you.

Tune in Frank Doyle with SIX O'CLOCK NEWS Every Weekday Evening...Radio Station KWK

ST. LOUIS Public Service COMPANY

CITY TRANSIT
SAFETY COURTESY SERVICE

St. Louis Globe-Democrat October 27th, 1946.

Car 1089 in late summer 1946 picks up men leaving Scullin Steel on Manchester before heading east. STLMOT

PCC car 1683 eastbound on Manchester at Hampton 1948. Ray Gehl/Mark Goldfeder collection.

"Peter Witt" 930, 12th Street at Olive circa 1951. A 1951 Nash is passing on the left, the old St. Louis Post-Dispatch building is on the right.
Ray Gehl/Mark Goldfeder collection.

"Peter Witt" cars 724, 725 on Midland at Wellington Avenue in University City, looking towards Olive Street Road in spring 1949. Car 725 is outbound to Creve Coeur Lake. Ray Gehl/Mark Goldfeder collection.

About 100 cars are visible in this evocative picture of the De Baliviere car house around August 1950. From left to right are cars 1317 (clearly on its last legs and perhaps already in open-air storage prior to scrapping), 744, 1583, 1671, 752 1734 and 1659. Most modern carhouses in St. Louis and Kansas City featured open-air storage, in spite of the climatic extremes. STLMOT

The materials yard at 39th and Park was standard gauge as opposed to the 4' 10" gauge of the St. Louis streetcar system. By the 1950s, it was worked by two locomotives and a crane. Here crane 400 is about to scoop a load from a Nickel Plate gondola car that has been switched in from the railroad connection by locomotive 97 circa 1951.

(Above) Highway 40 (I-64) is being extended towards downtown and a new bridge is needed for it to pass under Grand Avenue. Looking south on Grand circa 1954, PCC 1731 negotiates temporary tracks, installed because plans to replace the 1890 Grand Avenue Bridge (in the background) were incomplete and the line linked the main 39th and Park shops, located behind the Pevely Dairy plant in the center background, with the rest of the surviving system. Subsequent diversions for highway construction on Broadway, Jefferson and Forest Park Expressway were too expensive to contemplate and those lines were changed to buses. Grand too was changed on January 4th, 1960, when bridge replacement plans were finalized. STLMOT

(Left) PCC 1608 leaves Wellston Loop for a trip along Easton to downtown St. Louis, August 5th, 1961.

Another picture of the Grand detour in 1954, with PCC car 1745 heading north on Grand towards St. Louis University and mid-town. STLMOT

2. MINOR ST. LOUIS STREET RAILWAYS

A. City of St. Louis

i. **St. Louis Municipal Railway** In 1895 the city's water department expanded to a facility at Chain of Rocks on the Mississippi at the far northeast city limits. A single-track standard-gauge line was built from Humboldt Street to Chain of Rocks parallel to but east of Broadway, with a CBQ connection at Humboldt, that railroad handling all freight plus five daily passenger trains for Waterworks employees. In 1901, $4^{1/2}$ miles north of Baden Avenue was electrified. A trial run on September 28th, 1901 had St. Louis Water Commissioner Edward Flad and a few friends on board. Partial service began on November 1st, full service on January 5th, 1902 (possibly January 8th). One car made five daily round trips from Baden north to the Chain of Rocks settling basins, then northeast to end west of the coagulating plant. The public could ride the line, all within sight of the Mississippi, if they acquired free passes in advance at City Hall or Baden Station. Though floods could shut the line for weeks it was a popular ride.

The line was extended south in 1903 to Bissell's Point Water Station (East Grand) and a TRRA interchange, then southeast into Water Department's facilities.The public could not ride south of Baden as this competed with UR's Broadway line. Soon after, the city began its own freight and switching, buying the first of several steam locomotives for the job. To discourage joy-riding, a nickel was charged from August 18th, 1913. This had the opposite of the intended effect, making the line more, not less, accessible. Now one simply boarded and paid.

In 1914, passing sidings were installed at Chain of Rocks and Baden stations. In 1915, a new filtration plant was built. Diverted tracks left the old line south of the northeast curve, ran on the plant's south side and rejoined the old line on the east side of the settling basins. Ridership declined in the 1920s, and passenger service ended either May 1935 or May 1939—it is not clear. The cars were kept and when the city could not renegotiate a contract with a local bus company, cars ran three daily round-trips for employees from June 1st, 1944. In the 1950s, employees bought autos so the last cars ran April 30th, 1955. A new CBQ interchange was made south of St. Cyr Road and from about 1955 the CBQ resumed handling freight, the successor Burlington Northern Santa Fe continuing until the line closed a few years ago. The southern section was replaced by the Hall Street highway in the 1960s. In the 1980s and 1990s, a private group offered tourist railroad trips once a month. Car 10, fully restored, made its first runs at the St Louis Museum of Transportation over the 2001 Memorial Day weekend.

Free bridge upper road deck ramp looking east circa 1926, with never-used trolley tracks and lighting poles which also were to have carried the overhead wires.

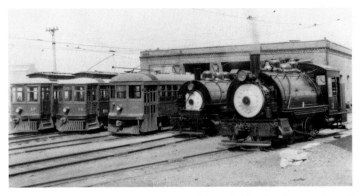

Left to right Waterworks cars 17, 12 and 10 plus locomotives 4 and 3, circa 1920.

Waterworks line car 13, 1931, Baden.

Incomplete Roster Notes

Car 2 (St. Louis, 1901) was a closed 48-seat car on St. Louis 23-A trucks with 2 GE 57 50HP motors. It was renumbered 12 in 1919.
Car 3 (St. Louis, 1904) was a closed 38-seat car, trucks and equipment unknown. It was remodeled as a line car circa 1915, and renumbered 13 in 1919.
Car 7 (American, 1910) was a closed double-end 48-seat car on Brill 27-GE2 4' 6" wb trucks, with 2 57HP GE motors. It was renumbered 17 in 1919 and is preserved at the St. Louis Museum of Transportation.
10, 11 (St. Louis, 1915) were closed 56-seat cars on St. Louis 23-EM trucks with 4 WH 306 50HP motors and K-35G controllers. These were pay-as-you-enter suburban cars on steel frames, designed to haul trailers. Car 10 has been restored and operates at the St. Louis Museum of Transportation.

ii. **St. Louis Municipal (Free) Bridge** This project, discussed from 1904 and backed by a voter-approved bond issue of 1906, was begun in 1910 but not completed until 1940. The bridge was intended to break the TRRA monopoly of Mississippi rail crossings which inflated the price of Illinois coal in Missouri. Thus its glacially slow creep to completion is puzzling. The road deck opened January 20th, 1917 (non-stop autos and trucks judging from opening-day pictures), yet the first train did not cross until September 24th 1930 and the Illinois rail approaches were not in full use from the east until January 15th, 1940. Nor was it a free bridge; initially all traffic paid tolls.

ERJ May 10th, 1919 (p. 931) said the city had not finished the bridge tracks, but the Board of Public Works had begun building a short standard-gauge loop in the city (not true, but the intention was there) and was stringing trolley wire on the bridge (poles yes, wires no). This "activity" was part of a broader city plan to get St. Louis-bound interurbans from

Waterworks car 10 Baden Station circa 1955. Ray Gehl/Mark Goldfeder collection.

London and Port Stanley cars 7 and 8 at Beach Terminal, Port Stanley ON, June 21st, 1944. Car 7 was originally built for the St. Louis and Monte Sano, only the first few miles of which were completed and subsequently operated as the Grand View line. These cars languished unsold at St. Louis Car until 1916.

Illinois onto a new standard-gauge downtown loop serving a proposed new inteururban "Union Station" on 9th Street, an idea that sprang from the abortive 1911 Southern Traction proposals (see below). This 1919 plan envisaged standard-gauge tracks on 9th Street from the Free Bridge north to IT's McKinley Bridge, relieving tie-ups at the Eads Bridge Plaza interurban terminal and at UR's adjacent 4' 10" gauge terminal loop at Washington and Third. A St. Louis-East St. Louis shuttle would run over the Free Bridge from July 1st, 1919. Its failure to open is one of St. Louis's enduring transit mysteries.

Incomplete Roster Notes

Two new Birney cars were bought for the shuttle. Not only did the city ignore the claims of local builders St. Louis and American to be the home of the Birney "Safety" car, they also ignored the "get the lowest bid but buy locally" custom. Instead Cincinnati Car got the order. The cars arrived late in 1919 (probably numbered 11 and 12), on 8' wb. Cincinnati #139 single trucks. They never ran, indeed may not have been tested. UR had little work for its own Birneys when they came in late 1920 and there was no chance they'd take over and re-gauge the city's pair. Instead they were stored until scrapped circa 1935. A 1923 plan to use them on a revived **St. Louis and Jennings** didn't gel.

B. Grand View Railroad Company. This suburban line had its roots in the defunct **St. Louis, Hillsboro and Southern Railroad Company**, planning a St. Louis-Hillsboro line via Bobring, Luxembourg and Fen-

ton, and the unrelated **Hillsboro, Kimmswick and Northern Railroad Company**, part of H. F. Vogel's Monte Sano Springs project at Kimmswick, which would *"give quick and frequent service to Kimmswick and the new resort by building from the Broadway line at Jefferson Barracks south to Kimmswick and...Hillsboro. About 28 of the 33 miles...will be in Jefferson County...We plan a 15-minute service between Kimmswick and the Barracks and hourly...between Kimmswick and Hillsboro."* (PD July 6th, 1906 p.8.) Construction was sub-contracted to Charles A. Gutke, one of the incorporators. SRJ July 14th, 1906 (p.85) claimed this project did not conflict with the St. Louis, Hillsboro and Southern, though both would serve Monte Sano Springs. Neither did.

The St. Louis, Hillsboro and Southern Railroad Company was chartered in 1902 to build a St. Louis-Hillsboro interurban. Its President was T. F. Sneed. A terminal building would be built between South Broadway, Kayser Street and the River Des Peres. It is unclear if third-rail or overhead wire was to be used. SRJ March 21st, 1903 (p.465) reported rock cuts being made. On December 15th, 1905 the P-D reported the compa-

Grand View car 1 at an unknown station, date unknown.

ny finishing surveys for a 60-mile line to Richwoods in Washington County, capital $1.25 million. R.Williams, president of the St. Louis Compressed Air House Cleaning Company now headed the project.

H. M. Bowen of Alton IL (General Manager) claimed capital was paid up and building (at $15,000 a mile) would start in March 1906. From Carondelet in St. Louis County, 200 yards from the St. Louis city line, it would run south for forty miles, 20 miles from either the MoPac (Iron Mountain) or Frisco, serving a population of 130,000 and tapping a *"rich lead-mining belt"* with passenger and freight trains. SRJ July 28th, 1906 (p. 35) said construction had been let *"to an eastern concern"* which would begin grading in 60 days. From South Broadway it would run via Bobring, Sappington,Luxembourg, Fenton, High Ridge, House Springs, Cedar Hill and Hillsboro.

Extensions to De Soto, Potosi, the Ozarks region and Yellville AR, were contemplated. In 1907, it reported 40 miles of standard-gauge track, eight passenger cars and 200 freight cars, a head office at 722 Pierce Building, St. Louis and a power station at "Jefferson County" MO. This was wishful thinking, for later in 1907 it merged with the Hillsboro Kimmswick and Northern. In August 1906, St. Louis County had given the latter a franchise for private right-of-way from Jefferson Barracks southwest to the Meramec River, with the right to bridge the Meramec near Telegraph and Fine Roads. Jefferson County franchised the line from the bridge to Kimmswick, plus Kimmswick-Hillsboro. But later in the year the company reapplied to St. Louis County, preferring not to build on right-of-way in the county, possibly because the owners of the parcels of land needed had jacked up the price.

In March 1907, the St. Louis, Monte Sano and Southern Railway Company was established as a merger of the two projects. It would be a 65-mile standard-gauge St. Louis-Flat River interurban via Monte Sano Springs and De Soto, with Hillsboro and Festus/Crystal City branches. It would link with the St. Francois County line (see Farmington) at Flat River. SRJ October 26th, 1907 (ad p. 28), incorrectly reporting it as the St. Louis, Monte Sano and Southeastern Railroad, said building began when *"seven carloads of ties were unloaded and hauled along the Lemay FerryRoad ...1000 tons of steel rails, representing the first shipment, are in transit. Charles W. Gutke is president..."* Attorney Lee A. Hall of St. Louis, company secretary and counsel had petitioned *"to alter the gauge to 4' 8 1/2 inches...to change it from an electric to steam road and to build one instead of two tracks."*

In 1908, the company had $1 million preferred stock, $3 million common stock and $2.5 million of funded debt. It claimed to have sixty cars and an office at 1114 Chemical Building, St. Louis but by March 1908, it had placed orders with St. Louis Car only for eight (four motors, four trailers) plus two motor baggage cars. The order was later cancelled but not before these cars were completed. They languished at St. Louis Car until 1916, when three were sold to the London and Port Stanley Railway in Ontario.The rest went to the Washington, Baltimore and Annapolis in 1918 as 88-92. In 1915, one baggage car became L&PS E1, the other Toronto Suburban Railway 201 in 1917. By 1911, the Monte Sano had either absorbed or was calling itself the St. Louis, Hillsboro and Southern Railroad Company, but completed only a few miles of roadbed before it went bankrupt. It was bought at foreclosure by George Baumhoff who reorganized it as the Grand View Railroad Company with $200,000 of capital.

Known as the "Green line," it opened August 1st, 1912 on much of the Monte Sano's completed roadbed. From its carhouse and station just inside the city close to UR's Broadway line at River Des Peres, it ran northwest on right-of-way for 100 yards by the River Des Peres, entering St. Louis County parallel to Fannie Avenue, going onto Fannie (a westerly extension of Virginia Avenue) at 5th Street, northwest on Fannie across Military Road and Fodor Avenue, southwest on Lemay Ferry Road for a mile, then northwest on right-of-way near Telegraph Road, crossing Gravois Creek, then southwest at milepost 2. From here, on right-of-way paralleling MoPac's Kirkwood branch, it crossed Barracks and Green Park Roads to Continental's cement plant.

The first transit service to the plant, the Grand View was seen as a blessing. A further mile to the powerhouse at Tesson Ferry Road was built but

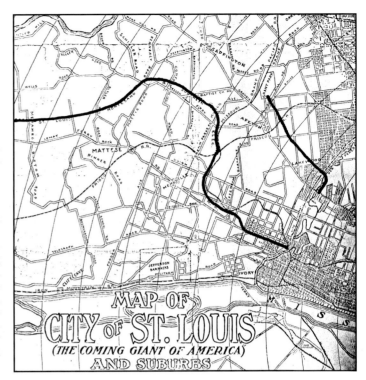

Map showing part of the St. Louis and Monte Sano (the Grand View line) plus (right), the shorter Grant Park line.

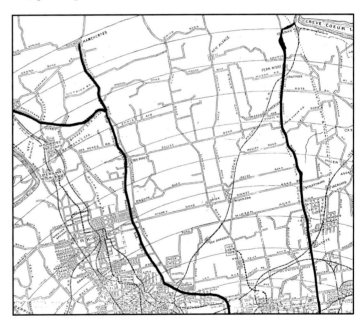

Map showing the proposed St. Louis Webster and Valley Park Electric Railway's line of route (left), and the proposed St. Louis, Creve Coeur and Western (right) on Olive Street Road, circa 1909.

not regularly used. It followed MoPac's Kirkwood branch northwest for a mile, crossed Tesson Ferry Road and ended a few yards beyond at Gravois Creek on a northwest to west curve. A 1913 plat shows the line bridging the creek, then ending. The Monte Sano was to continue west and southwest, a few hundred yards north of but parallel to Tesson Ferry Road, crossing Baptist Church Road. This segment may have been graded. With the extension, the line was six miles long. It crossed Gravois Creek four times.

The two first-day cars were swamped by thousands anxious to ride the new line. Powerhouse capacity was adequate for 25 cars, suggesting

Intramural cars 99 (left) and 2 (right), plus others outside one of the Fair's deceptively permanent-looking structures, in this case the Palace of Transportation.

extensions were foreseen. The Luxembourg area around Lemay Ferry Road was a growing suburb while the cement plant was a guaranteed source of revenue. A possible northeast extension to Etzel Avenue and west on Olive Street Road to Creve Coeur Lake would *"cross every steam and electric railroad entering St Louis, and land residents of Webster Groves, Kirkwood and othercommunities...on the South Side in about half the time heretofore required."* (St. Louis Watchman-Advocate August 2nd, 1912 p. 1.)

By 1918, there were five one-man cars, but auto competition was undermining the Grand View. It struggled through the next few years, discontinuing passenger service in 1926.*"The Grand View Railroad, a six-mile line in Kirkwood (sic), has been discontinued.The St. Louis Bus Company, a subsidiary of UR...(is) to substitute buses...The route the bus company would operate is two miles...(and) would connect with the Broadway and Bellefontaine car lines"* ERJ February 13th, 1926 (p. 299). This was the 2.2 mile Lemay Ferry bus line. Freight service continued until 1931.

Incomplete Roster Notes

In 1915 there were four closed cars, one single-truck open car and a few oddments, believed to be UR hand-me-downs. By 1918, there were five cars of unknown type, converted to one-man operation by the early 1920s.

C. **Louisiana Purchase Exposition Company Intramural Railroad**
Technological change in electric traction was as rapid as change in digital technology today, as the Intramural Railroad of the 1904 St. Louis World's Fair was intended to demonstrate. Built in 1903, it had seven miles of double track and seventeen stations. A mile of oak forest was traversed within Forest Park and more than two miles ran through the showier parts of the Fair. An unwired connection from MoPac's Manchester Road tracks ran to the north and into Forest Park to link with the Intramural. Some of this was used until relatively recent times for local railroad switching and though disused, a small section is still in place. Frustratingly, though the line was seen and ridden by millions in its short life, few photos have survived. Its first six cars arrived in January 1904. On the 27th the "Arkansas" (the first into service) made two trips. Twenty members of the General Passenger and Ticket Agents Association rode on one, delegates to the National Auditors' Association on the other. On opening day (April 30th, 1904), the line opened at 4:00 p.m and forty cars went out on a three-minute schedule. The line was not laid out for continuous loop service as stations one and seventeen (east and west Lindell at the main entrance) weren't linked, though within 600 feet of each other.

A typical Intramural station, with heavy-duty turnstiles (left) and crowd pens behind the solitary standing woman (right). The dual tracks allow freight trains with wider cars to pass through without hitting the platforms. The junction in the foreground is unidentified; it may be a spur to the car house.

In retropsect this was a mistake, but at the time it was felt this broad avenue between the stations was needed so as not to*"deface the fine central view of the 'main picture'"* (SRR June 20th, 1904 p. 349). There was criticism that much of the line wasn't built in front of the spectacularly-landscaped pavilions but instead skulked around back-stage, international tourists being treated to the unedifying spectacle of the Fair in not-ready-for-prime-time mode. This was an unavoidable consequence of its dual purpose as in-house railroad for the Fair's construction and demolition, and in-house transit system during the Fair. For almost a year prior to the April 1904 opening, and for weeks afterwards, steam freights used the Intramural to deliver building materials and exhibits to the pavilions.

Initial car service was 8:00 a.m. to 11:00 p.m. as the line was still needed for rail delivery of late exhibits. This was not good enough. Long lines of passengers remained nightly at 10:45 when cars were already dead-heading to the barns. Tempers flared but the crush of waiting freight cars could not be ignored. A G-D report on May 3rd claimed 639 freight cars had arrived in the last two days alone. Some pavilions were incomplete until June and sometimes the line had to be given over to all-day rail-freight deliveries, passenger cars not going out at all. Once things settled down cars ran multiple-unit on most trips until midnight, taking between 40 and 60 minutes from end to end.

Car 101 at St. Louis Car, December 21st, 1911, awaiting delivery.

However, the two St. Louis trolley systems stole the Intramural's thunder, daily delivering to the Fair a hundred thousand or more between them and taking them away again with comfort and safety and dispatch. It's not known when the wires came down, but the line itself wasn't dismantled until at least the end of 1905; it took nearly a year just to tear down the Fair and the line was constantly used by railroad freights, hauling away exhibits and debris.

Incomplete Roster Notes

Fifty cars were built by St. Louis Car in 1903/4, on Saint Louis 23-A trucks, with 4 GE 70 40HP motors, GE type-M multiple-unit train control, Van Dorn couplers and Christensen multiple-unit air-brakes. They were dark blue and either numbered 51-100 or named for a U.S. state or territory. Only a few poor photos survive, but a couple confusingly show the cars without state names and with numbers

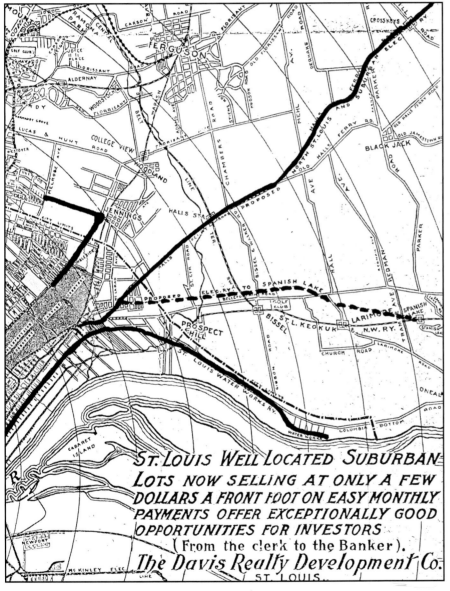

Map (from left) showing the St. Louis and Jennings from Robin Avenue, via West Florissant to Helen Avenue, then Helen Avenue to Melrose. This 1909 map precedes development of the area that fed the trolley. Next comes the proposed North St. Louis and Suburban Electric Railway, about which nothing is known, running from the Baden Torea on Halls Ferry Road past Cross Keys to the river. A branch to Spanish Lake, roughly paralleling Bellfontaine Road was no more than talk. Finally the Waterworks line is shown.

During the 1919-1926 United Railways bankruptcy, the clamor for route extensions went unheeded until the bankruptcy judge in 1924 allowed UR to operate buses, using its new St. Louis Bus Company subsidiary to counter competition from other companies. The first buses were run as suburban feeders to existing street railway lines and a little later as replacements for the St. Louis and Jennings. This advertisement was placed in local newspapers on January 12th, 1925.

A train of 600-class cars for the Pacific Electric Railway, Los Angeles, hauled by St. Louis Car Company Locomotive 1 in 1924, approaches the plant's set-out point for TRRA locomotives to pick up the trains.

ranging from 2 to 99. A rolling exhibit for suppliers such as GE and St. Louis Car, they sported air whistles and an automobile horn. Ten 14-bench open cars (1-10) on St. Louis 47 trucks were also built. SRR June 20th, 1904 (p. 348) however, says there were 51 closed cars and 7 opens, perhaps an error so far as the opens are concerned, but St. Louis Car did build a closed postal car for the Intramural in 1903. Whether it ran on the line and what became of it, isn't known. After the fair, ten closed cars went to the Chicago, North Shore and Milwaukee as 29-38, the rest went to KC's MET as 220-259. Of the opens, 1-6 went to the MET as 685-690 and were later rebuilt as closed cars. The fate of the rest is unknown, though two possibly showed up in Nevada MO. After the Fair closed, it's not known if there were further electric movements on Intramural tracks.

D. **St. Louis and Jennings Railway Company** This suburban real-estate line was backed by David P. Leahy, who sold 700 lots in the 2500-lot sub-division once he received his franchise; a record as the property had been on the market just four months (P-D July 9th, 1911).From December 19th, 1911 to early 1923, cars ran every 15 minutes (for a three cent fare) from UR's Union line terminal at Robin Avenue via West Florissant Avenue to its car house at Jennings Station Road. At busy times there was a six-minute service. A 6-block extension on Helen Avenue to Melrose opened at the end of 1915 (the West Walnut Manor line). There were unfulfilled plans to go downtown. Jitney competition bankrupted the company but a 1923 citizens' committee bought it for $35,000, intending to use the city's two Birneys once they reopened the line. Why their plans failed isn't known.

Incomplete Roster Notes

Four cars may have been owned, but reports conflict. One version says two cars (101/2) on St. Louis 47 trucks were built new by Saint Louis Car in 1911 and repaired by them about 3 months later and that the other two cars were single-truck. Another version is that 101/2 were ex-St. Louis and Suburban/UR Robertson-sill "Palace" cars and the other two unidentified single-truckers for the Helen Avenue shuttle, possibly ex-UR.

E. **St. Louis Car Company.** The 64-acre Baden plant stretched from present-day Hall Street to the railroad tracks by the Mississippi. It had electrified mixed-gauge test, switching and dispatch tracks, the first laid when the plant opened on this site circa 1897. These interchanged with the TRRA and other local railroads. The adjacent Waterworks line was sometimes used to test cars and locomotives on a longer stretch of road. Electric operation ceased in the 1960s but most tracks were used until

A transformer wagon for Stone and Webster Corporation sits on the transfer table, waiting to be picked up by locomotive 3 and towed through St. Louis Car's deserted shipping yard early in 1931. Locomotive 1 (right) is missing a set of wheels.

1974. In later years there was a remarkable selection of switchers including IT Class B locomotives 1567, 1568 & 1575, the last now at the St. Louis Museum of Transportation.

F. **St. Louis, Lakewood & Grant Park Railway Company** This standard-gauge line was a project of the Nicholls-Ritter Real Estate and Financial Company to develop new suburbs. SRJ September 7, 1907 (ad p.40) noted two miles were graded and that five summer cars, four box cars and three flat cars would be bought. It ran on a mile of right-of-way, from UR's Cherokee terminal on Gravois at Germania to Lakewood, Forest Heights and Grant Park, still farmland when the line opened in 1908, by which time it had changed owners several times. Until 1912 a car ran hourly—but profitably since the terminal boasted several new sub-divisions.

A branch was officially known as the Carondelet and Webster Groves Railroad Company. It was to have been eight miles long and independent of the Grant Park (SRJ November 9th 1907 ad p. 20). Willard E. Winner (the Kansas City developer) was its promoter so it may have been intended to serve further new suburbs. However, when opened in early 1908, it was a simple one-mile freight-only branch, serving a stone quarry. In 1909, the Grant Park was said to be building an extension with the quarry line as a jumping-off point, to connect with UR in Webster Groves. Two miles was reported ready for opening as of May 15th, 1909 (American Street Railway Investments, 1909), with the rest by summer, but it's doubtful a single yard was built.

Winner was now general manager and early in July 1912 extended the line closer to Affton, hoping to reach the Sunset Inn by fall, Fenton and the Meramec river after that. Grading on a Fenton extension did begin in 1912 (G-D, July 13th, 1912) but was never finished. On August 19th 1915, floods washed out a bridge over the River Des Peres and all service ceased. President Henri Chouteau's decision to quit jeopardised the securities of several stockholders including a Mrs. Margaret Milford who in 1917 petitioned for a receiver. Outstanding capital was $300,000 and funded debt $85,000. An April 17th, 1918 Circuit Court ruling allowed the rails to be sold for the war effort. Hoffman and Company bought it all, including 3 cars, for $20,527. The right-of-way was not sold until 1924.

Incomplete Roster Notes

Initially there was one passenger and three freight cars. Cars ran hourly, UR supplied power. ASRI 1909 reported three cars with 2 WH 800 25HP motors and no air brakes. In May 1910, former Baltimore City and Suburban car 73 (Fowler, 1894, by now Baltimore United Railways #2309) arrived. Poor's 1912 noted two passenger and three freight cars, one a single truck water sprinkler (for weed killing) which may have been UR sprinkler 61 or 62 (Lindell Railway circa 1895). It is not clear if freight cars for stone-hauling) were motored. McGraw 1914 claimed eight cars, but by 1915 only one single-truck and two double-truck cars survived, possibly former UR cars. UR was paid for neither the cars nor power, these being Grant Park debts when the receiver was called in.

G. **St. Louis, St. Charles and Western RR Co.** In June, 1896, the Wellston, Creve Coeur Lake and St. Charles Railway Company was incorporated by J. .D. Houseman and J.B.C. Lucas. Houseman had at least one real estate development along the line and possibly an interest in Camp Marvin. On July 8, 1899, it opened from Wellston to Lucas Park (now Normandy Golf Club), mostly along St. Charles Rock Road. It reached the German Protestant Orphan Home (now the Evangelical Children's Home) in Pattonville at the end of 1900.

At this time, it was renamed St. Louis, St. Charles and Western and began building a branch north from St. Charles Rock Road into Bridgeton which opened in 1901, the main line reaching the Missouri River soon after. Passengers completed their trip to St. Charles in a Company-owned ferry. Its captain and Houseman were on poor terms having at least one, possibly more, knock-down, drag-out fist fights over the ferry's erratic operation. Once a bridge opened on April 18th 1904, the line was extended over it into St. Charles. But it was in difficulties and was sold at foreclosure on July 24th 1905 to UR interests which ran it until July 1908, when the **Missouri Electric Railroad** was incorporated as a UR subsidiary to run the line and its two branches-St.Peter's (the old St. Louis County Street Railway horse line on Lucas & Hunt) and Bridgeton. This was done in part so a higher fare could be charged on this loss-making rural interurban. However, by 1925, the area east of Woodson Road had built up to the point that additional short-turn service (UR's Woodson Road line) was needed.

The line was cut back to Coles Avenue (Overland) in January 1932 to facilitate a federal highway widening and realignment project and avoid a grade crossing over Lindbergh Boulevard, then under construction. Bridging Lindbergh was not an option. The St. Charles service continued with buses, which had already replaced the branches a few months earlier and had supplemented the cars for years. The Woodson Road cars were extended a few hundred yards west to Coles Avenue. The separate corporate existence continued until 1939, as Missouri Electric's assets and property were not part of the 1933-39 SLPS bankruptcy. In 1909, sixteen cars ran the line, mostly numbered in the 3000 series. All were gone by 1936 except for 3009, which soldiered on for years. The Woodson Road line closed in December 1948.

H. **United Railways/Saint Louis Public Service Company** had a materials yard at the 39th & Park facility. Several tracks were standard gauge, served by home-built locomotives 97-99. For decades, supplies came by rail and the locomotives switched railroad cars to where they were needed for loading and unloading. The yards opened circa 1900 and survived closure of the 70-Grand line on January 3rd, 1960 by several years.

3. ST. LOUIS INTERURBANS (OPERATING, PART-BUILT AND PROPOSED)

General note Only Illinois Traction had significant St. Louis trackage. The other Illinois lines ended at Eads Bridge Plaza, feet away from but not connected to UR's 4' 10" gauge lines looping at Third and Washington. Cars crossed the TRRA-owned Eads bridge using trackage rights over TRRA's **St. Louis and East St. Louis Electric Railway** subsidiary, which linked to the East St. Louis and Suburban system. All these companies were for a time owned or controlled by Julius Walsh, a local magnate who at one time was president of the TRRA and the St. Louis **Union Depot Railway**. Thus East St. Louis lines were initially to St. Louis's 4' 10" gauge. Walsh sold his East St. Louis lines in 1902 to the E. W. Clarke

Mitchell viaduct circa 1906, showing ramps and steep curves onto and off the bridge.

AG & STL car 31 at American Car August 28th, 1909, awaiting delivery.

The Great Street Car service of Granite City, St. Louis Post-Dispatch, October 31st, 1905.

ny bought the Bellefontaine bus line with routes from Baden to Black Jack, Spanish Lake, Riverview Gardens and (seasonal) Chain of Rocks. It also had an isolated car line between Brooklyn/National City (Collinsville and St. Clair Avenues) and North Venice which interchanged with East St. Louis lines. Cars ran hourly (half-hourly at rush hours) until closure on April 6th, 1929. In March 1931, the IT took over the Alton, over which it had enjoyed trackage rights since November 14th, 1906, to avoid its closure cutting off access to the McKinley Bridge. All cars were diverted onto IT's relocated St. Louis tracks in 1931. On February 4th, 1932 the Mitchell-Edwardsville branch closed. In 1936 the main line on Alton's streets was diverted to newly-electrified tracks once belonging to the Alton and Eastern and Chicago, and Peoria and St. Louis railroads. The Alton line closed March 7th, 1953, St. Louis-Granite City, June 22nd, 1958.

ii. Alton Granite and St. Louis Traction Company Alton itself, on the Mississippi River about 25 miles north of St. Louis, had horse cars from 1868 and electrics from 1893. Competition and mergers led to consolida-

(Philadelphia) syndicate. All ESTL lines became standard-gauge in 1905 when it was clear McKinley's Illinois Traction was targeting the city on its long march down from Danville, Peoria and Springfield.

1. **Alton Granite and St. Louis Traction Company** and successors.
i. Alton Granite and St. Louis Traction Company Incorporated February 1904 and capitalized at $100,000, the first segment from Nieder-inghaus Avenue (Granite City) to Long Lake (Wood River) opened June 13th 1904 for Sunday afternoon trips. Alton-Mitchell opened February 2nd 1905, the full line to Granite City and the Venice ferry (for St. Louis) on March 1st. Laid to 4' 10" gauge, it was re-gauged to standard in 1905. Mitchell-Edwardsville (**Edwardsville, Alton and St. Louis Railway**) opened circa 1906. In August 1920, inflation and low fares put the Alton into receivership until sale to North American and reorganization as the **St. Louis and Alton Railroad** on December 1st, 1926. The rest of the Alton's utilities were sold to North American separately. In 1927 there were 27 cars (three inoperable), a trailer, two box cars and a line car. Cars ran hourly plus six daily "limiteds."

From 1926, buses ran St. Louis-Alton and on June 12th, 1928 the compa-

AG & STL interurbans 3 and 7 at Eads Bridge Plaza circa 1912.

AG & STL interurban 8, Eads Bridge Plaza circa 1925.

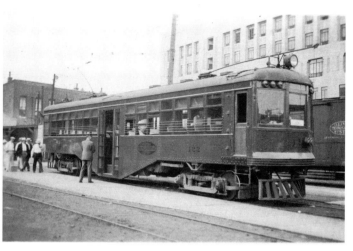

From 1931, the former AG & STL became part of the Illinois Terminal system. Car 123 at the temporary IT St. Louis station, July 3rd, 1932. R. V. Mehlenbeck.

tion of its city lines into the Alton Railway Gas and Electric Company by 1904, a subsidiary of the AG & STL and thus part of the East St. Louis and Suburban. Further reorganization in the 1920s spun off the city lines from the parent AG & STL into a new Alton Railway Company.

In 1927 there were 26 cars (six inoperable) of which nine were Birneys, plus three work cars and a training car and about 16 miles of track. When Illinois Terminal bought the property from Union Electric in March 1931, a further 14 Birneys were transferred to Alton from Galesburg Il. City service ceased early a. m. August 27th, 1936. However, IT continued run-

Interurban 101, Alton circa 1949. The drumhead reads Alton-St. Louis local, Electric Way, the Mississippi is on the left. Ray Gehl/Mark Goldfeder collection.

Beyond the Alton grain elevators, the electrified line petered out (wires visible to the left) and a non-electrified line ran alongside the Mississippi to Grafton. In its latter years passengers were served by a 1939 White bus converted to run on rails. Ray Gehl/Mark Goldfeder collection.

(Left) Illinois terminal car 104 at Federal, IL, circa 1952. This car now operates at the St. Louis Museum of Transportation. Ray Gehl/Mark Goldfeder collection.

(Above) Alton Birney 169 on Alby at 6th Street on Memorial Day 1935. Stephen M. Scalzo collection.

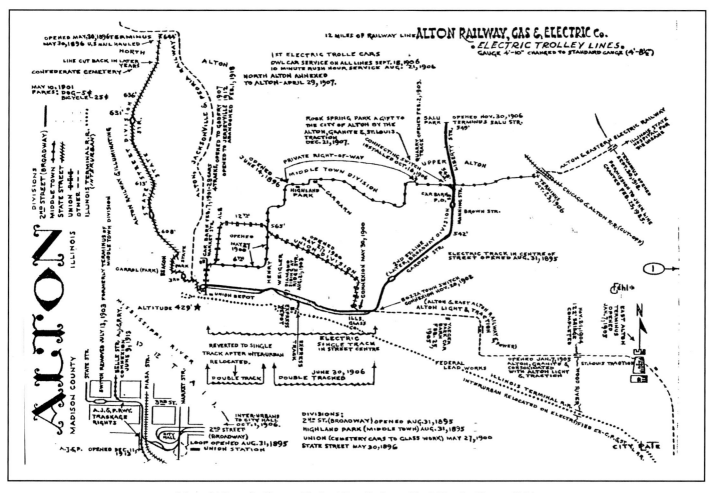

Map of Alton city lines, with the Alton Jacksonville & Peoria. George Fehl.

ning a Birney over former St. Louis and Alton street trackage from Cut Street in Alton down to Wood River until October 28th, 1936.

2. **Alton, Jacksonville and Peoria Railway Company** Branded by Hilton and Due as *"one of the most complete failures of all interurbans,"* the *"Piasa route"* in fact had a longer and marginally more successful life than Missouri's Mexico Perry and Santa Fe. Incorporated in November 1904, it planned an Alton-Peoria line (140 miles to the northeast) via Jerseyville, Carrollton, White Hall, Rood House and Jacksonville, on or close to today's U.S. 67. It was to parallel existing railroads much of the way, but the promise of speedy localized service, shorter route, cheaper fares and cleanliness of electric travel must have been irresistible. It was capitalized for $800,000 and most officers and investors were Jerseyville and Alton folk including Andrew W. Cross and Aaron A. Auten. J. J. Cummings of the McGuire-Cummings Car Manufacturing Company,Paris IL was also involved.

In practical terms, however, the six-mile line to Godfrey in Madison County merely fed Alton's city lines and the interurban to St. Louis. It opened August 20th, 1907 using hired Alton cars until their own car (a pre-owned single-trucker) was put into hourly service on August 29th. Three refurbished double-truck cars came from St. Louis's UR soon after

Alton cars 19 and 24, Public Square, Alton City Hall in back, circa 1910. Stephen M. Scalzo collection.

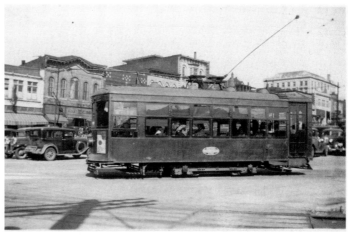

Alton Birney 170, Public Square circa 1933.

Alton Jacksonville and Peoria car 1 (a former 1890s UR of St. Louis vehicle of the 300-399 group) on Belle Street, Alton circa 1912. Stephen M. Scalzo collection.

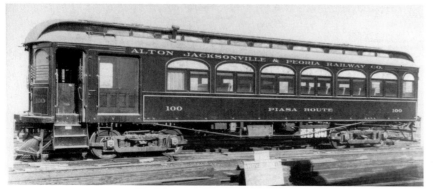

Combine 100, awaiting delivery at American Car, November 5th, 1911. Because the AJ&P couldn't pay for it, this and its four companions never ran on the line.

and service became half-hourly. It began at Third and Belle in Alton. By 1913 it had been extended down to the river landing and a connection with Alton's State Street line. On Belle it ran to just north of Valley Road, then right-of-way north to West Delmar, west on West Delmar and Chouteau to its first stop, Greenwood Cemetery in North Alton. From there it mostly used the road (U. S. 67), veering off before reaching Godfrey.

So it might have remained, jogging along in barely-just-better-than-break-even mode, but for the desire to build onwards to Peoria. The man with the most money in the line (A. W. Cross) died in February 1909. Hopes were pinned on his resources being able to carry the line the next sixteen miles from Godfrey to Jerseyville and that still seemed possible when his son-in-law Ed Davis took over. Instead, a 1910 bond issue financed the extension, which took an odd and difficult route via the Piasa Creek valley to McCluskey, ducked under the Chicago Peoria and St. Louis Railroad, then paralleled it into Jerseyville. With its twists and turns, bridges, culverts and rocky terrain, building expenses exceeded resources and the line went bankrupt in July 1911. Davis then skipped town with the company's cash and didn't resurface until October, where he was found in Los Angeles along with his brother, the line's treasurer. It took until 1914 to get them convicted of embezzlement

J. J. Cummings had provided cash and loans to reorganise the company. He now took direct control. Rumors a Jerseyville-Fieldon-Hardin branch opened January 23rd, 1911 are untrue but money was spent surveying the route; indeed as the **Central Traction Company** of 1904, it pre-dated the AJ&P. A. W. Cross and A. Auten were behind this project also, convinced that reaching the Illinois River via an area rich in resources and poor in transport, would be a sure-fire winner. The AJ&P's Godfrey-Jerseyville section began December 14th, 1912, with a formal opening on the 20th. It proved useless as a traffic generator. About 1800 feet of track was laid on Jerseyville's State Street from Barr south to Hickory but as the receivership and litigation continued, the town

A view along the East St. Louis and suburban's Edgemont-O'Fallon division August 18th, 1918. On the adjacent rail siding is a string of wagons including one of the East St. Louis & Suburban. STLMOT

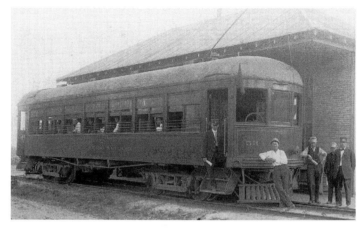

AJ & P interurban 53 at Jerseyville station December 16th, 1912 (first day). Bill Volkmer collection.

AJ & P interurban 53 at Jerseyville station circa 1915. Stephen M. Scalzo collection.

chose to distance itself from the AJ&P and embargoed the tracks within its limits. They were never used. The line ended just south of the city limits at Jersey Landing Road, a half mile short of downtown.

A May 1914 foreclosure led to a July reorganization as the **Alton and Jacksonville Railway Company** and more modest ambitions; Jacksonville being but 50 or so miles northeast of Jerseyville. The new owners were J.C. Van Riper (President of the American Trust Company) and a St. Louis syndicate. The Trust Company provided loans to pay receivership costs and all A&J securities were held by them as collateral. Operating profits of a few thousand dollars were made, but no paymernts were made on the bonds and further lawsuits began at the end of 1916.

It was believed Cummings had an agreement with the Clarke syndicate (East St. Louis and Suburban) to take over the A&J, but in November 1916 the line was sold to pay off Trust Company loans. The collateral still languishing in the Trust Company's vaults was bought by McKinley of the Illinois Traction. It was now the **Alton and Jacksonville Railroad**

Company but 1917's inflation and a quicker-than-expected deterioration of the many bridges and culverts wrecked the company within a few months. An attempt was made to close the Jerseyville extension in July 1917 but a restraining order was issued by the Illinois Public Utitlites Commission early in August, just as the wrecking crew was about to begin. Later in the month, the A&J applied for total closure, Alton-Godfrey being offered to East St. Louis and Suburban for scrap value, to be merged with Alton's city lines.

But it was losing too much money, was still in default of bond interest payments and was thousands of dollars in tax arrears. The Illinois Public Utilities Commission, hearing the abandonment application, was told that $65,000 to $90,000 was needed for repairs. It approved closure, remarking that the *"territory through which...(it) operates is not such as demands the operation of such a road, nor...make operation...under the most efficient management a profitable undertaking,"* suggesting it should never have been built in the first place (ERJ February 2nd, 1918

East St. Louis car 603 and passengers in the Eads bridge Plaza Station circa 1921. Just discernible in the murk behind the car is the Missouri Athletic Club on Washington; still a St. Louis landmark in 2006. STLMOT.

p .

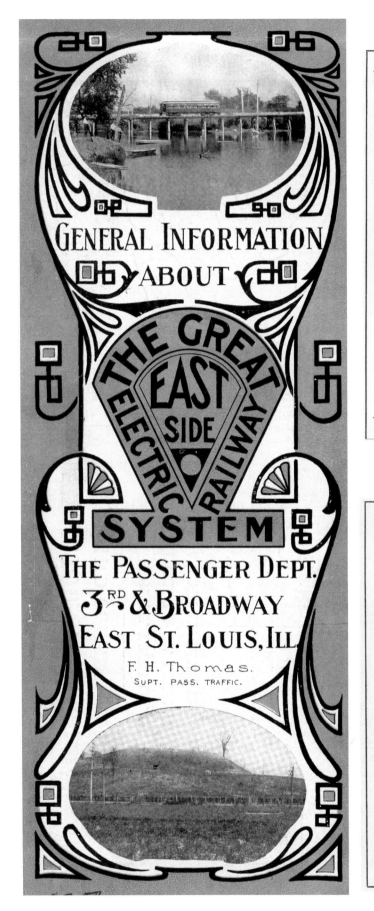

GENERAL INFORMATION ABOUT

THE GREAT EAST SIDE ELECTRIC RAILWAY SYSTEM

THE PASSENGER DEPT.
3RD & BROADWAY
EAST ST. LOUIS, ILL.

F. H. Thomas.
SUPT. PASS. TRAFFIC.

East St. Louis is just across the Mississippi River—a prosperous city of 85,000 people

East St. Louis, the second city of the great State of Illinois whose population and commercial importance have vastly increased during the past ten years.

The four-story structure on the left is the handsome new fire-proof building of the East St. Louis Railway Company. The General Offices of the East Side Electric Lines and related properties occupy this entire building.

STREET CARS PASS THIS POINT EVERY MINUTE

ENJOYABLE AND INTERESTING RIDES NEAR HOME

A bridge protected by heavy guard rail.

In conclusion, a trip around the Scenic Loop Route is an inexpensive but enjoyable evening's outing. Try it some hot evening when you are trying to cool off, and you will return to your home refreshed in mind and body and be ready for a night's sound sleep.

On the line.

One of the electric sprinklers used by the East Side Electric Lines, a powerful factor in overcoming dust and rendering street car riding more pleasant.

SEE YOUR OWN COUNTY'S BEAUTIES FIRST

600 ELECTRIC TRAINS A DAY LEAVE EADS BRIDGE TROLLEY STATION

THIS is the time of year when people who cannot afford to go far away to spend their vacation, are seeking some nearby-places to catch relief for a few days or hours from the humdrum of busy life. The Scenic Loop Route offers just such recreation. A ride on swiftly moving trolley cars through the country, with its fresh air and pastoral scenes, pleasing to the eye, affords real comfort and refreshment to a weary one. This opportunity is now right at your door. Take a trolley car at Eads Bridge Station, Third and Washington Avenue, St. Louis; get away for even a few hours from the sun-scorched confines of a crowded city, out into the freshness of the country on the Great East Side, and ride around the Scenic Loop Route, which embraces about 50 miles and gives you two and one-half hours of health-giving fresh air. Crossing the delightful and breezy Mississippi River, through East St. Louis, Granite City (famous for its rolling mills, steel plants, car works and granite ware mills), thence passing various fishing resorts, Eagle Park Lake, Long Lake and Chouteau Slough, the trip continues through rich fields of green corn many acres in extent. This is the most beautiful and fertile agricultural section of the State.

At Mitchell, the Loop Route diverges to the right as the car travels towards Edwardsville. From Mitchell the view in the distance of the green covered ranges of the Illinois Bluffs extending to the south and the north as far as the eye can reach, is one of beauty and grandeur, rivaling even the most pretentious mountain scenery.

EADS BRIDGE TROLLEY STATION, ST. LOUIS, MISSOURI, the Electric Gateway to the Great East Side, through which thousands of busy people pass daily and are brought into quick communication by the East Side Electric Lines with more than a dozen prosperous Illinois cities, and many places for recreation.

DUSTLESS, DIRTLESS, SMOKELESS—THAT'S THE ELECTRIC WAY

Away from the city's maddening noise, "where stillness like a poultice heals the wound of sound."

A quiet shady stream on the Mitchell-Edwardsville Line "There would I loiter, ponder, sit and read. Never, never taking heed. . . ."

Surviving East St. Louis city lines circa 1931.

A. *Stockyards, from Eads Bridge via Broadway, Collinsville and St. Clair. Cars ran every 12 minutes, six minutes in rush hours.

B. *Lansdowne, from Eads Bridge via Broadway, Collinsville, St. Clair, 13th, Nectar and Lincoln. A branch left here along 25th and east on Natalie to 29th Street and Jones Park, but this was only used occasionally. The main line continued on from Lincoln to Waverly. Here there was a junction, one branch going via Forest Park to the Alton and Southern tracks in Washington Park, the other via Caseyville Avenue to Kingshighway in the Rosemont subdivision. Cars ran every 10 minutes.

C. *State Street, from Eads Bridge via Broadway, Collinsville, Illinois and State Streets to 42nd Street. Cars ran every 15 minutes. However, St. Louis-Belleville cars also used this line every 15 minutes, so giving an overlapping service of 7.5 minutes as far as 42nd Street.

D. Cleveland Avenue. From Relay depot (west of 1st Street on Missouri Avenue) via Missouri, 14th, Cleveland, Illinois, Louisiana and 27th Streets to the St. Louis and Belleville right-of-way. Cars ran every 15 minutes.

E. Broadway, from Main Street and Southern Railroad crossing via Broadway, 22nd and Missouri Avenue to 32nd Street. Cars ran every 18 minutes, 12 in rush hours.

F. Alta Sita-Main, from Broadway and Main via Main, Converse, 6th and Piggott to 15th and from Broadway and Main via Broadway, 15th and Bond Avenues to 43rd. Cars ran every 15 minutes, 12 in rush hours.

* These lines operated through to Eads Bridge Plaza, St. Louis. There were also four bus routes by 1929 of which St. Clair Avenue incorporated the former Black Bridge to 18th and Lynch car line.

---

248). It closed on February 1st 1918. A move to have the Alton, Granite and St. Louis run it for 90 days from July 26th 1918, failed.

Incomplete Roster notes

Three maximum-traction cars (1-3), one nicknamed "Canary," were bought from UR, part of their 300-399 batch built in 1897 for an unknown predecessor. Ex-Baltimore single-truck car 317 (Brill, 1893) was AJ&P 42. Five interurbans (100-104, American, 1911) came early in 1912, but the company couldn't pay for them. 102-4 were sold to East St. Louis Columbia and Waterloo as their 20-22. 100/1 were sold to the Kankakee and Urbana Traction Company of Urbana IL. In December 1912, four more cars (50-53) came to the AJ&P from Cummings, but were sold in 1917/18 to Manhattan KS.

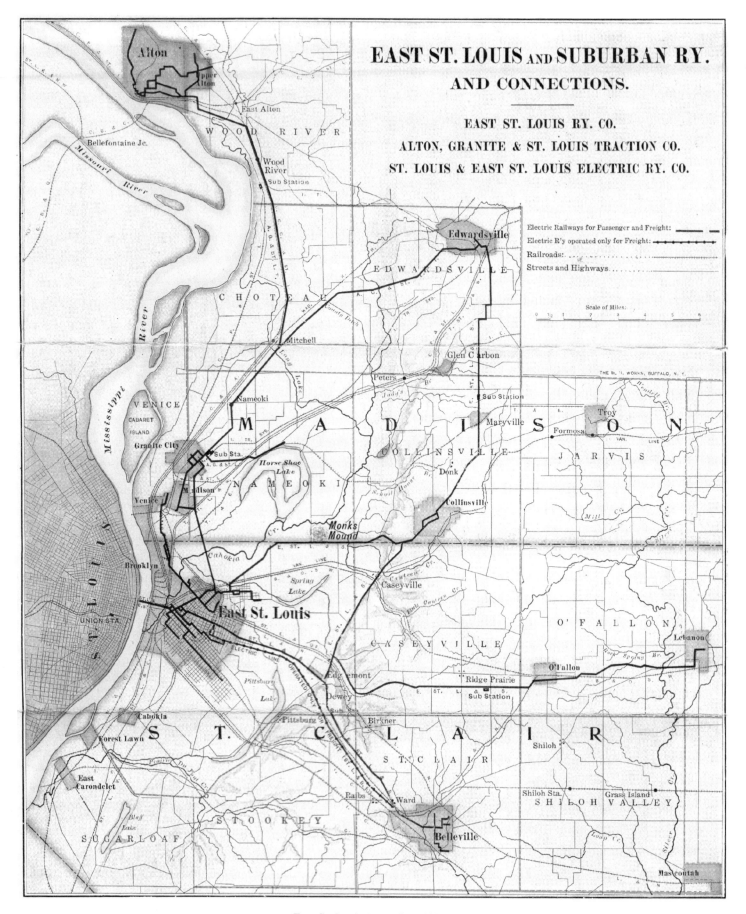

East St. Louis Area, circa 1905.

Eads Bridge looking east over the Mississippi, circa 1933. Mark Goldfeder collection.

Car 613 and another, Eads Bridge Plaza, St. Louis, looking west circa 1930. David J. Neubauer collection.

Broadway near 19th Street, East St. Louis Fall 1933. The track is serviceable but worn, the brick-paved road surface, however, has sunk around the railheads. STLMOT

A new Chicago and West Towns car came from McGuire-Cummings to run Alton-Godfrey from January 3rd 1918 until closure.

3. Chicago and St. Louis Electric Railway Company A visionary idea of St. Louisan Dr. Wellington Adams, wedge-nosed multi-phase electric locomotives were to haul trains at speeds up to 100 mph on a dead-straight double-track line, missing every significant town between Chicago and St. Louis on a 150 to 180-minute 248-mile run. (SRJ March 1892 p. 174). The shortest steam line was 284 miles. Passenger trains would run until 9:00 p.m, freight, express and mail would run at night. There would be no Pullman sleepers, the fast trip would make them unecessary. It would be ready for the 1893 Chicago Fair. By summer 1892 it had $6.5 million capital, mostly subscribed in New York and St. Louis, the rest backed by bonds. By December, the line was *"more prominent before the public than ever, notwithstanding the great mystery which surrounds all its actions."* (SRJ December 1892 p. 757). Six miles was graded north of Edinburg IL, but no track or overhead was installed.

4. East St. Louis and Suburban Railway Company This holding company, set up in 1901 as the **St. Louis and Illinois Interurban Railway** changed its name in 1902 to ESTL&SRC when the East St. Louis properties were acquired from Julius Walsh and the TRRA by E. W. Clark's Philadelphia syndicate. Between then and 1906 it merged the East St. Louis Railway, St. Louis and East St. Louis Railway (Eads bridge tracks into Missouri) and the East St. Louis and Suburban Railway, its operating arm. It also owned all Alton Granite and St. Louis stock, the St. Louis and Belleville Electric Railway plus city lighting utilities of Alton and East St. Louis. Edwards Whitaker and David R. Francis, two of the "big cinch" movers and shakers behind St. Louis's United Railways and members of its board of directors, were also on the East St. Louis & Suburban's board.

The city system was compact, with many short, heavily-traveled lines. All were one-man operated by the 1920s. The longer interurban lines were superimposed onto city tracks, going out to Alton, Belleville, Collinsville, Edwardsville, Granite City, Lebanon, Madison, O'Fallon and Venice. In the early 1900s these were cherished Sunday-afternoon outings for bi-state folks. In the 1906-1910 period there was 175 miles of track, about 150 cars, three express cars, 21 work cars, two electric locomotives, two steam locomotives and

610 coal cars, these last used on the all-freight St. Louis and Bellville Electric Railway (opened 1898) which ran from East St. Louis to an interchange with the Illinois Central Railroad just west of Belleville.

St. Louis trackage was confined to the western (Missouri) half of the Eads Bridge road (top) deck, ending at Eads Bridge Plaza at 3rd and Washington. The Eads Bridge horse-car shuttle between St. Louis and East St. Louis began in 1874 when the bridge opened. After a hiatus of a few years, it was electrified in 1889. Initially, ESL&S cars were banned as too heavy for the road deck. Runs thus ended in East St. Louis, riders transferring to the smaller electric cars into St. Louis. Later, bigger cars were allowed across the bridge to the Plaza.

Years of deferred maintenance, ridership decline and losses killed this impressive transit sysem. The Clarks in 1923 sold it ro the North American Company, on behalf of its subsidiary Union Electric Company, the St. Louis electric utility. The purchase was made to acquire the electric utility business in East St. Louis and vicinity; the trolleys came as part of the package. Union Electric bought the properties from North American in 1928 but leased the Alton Granite and St. Louis subsidiary (now the St. Louis and Alton) to Illinois Terminal from July 1st, 1930. It sold the Alton Railway Company (Alton's city lines) to Illinois Terminal on March 1st, 1930 for $10,000

In Belleville, the Oakland line went bus on July 1st, 1924, the other Belleville city lines on June 1st, 1926, due to operating losses, reconstruction costs of $40,000-plus and demands for extensions which there was no money to build. Blue Goose buses replaced the Edwardsville (via Collinsville) and Edgemont-Collinsville (via French Village) lines from October 14th, 1928, Lebanon via O'Fallon on December 1st, 1928 and the Belleville interurban early on July 24th, 1932. Vandalia Bus lines replaced the Collinsville interurban on the same day and State Street city cars weere extended over the Belleville interurban as far as Edgemont (89th Street).The last East St. Louis cars (and the bridge line) went bus in October 1935. The St. Louis and Belleville electric freight line was now owned by Union Electric. Dieselized by 1951 and bought by Peabody Coal in 1958. it ran until the 1970s.

Belleville Public Square (Main and Illinois) circa 1905. Stephen Scalzo collection.

The St. Louis and Belleville began as a passenger-carrying interurban in 1898, but unlike its rival a few blocks further north, could not access St. Louis via the Eads Bridge. Once the two Belleville lines came under common East St. Louis ownership, the St. Louis and Belleville was turned over to heavy electric freight operation, its miles of private right-of-way being ideally suited to this purpose. Car 4, one of eight ordered for the line's inauguration, is seen at the new St. Louis Car plant in 1898, before delivery.

St. Louis & Belleville Locomotive 600 and train, Centerville, circa 1947. Stephen M. Scalzo collection.

Columbia. The trip took 75 minutes and cars eventually ran every 90 minutes, but sometimes hourly.

The East St. Louis terminal was extended to Broadway and Collinsville Avenue on June 26th, 1913 to avoid a double transfer by St. Louis-bound passengers; onto East St. Louis Alta Sita line cars and then onto Eads bridge cars. A stub track for layovers was built south on Third. Through one-seat service across the Mississippi into St. Louis's Eads Bridge Plaza began on June 5th, 1915. Freight services, however, were confined to Illinois.

In 1914, capital was $1 million, though $750,000 was outstanding. E. H. Conrades was president, E. C. Donk vice-president, both of St. Louis. 600V D.C. Power was bought from the ESTL&S's Winstanley plant. There were connections with the Alton and Southern in East St. Louis, with the TRRA and MoPac in Dupo, and the Mobile and Ohio Railroad in Columbia. Spur tracks served the Schorr Brewery and the Petri and Hill lumber yard in Waterloo and other customers at various points on the line.

It was sold early July 1924 for $335,000 to a St. Louis syndicate headed by Charles H. Lemp, Vice-President of Liberty Central Trust Company, owned by Merchants and Manufacturers Investment Company which also owned Donk Brothers' Coal Company stock and the coal-hauling Troy and Eastern steam railroad. Lemp claimed to have bought it as an investment and it certainly had paid until his purchase.

However the new concrete Illinois Route 3 was opened in 1925, paralleling almost every inch of the line, after which things tanked. On April 19th, 1932, $92,321 damages were awarded to E. W. Foristel, Charles A. Lemp and Mrs. Marie Finch for money loaned to the line on promissory notes. Within weeks, the St. Louis, Red Bud and Chester Motor Bus and Service Corporation put on buses, the line decided not to compete and the last interurban ran on May 31st, 1932.

Freight continued, but the line declared bankruptcy on October 31st, 1934. It is not clear if subsequent trains were hauled by electric or steam traction; certainly by the

5. East St. Louis, Columbia & Waterloo Railway

With 22.9 miles of standard-gauge track, this company had an additional 2.5 miles of trackage rights over the Eads Bridge and on East St. Louis tracks on Broadway, 15th and Bond Avenue to reach its own tracks at Nineteenth and Bond Avenue. This was street running, repeated in Columbia and Waterloo, but otherwise it ran on right-of-way, sometimes cross-country, sometimes side-of-road. It entered Waterloo along Main Street, ending in a wye at Mill Steet and the courthouse in the town's main square. Incorporated in 1906, it was capitalized at $10,000. In 1907, while raising more money, there was talk of reaching Cairo IL via Red Bud, Sparta and Murphysboro, taking in the coal and oil belt.

Ultimately the line was financed by selling almost all its stock to the Merchants and Manufacturers' Investment Company. Construction began in east St. Louis during 1910 and on the remainder in the summer of 1911. A test car ran on May 24th 1912, the first eight-mile section opening from Bond and 19th to Dupo next day (fare-free until June 1st). A six-mile section opened to Columbia on August 12th and the last into Waterloo on December 20th, the line now running from 19th and Bond in East St. Louis to Waterloo via Cahokia, Prairie Du Pont, Dupo and

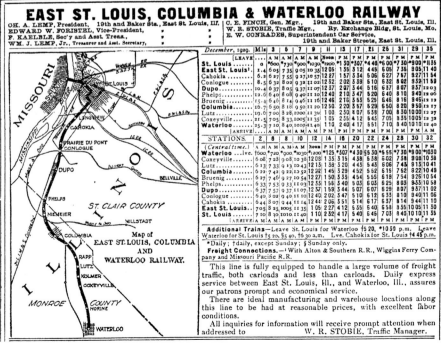

EAST ST. LOUIS, COLUMBIA & WATERLOO RAILWAY

CH. A. LEMP, President, 19th and Baker Sts., East St. Louis, Ill.
EDWARD W. FORISTEL, Vice-President,
F. KAELBLE, Sec'y and Asst. Treas.,
WM. J. LEMP, Jr., Treasurer and Asst. Secretary,
C. E. FINCH, Gen. Mgr., 19th and Baker Sts., East St. Louis, Ill.
W. R. STOBIE, Traffic Mgr., Ry. Exchange Bldg, St. Louis, Mo.
E. W. CONRADES, Superintendent Car Service, 19th and Baker Streets, East St. Louis, Ill.

Map of EAST ST. LOUIS, COLUMBIA AND WATERLOO RAILWAY.

Additional Trains—Leave St. Louis for Waterloo †5 20, *10 30 p.m. Leave Waterloo for St. Louis †5 20, §5 40, †6 30 a.m. Lve. Cahokia for St. Louis †4 45 p.m.
*Daily; †daily, except Sunday; § Sunday only.
Freight Connections.—† With Alton & Southern R.R., Wiggins Ferry Company and Missouri Pacific R.R.

This line is fully equipped to handle a large volume of freight traffic, both carloads and less than carloads. Daily express service between East St. Louis, Ill., and Waterloo, Ill., assures our patrons prompt and economical service.
There are ideal manufacturing and warehouse locations along this line to be had at reasonable prices, with excellent labor conditions.
All inquiries for information will receive prompt attention when addressed to W. R. STOBIE, Traffic Manager.

Waterloo car 1 at American Car circa 1912, awaiting delivery.

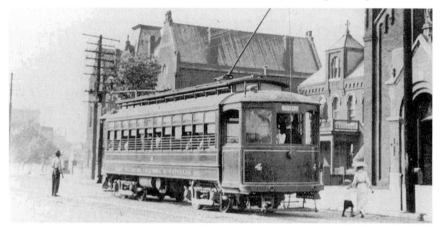

Waterloo car 4 believed to be Columbia IL circa 1913. Bill Volkmer collection.

time the last freight train ran on July 31st, 1936 it was by steam. By now the line was losing $30,000 a year, and was sold for its $58,000 scrap value. Some of the right of way was bought for an additional $16, 000 by St. Clair and Monroe counties and used to straighten Illinois Route 3. Unfortunately, the line's total debts topped $145,000

Incomplete Roster notes

(These notes were compiled with the help of Roy G. Benedict)

1-5 (American, 1912). 48-seat passenger cars with smoking compartments, air brakes, Brill 27-MCB1 6' wb. trucks GE airbrakes and 4 GE 203 50HP motors. They were painted red, Pullman green later and burnt sienna later still.

20-22 (American, 1910) Originally Alton Jacksonville and Peoria interurbans 102-4, the AJ&P couldn't pay for them and never ran them. They came to the Waterloo line in 1913, but were sold on to the Nipissing Central Railway in Ontario during 1917 (possibly earlier) as their 22, 24, 26. 30, 31 (American, 1913). Open trailer cars, sold to the Sand Springs Railway Oklahoma in 1915 as their 51 and 53, but destroyed in a barn fire December 18th, 1924.

100 (Wells and French 1895). Single-truck line car, believed once to have been North Chicago Street Railroad passenger car 938, later Chicago Railways 4038. It came to the Waterloo line in early 1912.

101/2 (Russell, 1912) Snow Plow.

200 (American, 1913). Baggage/Express car on Brill 27-MCB1 trucks, with 4 WH 317 75HP motors.

300 (St. Louis, 1920). Steel-bodied express car on St. Louis 23-ES trucks, with 4 WH 317 75HP motors.

McGraw 1918 calls cars 1-5 "light interurbans" plus single-truck line car 100), motor freight car 501 (sic) and 1 freight trailer car. McGraw 1928 reported five motors, two express cars and one motor service car, a three cents a mile fare and 600v D.C. power. By 1930, there were five passenger cars and one motor service car. Three cars are thought to have survived in dead storage at the line's 19th and Baker East St. Louis car barn until 1936.

6. **Hillsboro, Kimmswick and Northern Railroad Company**

See Grand View Railway Company in section 2 above.

Car 2 and what appears to be a school party, Waterloo IL, circa 1915. Bill Volkmer collection

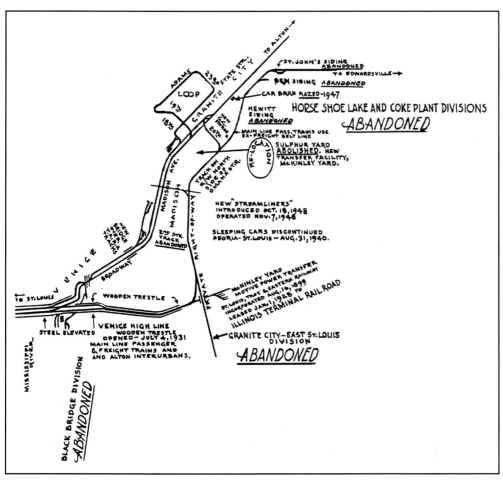

Street Railways and interurbans in Granite City IL circa 1940. George Fehl

the Indiana interurbans to create a through St. Louis-Port Huron-Detroit MI route to access Toledo and Cleveland OH and Erie PA. (SRJ July 6th, 1907 p. 38). But the gap between the IT at Danville and the nearest Indiana interurban, while small, was never bridged. Nor were interurbans ever built to or from Jefferson City though McKinley did have the idea in mind when he bought that city's town cars in 1912. Money was the issue. The IT couldn't fund a through line to Chicago plus build a bridge into St. Louis and onwards across Missouri, so McKinley (and his Canadian and British backers) eventually dropped Chicago to focus on the bridge and a short but crucial two miles in St. Louis. Known as the **St. Louis Electric Terminal Railway**, this IT subsidiary ran from the west bridge ramp at Salisbury Street, south on 9th Street onto a short right-of-way jogging over to 12th Street, then south on 12th to a terminal at Lucas.

The first test was on September 21st, 1910, when car 221 was towed over the bridge by a locomotive. On the St. Louis side, it ran under power. The bridge opened to traffic on October 1st, with a formal ceremony ten days later. From the outset, the IT ran freight over the bridge but St. Louis insisted that no more than two cars be hauled within city limits at night and one during the day, a restriction not relaxed until 1925. Express motor 1006 was rebuilt to resemble a passenger

7. **Illinois Traction System** This huge and long-lived interurban system was headed by William Brown Mckinley. Born September 5th 1856 in Petersburg IL, in 1887 he went into the banking and mortgage loan business. He assembled the IT out of local lines in Danville, Champaign Urbana from about 1901 and expanded it in stages over the next decade, ultimately linking Danville, Springfield, Bloomington/ Normal, Champaign/Urbana and Peoria with St. Louis. An isolated northern Illinois segment interchanged with Chicago-bound lines in Joliet, but the intention was that IT lines should link Chicago and St. Louis using its Ottawa-Streator branch, plus a never-constructed line from Streator to existing southern routes, possibly via Peoria or Mackinaw junction.

Denied access to the Merchants and Eads bridges by the TRRA, the IT decided to reach St. Louis with its own bridge, receiving a franchise on March 28th, 1907. Next day, the Jefferson City Tribune ran an ecstatic page one article claiming there was no further obstacle to the IT crossing Missouri *"and reaching the next important point, which is Kansas City."* Jefferson City eagerly anticipated the arrival of such a trans-Missouri electric line, believing McKinley interests were the most likely to get the job done if it was going to be done at all. Bridging the Missouri at least twice plus the not-unimportant question of raising cash for so huge a project, were matters the city ignored.

Mckinley instead began negotiating agreements with

IT PCC 450 on 19th Street at State Street, Granite City in 1958. Granite City Steel is in the rear, with plenty of sleek looking autos parked by the "Leader" Department Store, including a 1957 Cadillac De Ville on the left of the trolley (to which a passenger is slowly walking), a 1953 Ford Mainline to the trolley's right and partly cut off on the right a 1957 Mercury Montclair. Ray Gehl/Mark Goldfeder collection.

PCC 450 on Broadway, heading for Granite City in 1958, though incorrectly signed. The McKinley Bridge and Venice IL are in the background. Ray Gehl/Mark Goldfeder collection.

car (numbered 1514, later 1524) specifically to haul freight from Venice into St. Louis, again so as not to infringe city sensitivities. There were similar limitations in Illinois, the IT eventually having to spend serious cash to build belt lines around Springfield and other towns to get freights off city streets.

In St. Louis, a 1931 relocation saw IT's main line relocate to a new "high line" at Venice and onto the bridge. At the Missouri end of the bridge, the line was re-routed to a new terminal at 12th Street almost all on its own right-of-way. This took IT vehicles off St. Louis streets, except for a short stretch of Hadley between Howard and Cass.

In 1905, McKinley was elected a U. S. Congressman and except for 1912-1915, he remained so until elected a U. S. Senator in 1921. He died in office on December 7th 1926. As his political career gathered momentum, McKinley lost interest in the IT, ownership passing through several hands until in 1926 North American and Samuel Insull assumed ownership through the Illinois Power and Light Corporation. Under the 1935 Public Utilities Holding Company Act, North American sold IT to St. Louis investors who in the 1940s began shrinking and dieselising the system. In 1956, it was sold to a syndicate of eleven Class 1 railroads and the last interurban ran between Springfield and St. Louis on March 3rd 1956. The IT then became a diesel-powered freight hauler except for St. Louis-Granite City suburban cars and a few feeder buses. The last Granite City car ran early June 22nd, 1958, ending all IT electric (and bus) services.

Between 1956 and 1981 IT freight trains were diverted to the lines of one or other of its parent railroads.Few original IT alignments remained in use when in 1981 the IT lost its identity after absorption by the Norfolk Southern. Most of the 1931 St Louis diversion ran until June 2004, with a Railroad Switching Services of Missouri diesel hauling cars of newsprint once or twice a week from the Branch Street interchange with the Norfolk Southern to the St. Louis Post Dispatch, in whose basement (formerly that of the St. Louis Globe-Democrat) from 1931 to 1958 was IT's St Louis subway terminal. The Mckinley Bridge was closed in 2001, severing a major Mississippi road and rail crossing. The road deck has been removed.

8. **Kansas City-St. Louis Short Line Electric Railroad Company** Most of what is known of this project comes from its March 23rd 1925 MOPSC application, which stressed its utility to the Columbia area. Columbia Commercial Club was in favor of the line, suggesting the University of Missouri had not progressed as they would have liked due to the city's inacessibility by rail. The Centralia station, transfer point for the Columbia line, was little better than a boxcar, said one witness. A similar plea was made on Fulton's behalf. (UM March 23rd, 1925 p. 1.)

William E. Stringfellow, the project's attorney, claimed the need for the line was self-evident. Its presence would lower railroad rates all round as it would run through and local freights, attaching the latter to fast through trains at the nearest division point. The 237.5-mile double-track St. Kouis-Kansas City line would be financed by issuing $40 million of bonds for roadbed and $20 million for rolling stock. MOPSC refused the application as the company could not prove it was financially able to carry through the $55 million project. The next two years were spent going through the judicial hierarchy, the Missouri Supreme Court again turning down the application in September 1927.

Despite unrelenting opposition from the steam railroads, the company tried again. J. B. Collins of Kansas City, a promoter, testified before the MOPSC on December 9th saying he believed *"bus and motor truck competition…was not the bugaboo that the steam railroad officials believed it to be."* (ERJ December 18th, 1927 p. 998). When asked how the line would support itself once built, he claimed $5 million per year of new business would come from setting up on-line industries and utilizing presently-dormant resources. That figure was challenged as being more than the annual business of any single railroad linking St. Louis and Kansas City. Collins responded that his line would get most of the business as it would be the shortest. Through trains would take five hours rather than the seven of the steam lines. In June 1928, the permit was again denied, on the same grounds.

9. **St. Louis trnd Southeastern Railway** An unknown proposal to build from to St. Louis 75 miles to Esther in St. Francois county (SRJ October 20th, 1906 p.45)

PCC 451 has just come off the McKinley Bridge ramp in Venice IL. The IT "High line" runs left to right onto the bridge in the middle back ground. A 1952 Ford Custom Line is parked outside the tavern at left. Ray Gehl/Mark Goldfeder collection.

10. **St. Louis and Western Traction Company.** This J. D. Houseman project (incorporated July 25, 1912) was to run 25 miles from West End Heights to the Missouri river opposite Weldon Springs. Capitalised at $300,000, it would serve Des Peres, Valley Park, Manchester and Ellisville before turning northwest. Houseman said he'd bought all the old St. Louis, Webster Groves and Valley Park, already graded to Kirkwood. The new line would give rapid transit to St.Louis and to county towns, some of which had no railroads. It would also be the St. Louis entry for a proposed St. Louis-Kansas City Electric Railway Company's cross-state interurban. At West End Heights the line would feed into a planned subway to downtown St. Louis. Franchise conditions included a paving obligation and a requirement for electric street lights to be lit until midnight.

On November 8th, 1912, the St. Louis and Western Traction (plus the

PCC 455 at the top of the Venice ramp onto the McKinley Bridge in 1958 as a 1957 Ford Custom heads into Illinois. The "High Line" continues on the right. Ray Gehl/Mark Goldfeder collection.

There were two intermediate stations on the IT's 1931 diversion line. This is Blanton, serving Mallinkrodt chemical (on the left). The Mississippi is on the right, under the bridge span. PCC 455 is rolling towards St. Louis in 1958. Ray Gehl/Mark Goldfeder collection.

11th, 1911) reporting the award of a 50-year St. Louis franchise to it on April 1st, on condition that the city control the line's depreciation fund and dictate how much the fund should contain and the sums disbursed from the fund for line betterments. The franchise allowed the city to buy the line any time it chose, the price to be settled by arbitration plus an extra 20% if bought within the first 25 years of the franchise. Should the line not be finished, the city would do the job, charging the cost against the bond given the city by the promoters. All this came from suggestions of the city's Public Service Commission.

The promoters, relying on the assurances of their civil engineer E. R. Kinsey, said work would begin soon. From Grand Avenue and Wyoming it would run five miles southwest to Bancroft Avenue, then to Arcadia in the Missouri lead district, about 65 miles south and 20 miles southwest of Farmington. But by June, with capital of just $250,000, the company claimed its route within St. Louis would not pay without a downtown connection. (St. Louis Republic June 9th, 1911) Whether this meant they wanted a transfer station at Grand and Wyoming, or trackage rights over UR to go downtown, isn't clear. Either way, they would not build without the connection, and only a 15-mile segment to Fenton was now being considered. At no time was the "Jefferson City" in the company's title explained.

12. St. Louis, Collinsville and Eastern Electric Railway Company SRJ September 1892 (p.560) reported this company filing for incorporation with $1/2 million in capital.

St. Louis County Belt Railroad and the Illinois and Eastern Traction) was deeded to F. E. Niesen, a real estate dealer, in trust for the stockholders. (R. S. England had quit his claim to St. Louis and Western property acquired at the January 1911 foreclosure.) The new promoters wanted to build a St. Louis-Manchester line, cross the Missouri near Gumbo and head for St. Charles County, possibly Weldon Springs. The St. Louis County Belt Railroad would run round St. Louis, cross the Mississippi on a proposed bridge north of Chain of Rocks, connect with the Wood River, East Alton and Bunker Hill Traction Company), go northeast to Pana IL, and hook up with the "Indianapolis Interurban system."

However, Houseman was still involved. On January 31st 1913, the St. Louis Watchman-Advocate quoted him as saying the line would run *"from West End Heights, following the road graded some years ago by Paul Cable to Kirkwood and from there through Manchester, Ballwin, Ellisville, Gumbo, across the river at Weldon Springs and then to Wentzvile in St. Charles County,"* in other words, the original 40-mile long St. Louis and Western Traction proposal. He wanted cars running on the 71/2 miles already graded from West End Heights (southwest corner of Forest Park) to North Kirkwood by August 1st, 1913. He would use gas-electric cars, which would also handle freight. He claimed the company was adequately capitalized to build without delay, but property owners had to donate the parcels still needed for right-of-way. The story seems fragmented and confusing and the fact that no more was heard of it suggests the harded-headed financial community thought so as well.

11. St. Louis, Arcadia and Jefferson City ERJ (March 4th, 1911 p. 400) noted this company wanting a St. Louis franchise for an electric line serving Carondelet Park, Arloe, Gratiot and Lindenwood. The P-D (April

PCC 457 outbound to Illinois has just left North Market station and is crossing North Broadway (St. Louis) circa 1952. David J. Neubauer.

13. St. Louis, Creve Coeur & Western Railway Company See St. Louis Fern Ridge & Western below.

14. St. Louis, Fenton and Southwestern Railway SRR July 1897 (p. 470) reported an April franchise for a St. Louis-Morse Mill (west of Hillsboro) interurban. SRR April 1899 (p. 283) noted the McCoy Construction Company (President Thomas F. Sneed, former superintendent of the St. Louis and Suburban and later Belleville IL city cars) would build 28 miles (sic) from Carondelet to Fenton at once. Poor's 1901 reported the line already operating, but construction had not begun and its 44 miles of standard-gauge track, ten cars and twenty trailers represented hope deferred, not accomplished fact. Capital was $1 million, as was bonded debt of which $350,00 was outstanding at 6% interest. Sneed was President, W. K. Kavanagh Vice-President and J. B. Clayton Secretary. Offices were in

PCC 451 rolls off the diversion's right of way at Howard to head south down Hadley, St. Louis in 1958. Ray Gehl/Mark Goldfeder collection.

downtown St. Louis. Nothing was heard after 1904.

15. St. Louis Fern Ridge & Western Railway Company

SRJ June 2nd, 1906 (ad p. 2) noted a franchise granted to this company November 20th, 1905. An estimated $300,000 would let them build from Saint Louis to Creve Coeur Lake via Olive Street Road. This project was financed mainly by St. Louis county men, William F. Pfister of Fern Ridge, President. UR's Creve Coeur Lake (05) line of 1898-1900, had rejected this route as it would reach the lake at ground level and be subject to flooding and washouts. Instead, their line ended on bluffs above the lake.

SRJ November 17th, 1906 (ad p.32) said the line would run from De Hodiamont via Etzel Avenue and right-of-way to Olive Street Road, west on Olive Street Road and north on Creve Coeur Mill Road to Studt's Park (Creve Coeur Lake) if the company graded and widened Etzel to 60' under the supervision of the County Commissioner of Roads and Bridges. If the County felt it necessary, the line would cross the Wabash (today's MetroLink) line on a bridge. The company, unhappy with this, petitioned for changes, including a 30-cent rather than a 5-cent fare, hourly rather than half-hourly service, the right to run mail and express cars and to use Telford rather than brick paving. Without these revisions outside money would be impossible to find. (SRJ December 22nd, 1906, ad p. 35).

The enterprise foundered and was reorganized as the **St. Louis, Creve Coeur and Western Railway Company** on January 18th, 1909 with the same promoters plus JudgeWarremeyer of Clayton. Its $140,000 capital was soon increased to $750,000. There would be two terminals, one at Studt's Pavilion, the other at Upper Lake. Money was subscribed by local farmers and property owners. It would be single-track but if unnamed eastern capitalists put up money, it would be double-track. Suburban real estate

IT's St. Louis trackage was used by suburban services to Granite City and to Alton and interurban services to Springfield, Peoria, Bloomington, Champaign/Urbana and Danville. This is a two-car final fantrip to Danville rolling north along Hadley, having just left the subway. The trip was sponsored by the Louisville chapter of the National Railroad Historical Society and probably held on April 26th 1952, the last day of the Danville service. Ray Gehl/Mark Goldfeder collection.

would be developed along the route, the main motivation for the project. ERJ March 27th, 1909 (p.572) claimed Union Finance Company of New York would provide money and experiment with a storage-battery car and a gasoline motor car.

PCC 451 at Hadley and Cass in St. Louis, about to head into the subway terminal circa 1958. Ray Gehl/Mark Goldfeder collection.

The <u>Saint Louis Republic</u> (May 3rd, 1910) reported a May 2nd contract for *"the Olive Street Road line to Creve Coeur Lake."* Estimated costs were $210,000, of which $75,000 was pledged by locals, half to be paid when track reached their properties, the other half when cars began running. The Frederick-Essen Company managed the project for the promoters (the Olive-Stratmann Improvement Association). <u>ERJ</u> June 4th, 1910 (p.1008), reported $300,000 of stock had been issued, plus $300,000 in bonds. Construction would start in July and the line would be electric: power would come from Union Electric or UR. Again, nothing happened.

In April 1912, a new **St. Louis Creve Coeur and Western** was franchised, *"a new company, which has taken the rights of the original...whose stockholders were farmers living on Olive Street Road. The old company turned over its rights on April 1st 1912. Tracks may be laid on Olive Street Road or on a private right of way 1000' south of Olive Street Road. Fares will be 5 cents to Ballas Road and 10 cents out to Creve Coeur Lake. Cars will run every half-hour from 5 am to 8 pm., then hourly to midnight. In the five years since the road was organized, there have been many attempts to get the road started, but little was done. Frederick Heskert (of the Heskert and Meisel Trust Co.) is president."* (<u>St. Louis Watchman-Advocate</u> April 5th, 1912). This attempt also failed.

16. St. Louis, Hillsboro and Southern Railroad Company. (See Grand View Railroad in section 2 above).

17. St. Louis-Kansas City Electric Railway Company See Columbia

18. St. Louis, Monte Sano and Southern Railway Company (See Grand View Railway Company in section 2 above). <u>SRR</u> April 1899 (p.283) briefly noted that J. D. Houseman was president of a company making surveys for a proposed electric line to Monte Sano, on a route taking it through Jefferson Barracks. Nothing else is known.

19. St. Louis, Mountain Grove and Southern Railway Company A 30-mile line from Mountain Grove in Wright County south to Bryant Creek in Ozark County, chartered in June 1907 with $400,000 capital (SRJ July 6th, 1907 p. 38).

20. St. Louis, Webster Groves and Valley Park Railway Company An "almost" interurban, incorporated in late 1904, promoted by Paul D. Cable of Maplewood (Vice-President). Markee and Company of Philadelphia financed it, predicting a July 1st, 1905 opening. From UR's Chouteau Avenue line terminal, it would run fifteen miles to Valley Park (with a Manchester branch) via Webster, Kirkwood and Des Peres on right-of-way close to Manchester Road. Shops and power station would be at Menfos. Offices were in room 225 of the St. Louis Wainwright Building.

Within six months, an irritated <u>P-D</u> reader wrote that Manchester still had no connection with St. Louis *"other than a roundabout way of five miles by (horse) bus line, and is now suffering from an increase in rates on the Missouri Pacific Railroad to suburban passengers."* Several companies had already defaulted on franchises, the latest being this one's Manchester branch. *"Now I'm told they're working on both ends of the Valley Park line and have abandoned the other. I protest."* (December 15, 1905 p. 7.)

In April 1909 the company said 24 miles was finished, the rest (48 miles) being built. Some grading had been done, but the claim of 72 miles of track under construction was untrue. At the time, the company claimed only $600,000 of capital and $600,000 of funded debt, enough to have complete surveying and rough grading, but insufficient to pay for cars, tracks, electrical supplies and the rest.

The <u>St. Louis Watchman</u> February 3rd, 1911 reported a foreclosure sale, bought for $7,000 by Robert S. England of Festus. Grading was complete to Valley Park though rail and ties hadn't been laid. England had done the grading and in January 1910 had filed a $12,867 mechanic's lien that precipitated the sale. He said he'd have the line reorganized by April, then extend it to Pacific. Soon after, however, England refused to discuss the future.

The <u>G-D</u> (June 18th, 1912) reported a franchise for a 2-mile electric line to run from a point 300' south of Clayton Road (St. Louis city limits) to the Kirkwood-Ferguson (01) line. It would run south of Clayton and a short distance north of Eager Road, rather than close to Manchester, but otherwise on a similar grade to the abortive Valley Park, crossing Belle-

Car 470 heading up the ramp out of the subway and onto Hadley Street, St. Louis May 15th, 1953. David J. Neubauer .

vue, Pennsylvania and Hanley. Some of the graded roadbed might be reused. Nothing happened.

21. **Southern Traction Co** Southern Traction was set up in 1908 to build a standard-gauge East St. Louis-Belleville electric line with extensions to Murphysboro and Cairo. An initial foray that would have taken it over Eads Bridge into St. Louis failed, though it soon received a 50-year franchise to use the Municipal Free Bridge and 4th Street in St. Louis, the first of many plans for a standard-gauge downtown St. Louis trolley loop.

There were three hurdles. One was the bridge itself, complete but minus ramps due to lack of money to build them. A second was the April 1911 fifty-year St. Louis franchise, denounced for ST's criminal effrontery in bribing the House of Delegates to get it. A third was the threat ST would bottle up the city, as the TRRA had done on the Eads and Merchants bridges, a sore spot in St. Louis as existing TRRA river crossing "tolls" doubled the price of rail-delivered Illinois coal.

There were also suspicions ST was a front for the TRRA or the IT (or both), either of which could monopolize the Free Bridge. Paranoia on this issue was so intense, it was soon (mistakenly) taken as fact, since later plans envisaged ST running on its own tracks through downtown St. Louis to IT's 12th Street station on the north side. The city-sponsored standard-gauge downtown interurban loop idea sprang from this notion, as did the interurban "Union Terminal" idea the St. Louis City Engineer was to champion for the next decade.

Southern Traction as built began at 4th and Broadway in East St. Louis, went southwest on 4th to Brady, jogged to 5th on Brady, southwest on 5th to Market and southeast on Market to 17th, jogging southwest on 17th a block to Piggott Avenue, then southeast on Piggott Avenue, Elizabeth Avenue and Central, working its way over to the American Bottoms to

parallel the Illinois Central Railroad through The Bluffs. It entered Belleville on a wooden trestle across Highland Creek, east on Garfield, north on First to the courthouse on West Main, Belleville.

Once its tracks were laid circa 1910, ST began projecting a Belleville-Duquoin IL line, with a Chester branch. The St. Louis Star (May 17th, 1911) then noted ST buying franchises and property of the unbuilt Illinois and Indiana Electric Railway. On June 3rd, 1911, the paper said ST had bought the Wabash, Chester and Western Railroad (Chester-Mt. Vernon IL, 65 miles) from the Hippard interests, intending to electrify it. The deal included two coal mines near Belleville. ST was originally capitalized at $1 million, soon upped to $7 million to pay for these purchases, plus a new Belleville-Pinckneyville link line (40 miles) to the WC&W RR. At this time, ST was rumored to be planning a name change to Southern Illinois Traction Company.

The contentious St. Louis franchise was revoked early in July 1912, but ST came up with a new plan a few months later, summarized by this wordy April 15th 1913 St. Louis Times headline."*Southern Traction Company of Illinois to tap rich country and establish a 5 cent fare between East St. Louis and St. Louis. Residents of many counties eager to trade in St. Louis and are counting days until electric cars crossing Free Bridge will pass their doors giving them hourly service for passengers and freight to and from Metropolis of the Mississippi Valley.*"

In brief, H. D. Mepham (along with Jeptha Howe), ST's promoters, were promising cars would run by October 15th, a claim repeated in the St. Louis Republic (June 27th, 1913). "*Southern Traction's first division will be completed by November 1st...but for the unfinished condition of the Free Bridge*" Division one was their East St. Louis-Belleville Line. Edison storage battery cars would handle passenger service. ST's second division (Belleville-Marissa) would open in July 1913 and ST's third division (Marissa-Duquoin) would open in December. The Free Bridge was the rock on which all hopes foundered. No division ever opened; it's not clear divisions two and three were even graded.

Six 38' interurban combines ordered from St. Louis Car (St. Louis 23-EM trucks) on April 27th, 1914 were cancelled some weeks later, by which time ST's affairs were so badly tangled elsewhere that despite having spent $1.5 million and with division one ready to open, it spent the next few years in litigation.This arose out of former U.S. Senator William Lorimer's financial difficulties. He headed Lorimer-Gallagher Construction, which had built ST's division one, lost money doing so, then had lost more in the 1911 failure of the LsSalle Street Trust and Savings Bank of Chicago, of which he was President. Still the company persisted. In 1917 it was back at St. Louis City Hall to ask that its coal trains use city car tracks. As St.Louis civic attitudes to on-street freights was unchanged ("what part of no don't you understand?"), one has to question the ST's board's judgement on this point.

The ST was foreclosed in 1919 and bought for $400,000 by H. D. Mepham and associates. The city's policy now was to make the Free Bridge bridge available to all, including ST, which was advised to reapply for a franchise. (ERJ (August 2nd, 1919 p. 252). Mepham said that

was fine with him and within 60 days ST passenger cars would use the bridge and loop downtown St. Louis. He'd rebuild bridges, repair roadbed, maybe extend to Duquoin, spend $1 1/2 million for new cars and carry coal within Illinois. To acquire ST, Mepham had outbid Judge E. C. Kramer, acting for a group of St. Louis financiers. but didn't make payment in full by December 17th as agreed. He stood to lose the $30,000 earnest money he'd put down, plus $75,000 of other expenses. (ERJ November 15th, 1919 p. 952).

With court approval, he transferred his rights to C. B. Cox, President of the Alton and Southern Railroad and the Aluminum Ore Company.*"The Aluminum Company owns coal property near Tilden IL 45 miles southeast of East St Louis.Southern Traction's right-of-way runs within a short distance...Rail was laid about 10 years ago from 4th Street and Broadway to Belleville, but passenger service was never installed. Freight trains have run over the line from... the east section of East St. Louis to Belleville."* (ERJ December 20th 1919 p. 1018.) These trains ran because ST east of TRRA tracks on East St. Louis's 20th Street had become part of the St. Louis and Ohio River Railroad, later a part of the Alton and Southern.The on-street tracks in Belleville were never used, not being lifted until the fall of 1939.

SEDALIA

1880	**1890**	**1900**	**1910**	**1920**	**1930**	**1940**	**1950**	**1960**	**1970**	**1980**	**1990**	**2000**
9,561	14.068	15,231	17,822	21,144	20,806	20,428	20,354	23,874	22,847	20,927	19,800	20,339

En route to Kansas City from St. Louis, the Missouri Pacific railroad avoided Georgetown, then the Pettis County seat, to traverse the area where Sedalia now stands. Established in 1857, Sedalia owes its existence and livelihood to the railroad, but also to Texas longhorns and cattle drives. As a railroad division point, (the MKT was also here), Sedalia soon became the Pettis county seat and fairgrounds were built in the 1880s for the county fair, the trump card in the city's successful bid to be the Missouri State Fair's permanent home from 1901.

In 1876 a street railway was franchised but didn't build. A **Sedalia Street Railway Company** was franchised in 1881 to Joseph D. and Frank F. Sicher, A. D. Jaynes and P. T. Gentry and by September, they'd built a mile of track west on Third Street to Sicher's Park. The first cars ran in Fair Week early that month.

1 2 3 4 5 6 7 8 9 10 11 12 13 14 15 16
17 18 19 20 21 22 23 24 25 26 27 28 29 30 31

The Railway and Electric Co. of Sedalia, Mo.
Good for one continuous ride over the Division indicated by punch marks, when used by the party accepting it and presented to the Conductor on Car AT JUNCTION WHERE TRANSFER IS MADE within 15 minutes of time cancelled; subject to rules of the Company.

A.M. | 16th South | 16th West | 3rd South | 3rd West | 13th South | 13th East

	1	20	40
2	20	40
3	20	40
4	20	40
5	20	40
6	20	40
7	20	40
8	20	40
9	20	40
10	20	40
11	20	40
12	20	40

Ohio east to Engineer opened March 1st, 1882 and the entire Third Street line was two miles long. Real estate was the stimulus. SRJ Directory (February 1887) said the *"Third Street horse line"* had route 2.4 miles, 4' 10" gauge tracks, six cars and 25 horses.The gauge suggests cars might have been hand-me downs from St. Louis. By 1889, there were 3.25 route miles, six cars and 35 horses.

A company with $200,000 capital was chartered March 17th, 1890, a pole for overhead wires was planted on the 19th and the SSRC's Third Street line was taken over March 28th, 1890, renamed **Electric Railway, Light and Power Company of Sedalia** in May. SRJ May 1890 (p. 249) noted Third Street would be electrified in a year now that *"Judge Metsker (of Topeka KS was) the heart and soul of this concern."* An electric line from Fifth and Hancock south to Tenth, Tenth to Ingram, south to Thirteenth,

west on Thirteenth to Ohio, and north on Ohio to MoPac tracks, opened July 4th, 1890 (Sedalia Democrat October 4th, 1931 p. 2). No grade crossing was made; passengers walked over railroad tracks where (ideally) another car waited to take them on to the cemetery. Other reports, however, suggest the new line was a belt including Ohio, Main, Lamine and 5th Streets.

The SSRC and the ERL&P kept their separate identities. SRJ June 1891 (p.325) said the SSRC had four route miles, four cars and six others, the ERL&P had seven standard-gauge route miles, five cars and ten trailers. D. C. Metsker remained Secretary, Treasurer and General Manager. Offices were at 207 E. 3rd Street in Sedalia. After the last horse car, the gauge was changed (date unknown) and the two companies were fully merged. Modest profits were made and the 1890s saw expansion; by 1897 there were twelve route miles, ten cars and five trailers. This was not bad for even at its peak, competition came from pedestrians (it was not difficult, though it took longer, to walk any of the routes), bicycles and buggies. Demand was high in summer as open cars allowed folks to cool off on muggy nights. But in winter, cars were underused. Poor conditions underfoot made walking, even to a car stop, a nightmare.

The company ran the four-mile **Sedalia and Brown Springs Railway** (opened August 1st, 1896), under lease until October 1898 when the ERL&P took it over and renamed itself **Sedalia Electric and Railway Company.** It had a blanket franchise to run over all city streets; a monopoly never exercised. Ten new open and seven new closed cars (all motored) were bought, generating capacity was increased and tracks relaid with heavier rail. A new subsidiary (**Sedalia Electric and Heating**

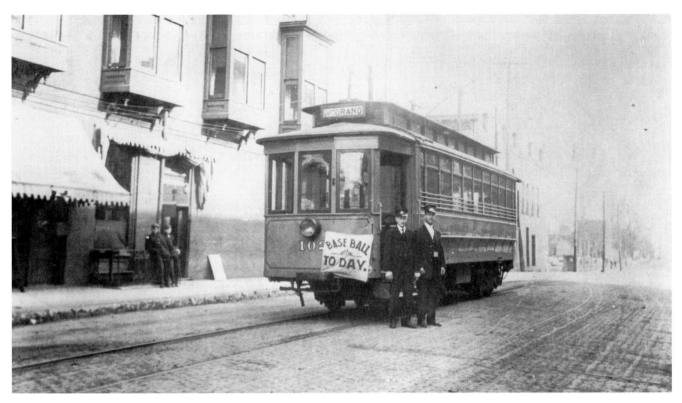

Car 102, on Ohio at Main, about to leave for South Grand, circa 1905.

Company) sold surplus power and exhaust steam from the street railway's generating plant. But the company was overextended, receivers were called in on February 16th, 1900 and it was sold on March 15th, 1901 to a bondholders' committee who reorganized it as **Railway and Electric Company of Sedalia**.It opened the Fairgrounds line in 1902 and by 1903 had nine miles of track and eighteen cars. In 1904 it became the **Sedalia Transit Company,** with barns at Ninth and Ingram. A merger with Sedalia Electric Light and Power and Sedalia Gas and Fuel saw STC lose its identity within a **Sedalia Light and Traction Company** from December 17th, 1906.

Capitalized for $1 million plus $710,000 in bonds, the President was E. M. Dean of the Edward M. Dean Company, Grand Rapids, MI, SL&TC's new owners. A small five-figure profi was made on operations, though the debt continued and on June 1st 1910 it defaulted again. Closure of Forest

Park-Brown Springs at this time may have been linked to this. The bondholders contracted with Cities Service Company of New York and a new **City Light and Traction Company** was incorporated on July 23rd, 1912 with $5 million capital ($500,000 in preferred stock) and $2.5 million of 5% first mortgage bonds, $400,000 to be issued at once. Bondholders of the old company got 50% of their holdings in new bonds and 50% in preferred stock, dividends on the latter being guaranteed by Gas Securities Company of New York.

With the agreement, Sedalia's public utilities now had huge resources behind them. In 1912 Cities Services owned or controlled about 200 companies including traction, light, heat and water utilities, and rapidly becoming big in oil and gas. By 1914 the new company's board remained mainly Sedalia people, responsible for 8.3 miles of track, nine closed cars, seven open cars, nine open trailers and three work cars. As in St. Joseph,

Sedalia's street railway routes, 1904.
These changed and merged in later years.

A. From Ohio and Main to Forest Park, 3 miles. Initially, the MoPac grade crossing on Ohio was a major headache. The railroad did not allow the cutting-in of a crossing. Brown Springs cars ran from the far side of the crossing.

B. From Ohio and Main to East Sedalia via Ohio (south) to 13th, east on 13th to Ingram, north on Ingram to 10th, east on 10th to Hancock, north on Hancock to 5th and (later) east on 5th to Engineer.

C. From Ohio and Main to MKT shops and Missouri State Fair Grounds via Ohio (south) to 16th Street, west on 16th to Grand Avenue, South on Grand to 20th Street, west on 20th to the MKT shops and then to the Missouri Fairgrounds. (The Fairground extension was not opened until circa 1902.)

D. From Ohio and Third west to Liberty Park (Sicher's Park had been absorbed into Liberty Park in the 1890s.) **(end)**

marketing was Cities Service strength to stimulate ridership multi-pack books of tickets were introduced, 6 rides for 25 cents to 120 rides for $5.00—often cut by another 30 cents. In January 1916, house-to-house canvassing began and ads were placed in newspapers.

In November 1915 the rear doors of closed cars were blocked off and near-side one-man operation began in which riders entered and exited at stops sited before rather than after a street crossing, using a double doorway at the front, with separate entry and exit streams. Judged a success, eight new lightweight double-end single-truck cars were ordered. Delivered in summer 1916, they ran all base service on the system until it closed. Older cars were kept for extra service, the fleet now consisting of nineteen cars and six trailers. As a result, Sedalia's trolleys were able to withstand inflation and World War One when each hit. Moreover by 1919, despite the newly-paved streets,

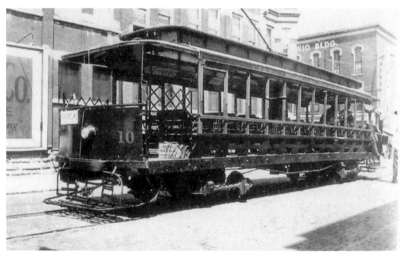

Open car 10 on Main at Ohio about to head for the Fairgrounds circa 1910.

Sedalia had not yet seen a major influx of automobiles. This may be attributable to local circumstances such as the presence of MoPac and MKT shops and the State Fair Grounds. But continued good trolley service was the result. In 1919, one line ran from Liberty Park, east on Third and Broadway to the MoPac shops. A second line ran south on Ohio from Main to 16th Street, then west and south to the State Fair grounds, looping back past the Katy shops. A branch at Ohio Avenue ran east on 13th Street through east Sedalia, ending at 15th Street and Brown Avenue. Schedules varied between 10 and 20 minutes. The system remained profitable in the early 1920s and in 1924 had 8.3 miles of single track (7.5 miles operating) of which 6.25 miles were in paved streets. The car fleet was unchanged from 1916.

Early in 1926, the city decided seven blocks on West 16th Street should be paved. Under the franchise, when the city made such a decision, the company had to pave the space between its rails and a foot outside with like material. Cities Service wouldn't do this, inviting the city council to exercise its option and remove the tracks instead, so opening up the whole issue of continued trolley operation. By Fall, Sedalia's mayor, council and other movers and shakers were saying that for a town of its size, replacing cars with buses would be in keeping with current transit trends.

In July 1927 company officials made a fact-finding tour of Missouri cities for information on the kinds of bus being used for trolley replacement and the different operating methods required. Meanwhile, the trolleys went

An unidentified lightweight car seen toward the end of its days.

into decline, losing $11,608 in 1928. MOPSC gave its assent to substitute motor buses on October 1st, 1931, on the grounds of declining revenue and failure to meet fixed charges. Gross revenue was $13,751, operating expenses $25,535, an operating deficit of $11,784 in the year ending August 31st. The system's appraised value had fallen from $300,000 in 1926 to $241,000. (The Sedalia Democrat, October 1st, 1931 p. 1.) The trolleys ran their last miles on October 3rd, 1931 on West Third Street and East Sixth Street. Cities Service ran the buses initially, but wanted out of Sedalia transit and sold them to locals. In 1942 Mary A. Siegel's Sedalia Bus Company ran seven buses in and around Sedalia on 31 route miles, while Olen and Michael Howard ran buses until the early '50s.

Incomplete Roster Notes

No records have been found. SRJ directory 2/1887 claims six cars and 25 horses. Many cars were electrified in the 1890s. Car 6 (with eight narrow windows per side) and Crown Hill cemetery car 7 were two, each on a St. Louis Car patent single truck. Car 8 was another converted horsecar, slightly different, with 6 round-top windows per side, similar to car 10 (#1) and on a Brill #4 single truck. Car 10 (#1) may have been new, but looks like a circa-1890 closed horse car body with round-top windows (6 a side) on a Brill #4 single-truck.

Car 10 (#2), 11 were 14 bench opens with deck roof and maximum traction double-trucks. Still in service 1931.

Car 13, a 10-bench single-truck open on a Peckham Cantilever #8 truck, may later have been renumbered #23.

Car 14 a 10-bench single-truck open, probably came from the Detroit and Mackinac Island Street Railway Company.

Cars 18, 19 were 10-bench single-truck opens on Peckham Cantilever #8 trucks.

Cars 20,22,24 were enclosed single-truck city cars on Peckham Cantilever 38 trucks.

One-man cars 50-57 (American, 1916) used 9' wheelbase (very long) wide-wing Brill 21-E trucks and double-door "nearside" front entrances. Their 14,000lbs weight was 75% less than the heaviest older cars.

Car 102 was a double-truck closed city car, possibly like car 104, a double-truck maximum-traction closed city car, said to have been bought in 1904 after use at the St. Louis World's Fair.

Cars 106-108, single-truck closed winter cars were bought used from St. Joseph MO in 1913, at the same time as six trailers (origins unknown) were bought used from broker Lloyd J. Smith of Chicago, all for heavy State Fair traffic. Unknown number. Single-truck 10-bench trailer (perhaps more than one) believed to have been bought from the Electric Springs Railway Company (Warrenburg MO-Pertle Springs MO), a mule line.

Interurban Proposals

SRJ November 1896 (ad p. 55) noted Edward Wood of Chicago, acting in the interests of unnamed New York and Boston capitalists, proposing a line from Monett in Lawrence County (southwest Missouri) to Sedalia. A branch from Leesville would run west to Butler via Clinton and from Leesville to Osceola and Stockton in today's Harry S. Truman Reservoir area in Mid-Missouri's Lake of the Ozarks region. No more was heard.

1. Sedalia and McAllister Springs Electric Railway and Power Company SRJ November 1897 reported this as a 25-mile long, ten-car line, promoted by a Woodford Brooks of Sedalia. No franchises were granted

2. Missouri Interurban Railroad Company Jefferson City-Sedalia. See Jefferson City interurban proposals.

3. Versailles and Sedalia Railway Company SRJ April 6th, 1907 (ad p. 42) said the new owner of this line (implying there had been one previously) intended to extend to Sedalia, then south to Springfield. Surveying was proceeding. No more was heard. The V&S may have been planned as a steam railroad; the report is ambiguous.

4. Kansas City and South Eastern Railway Company See Kansas City interurban proposals.

SHELBINA

Line 1 Shelbina. Line 2 Shelbyville. Line 3 Labelle.

1880	**1890**	**1900**	**1910**	**1920**	**1930**	**1940**	**1950**	**1960**	**1970**	**1980**	**1990**	**2000**
1. 1,289	1,691	1,733	2,174	1,809	1,826	2,107	2,133	2,067	2,060	2,169	2,172	1,943
2. 619	486	777	685	690	704	756	635	657	601	645	582	682
3. 340	702	966	1,017	878	820	833	840	866	848	845	745	669

SRJ July 30th, 1906 (p. 36) reported surveyors working on an 8-mile electric line north from Shelbina to Shelbyville in Shelby County, Shelbyville being the county seat. More than $100,000 had been subscribed and the line was to extend north to Labelle in Lewis county (on the O. K. railroad), and south to Mexico. (See Bevier, Huntsville and Macon)

SPRINGFIELD

1880	**1890**	**1900**	**1910**	**1920**	**1930**	**1940**	**1950**	**1960**	**1970**	**1980**	**1990**	**2000**
6,522	21,850	23,267	35,201	39,631	57,527	61,238	66,731	95,865	120,096	133,116	140,494	151,580

Springfield and North Springfield were originally separate townships. Springfield began circa 1830 after the Kickapoo and Delaware tribes were removed from southwest Missouri. Outlaws and heroes of the old west marked its early history; Wild Bill Hickok, for example, made his name here in 1865. But once the towns merged, Springfield became the Greene County seat and took on a settled, urban character as a railroad town and evangelical Christian center. One of many Midwest cities to see themselves as the "buckle on the Bible Belt," it also calls itself "Queen City of the Ozarks." North Springfield grew around the Atlantic and Pacific (later Frisco) railroad station which opened in 1870. The two towns were linked by H. F. Denton's horse buses. A College Street livery stable owner, his buses ran into the 1880s. Streetcars, however, were considered. In 1869, the **Springfield Railway and Transfer Company** was given a blanket franchise to use any street, but did not build. A similarly-named company made another attempt in 1874.

In October 1880, a **Springfield Railway Company** got a 20-year franchise for a Springfield-North Springfield line. Incorporators included Colonel Homer F. Fellows, Robert J. McElhaney and James A. Stoughton, well-known local lights. Stoughton kept what was quaintly termed *"a beverage establishment,"* Fellows owned the Springfield Wagon Company and McElhaney ran a bank at the southwest corner of Benton and Commercial. Capitalized at $25,000 the line opened April 15th, 1881 from Public Square, runing north on Boonville to Commercial, then east on Commercial to Benton just short of the railroad depot. It was unprofitable, despite the dime fare and 1884's track doubling. A line on Commercial west to the city limits was authorized but ran only to Grant.

Within days of opening, a rival **People's Railway Company** was fran-

Southwest corner of Public Square circa 1885. Other than for the car tracks, the square is little changed since Wild Bill Hickock's days twenty or more years earlier. The streets are unpaved but plenty of vehicles can be seen including two animal cars of the People's Railway Company. Crowds are gathering for a public event. History Museum for Springfield-Greene County

need to raise and spend more capital sums. Clearly this was not presently possible.

Though Citizen's was not involved directly, some of its board and stockholders began a new project. The **Woodland Heights Rapid Transit and Improvement Company** franchise of April 6th, 1889, gave it the right to build on many streets. A November supplement gave more, including a line to Talmage, Zoo Park and Doling Park. What is unclear, however, is what the new company actually built. SRJ May 1890 (p.250) reported tracklaying had begun on Walnut and 2 miles would be built "soon" on a line from Commercial to Doling Park. A mile was finished in May 1890. An unreliable steam "dummy" and trailer ran for a few months in 1889/1890, but on what streets and how far isn't known. The line served a new real estate develpoment of its backers, who included St. Louisan B. F. Hobart (the Citizen's President) and was also interested in leisure traffic for the Zoo and Dolling Park.

SRJ June 1888 (p. 165) reported a franchise allowing the Detroit Electrical Works to build a Fisher electric motor railway, work to start within a month of April 19th, two miles operating inside four months. However, SRJ October 1888 (p. 283) reported cancellation for non-compliance. Springfield officials remained skeptical of mechanical power and it took a trip to St. Joseph to convince them electricity was the coming thing. How to pay for it was not the city's problem; it was just that they now were willing to grant franchises for such work and previously they weren't.

An October 3rd, 1889 ordinance allowed Citizen's to change motive power, extend the existing franchise to 1924 and get into city electric lighting. Anticipating passage of the ordinance, Citizen's on September 10th had increased capital from $120,000 to $200,000, but soon

chised, incorporators being south-side businessmen. Its first cars ran October 15th, 1881 on South Street from Public Square to Madison. Later People's lines ran from the Square west on College and north on Main to Water (later to Nichols), from the Square east on St. Louis to Jefferson then north on Jefferson to Central. The company intended to go north of Division Street to the railroad depot on Commercial in North Springfield. Franchises were obtained but not acted on and while at some point it had lines running into North Springfield, that lasted less than a year. Another People's line (Benton, from Division to Commercial) ran for a year before a new **Citizens Railway Company** took over in August 1886.

This was a merger of the People's and the Springfield Railway Company, capitalized at $120,000. Again, most of the board were locals. The SRC's single route with its western branch to Grant was unchanged and it was the People's that brought the most routes and cars to the merger. Little was done to extend the lines, though links between the two systems were put in. Some single track was doubled and in March 1887, SRJ's directory (p. 276) noted seven miles of Citizen's tracks, fifteen cars, 28 horses and 48 mules. SRJ June 1888 (p. 134) noted Citizen's completing 11/2 miles of double track on Booneville, giving double track from the Ozark Hotel and Frisco Depot to Public Square.

The merger saw a universal nickel fare replace the dime charged on some lines. For Citizens, this gave sustained ridership increase and profits. Poor's 1889 reported Citizen's gains as $16,000 in 1888 and $18,000 in 1889. But $80,000 funded debt in 7% bonds (payable by 1890) was a problem now that cable, steam and electricity were vying with each other as replacements for animal traction. Any such change brought with it the

Another view of Springfield Peoples Railway car 3, this time on South at Walnut, running up to Public Square in the background circa 1885. History Museum for Springfield-Green County.

Though Springfield's <u>MET</u> had the biggest share of city traction business, it was not a complete consolidation. Six further companies were established after 1890. Not all made it into operation.

1. <u>Kickapoo Transit Company</u> A March 1890 franchise allowed KTC to build an animal line from Public Square to the "Poor Farm," with a future extension to the National Cemetery. The "Poor Farm" was on the former "Kickapoo Prairie," later occupied by the Normal school at Pickwick Avenue just south of Cherry. The line ran east on St. Louis from Public Square to Jefferson, south on Jefferson to Elm and east on Elm to National. This nickel-fare two-car mule line opened in summer 1890 and soon ran to the Poor Farm on Pickwick. A car barn was built, with a branch on Cherry to serve it. The line was built to promote real estate planned by its backers. Within a year, the "Poor Farm" had sold its 40 acres of land and moved to Nichols Street. The land was platted and sub-divided as the "Pickwick Addition." Mules powered the line until October 15th, 1903, when electric trolleys took over. It was independent until 1905 and had 2.2 miles of standard-gauge track.

2. <u>Walnut Street Railway Company</u> This company's 1889 franchise was for a line on West Walnut from South to Fort. An 1890 amendment added East Walnut from South to National. A National Cemetery extension was planned but not built while access to Public Square over the Citizen's lines was blocked. Incorporated July 1890 with $40,000 capital stock, R. L. and R. J. McElhaney were behind the company. Operations began some time in 1890. It never became part of the MET and results were so poor that it ceased running August 7th, 1894.

3. <u>Union Rapid Transit and Improvement Company</u> Set up in the late 1880s, an 1890 franchise allowed it to run on Campbell from College to Commercial, on Scott from Commercial to the west city limits, on College from Campbell to the west city limits, and to link with the Springfield and Nichols Junction (see 4 below) at or near the city limits and Scott Street. Most was built and operated, but money troubles prompted a sale in 1891 to the Springfield Electric Street Railway Company (see 5 below), which then sold it to the MET. SRJ August 1892 (p. 498) said there was a petition to have the MET *"equip the abandoned road on Campbell Street with electricity."*

4. <u>Springfield and Nichols Junction Rapid Transit and Improvement Company</u> Almost nothing is known of this. Its franchises were turned over to the Springfield Electric Street Railway Company in April 1891.

5. <u>Springfield Electric Street Railway and Improvement Company</u> This was a merger or buy-out of Union Rapid Transit and the Springfield and Nichols Junction, approved by the city in April 1891. It not known if this company built more than lines on Campbell (from College to Scott), Johnson and Calhoun to the west city limits. For a time, this line went a further 1 1/2 miles west of the city limits to "the old Fullbright Farm," on the line of Calhoun Street had it gone that far. Despite the name, only horse and mule cars were ever run.

6. <u>Robberson Avenue Street Railway</u> Another project in which the McElhaneys were involved, it built on Peach Alley and Robberson Avenue, (both Robberson Avenue now) to a point between Pine and Phelps, where a viaduct was built to cross Water Street, ending at Olive. Heavy construction costs tapped out fiscal reserves, the line was not completed and no car ever ran. It was sold to Springfield Traction (see below) in 1900.

found this insufficient given their bonded indebtedness. Other sources of money had to be found. Enter the **Metropolitan Electric Railway Company**. Organized in May 1890 with $1/2 million capital, mostly from St. Louis investors, it took over the Citizen's and the Woodland Heights on June 16th, 1890. The power generating plant was jointly owned with the new Springfield Lighting Company. On July 11th, 1890, wire was strung and poles planted. Lines were rebuilt, four miles of single track added and fifteen cars and fifteen trailers ordered. The first test car (car 26) ran December 4th, 1890 and on January 4th, 1891 electric cars began regular service.

The MET fell to the 1893 Depression, going bankrupt on October 23rd. The **Springfield Traction Company** rose from its ashes in November 1895. Board and stockholders were holdovers, mostly St. Louisans. But business was poor. Late-1890s service needed only ten cars. STC added no new tracks, though doubling took place. Activity was instead focused on acquisitions. The St. Louisans, plus the Robberson Avenue and Kick-

apoo companies were subsequently bought out and their securities sold to Springfield Gas and Electric (established circa 1902).

In March 1906 a new **Springfield Traction Company** was organized with George Macomber President, F. W. Little Vice-President and W. A. Bixby General Manager. It began rehabilitating the property and improving services. SRJ August 4th, 1906 (ad p. 71) noted Bixby on a recent two-day car-shopping trip to St. Louis. New cars were bought and heavier rail laid on Boonville and Commercial Streets plus lines to Dolling Park. Yet service remained minimal. Center and State Streets saw only a car an hour, Monroe slightly more. Only Boonville had good service. This contravened franchises which stipulated schedules, but the city did not enforce them and the service levels suited the company.

There were plans to build an interurban to Carthage. ERJ January 1st, 1909 (p. 49) reported two possible routes, one paralleling the Frisco's Springfield-Carthage line, the other a sixty-mile run via Miller and Avil-

Car 61 negotiates the traffic circle in Public Square circa 1905 on its way to Monroe. This line was extended circa 1909 to the State Teacher's College at Lombard and Kings Avenue. History Museum for Springfield-Greene County.

la. ERJ February 27th (p. 394) said surveying had begun on the latter, but the project stalled when Springfield turned awkward. This STC-sponsored interurban wanted to enter from the west over Nichols, linking with Boonville's tracks. North Springfielders, however, wanted it to come in on Commercial near the stations. The Greene County judge hearing the application decided the latter route was better and refused a Nichols Street permit. STC immediately dropped the project.

ERJ September 24th, 1910 (p. 487) claimed a **Springfield and Western Railroad Company** planned a similar interurban (Hector D. Mackay of Springfield President, Mortimer Hollenback Chief Engineer). Capitalized at $2 million, it would run via Bennetts, Plano, Halltown, Paris Springs, Miller, Red Oak and Avilla. A 28-mile Paris Springs branch would go southwest to Pierce City via Mount Vernon and Monett. Surveys began from Springfield and by May (ERJ May 13th 1911 p. 859) a contract for Springfield-Carthage-Joplin was wrongly reported as signed. ERJ June 3rd 1911 (p. 997) corrected this and reported a $1 1/2 million bond issue. ERJ March 6th, 1912 (p. 448) said the Paris Springs survey was done while ERJ January 10th 1914 (p.106) reported preliminary surveys from Mt. Vernon 45 miles west to Joplin via Stotts City, Clarkson, Sarcoxie and Duenwag, plus a nine-mile Jenkins Creek to Carthage branch. The franchise expired January 1917 if 10 miles of line weren't open. They weren't.

In 1909, new tracks were laid on Dollison south from Monroe to Lombard and east a block on Lombard to Kings. This short addition served new buildings of the State Teacher's College (Normal School). A connection linked North and South Jefferson tracks at St. Louis but was little used and removed in November 1929. As finances became strained, President

Car 75 southbound on Boonville with Commercial Street in background, October 2nd, 1911. STLMOT

Macomber and Vice-President Little supplied most funds personally. By 1909 Macomber was ready to sell but defects in the franchises deterred potential buyers. Eventually it was agreed that in return for a new franchise, STC would build more tracks and improve service. A July 14th, 1909 vote approved this and the new franchise was granted on August

Atlantic and Broadway looking east on Atlantic. A Dolling Park car turns north onto Broadway circa 1912. STLMOT

property damage as the city had not protected it during the strike. Issues were unresolved when the strike petered out and a further three-week strike in August 1918 was only settled when a new wage scale paid a penny an hour extra to all.

In 1919, twelve Birneys took over base services. A further eight came in 1921. But crumbling tracks on Center Street, a short, poorly-paying shuttle, made buses look like a sure thing. An August 2nd initiative election approved STC's request for exclusive rights to run buses and convert weaker car lines. STC then took over all jitneys though initially it had no facilities to house or maintain them. By early 1924 there were five bus routes, the longest just over two miles with three buses, the rest 1.25 miles with a bus each, except at rush hours when there were two. All routes had twenty-minute service, but lost money from the start. In 1926, trying to raise bus fares from five to seven

23rd. All previous rights were extended to 1944 and STC would build new lines on Nichols to the west city limits (Kansas Street), north on Park from Nichols to Division and on Atlantic from Broadway to Kansas Street.

It would also dedicate a lot on Grant north of Commercial to build a subway under the Frisco tracks and run a line through from Commercial to Atlantic, then west on Atlantic to Broadway. To avoid duplication, tracks would be removed on Commercial from Grant to Broadway, on Broadway from Commercial to Atlantic and on Springfield from Turner to Kearney. Tracks would be modified around St. Louis Street at Public Square. The nickel fare would remain. The Atlantic line was the first to open on September 16th, 1909.

Macomber and Little hosted several sales prospects during 1910, including Henry L. Doherty who withdrew grumbling he'd been given an option but Little had asked too much for it. At the end of 1910, Little contacted Harrison Williams of New York City whose clients had connections with Federal Light and Traction. On March 1st, 1911 FL&T bought Springfield Railway and Light, STC and Springfield Gas and Electric. Between then and 1913, $350,000 was spent on the system but more than 500 new autos were bought by locals, many of which made up the plague of unlicensed jitneys which in 1914 descended on the town. On the worst day, 200 were on the streets. They were speedier than the trolleys and it was two years before new tax and licensing laws cut them down to fifty. A State Street extension (ERJ July 7th, 1915, p.130) from New Street west to Fort, and south on Fort for three blocks to Grand, was never built.

Strikes from February 19th to 23rd, 1916 and October 4th, 1916 to June 25th, 1917 exposed Springfield to arson, bombs and armed vigilantes murdering strikers and bystanders. In February the issues were diffuse, rooted in malaise, inflation and unresponsive management. The October strike was about union recognition, a closed shop, and pay matching inflation. Both sides dug in, STC hiring strike-breakers. What was quaintly referred to as a dynamite attack in February 1917 wrecked a car on Nichols. In March STC sued claiming $200,000 compensation for

Springfield car lines, 1931
(every 15 minutes unless stated otherwise)

<u>Atlantic</u> From Public Square, north on Boonville to Commercial, west to Grant, north to Atlantic, west to Park. After 6:00 p.m., this became a shuttle along Atlantic only from Broaway to the end of the line.

<u>Belt</u> From Public Square east on St. Louis to Jefferson, north to Center, east to Benton, north to Commercial, west to Grant, south to Nichols, east to Main, south to College, east to Public Square. This ran in the reverse direction also.

<u>Boulevard</u> From New Street east on State to South, north to Public Square, north on Boonville to Commercial, east to Boulevard, north to Turner, west to Boonville, north to Doling Park.

<u>Center</u> From Benton and Center, east on Center to Fremont, north on Pythian (shuttle service).

<u>Doling Park</u> From Pickwick and Catalpa, north on Pickwick to Elm, west to Jefferson, north to St. Louis, west to Public Square, north on Boonville to Commercial, west to Grant, north to Atlantic, west to Broadway, north to Talmage, east to Doling Park at Boonville.

<u>Elm</u> From Doling Park at Boonville south on Boonville to Turner, east to Boulevard, south to Commercial, west to Boonville, south to Public Square, east on St. Louis to Jefferson, south to Elm east to Pickwick, south to Catalpa.

<u>Nichols</u> From Grant and Nichols, west on Nichols, north on Park to Division and West Frisco shops. (30 minutes.)

<u>State</u> From Doling Park west on Talmage to Broadway, south to Atlantic, east to Grant, south to Commercial, east to Boonville, south to Public Square, south on South Avenue to State, west on State to New.

<u>Teachers College</u> From Public Square south on South Avenue to Monroe, east to Dollison, south to Lombard, east on Lombard to college. (10 minutes.)

Hourly owl car service served Main, Square, Boonville and Commercial to Benton.

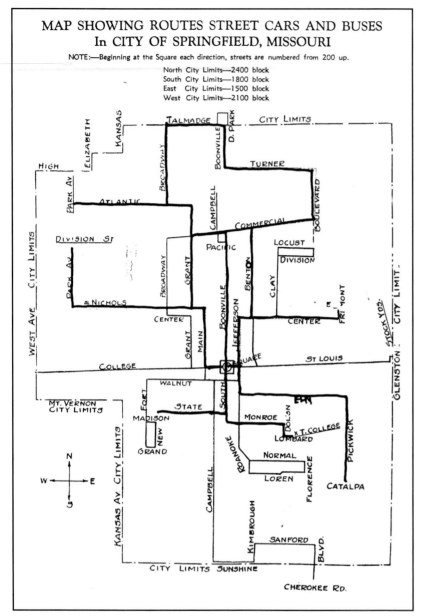

MAP SHOWING ROUTES STREET CARS AND BUSES
In CITY OF SPRINGFIELD, MISSOURI

NOTE:—Beginning at the Square each direction, streets are numbered from 200 up.

North City Limits—2400 block
South City Limits—1800 block
East City Limits—1500 block
West City Limits—2100 block

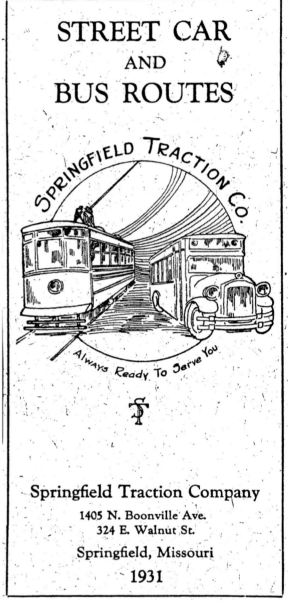

STREET CAR
AND
BUS ROUTES

SPRINGFIELD TRACTION CO.

Always Ready To Serve You

Springfield Traction Company

1405 N. Boonville Ave.
324 E. Walnut St.

Springfield, Missouri

1931

cents to match the trolleys, STC stated it lost $49,000 between September 1st 1924 and September 30th, 1925. MOPSC declined to hear the case, saying it had no jurisdiction over buses, even those linked to car operation.

Federal Light and Traction merged STC and Springfield Gas and Electric in July 1927 as the **Springfield Electric Company.** STC was valued at $1,740,944, capitalized at $400,000 and owed $1,242,773, $1/2 million being 5% first mortgage bonds. SEC's 1927 MOPSC report claimed 23.3 track miles, 20 miles of bus route, 52 closed cars, two closed and three open car trailers (all one-man), two work cars, seven work trailers, a snow sweeper, a "miscellaneous" work car, plus 14 buses. In the 1930s, voltage was increased from 550 to 600V D. C. Annual losses of circa $50,000 made by cars and buses during the 1930s were cross-subsidized from Federal Light and Traction's other Springfield utilities.

In 1936 the city and company agreed general rate reductions and transit improvements, including new buses to replace the trolleys. Their last day was a great occasion. Downtown retailers held huge sales, trolleys were fare-free and they were packed. A closing parade of trolleys and replacement buses followed the route of the first animal line of 1881, running west on Commercial to Boonville and south on Boonville to Public Square. The first bus broke a blue ribbon before starting the parade at 7:00 pm. After it was over, trolleys maintained normal schedules, the last leaving Public Square at 12:06 a. m. on Sunday August 29th. The buses

went to the barns for a dedication ceremony. In March 1945 the new **City Utilities of Springfield** took over. It has run Springfield's buses ever since.

Incomplete Roster Notes.

Nothing is known of 1890s electric cars. Most were worn out by 1905. Many numbered below 50 were former horse cars, often towed behind electrics for heavy summer traffic. They were used to 1917 and some were derelict in the car barn yards in the 1920s. Some may have survived to the end.

60-63 (St. Louis, 1903) were closed city cars on St. Louis 25 single trucks.

65-69 (American, 1906) were 28-seat cars, 70-81 (American, date unknown)

82-84 (Danville Car, date unknown) were 32-seat cars, all semi-convertibles on Brill 21-E single-trucks.

300-305 (Jewett, 1907) were 40-seat city cars on Baldwin double-trucks. Four single-truck closed city cars (Kuhlman, 1907), numbers unknown.

100-101 (St. Louis, 1907) were 44-seat cars on St. Louis 47 double-trucks.

102-103 (American, 1909) were 56-seat trailers on Brill 39-E double-trucks.

Four single-truck closed city cars (American, 1909), numbers unknown.

Postcard showing a car entering St. Louis Street, circa 1912, with Public Square in the distance.

nough pitched this to the Springfield Club on November 27th, 1906, calling it the **Kansas City and Springfield Southern Railway Company** and asked for a $20,000 cash bonus. The project General Manager (C. C. McMann of Nevada), said building would start in 60 days, that all but nine miles of right-of-way had been bought and that only Stockton and Springfield had yet to give franchises.

SRJ April 6th 1907 (ad p. 42) said building the 146-mile Springfield-Stotesbury via Nevada line (no mention of a Kansas City extension) with a cross line from Stockton to Sylvania would begin in 2 months. SRJ January 4th, 1908 (ad p. 35) said the main line would be Springfield-Nevada, with a Carthage branch. Surveys were complete, but not the increase of capital to $4,250,000 from $3,750,000. The powerhouse would be near Arcola, with an amusement park near the Sac River. No more was heard other than the manager (SRJ April 25th 1908 ad p. 35) saying that no building would be done this year *"because of financial conditions."*

2. Springfield, Nixa and Southern Electric Railway First noted in ERJ June 27th, 1908

Single-truck work car 9, (home-built, 1909).
One double-truck work car (home-built, 1909), number unknown.
Single-truck snow sweeper 12 (McGuire-Cummings, 1909).
Single-truck snow sweeper (McGuire-Cummings, 1910), number unknown.
Four Brill double-truck closed city cars (American, 1910), numbers unknown.
104 and 108 (St. Louis, 1905) were 40-seat cars on St. Louis 23-A double-trucks. They were bought used from Las Vegas NM (LV #101, 102) at an unknown date.
105-107 (St. Louis, 1905) were 36-seat cars on St. Louis 23-A double-trucks, bought used from Las Vegas NM (LV # 103-105) at an unknown date.
110-112 (American, 1910) were 84-seat trailer cars on Brill double-trucks, bought used from an unknown Texas property at unknown date.
Springfield had 24 Birneys. 200-211(American Car, 1918) were bought new from brokers *"St. Louis Rail and Equipment Company"* on October 2nd, 1918. 212-219 (Cincinnati, 1918) may have been bought direct. 220, 221 (Brill, 1920) were originally cars 70, 75 of Orange County Traction Newburgh NY. They were sold to Fishkill Electric Railway, Beacon NY in 1923 and became their #32 and #37, and came to Springfield in 1930. 222, 223 (Brill 1921) came from the New York City Department of Plant and Structures (Staten Island) part of the #201-233 series. They were sold to Fishkill Electric in 1927 as #38 and #41 and sold to Springfield in 1930.

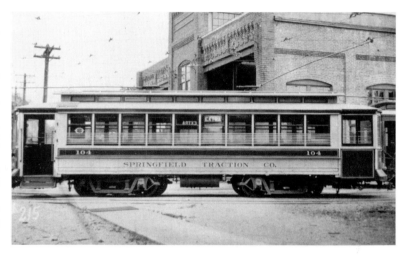

Car 104 outside the car barns, circa 1915.

Springfield Interurban Proposals

1. Kansas City, Nevada and Springfield Electric Railway SRJ September 8th, 1906 (ad page 35) said T. P. McDonnough, a New York promoter and H. C. Kehm a broker, had talked to the Springfield Club of a 90-mile Springfield-Nevada electric line via Dadeville, Jerico Springs and larger towns in Cedar County's mining districts. On September 15th 1906, SRJ (ad p. 39) reported Nevada agreeing a $15,000 bonus, a franchise and land for the terminals. Hydro power would come from the dammed Sac River, thirty-seven miles northwest of Springfield. McDon-

Advertising car on northwest corner of Public Square circa 1924. City Utilities Transit.

Sweeper 12, car barns circa 1930. STLMOT

Birney 218 heading north on Boonville, passes the old City Hall, August 28th, 1937. History Museum for Springfield-Green County.

Birney 218 on Commercial at Boonville, August 28th, 1937. History Museum for Springfield-Greene County.

(p.109), surveys for this $350,000 line had begun south from Springfield to Nixa. Hydro-electric power, generated at Nixa, would be used. ERJ (July 9th, 1910) noted H. M. Wilson and W. H. Schreiber were promoting the line.

3. Osage, Ozark and Springfield Electric Railway Company. First noted in ERJ April 1st, 1911 (p. 619), this was to be a Springfield-Warsaw line (Warsaw being at the west end of the today's Lake of the Ozarks) running via Fristoe, Cross Timbers and Buffalo. ERJ April 15th 1911 (p. 694) noted the OO&SERC, would have power stations at Warsaw and Brunetts and this 80-mile line would be built as soon as it had financial backing. Though money had been subscribed for preliminary surveys, no more was forthcoming.

TRENTON

1880	**1890**	**1900**	**1910**	**1920**	**1930**	**1940**	**1950**	**1960**	**1970**	**1980**	**1990**	**2000**
3,312	5,039	5,396	5,656	6,951	6,992	7,046	6,157	6,262	6,063	6,811	6,129	6,216

The Grundy County seat, 90 miles northeast of St. Joseph and 25 miles north of Chillicothe, Trenton began in 1840 as Bluff Grove. It was renamed in 1842 but why, or if the name refers to its New Jersey namesake, isn't known. SRJ November 1890 (p. 574) said W. E. Bailey and associates had a city franchise for two electric lines. One was from Trenton Avenue (7th Street) on Water Street to Elm, north on Elm, east on Bridge across the Rock Island tracks to Lulu Street, then north on Lulu to the city limits at Holt's addition. A Fairgrounds extension would come later. The other would run from the Rock Island depot west on Prospect, north on Norton to Moberly Park, then west on an unamed street to link with the Holt's addition line. Horse cars were to have run initially, but the lines were not built.

SRJ did not say that a second group, headed by N. A. Winters was given

a city franchise on October 2nd 1891 to run from the Rock Island depot west on Prospect to Mabel, w\here its line split, one branch going north on Mabel, east on 17th and north on Princeton to the fairgrounds, the other to 9th and Main, then east on Main to Avalon College, later the site of the high school. A spur would serve the southwest corner of the courthouse block. Other streets were also granted, a total of four miles. However only a portion was built, opening on December 4th, 1890 as an animal line. A dedication ceremony with the mayor and the town band was repeated at the Rock Island railroad depot, where the line stopped just 40 feet from the tracks. There was no schedule; cars ran in connection with the trains. There was little business and it closed in 1896. A **North Side Electric Railway Company**, was noted in the March 1897 SRJ directory as having three cars and three miles of track. Nothing is known of this.

WARRENSBURG

1880	**1890**	**1900**	**1910**	**1920**	**1930**	**1940**	**1950**	**1960**	**1970**	**1980**	**1990**	**2000**
4,049	4,706	4,724	4,689	4,811	5,146	5,868	6,857	9,689	13,125	13,807	15,244	16,340

The Johnson County seat, about 45 miles southeast of Kansas City and 30 miles west of Sedalia, was established around 1837 and named for Martin Warren, a surviving veteran of the Revolutionary War who settled here in 1833 after leaving his native Kentucky. The town expanded with the arrival of Missouri Normal School #2 in the 1870s (today's Central Missouri State Teacher's College). Electric Springs and Pertle Springs, two

separate locations, were developed for tourists in the 1880s. Pertle Springs was for many years on the Midwest Chautaqua circuit.

1. Electric Springs Railway Company Electric Springs, on the town's northwest edge was owned by George W. Colburn who sold it in the early 1880s to a pair remembered as being "from abroad," who platted the property for residential building and in 1887 installed an animal street railway through downtown, past the railroad station and along South Street to its west end. The pair soon went bankrupt and Colburn resumed control. The mineral springs spawned the Oates Hotel and a bowling alley, but no residential development occurred. The line had no purpose, though Colburn felt it was worth keeping. Poor's Manual 1890 reports 0.75 miles of 4' gauge track, four cars and four horses. A daily franchise run was made in the charge of an Irishman paid $1.00 a day for the privilege.

The P-D August 10th, 1896 p. 10) noted a *"1.3 mile [sic] line...part of a scheme to make a great summer resort of Electric Springs, where a large hotel was built. The franchise...required cars run...every month...So to hold the franchise, an old rickety bobtail car is run...once a month and mules attached to it. A man drives over the line and back and then puts the car in the barn.The rails are twisted and the car jumps the track often. Sometimes it takes ten days to make the round trip..."* By the late 1890s it was down to one run per month. It's not known when it closed; a picture of an old horse car adorned with a banner proclaiming *"the last trip, May 17 '09. Started 1887. Goodby dear donkeys, goodby,"* is thought to be the last run but the car is generically labeled "colleges, hotels and hospitals," with no evidence tying it to Warrensburg and Electric Springs. The Oates hotel burned in 1906.

2. Pertle Springs No formal name has been found for this line. Colonel J. H. Christopher bought Purtle Springs in 1884, developing the place as a resort and changing the spelling to Pertle to make a more attractive word. SRJ March 1890 (p. 141) said he would arrange to build a Warrensburg-Pertle Springs electric line which he'd already graded. It would open in May 1890 and cost $40,000. The one-mile line did open that year but was always powered by a steam dummy. It ran from a two road terminal at the Estes Hotel, across from the MoPac station, to Pertle Springs, going east on Commercial, south on Miller, west on South Street a half- block, south on Normal Avenue, past the west side of the Normal School campus onto its own right-of-way between Clark and Hunt Avenue, southwest into Pertle Springs Park, past Lake Cena (named for Christopher's granddaughter) and ending close to the Minnewawa Hotel, another Christopher project. Fare was a dime one-way, 15-cents round-trip.

It was heavily used in season. A big Chautauqua could generate 8,000 daily riders. Base service was eight daily three-car trains. The 0-4-0 steam dummy had an extended rear frame for a fuel bunker, under which was a pair of small carrying wheels. It's not known if there was a second dummy. Two trailers were 14-bench double-truck street railway type opens with railroad roofs; a third car had a different appearance. All were painted orange, with aluminum and black trim. It is not clear if the line ran out-of-season. It didn't by 1900. The Warrensburg Daily Star-Journal (May 27th, 1960, p. 1) published Jackson Hackly's reminiscences. This 75-year old retiree took a summer job on the Pertle Springs steam dummy as a teenager in 1901, before joining a main-line railroad. He recalled April was spent getting the locomotive and cars repaired, cleaned and painted. The first Sunday in May saw the train pull out at 8:30 a.m. About ten trains were run normally, the last returning about midnight. *"On holidays,"* Hackley remembered," *we made as many as 30 trips a day, going and coming just as fast as we could."* By the 1920s mineral springs, chautauquas and similar entertainments were out of fashion. The dummy line closed in 1922 and the hotel Minewawa, barely used for years, burned in 1926. Christopher lived until 1931. His granddaughter wrote plays and books into the 1970s, based on her early life in Warrensburg with him.

APPENDIX
ABBREVIATIONS AND GLOSSARY

American = American Car Company, St. Louis.
ASRI= American Street Railway Investments.
BLW=Baldwin-Westinghouse.
Brill=J. G. Brill Company of Philadelphia.
CB&Q= Chicago, Burlington and Quincy Railroad Company.
Chautauqua = an outdoor educational gathering that included lectures, entertainment and summer school instruction.
Danville= Danville Car Company, Danville, IL.
ERA= Electric Railroaders' Association.
ERJ= Electric Railway Journal.
ESTL&S= East St. Louis and Suburban Company.
ETW=Electric Traction Weekly.
Frisco=St. Louis and San Francisco Railroad Company.
G-D = St. Louis Globe-Democrat.
GE = General Electric Company.
IT = Illinois Treaction System or Illinois Terminal Railroad.
KCKS= Kansas City, Kansas.
KCMO = Kansas City, Missouri.
KCPS=Kansas City Public Service Company.
KCS = Kansas City Star.
Laclede = Laclede Car Company.
LCL= Less than carload freight.
McGraw = Mcgraw Electric Railway Directory/List/Manual.
MET= Metropolitan (Kansas City).

M(D or W)I = Mexico (Daily or Weekly) Intelligencer.
MKT = Missouri Kansas Texas Railroad Company (the Katy)
MoPac = Missouri Pacific Railroad Company.
MOPSC = Missouri Public Service Commission.
PAYE = Pay As You Enter.
P-D = St. Louis Post-Dispatch.
Poor's = Poor's Maual of Street Railroads/Manual of Public Utilities.
Russell = Russell Car and Snow Plow Company, Ridgeway PA.
Santa Fe = Atchison, Topeka and Santa Fe Railroad Company.
SLPS = St. Louis Public Service Company.
STLC = St. Louis Car Co., St. Louis.
SRG = Street Railway Gazette.
SRJ = Street Railway Journal.
SRR = Street Railway Review.
STC = Springfield Traction Company.
TRRA = Terminal Railroad Association of St. Louis.
UM = University Missourian, the local newspaper of Columbia, MO.
UR = United Railways of St. Louis.
Wb = Wheelbase.
WH = Westinghouse.

BIBLIOGRAPHY

A. Books and unpublished manuscripts

Alton Jackonville and Peoria Railway Company by James J. Buckley. Unpublished monograph compiled circa 1986 from local newspapers, made available courtesy of Roy G. Benedict.

Andrew County; a community. No author cited. Andrew County Historical Society, Savannah MO 1980

At Ease: stories I like to tell friends by Dwight D. Eisenhower, Doubleday, Garden City NY 1967.

The "Big Cinch:" A business elite in the life of a city, St. Louis 1895-1915 by Alexander Scot McConachie. Unpublished Phd. thesis, Washington University St. Louis, 1976.

The Birney Car by Harold E. Cox, Self-published, Forty Fort, PA 1966.

The Cable Car in America by George W. Hilton. Howell-North Books, Berkeley CA, 1971.

The Consolidation of Street Railways in the City of St. Louis, Missouri by James Lee Murphy. Unpublished MA thesis, St. Louis University, 1964

The Day the Streetcars Stopped; the Cape Girardeau-Jackson Interurban Railway Company by J. Scott Taylor. Unpublished thesis, Southeast Missouri State University, Cape Girardeau MO 1984.

The Electric Interurban Railway in America by George W. Hilton and John F. Due, Stanford University Press, Stanford CA 1960.

Financial History of Street Railways in St. Louis, by Arthur Vieth. Unpublished MA thesis, Washington University St. Louis MO 1943.

The First 150 years in Cassville by Senator Emory Melton. Self-published, Cassville MO 1995.

The First Hundred years; a History of Lebanon Missouri compiled by Frances Gleason. Laclede County Centennial inc., Lebanon MO 1949

Heartland Traction, the Interurbans of Kansas City by Edward A. Conrad, Heartlandrails publishing, Blue Springs MO 2006.

History of Henry County Volume 1 by W. Lamkin, Historical Publishing Company, Topeka KS 1919.

A History of Missouri, The Missouri Sesquicentennial edition vols. 1-6, William e. Parish ed. University of Missouri Press, Columbia MO 1971-2004.

How a good car differs from a poor one, and how to get it by Frederick B. Brownell (uncredited), Brownell Car Company, St. Louis MO (no date but circa 1895).

Illinois Terminal, the Electric Years by P. Stringham. Interurbans Special 111, Interurban Press, Glendale CA. 1989

Kansas City Streetcars Remembered by Henry Elsner, N. J. International, Hicksville NY 1991.

King Trolley and the Suburban Queens, St. Louis County Streetcar Service from 1890-1950, by James F. Baker, Meramec Highlands Books, Kirkwood, MO. 2005.

Lafayette County, MO, by Will Young. B. F. Brown and Co., Indianapolis IN, 1910

Missouri Highways, the first 200 years Missouri State Highway Commission, Jefferson City MO, 1966

Pioneers of Electric Railroading, Their story in words and pictures Edited by John R. Stevens, Electric Railroaders' Association "Headlights" volumes 51 & 52, 1989-1990, New York NY 1991.

Progress and enterprise, a report of the Development of Mass Transit in St. Joseph Missouri by David Fox. Unpublished report, prepared for the Department of Public Works and Transportation, City of St. Joseph MO, 2002.a

Quality Shops, The History of the St. Louis Car Company by Andrew D. Young and Eugene F. Provenzo Jr. Howell-North Books, Berkeley, CA. 1978

The first 100 years; a history of the city of Sedalia 1860-1960. Centennial History Committee, Sedalia MO. 1960.

St. Joseph Light and Power Company, a century of Progress, a century of Service 1883-1983, by Robert L. Slater. St. Joseph Light and Power Company, St. Joseph MO. no date (circa 1984)

St. Louis and its Streetcars, the way it was by A. D. Young, Archway Publishing, St. Louis MO 1996.

The St. Louis Streetcar Story by A. D. Young, Interurbans Special 108, Interurban Press, Glendale CA. 1988

The St. Louis Waterworks Line by Bill Cordes. Tower Grove Press, St. Louis MO 2004.

A Splendid Ride, The Streetcars of Kansas City 1870-1957 by Monroe Dodd,(based on material researched by Terence Cassidy), Kansas City Star, Kansas City MO 2002.

The Street Railway Post Offices of St. Louis by Robert G. Schultz. Street Car Monograph series, Mobile Post Office Society, Chicago 1984.

Streetcars, Light Rail and Utility Cars of St. Louis by A. D. Young, Archway Publishing St. Louis MO 2003.

Streets & Streetcars of St. Louis, a sentimental journey by A. D. Young, Archway Publishing St. Louis MO 2002.

Tri-State Traction, the Interurban Trolleys of Southwest Missouri, Southeast Kansas and Northeast Oklahoma by Edward A. Conrad, Heartland Rails, Blue Springs MO, 2005.

Trolley Through the Countryside by Allison Chandler, Sage Books, Denver CO, 1963

Tweed Days in St. Louis, one of several articles collected in **The Shame of the Cities** by Lincoln Steffens, McClure, Phillips & Co, New York, NY 1904.

Untitled unpublished 1929 memoir by N. C. Cunningham, a Springfield Traction Company officer until 1919. The manuscript is in the St. Louis Museum of Transportation's archival collection.

B. Magazine and newspaper articles

East St. Louis and Suburban Railway Co. by Mark Godwin, The Flyer, Spring 2001, Illinois Traction Society, Decatur, IL.

The Excelsior Springs route, Life & Death of a Missouri Interurban by H. Roger Grant, Missouri Historical Review (pp 37-50).

The Interurban, a Victim of the Auto by Berl Katz, Waterloo Republican May 15th, 1974 (East St. Louis, Columbia and Waterloo).

Lightweight Street and Interurban Cars by Donald Engel. Branford Electric Railway Journal, Branford Electric Railway Association, East Haven CT 1998.

Missouri Short Line by Terence W. Cassidy, Steel Rails magazine July 10th, 1953 (p.4-6)

St. Louis by Andrew D. Young, Motor Coach Age January-March 1998 PP. 3-37 (History of St. Louis buses and bus services 1843-1960).

The St. Louis Municipal Bridge Railway by Richard M. Castagna, Lawrence Thomas et al, Terminal Railroad Association of St. Louis Historical and Technical Society Inc. issue 65, Summer 2005.